The Aesthetics of Antichrist

The Aesthetics of Antichrist

From Christian Drama to Christopher Marlowe

JOHN PARKER

Cornell University Press ITHACA AND LONDON

Cornell University Press gratefully acknowledges receipt of
a subvention from Macalester College, which aided in the
publication of this book.

First published 2007 by Cornell University Press

Printed in the United States of America

Library of Congress Cataloging-in-Publication Data

Parker, John, 1972–
    The aesthetics of Antichrist : from Christian drama to
Christopher Marlowe / John Parker.
        p. cm.
    Includes bibliographical references and index.
    ISBN 978-0-8014-4519-4 (cloth : alk. paper)
    1. Marlowe, Christopher, 1564–1593—Religion.   2. English
drama—Early modern and Elizabethan, 1500–1600—History
and criticism.   3. Christian drama, English—History and
criticism.   4 Christianity and literature—England—History—
16th century.   5. Antichrist in literature.   I. Title.
PR2677.R4P37 2007
822'.3—dc22

2007018959

Cloth printing   10 9 8 7 6 5 4 3 2 1

Contents

Preface

With the advent of a commercial theater in London, traditional drama was dying, or already dead. Almost completely destroyed were the plays that had staged the miraculous lives of saints or explained the Catholic sacraments as a certain avenue to posthumous benefits. For centuries before, daylong cycles honoring the Feast of Corpus Christi had brought to northern England the history of the world from creation to judgment. Now judgment came to them. In 1576, the same year James Burbage founded his Theater, the inhabitants and local authorities of Wakefield received instructions from the ecclesiastical commissioners at York to cease staging anything "wherein the Majesty of God the Father, God the Son, or God the Holy Ghost... be counterfeited or represented."[1] Notwithstanding a brief vogue later in London for plays drawn from Old Testament narratives, throughout the country it was increasingly unfashionable, if not also illegal, to put explicitly religious scenes on stage. Over the next quarter century the dramatic representation of godhead would all but disappear. In its place there flourished, for a while, an openly for-profit theater without obvious precedent.

---

1. Glynne Wickham et al., ed., *English Professional Theatre, 1530–1660* (Cambridge: Cambridge University Press, 2000), p. 69. On the demise of religious drama over the last quarter of the sixteenth century, see Michael O'Connell, *The Idolatrous Eye: Iconoclasm and Theater in Early-Modern England* (Oxford: Oxford University Press, 2000), pp. 20–27; on the brief, ineffectual fashion for Old Testament drama that I mention in the following sentence, see pp. 91, 107–14.

No one who wrote for the new venue has a more debated relation to sacred drama than Christopher Marlowe. In general the scholarship on him
has been tempted either to stress his novelty or to deny it. Either he produced a radically new sort of theater, at odds with the old superstitions and
no longer blinkered by faith; or he recapitulated with only minor deviations
solidly Christian conventions. Either his plays gave voice to Protestant ortho-
doxies just as medieval dramatists had underwritten, in their own complex
fashion, the prerogatives of the church; or else he broke with religion by
twisting Christian idioms into the radically ironic formulations of modern
atheism. Either Marlowe the Christian or Marlowe the Antichrist.

It will be the task of this book to argue that Marlowe separates sacred
and secular drama—the Middle Ages, as it were, from High Renaissance—
the way a common wall divides adjacent rooms. We debate whether the
rooms are entirely separate or perfectly conjoined, but really this amounts
to the same thing. Medieval and Renaissance drama are divided by what
they share. Their Antichrists are exclusive and mutual.

My account of Marlowe could be said for that reason to emerge dialectically from the truth of both approaches to his work—as the short-circuit between them, so to speak. If Marlowe preserves certain elements of medieval
drama, should this not, for example, be allowed to imply that his medieval
predecessors achieved by means of the Bible a drama almost as dodgy as
his? My first three chapters pursue that implication at length. A medieval
Marlowe, I want to say, should allow us to see all the better how Marlovian
the Middle Ages already were. By the same token, those who argue that
Marlowe's work is fundamentally at odds with "real" Christianity—either as
an early expression of secular atheism (e.g., Dollimore) or as the recovery
of atheism's classical analogues (e.g., Riggs)[2]—should begin to seem, in
light of these chapters, of all things unconsciously pious. I suspect the radical Marlowe looks so modern because his champions cannot easily stomach
the "ambivalences" of medieval drama,[3] much less of the old-time religion
this drama reflects, and in the reflection, partly constitutes.

"The vanity of scholarship," writes Harold Bloom, "has few more curious
monuments than this Christianized Marlowe. What the common reader
finds in Marlowe is precisely what his contemporaries found: impiety,
audacity, worship of power, ambiguous sexuality, occult aspirations, defiance

---

2. Jonathan Dollimore, *Radical Tragedy: Religion, Ideology, and Power in the Drama of Shakespeare and His Contemporaries*, 3rd ed. (New York: Palgrave Macmillan, 2004), and David
Riggs, *The World of Christopher Marlowe* (London: Faber, 2004).

3. A term I borrow from Rainer Warning, *The Ambivalences of Medieval Religious Drama*,
trans. Steven Rendall (Stanford: Stanford University Press, 2001).

of moral order, and above all else a sheer exaltation of the possibilities of rhetoric."[4] This verdict makes sense only if you assume that Christians by definition never worship power, aspire to the occult, audaciously defy the moral and sexual "order," or exalt in rhetoric. Such a criticism, though ostensibly secular, actually projects onto Christianity a religious fantasy of what religion at bottom is really like: prim and spiritual, ravished at the touch of worldly influence. Christianity touches on nothing else. That is why the New Testament and the interpretations of it given by the Fathers, by medieval and early modern reformers, are so saturated with polemic *against other Christians*—against, that is, the members of Antichrist—for being, by turns, too pagan or Jewish, too fractious, too exclusive, or for tolerating Satan and including too many. Through such negations the "orthodox" (whoever they are at any given moment) would produce an *effect*: the truth and transcendence of their own alleged faith.

One final example of the position that finds in Marlowe a worldliness lacking from earlier drama (and therefore presumably lacking from the Bible) should suffice to outline the problem. According to John Cox, for all Marlowe's indebtedness to the sacred tradition, in fact he "deconstructs" the official binaries of religious drama. So in *Dr. Faustus*, for instance, "Marlowe's implicit reduction of the Reformation to a struggle for power is an acute response to the secularization introduced by the Tudors, not because struggles for power were invented by Protestants but because Protestants made religion a matter of crown policy and thus, comparatively, a matter of mere power."[5] What gets me here is the word "comparatively." Compared to what, exactly? Not compared to the medieval papacy. Power politics were as traditional there as apostolic succession. Henry VIII did *not* introduce into formerly "religious" questions an element of *Realpolitik* which the church, in its innocence, had never allowed to darken its mission. Accounts of Marlowe as a novel deviant, I think, all too often tend secretly to assume, against everything we know about the Middle Ages, that there existed prior to the Reformation some form of Christianity free at its core from psychological, social, political, and economic determinations; that before undergoing secularization (to the extent that it did), Christian drama must have been *purely* spiritual—only later was it tarnished with ulterior motives.

I have tried in the pages that follow to modify this widespread view by arguing a stronger, more provocative version of its presupposition: namely,

---

4. Harold Bloom, ed., *Christopher Marlowe* (New York: Chelsea House, 1986), p. 1.
5. John Cox, *The Devil and the Sacred in English Drama, 1350–1642* (Cambridge: Cambridge University Press, 2000), p. 114.

that a pure spirituality *does* inhere in Christianity, but it is neither pure, nor spirit, because it is art.

Some will blush at these terms and want to start in about history, but I am impenitent. History is catastrophic. This book concerns aesthetic responses to it that have, in the name of Christ, been more or less worshipped. I focus specifically on the figure of Antichrist because Antichrist gives such a powerful indication of the centrality to Christianity, through its many permutations, of playacting. His second-order, mimetic reconstitution of Christ's actions is of course a travesty—a parodic and false approximation of what is supposed to have no immediate proxy other than itself: God's "persons." Those persons, however, already owe a great deal to the masks or *personae* of pagan theater. The travesty of Antichrist, akin to what medieval actors performed all the time, stems moreover from Christ's prior inability to exonerate himself or his followers from the accusations of magic, robbery, and con artistry—in sum, the theatrical sin of hypocrisy—that led to the cross. Impotent and false in themselves, (anti)christian figurations consequently augur, as did Christ's first coming, the deferred arrival of yet another, more effective messiah. This one may or may not come in glory, but till he does, the mimetic limitations of every precursor will have to anticipate on his behalf the final revelation, such as it is. To put this another way: the aesthetic of Christ and his doubles depends above all on the power of fallen material to represent the pure and immaterial, of history to signify the timeless, of human finitude to approximate the infinite as an asymptote approaches its impossible limit.

"The theological heritage of art," writes Adorno, "is the secularization of revelation—the ideal and limit of every work. To contaminate art with revelation would mean to repeat in theory, without reflection, its inescapable fetish character. To eradicate all trace of revelation from art would degrade it to the undifferentiated repetition of what is."[6] With this book I hope

---

6. *AT* 162; trans. 106. I cannot tell which is greater, the influence of Adorno on the present study or the influence of messianic thought on his aesthetics: "In the incineration of appearance," he writes, "artworks break away in a glare from the empirical world and become the counterfigure of what lives there; art today is scarcely conceivable except as a form of reaction that anticipates the apocalypse" (*AT* 131; trans. 85). For a defense of Adorno's continuing importance to literary studies, see another major influence on my thinking, Fredric Jameson, *Late Marxism: or, Adorno and the Persistence of the Dialectic* (London: Verso, 1990). Adorno's specific relevance to the Middle Ages has been defended by Maura B. Nolan, "Making the Aesthetic Turn: Adorno, the Medieval, and the Future of the Past," *Journal of Medieval and Early Modern Studies* 34.3 (Fall 2004): 549–75; this same issue includes an essay of mine that provides some theoretical underpinning for the argument to come: "What a Piece of Work Is Man: Shakespearean Drama as Marxian Fetish, the Fetish as Sacramental Sublime," pp. 643–72.

to add that eradicating art from the specifically Christian revelation would be to eradicate the religion's sensuous specificity. Trying to imagine the Christian God without the fables of scripture, liturgical performance, the splendors of iconography, music, architecture, and (above all) drama is like imagining *Dr. Faustus* without any props, any costumes, any written poetry or speaking actors. It reduces him to a historical figure. When Christians in the sixteenth century tried to effect precisely this reduction with respect to Christ, and to sustain their religion without traditional theater, they helped give rise to plays like *Faustus*. Throughout the book I will be arguing that few people more radically assert the uncanny, revelatory power of drama than those who discern in it an anti-church, exactly like the real church, but hideous. Few come closer to confessing the innermost kernel of the Christian faith than the antitheatricalists who see a vapid aestheticism in the wrong sort of Christians, are horrified, and strive in vain to rectify matters by focusing exclusively on scripture—as though this weren't to prefer, in place of performance, the script on which it had always been based.

To make in any way good on these claims will obviously require something more complex than the usual progression from *Mankind* to Marlowe. I am going to try, by contrast, for a wholesale revision of the terms through which medieval drama has traditionally been read: as a species of "miracle" or as fundamentally "typological" (chapter 1) or "sacramental" (chapter 2) or "parabiblical" (chapter 3). I do not think we have begun to grasp the extent to which each of these conventional terms is involved in a critical discourse that animates medieval drama, and religious culture more generally, long before the revolt of Marlowe (chapter 4). My point is that the Marlovian revolution in drama revolves around traditional instabilities. He models three of his heroes, for example, on scriptural personages that medieval exegetes had always taken as types of the Antichrist: Barabbas for Barabas, of course, and Simon Magus for Faustus. Tamburlaine presents a special case, connected as he is to Paul, a former persecutor, who according to tradition began as an Antichrist but ended a Christian. In medieval drama demonic antics such as those of Marlowe's heroes always promised at some future point their eschatological reversal (just as Paul's persecutions had somehow "prefigured" his coming conversion) and were consequently, for an audience, a source of enormous pleasure. In my view Marlowe's drama capitalizes on this ancient impulse, but with a new result, such that his carnage gives rise less to any hope of its ending in apocalypse, or its eternalization in hell, than to open admiration of its sinister and semiautonomous beauty.

Acknowledgments

I am firstly grateful to Beatrice Kitzinger, whose research assistance has been indispensable to this book's completion. Other friends and colleagues who took the time to comment on my work have also been a great aid: Ilana Blumberg, Sophie Gee, Erik Gray, John Heon, and Mike Magee all lent a hand at various stages. Sarah Beckwith, Jim Engell, Stephen Greenblatt, Lisa New, David Quint, James Simpson, Gordon Teskey, and Nicholas Watson gave their keen attention to hundreds of pages. The manuscript received a great many anonymous readings in the course of a promotional review, and these unnamed, too, have my heartfelt thanks. Roger Haydon and the editorial staff at Cornell have made a huge difference. Holger Schott Syme helped with hard German, Dan Shore with proofreading.

I owe a special debt of gratitude to my *Doktormutter*, Margreta de Grazia. Her intelligence and friendship have been the polestar for two projects now, spanning ten years. Thanks also to the other members of the Med/Ren colloquium at the University of Pennsylvania, which has always provided an ideal model of cross-pollination between usually separate fields. The influence of Peter Stallybrass will be evident throughout these pages.

I could not have managed without Emily Ogden.

In a book this dependent on others it is a small relief to be able to claim at least the faults for myself. There are many, I am sure, and these cannot be shared. What I have written, I have written.

JOHN PARKER

Saint Paul, Minnesota

Note on Texts and Translations

When quoting from texts in other languages, I cite in addition to the original a published translation whenever possible, though I have not always been faithful to its wording. The dual citation makes in places for some bulky parentheticals but is intended for ease of reference across a range of potentially unfamiliar texts. "Ibid." in a parenthetical citation refers to the previous in-text citation (ignoring intervening references to the Bible); "op. cit." refers to a citation in the previous footnote. I normally omit the name of the translator in a series (ANF, NPNF, etc.), with the exception of FC, whose volumes can be otherwise tough to find in the library. I transliterate Greek when it appears in the main text but not in quotations from other scholars or in the notes, save where an important stem word, operative also in English, makes an appearance. For English works I quote the text as I found it with the exception of italics, the long *s,* and abbreviations, which I expand. In the footnotes, the first citation of a text appears in full within each chapter; I shorten subsequent references but indicate parenthetically the earlier full citation if it isn't nearby. Any sustained discussion of a single work, after the first footnote specifying the edition I am using, gives citations in the main text. Quotations from Marlowe are keyed to the Revels Plays, which I likewise cite in full only on first appearance.

Quotations from the Bible generally follow the Revised Standard Version (RSV) unless otherwise noted. Early modern English Bibles, for the most part now available on-line, are quoted from first editions with the exception of the Geneva, where I have used both the 1560 and its 1587 revision. For the Greek I have relied on *The Greek New Testament*, ed. Barbara Aland et al., 4th ed. (Stuttgart: Deutsche Bibelgesellschaft, 1993), and *Septuaginta*, ed. Alfred Rahlfs, 6th ed., 2 vols. (Stuttgart: Privilegierte Württembergische Bibelanstalt, 1959); for the Vulgate, *Biblia sacra: iuxta Vulgatam versionem*, ed. Bonifatius Fischer et al., 4th ed., 2 vols. (Stuttgart: Deutsche Bibelgesellschaft, 1994).

Abbreviations

AB	Anchor Bible
ANF	Ante-Nicene Fathers. 10 vols. Reprint. Grand Rapids: Eerdmans, 1950–53.
AT	Adorno, Theodor W. *Ästhetische Theorie.* Frankfurt am Main: Suhrkamp, 1970; *Aesthetic Theory.* Translated by Robert Hullot-Kentor. Minneapolis: University of Minnesota Press, 1997.
C. Celsum	Origen. *Contra Celsum.* Translated by Henry Chadwick. Cambridge: Cambridge University Press, 1953. Original in SC 132, 136, 147, 150, 227.
CCSL	Corpus Christianorum, Series Latina. Turnhout: Brepols, 1953–.
Chester	*The Chester Mystery Cycle.* Edited by R. M. Lumiansky and David Mills. EETS s.s. 3, 9. London: Oxford University Press, 1974–86.
CM	Kuriyama, Constance Brown. *Christopher Marlowe: A Renaissance Life.* Ithaca: Cornell University Press, 2002.
Conf.	Augustine. *Confessions.* Edited by James J. O'Donnell. 3 vols. Oxford: Clarendon Press, 1992. Translated by R. S. Pine-Coffin. Harmondsworth: Penguin, 1961.
CSEL	Corpus Scriptorum Ecclesiasticorum Latinorum. Vienna, 1866–.
DMC	Young, Karl. *The Drama of the Medieval Church.* 2 vols. Oxford: Clarendon Press, 1933.
EETS	Early English Text Society
FC	The Fathers of the Church: A New Translation. Washington, D.C.: Catholic University of America Press, 1947–.
GCS	Die griechischen christlichen Schriftsteller der ersten drei Jahrhunderte. 53 vols. Leipzig: Hinrichs; Berlin: Akademie-Verlag, 1897–1969.
KEM	Origenes. *Der Kommentar zum Evangelium nach Matthäus.* Translated by Hermann J. Vogt. 3 vols. Stuttgart: Anton Hiersemann, 1983–93.

LCL	Loeb Classical Library. Cambridge: Harvard University Press, 1912–.
L&S	Liddell, Henry George, and Robert Scott. *A Greek-English Lexicon*. 9th ed. Oxford: Clarendon Press, 1968.
Luz	Luz, Ulrich. *Matthew: A Commentary*. Vol. 1 translated by Wilhelm C. Linss. Minneapolis: Augsburg, 1989. Vols. 2–3 translated by James E. Crouch. Hermeneia. Minneapolis: Fortress, 2001–2005.
LW	*Luther's Works*. American edition. 55 vols. Philadelphia: Fortress; St. Louis: Concordia, 1955–86.
LXX	Septuagint
ME	Lubac, Henri de. *Medieval Exegesis*. Translated by Mark Sebanc and E. M. Macierowski. 2 vols. Grand Rapids: Eerdmans, 2000.
NPNF	Nicene and Post-Nicene Fathers, First Series. 14 vols. Reprint. Grand Rapids: Eerdmans, 1983.
NPNF II	Nicene and Post-Nicene Fathers, Second Series. 14 vols. Reprint. Grand Rapids: Eerdmans, 1983.
NRSV	New Revised Standard Version
NT	New Testament
NTA	*New Testament Apocrypha*. Edited by Wilhelm Schneemelcher. Translation edited by R. McL. Wilson. Revised ed. 2 vols. Louisville, Ky.: Westminster/John Knox Press, 1991–92.
OT	Old Testament
PG	Patrologia cursus completus, Series Graeca. 161 vols. Paris, 1857–66.
PL	Patrologia cursus completus, Series Latina. 221 vols. Paris, 1844–64.
RSV	Revised Standard Version
SC	Sources chrétiennes. Paris: Cerf, 1941–.
TC	Metzger, Bruce M. *A Textual Commentary on the Greek New Testament*. 2nd ed. Stuttgart: Deutsche Bibelgesellschaft, 1994.
Towneley	*The Towneley Plays*. Edited by Martin Stevens and A. C. Cawley. EETS s.s. 13–14. Oxford: Oxford University Press, 1994.
WA	*D. Martin Luthers Werke*. Kritische Gesamtausgabe. 61 vols. Weimar: Hermann Böhlaus Nachfolger, 1883–1983.
WSA	*Works of Saint Augustine: A Translation for the 21st Century*. Hyde Park, N.Y.: New City Press, 1990–.
York	*York Mystery Plays*. Edited by Richard Beadle. London: E. Arnold, 1982.

The Aesthetics of Antichrist

After Strange Gods

The Making of Christ and His Doubles

The Orthodoxy of Heresy

Antichrist appears by name first in the Johannine epistles and not again for about a hundred years.[1] By then a lot had happened. To flesh out the figure certain passages in scripture, originally unrelated, had to be connected. Extrapolation ran rampant. The lawless "man of sin" or "son of perdition" predicted to arrive before the innocent son of God could lawfully second his first appearance (2 Thess. 2:3, 8); the sea monster foretold by John to star in a devilish trinity comprising itself, a Dragon, and land beast (Rev. 11:7, 13:1–10);[2] the pseudo-Christs and false prophets enshrined throughout the gospels and apostolic epistles: under scrutiny from the learned these multiple demons had jelled into one. That

---

1. 1 Jn 2:18, 23; 4:3, and 2 Jn 7, ca. 100 CE. The development of an Antichrist figure prior to the New Testament has been laid out by Geert W. Lorein, *The Antichrist Theme in the Intertestamental Period* (London: T & T Clark International, 2003). Two others, L. J. Lietaert Peerbolte, *The Antecedents of Antichrist: A Traditio-Historical Study of the Earliest Christian Views on Eschatological Opponents* (Leiden: Brill, 1996), and Gregory C. Jenks, *The Origins and Early Development of the Antichrist Myth* (Berlin: de Gruyter, 1991), take the story through to the third-century Fathers. See also William C. Weinrich, "Antichrist in the Early Church," *Concordia Theological Quarterly* 49 (1985): 135–47. Wilhelm Bousset's seminal work, originally published in 1895 and now reprinted in translation, remains valuable: *The Antichrist Legend: A Chapter in Christian and Jewish Folklore*, trans. A. H. Keane (Atlanta: Scholars Press, 1999). The most comprehensive study is Bernard McGinn, *Antichrist: Two Thousand Years of the Human Fascination with Evil* (New York: Columbia University Press, 2000). I have borrowed from McGinn the phrase "dialectical counterpart" (37) at the end of this paragraph and will have subsequent occasion to quote from his superb work.

2. "Devilish trinity" belongs to Josef Ernst, *Die eschatologischen Gegenspieler in den Schriften des Neuen Testaments* (Regensburg: Pustet, 1967), p. 96. Richard K. Emmerson, *Antichrist in the Middle Ages: A Study of Medieval Apocalypticism, Art, and Literature* (Seattle: University of Washington Press, 1981), calls it a "parodic Trinity" (24), as do a number of other scholars cited by Jenks (*Origins*, p. 236 n. 29), though he finds such phrases anachronistic.

ominous composite then became in effect the dialectical counterpart to Christ, his doppelgänger and dark supplement.

Further corroboration for Antichrist's coming could be had from the texts on which these texts were based, Daniel especially, and the discernment of his presence here too, in the newly christened "Old" Testament, was of a piece with its christening. Antichrist provided yet another instance of continuity with the one tradition that Christians could not, except by continuing, otherwise supplant. The Jews had been right. They had rightly predicted their own intransigence. Evidently a number were still holding out (at least in the eyes of their Christian opponents) for a messiah who might deliver his people from worldly affliction, whereas Jesus had not. Even some of his own disciples seem to have wished for more than they got. "We had hoped," comes the sad confession in Luke, "that he was the one to redeem Israel" (Lk 24:21; cf. Acts 1:6). Hope such as this, true Christians in time had had to give up—or what amounts to the same thing, such hope had been spiritualized. Antichrist proved the gentiles' righteousness. It was *he*, not the real Christ, who would raise the kingdom of the Jews, end the Diaspora, and restore their nation.[3] Holdouts for a messiah other than Jesus would no longer get the Son of God but rather "the Son of the Devil" (*Antichrist* 15, 57 [GCS 1:11, 37; ANF 5:207, 216]).

Meanwhile Antichrist gave an indirect answer to the "Jewish" accusations, repeated emphatically by scripture and echoing through subsequent centuries, according to which *Jesus* is the real impostor, a "deceiver" who "leads people astray" (Mt 27:63; Jn 7:12) by equating himself with God (Jn 5:18, 10:33, 19:7) though really an "evildoer" (Jn 18:30) and blasphemer (Mk 14:64; Mt 9:3, 26:65).[4] Christians might now admit that these accusations

3. Irenaeus, *Adv. haer.* 5.25.4 (SC 153:318–22; ANF 1:554); Hippolytus, *Antichrist* 25, 54 (GCS 1:18, 36; ANF 5:209, 215). On Antichrist's relationship to Judaism, see Jenks, *Origins*, pp. 83–86; David G. Dunbar, "Hippolytus of Rome and the Eschatological Exegesis of the Early Church," *Westminster Theological Quarterly* 45 (1983): 322–39, specifically 331–32; and J. A. Cerrato, *Hippolytus between East and West: The Commentaries and the Provenance of the Corpus* (Oxford: Oxford University Press, 2002), p. 156.

4. These and similar accusations against Jesus are collected from multiple sources by Joseph Klausner, *Jesus of Nazareth: His Life, Times, and Teaching*, trans. Herbert Danby (New York: Macmillan, 1953), pp. 18–54; see also Wayne A. Meeks, *The Prophet-King: Moses Traditions and the Johannine Christology* (Leiden: Brill, 1967), pp. 55–56. The calumnies were picked up by Christianity's cultured despisers early on (e.g., Celsus, Porphyry, the emperor Julian) so that an extensive apologetics eventually developed to combat them. See, for example, Frederick W. Norris, "Eusebius on Jesus as Deceiver and Sorcerer," in *Eusebius, Christianity, and Judaism*, ed. Harold W. Attridge and Gohei Hata (Detroit: Wayne State University Press, 1992), pp. 523–40. For the argument that the charges involving magic were, in fact, historically true of Jesus, see Morton Smith, *Jesus the Magician* (San Francisco: Harper & Row, 1978).

were true after all, but only of Antichrist. According to Irenaeus, it is *he* who will come as an "an apostate and robber"; he who "wants to be adored as God and though a slave wants himself proclaimed king"; he whose reign will be "lawless" (*Adv. haer.* 5.25.1 [SC 153:308–9; ANF 5:553])—*not* the reign of Jesus, that humble King of Kings who could hardly be said to have freed his followers from the Law by way of apostasy since on the contrary Jesus had offered to it full and final payment (Mt 20:28; Mk 10:45; 1 Tim. 2:6). Granted he was crucified as a robber and "counted among the lawless" (Mk 15:28; Lk 22:37), but this was in accordance with prophecy (Isa. 53:12), so no one had the right to think him an outlaw in fact. Impossible. Or rather it was a possibility held open among Christians only in displaced and neutralized form as the thought of someone else who was really not even thinking about Christ but rather of his opposite. Antichrist bears the sins of Christ. If it so happens that Jesus shamefully took the form of a slave (Phil. 2:7) in contradiction to his godly claims, still, he was no such slave as Antichrist, nor half so presumptuous. Antichrist would "set aside all idols to make believe that he himself is God, raising up himself as the only idol" (*Adv. haer.*, ibid.), where Christ by contrast had as a child destroyed all pagan artifice and set in its place the artful icon of his genuine godhead.[5] Their careers were to be mirror images: the same, but opposed. Inversion, for Christ, is the ultimate complement.

"The true birth of Antichrist," writes Bernard McGinn, "is inseparable from belief that Jesus of Nazareth, an itinerant Jewish preacher active around 30 C.E., was the messiah....Antichrist was not an accident or a superfluous addition to Christian faith....Early Christians *needed* the legend of Antichrist."[6] What they needed above all was a way to deal with

5. Isa. 19:1 provides the scriptural impetus for the enormously popular medieval legend of the infant Christ destroying Egypt's idols during his childhood visit. If Irenaeus knew of the legend and means to invert it here, he would probably have known of it only in oral form, which predates the written versions we have today, as noted by François Bovon and Pierre Geoltrain, eds., *Écrits apocryphes chrétiens* (Paris: Gallimard, 1997), p. 109n. Irenaeus was among the first to condemn the spread of these kinds of legends (*Adv. haer.* 1.20.1) in favor of a fourfold gospel (*Adv. haer.* 3.11.8), but his condemnation obviously failed: if it hadn't, medieval drama would look very different. See, for instance, the destruction of the idols in *Chester* 10.285–88 + SD, whose editors cite contemporary examples of the same idea. I deal with the "parabiblicism" of medieval drama in chapter 3.

6. McGinn, *Antichrist* (n. 1), p. 33; my emphasis. He continues with the remark that the Antichrist legend "resulted logically from the opposition between good and evil implied in the acceptance of Jesus as divine Son of Man, Christ, and, later, Word of God." In what follows I offer considerable resistance to this viewpoint, on the grounds that the "logic" behind Antichrist is not that of binary opposition between good and evil but rather of dialectical cooperation. As McGinn himself notes, apocalyptic legends like that of Antichrist "imply a strong element of theodicy" (15), such that "no apocalyptic text considers evil to

the adamant rejection of Jesus by the far more numerous non-Christians who, if they thought of him at all, saw him as a hysterical libertine or magician, a would-be king or messianic pretender. Antichrist maintained but deflected these widespread suspicions. In the process he helped Christian churches redirect at their own undesirable or apostate members all the charges originally leveled against Christ and his followers. "Now there are many Antichrists," announces the first of three epistles insinuated into the canon under the apostolic name of John in order to oppose a group of "false prophets" (1 Jn 4:1) that by the writer's own account first originated from *within* the Johannine community: "They went out from us, but were not of us" (1 Jn 2:18b–19a).[7] From, not of. A succinct distinction, which captures the full genius of Christian self-justification when faced with the social fissures that faith in Christ historically induces. Antichrist is the part of itself the church would repudiate. Hence what McGinn calls the "external-internal polarity" (4) of the figure: Antichrist excuses animosity among differing Christians while acting as its chief expression. Even more than Christ he offers impunity. Any internal furor, any mutual recrimination that members of the Johannine community prove impotent to mend or actively wish to foment, they can disavow by way of Antichrist. He is the critical symptom of their faux collective and will come in time to bear the full burden of Christianity's mounting bad conscience, as well as the germ of its severest self-critique—and with that, its best claim to truth. The critique, as well as its truth, grows in proportion to Christian bad faith.

Witness Hippolytus, nominal author of the earliest known treatise exclusively on Antichrist and fated by Irony, the hardest god of church history, to enter the annals of scholarship as the first antipope.[8] His election to

---

be a separate principle or cause independent of God's will; hence, any form of ontological or cosmological dualism is ruled out" (21; cf. 23). There were of course surreptitious ways to reinstate that dualism (e.g., "moral or ethical dualism"), but as we'll see there were also ways to resist these evasions.

7. For discussion and full bibliography of the Johannine opponents, see Raymond E. Brown, *The Epistles of John*, AB 30 (New York: Doubleday, 1982), pp. 47–115, and Daniel J. Harrington, ed., *1, 2, and 3 John* (Collegeville, Minn.: Liturgical Press, 2002), pp. 84–94.

8. For Hippolytus the Novatianist, later reconciled and killed as a martyr, see Prudentius, *Liber Peristephanon* 11 (CCSL 126:370–78; trans. M. Clement Eagan, FC 43:242–59). His account borrows heavily from Seneca's *Hippolytus* in a nearly perfect example of pagan drama undergoing Christianization; it is therefore not a very reliable piece of evidence for the historical career of the person who actually wrote the Hippolytan corpus; nor is it likely to be "a fiction based upon misunderstood facts" as interpreted by the originator of the antipope theory, Johann Joseph Ignanz von Döllinger, *Hippolytus and Callistus, or the Church of Rome in the First Half of the Third Century*, trans. Alfred Plummer (Edinburgh: T & T Clark, 1876), p. 57. His thesis has held sway until recently, however, and is still repeated. For critique and bibliography, see Cerrato, *Hippolytus* (n. 3).

a schismatic's highest office, however historically dubious, captures the genuine spirit of his treatise, for like the majority of third-century commentaries it targets unbelieving Jews less fiercely than all-too-devoted Christians—those heretics and other losers who went for strange doctrines early enough in the tradition that, given time, their accusers too could still fall victim to the same accusation. No one yet knew who the true God was going to be. It depended on the winning faction.[9] Followers of Marcion who thought it possible to root out any residual Judaism from the emergent canon (and against whom Hippolytus supposedly wrote a now lost treatise)[10] were denounced by Tertullian, for example, as being in fact too much akin to Jews and therefore at bottom a bunch of "Antichrists,"[11] though Tertullian himself would later take fire from parties ostensibly more orthodox. "In reality," writes Martin Werner,

> if the newly developing Catholic Church be measured by the same rule by which it condemned other groups and tendencies as heretical, it is itself nothing other than a heresy, but certainly the most pregnant, which ultimately had driven triumphantly all others from the field. This victory it did

9. See Walter Bauer, *Orthodoxy and Heresy in Earliest Christianity*, ed. Robert A. Kraft and Gerhard Krodel (Philadelphia: Fortress, 1971), with appendices on subsequent scholarship; also Michael Desjardins, "Bauer and Beyond: On Recent Scholarly Discussion of Αἵρεσις in the Early Christian Era," *The Second Century* 8 (1991): 65–82; and more recently Bart D. Ehrman, *Lost Christianities: The Battle for Scripture and the Faiths We Never Knew* (Oxford: Oxford University Press, 2003), a major and clear-sighted contribution. I am going to be suggesting that certain elements of Ehrman's "lost" Christianities never wholly disappeared but rather continued to live on *within* the orthodoxy that as often subsumed as suppressed them. Medieval drama gives only one exceptionally colorful, widespread example of the thriving life of "heresy" within the confines of the church. Scholastic dispute gives another.

10. Eusebius, *Hist. eccl.* 6.22 (LCL vol. 2); Jerome, *De vir. ill.* 61.2 (PL 23:07A; trans. Thomas P. Halton, FC 100:88).

11. Tertullian, *Adv. Marc.* 3.8 (CCSL 1²:518; ANF 3:327). David Efroymson, "Tertullian's Anti-Jewish Rhetoric: Guilt by Association," *Union Seminary Quarterly Review* 36 (1980): 25–37, points out that Tertullian often tarred his opponents with the brush of Judaism in order to prove the incompatibility of their position, whatever it was, with "true" Christianity. His treatise against Marcion in fact incorporates large portions of his treatise against the Jews, a major irony (given Marcion's open hostility to Judaism) made more potent still by the possibility that Marcion, like Paul, was himself a convert *from* Judaism, as suggested by Adolph von Harnack, *Marcion: The Gospel of the Alien God*, trans. John E. Steely and Lyle D. Bierma (Durham: Labyrinth, 1990), p. 15. For a translation of Tertullian's *Against the Jews* and an introduction to the topic of early Christian hostility to Judaism with a good bibliography of the debate as it has raged since the publication of Rosemary Reuther, *Faith and Fratricide: The Theological Roots of Anti-Semitism* (New York: Seabury Press, 1974), see Geoffrey D. Dunn, *Tertullian* (London: Routledge, 2004), esp. pp. 47–51 and 63ff.

not in the end even owe to the fact that it had simply fought the opposing heresies, but to the fact that it had taken over from them very positive and important suggestions, which it had then proceeded to convert after its own fashion to suitable means for its own new construction of doctrine.[12]

We will return to this bracing definition, according to which defeated, "aberrant" opinions precede or otherwise determine the shape of their normative correctives. A microcosm of the resulting richness and complexity of the Christian faith, taken as a whole in the sum total of disagreements that form its faulted essence, can be glimpsed in the similarly ironic fate suffered by Hippolytus' contemporary and fellow Antichrist-hunter, Tertullian. At some point he chose to join the New Prophecy, an inauspiciously named apocalyptic movement that according to report he had previously attacked. (Novelty is the bête noire of would-be traditionalists.) Is it possible that Tertullian at first *reproached* his future, sectarian comrades? Augustine thought so.[13] Even if that supposition is not exactly right, it would not have been the only time a Christian's contempt has secretly expressed his utmost delight. Some lovers of the cross love everything condemned. They really do love their enemies. Condemnation keeps what they reject perpetually alive—not unlike the risen Christ, whose death sentence ensured an imperishable afterlife.

The morass of wrong doctrine and rapturous polemic of course started well before patristic heresiology, or the Johannine epistles. The gospels themselves repeatedly denounce a number of fellow travelers who *seem* like Christians, but really aren't. On that day, Jesus reveals, "many will say to me, 'Lord, Lord, did we not prophesy in your name, and cast out demons in your name, and do many mighty works in your name?' And then I will declare to them, 'I never knew you; depart from me, you evildoers'" (Mt 7:15, 22–23). Scholars have inferred from this passage and others like it a plenitude of competitors on the primitive Christian market

12. Martin Werner, *The Formation of Christian Dogma: A Historical Study of Its Problem*, trans. S. G. F. Brandon (New York: Harper & Brothers, 1957), p. 52.

13. *De haer.* 86 (CCSL 46:338–39; *WSA* I/18:54). David Rankin, *Tertullian and the Church* (Cambridge: Cambridge University Press, 1995), considers Tertullian's initial hostility to Montanus "an intriguing possibility" (50) in a book that otherwise marks a major increase in scholarly resistance to the ancient idea that Tertullian formally left the church and "wrote books against it," as reported (for example) by Jerome, *De vir. ill.* 53.5 (PL 23:661C–664A; trans. Halton, FC 100:74–75). Later Montanists unquestionably *were* separatists, as were the sectarians who called themselves Tertullianistae and so presumably traced their lineage back to Tertullian. What this tells us about Tertullian's own stance vis-à-vis the church is still open to debate.

who apparently had as much charisma as the correct apostles, equally impressive miracles, and an overall message every bit as electrifying as the once-and-for-all declaration to which the gospel communities wanted to hold as to a unique revelation. Who these charlatans actually were has been much debated among modern interpreters, but it would best befit subsequent conflicts if the Synoptic "false prophets" in certain instances referred to followers of Paul,[14] that former persecutor of Christians and renegade apostle from outside Christ's Twelve, the "dialectical disputant" (*C. Cresconium donatistam* 1.14.17 [PL 43:456]) beloved of Augustine and Luther, whose letters place vitriolic diatribe against one's fellows at the heart of the church—naturally in the name of greater openness, and tolerance. Whatever Paul's actual message or intent, his idiom would eventually come to express the flaming self-hatred continually stoked among Christians, as though the Pauline mission had become a permanent reminder of the intramural trauma at the religion's deepest origin and the guarantor of its perpetual renewal, lest there disappear with the internecine conflict any viable definition of a "true" Christian. As Paul had written to the infighting Corinthians, so would it be for the better part of Christian history: "There must be factions [*haireseis*] among you, that those who are genuine...may be recognized" (1 Cor. 11:19).

Infighting between these groups arguably produced the majority of documents that now make up the New Testament. Speaking specifically of Matthew's false prophets, David Aune remarks that whoever they were, they're best understood as "a form of antistructure which posed a great threat to the existing structure of the Matthean community."[15] The same could surely be said of the antichristian opponents facing every Christian community, with the added provision that such "antistructures," encoded in scripture, invariably help *constitute* the community. Their parodic bastardization of the true faith proves which members are serious. So that even once the supposed threat has lapsed, there is good reason to embellish, or at a minimum preserve, the imaginative possibility of its imminent reemergence—to apotheosize its coming, so to speak, as an impending

14. As suggested by Johannes Weiss, *Earliest Christianity: A History of the Period A.D. 30–150*, trans. Frederick C. Grant, 2 vols. (1914–17; repr. New York: Harper & Row, 1959), 2:753; also H. D. Betz, "Eine Episode im Jüngsten Gericht (Mt 7,21–23)," *Zeitschrift für Theologie und Kirche* 78 (1981): 1–30; here 28, conceded a little begrudgingly by Luz 1:442 as "some form of vulgar Paulinism." He provides further bibliography on the other interpretations (1:441 nn. 14–17). See also John K. Riches, *Conflicting Mythologies: Identity Formation in the Gospels of Mark and Matthew* (Edinburgh: T & T Clark, 2000), esp. pp. 202–28.

15. David E. Aune, *Prophecy in Early Christianity and the Ancient Mediterranean World* (Grand Rapids: Eerdmans, 1983), pp. 222–24.

apocalypse. And by "imminent" or "impending," I mean to stress that scripture stipulates an undiscoverable hour, one constantly deferred, so potentially ever present. Inevitable, but not quite yet.[16] That at least is how I understand the emphatic limitation that no one, neither the angels that are in heaven nor even the Son,[17] can say when history will reach its nearing conclusion, whereupon so many false prophets will appear, along with Antichrist, before the arrival, finally, of Christ "himself"—whoever that is going to be. This fundamental ignorance about the timing of his second coming seems to diffuse vigilance in such a way that the promise (which is also a threat) becomes timeless and permanent and would forever guarantee, symbolically at least, the integrity of those who tantalize themselves by means of it. Hence the ache and unstilled longing—in a word, the beauty—of apocalypse: the perpetual predictions and titillating deferrals serve all the better to secure a fallen collective around the cultivation of this common arousal. Under differing historical conditions and given differing personal temperaments, of course some Christians have felt the stirrings of a final consummation more deeply than others. This accounts for the difference in degree, less pronounced than one might think, between those with a truly apocalyptic outlook (i.e., those with a real sense of urgency) and their cooler counterparts who manage to contain their expectations within the more flexible framework of a generalized

16. Much of the scholarly debate on the pronounced biblical tension between the "already" of Christ having come and the "not yet" of his coming back (save for the abortive and enigmatic appearances after the cross) has centered on the related tension between what Jesus "actually" taught (regarding, for example, the Kingdom) and what his followers retroactively *thought* he must have taught (and chose to record) in light of subsequent events, chief among them the calamity of his death, the destruction of the Temple, and their persecution by Romans as a pestilent sect. Things are made a lot easier for the present study by reason of its relative indifference to the "historical" Jesus, though on the whole I tend to side with the school of thought sometimes called "consistent eschatology." For summaries of the many other scholarly positions (the existentialism of Bultmann, the "realized eschatology" of Dodd, etc.), too numerous to go into here and of limited relevance, see Hans Schwarz, *Eschatology* (Grand Rapids: Eerdmans, 2000).

17. Mk 13:32; Mt 24:36, though in some mss. of the latter case these words—"nor the Son"—have been suppressed, as has the whole passage in Luke (who says however in Acts 1:7 that no one besides God can foretell the final end). See *TC* 51–52 and Bart D. Ehrman, *The Orthodox Corruption of Scripture: The Effect of Early Christological Controversies on the Text of the New Testament* (Oxford: Oxford University Press, 1993), pp. 91–92. One lesson to take away from the textual struggle over the Son's ignorance about the timing of apocalypse is not that a potentially heretical stumbling block has been eliminated from scripture but that the stumbling block remains for all to see (in Mark), *despite* successful attempts to remove it elsewhere. Such residual "heresies" *within scripture* will have enormous consequences for medieval and early modern Christian factionalism.

eschatology.[18] In either case, everybody is going to wait. Presumably the wait that is torture to some has been sweet to others, and for still others the torture itself has been sweetest. For none should it have been a matter of indifference. Till Kingdom come, according to the gospels, Christians of all stripes can look forward in the meantime to increasing conflict and factionalism, as nation will rise against nation, kingdom against kingdom; there will be earthquakes, famine, pestilence, fearful sights and great signs from heaven. The worse things get, the better. For as Jesus himself has taught, "when these things begin to take place, then look up and raise your heads, because your redemption is drawing near" (Lk 21:28).

When Hippolytus quotes this passage in his Antichrist treatise (§64 [GCS 1:44; ANF 5:218]), it refers indirectly to the proliferation of his own enemies and would transform them, by means of the coded allusion, into a source, for his friends, of eschatological consolation. In Luke by comparison it likely refers to the recent destruction of the Temple (70 CE) predicted by the verses immediately preceding (19:41–44, 21:20–24) in what is the most direct, unambiguous reference of all the gospels to the Jewish uprising's catastrophic aftermath. "This addition is a striking one," writes Jonathan Knight, for it "makes the recent past a sign that Jesus will return."[19] And not just any element of the recent past, but the one

---

18. For this and other distinctions among the many premodern ways of contemplating the end of history, together with an account of the equally various (and incompatible) positions adopted by scholars on this topic, see Bernard McGinn, *Visions of the End: Apocalyptic Traditions in the Middle Ages* (New York: Columbia University Press, 1998), esp. pp. xiii–41. I have taken very much to heart his insight that the "apocalyptic author frequently differs from the merely eschatological one more in degree than in kind" (4). This is to say, if we set aside differences of "mere" degree, it should be possible to investigate a fundamental *sameness in kind* that establishes some real kinship between apocalyptic "in the proper sense of the term" and anti-apocalyptic writers (like Augustine) who nonetheless view history as progressing inexorably toward its cataclysmic conclusion.

19. Jonathan Knight, *Luke's Gospel* (London: Routledge, 1998), p. 189; against Hans Conzelmann, whose exegesis of this chapter, once in the ascendancy, now in eclipse, nevertheless helpfully explains how its eschatological aspect draws from the community's present suffering a form of "consolation." As he says, "the cosmic upheaval"—whenever it should come—"does not affect the elect; on the contrary it brings them liberation" (*The Theology of St. Luke,* trans. Geoffrey Buswell [New York: Harper, 1960], pp. 129–30). For an account and critique of those who would deny the role of contemporary history in these verses, see Joseph A. Fitzmyer, *The Gospel According to Luke,* 2 vols., AB 28, 28a (Garden City, N.Y.: Doubleday, 1983), 2:1253–54, 1342–44. The usual rationale for dating the other predictions of the Temple's destruction (e.g., Mk 13:2) to *before* its actual ruin is that Jesus' literal prediction does not come true. As medieval crusaders were perhaps surprised to learn, some of the stones continue to stand, one upon the other, which makes the prophecies in Mark and Matthew less likely to have been fabricated *ex eventu.* See E. P. Sanders, *The Historical Figure of Jesus* (New York: Penguin, 1993), pp. 256–57.

event that might have most threatened to attenuate the expectations of weaker Christians, unless Jesus himself could be shown to have predicted it. Failure itself could then fulfill their hopes. They only had to be strong of heart. They could otherwise relax. We will see in all that follows this repeated transformation of historical calamity into triumph, or rather the miscarriage of history as such into a sign of impending deliverance and the workaday world into a place where everything factual is to some extent false because if the good God exists and atrocity still happens, then events themselves must be at worst a divine figure of speech. Because to imagine events not only as events but also as a semiotic system through which God narrates his mystery is to view lived history as so many rhetorical elements of some overarching story—subject, *qua* sign, to all the analytic joy of literary criticism—whose godly author has a real knack for artistic foreshadowing, for orchestrating the exquisite pleasures of the tragic turn, and whose promise of redemption is therefore caught up in the whole enigma of aesthetic enjoyment.[20]

From Script to Scripture

Judaism was not the only religion whose fraudulence the Christian faith could not afford to jettison. Once the church began to win the majority of its converts from pagan as opposed to Jewish peoples, there remained an expectation that Christianity could invariably surpass a convert's earlier worship not through simple cancellation but through something more like typological fulfillment. The Christian anxiety of influence, clear enough with respect to Judaism, was consequently in places just as acute with respect to the Graeco-Roman theater, paganism's most lasting shrine and the staging ground for its resplendent mythology. "If the literature of the stage delights you," writes Tertullian, "we have literature in abundance of our own—plenty of verses, sentences, songs, proverbs," with the added benefit, he says, that the Christian script, for all its apparent artifice, is entirely real (*Adv. spect.* 29; LCL). Nor was Tertullian alone among the authorities,

---

20. The ideological and psychological functions of such enjoyment have been theorized with particular panache by Slavoj Žižek, e.g., *For They Know Not What They Do: Enjoyment as a Political Factor* (London: Verso, 1991). Žižek has increasingly insisted on the primacy of Christian thought in his own theoretical work. See, for two examples, *The Puppet and the Dwarf: The Perverse Core of Christianity* (Cambridge: MIT Press, 2003), and *The Fragile Absolute: or Why Is the Christian Legacy Worth Fighting For?* (London: Verso, 2000). On aesthetics specifically I am much beholden to Adorno's unsurpassed *Aesthetic Theory* (AT); see my preface, n. 6.

a lot of them converts, who knowingly or otherwise wanted to arrogate to Christian scripture and ritual the full authority of classical theater.[21] Somebody in the fourth century—some say Gregory of Nazianzus—patched together a cento from the plays of Euripides with Christ as the new tragic hero (SC 149). His groans and tears, writes Gregory elsewhere, were in any case already "dramatized and marvelously composed for us" (*Orat.* 30.6 [SC 250:236]). He means that the passion, though entirely historical, had been nonetheless *staged* by the Author of all history; therefore that Christ's suffering on behalf of others was just as beautiful, say, as the crushing of Oedipus, only Christ's drama could have even more lasting effects on an appreciative audience. It's a sensibility this study will touch on constantly. "The illustrations that Christ employed in his preaching," Jaroslav Pelikan points out, were often likened by the Cappadocians "to the costumes and stage props in the performance of Greek tragedies, which symbolized the truth being conveyed but were not identical with it."[22] Precisely this discrepancy between Christian truth and the unavoidable contingencies of its worldly conveyance will again and again draw its advocates back toward an aesthetic discourse, albeit one submerged in their antitheatricalism, as well as in their allegoresis. We will see that the hermeneutic eye almost by definition views sacred history in such a way that mere appearances— utterly corrupt in comparison to the invisible deity, hence open to endless criticism—nonetheless signify or represent his truest substance, which is beyond all reproach save for what his appearance itself inspires, absorbs, and in the absorption atones for. The scandal of mere theatrics acts here as a formal equivalent of grace.

Pelikan's warning that the tendency of theologians to compare their religious myths to classical theater "should not be permitted to obscure their attacks on the dramatic poets" (24) frankly seems to me far better off reversed: the theologians' war against theater should never obscure their radical debt to it, least of all where obfuscation seems to have been their unspoken goal. Only recently have modern scholars been willing to argue what the church Fathers and later medieval authorities appear to have suspected all along and sometimes state outright: namely, that the story of Christ really *is* dramatic—and not just metaphorically, it turns out, but as a matter of generic influence. No doubt this is the reason patristic attacks

---

21. On Augustine, see below, pp. 72–74 and 123. For Tertullian's former love of the spectacles he denounces, see *Adv. spect.* 19.5 (LCL), *Apol.* 15.5, 18.4 (CCSL 1¹:114, 118; ANF 3:30, 32).

22. Jaroslav Pelikan, *Christianity and Classical Culture: The Metamorphosis of Natural Theology in the Christian Encounter with Hellenism* (New Haven: Yale University Press, 1993), p. 23.

on the theater possess such a symptomatic intensity: the Synoptic tradition partly originates in classical drama. The gospel according to Mark—in all likelihood the earliest we possess and, if the dominant supposition is right, a key source for Matthew and Luke—specifically exhibits all the telltale traces of dramatic convention[23]: the developmental progress structured, as it were, into acts and building up, through the hero's *hybris* of claiming kinship with God, to a conventional reversal of fortune (*peripeteia*); the *anagnōrisis* or scene of recognition with Peter's confession, the repeated, Cassandra-esque predictions of a coming atrocity, the "final oracle" from Jesus in his apocalyptic speech, the *katastrophē* of his arrest, the *pathos* of crucifixion, the practically Euripidean *deus ex machina* when a youth from out of nowhere announces that Jesus is risen and therefore gone.[24]

These are not the only generic markers on display in the gospel, but they are arguably the ones that would have been most pronounced to the earliest "readers," since in its original context the gospel of Mark was not read. It was recited—performed even.[25] The evangelist would have assumed as a matter of course that his words, already modeled (consciously or not) on classical drama, would be read out loud, probably in a liturgical context. The parenthetical aside that occurs in the course of Christ's small apocalypse to "let the reader understand" (13:14), for example, likely results from the interpolation of a marginal note telling the lector to beware the grammatical solecism in the preceding phrase, over which his

23. For a discussion citing the major earlier studies, see Joel Marcus, *Mark 1–8*, AB 27 (New York: Doubleday, 1999), pp. 68–69, and the next two notes. A similar interpretation has since been taken up with respect to John: Jo-Ann A. Brant, *Dialogue and Drama: Elements of Greek Tragedy in the Fourth Gospel* (Peabody, Mass.: Hendrickson, 2004). For the theological argument in favor of Christianity's dramatic core, see Hans Urs von Balthasar, *Theo-Drama: Theological Drama Theory*, trans. Graham Harrison, 5 vols. (San Francisco: Ignatius Press, 1988).

24. Roughly following the point-by-point comparison of Martin Hengel, *Studies in the Gospel of Mark*, trans. John Bowden (Philadelphia: Fortress, 1985), pp. 34–37. See also next note.

25. Gilbert G. Bilezikian, *The Liberated Gospel: A Comparison of the Gospel of Mark and Greek Tragedy* (Grand Rapids: Baker, 1977), pp. 113–14, 118–19; Whitney Shiner, "Applause and Applause Lines in the Gospel of Mark," in *Rhetorics and Hermeneutics: Wilhelm Wuellner and His Influence*, ed. James D. Hester and J. David Hester (New York: T & T Clark International, 2004), pp. 129–44; Joanna Dewey, "The Gospel of Mark as an Oral-Aural Event: Implications for Interpretation," in *The New Literary Criticism and the New Testament*, ed. E. S. Malbon and E. V. McKnight (Sheffield: Sheffield Academic Press, 1994), pp. 145–63; Christopher Bryan, *A Preface to Mark: Notes on the Gospel in Its Literary and Cultural Setting* (Oxford: Oxford University Press, 1993), pp. 67–70, 167–71. For a more general study, with full bibliography, see Samuel Byrskog, *Story as History—History as Story: The Gospel Tradition in the Context of Ancient Oral History* (Tübingen: Mohr, 2000). He points out that the earliest Christian literature "had no life of its own; the written texts...were mostly 'transitional' in the sense that they presupposed and supplemented oral modes of communication, regularly returning to oral modalities" (127).

performance might otherwise trip.[26] From this internal imperative to incorporate into the text an unknown reader's imagination and voice, the gospel gains its most critical asset, namely, the formal refusal of any absolute completion. As a document written for communal recitation, it calls out for supplementation: let the reader read well! Yet as "mere" recitation, it remains forever contingent, a momentary actualization of the words— or Word—whose pure potential (transcendence even) such performance can realize at best only through betrayal: the man reading the words of the Lord obviously cannot read so well as to embody God's fleshy fullness. No matter how talented, his performance *must* fail to capture the Lord's full personhood; else the follower would usurp the position of Jesus and the performance cease to be a subordinate, mimetic form of worship. And in any case, who could imagine the slight lisp of today's celebrant, his gawky manners, wild red hair, or ill-timed cough had nonetheless captured without interference the true divinity of Jesus? All this has to be factored out on the authority of a script that contains by contrast nothing extraneous, even as it lacks, of itself, the contingent and compromised voicing from which it receives its fullest existence.[27]

Fredric Jameson's crowning insight that the ideology of any literary form constitutes at the same time its strongest utopian appeal—even while the form continues to emit various outmoded signals as recurrent symptoms of the previous struggles, repressed by its current function, into which it had earlier been co-opted—finds profound confirmation in the theological drama of Mark (a theology on which Jameson himself readily concedes a certain dependence).[28] It has been argued, for example, that Mark's appropriation of a dramatic form heavily coded or even stigmatized as pagan cuts against his gospel's Jewish content, so that the form itself aids in producing something like a "defiant manifesto of its enfranchisement from sectarian implications," as Gilbert Bilezikian writes, "and

26. See Ernest Best, "The Gospel of Mark: Who Was the Reader?" *Irish Biblical Studies* 11 (1989): 124–32.

27. Cf. the emphasis on the "living voice" at the root of faith in apostolic succession, as for example in the fragment of Papias: Eusebius, *Hist. eccl.* 3.39.4 (LCL vol. 1). In my consideration of this issue I am (indirectly) indebted to Derrida's seminal deconstruction of the philosophical tradition's similar faith in the spoken word (over and against the necessity of writing) as the guarantor of its truths. See Jacques Derrida, *Of Grammatology,* trans. Gayatri Chakravorty Spivak, corrected ed. (Baltimore: Johns Hopkins University Press, 1998).

28. Fredric Jameson, *The Political Unconscious: Narrative as a Socially Symbolic Act* (Ithaca: Cornell University Press, 1981), pp. 29ff. on Christian hermeneutics, pp. 98–102 on form, and pp. 285ff. on Marxism and Christianity.

a bold declaration of its universal relevance."[29] Given the subsequent realization of Christianity's universal relevance through the forced conversion or outright liquidation of uncooperative persons, this puts the Christian case perhaps a little too boldly. It could go without saying, if it were not so often unsaid, that historically the utopia of Christian universalism (as well as its Marxist variants) has itself been one of the more insidious forms of ideological sectarianism. That is why Theodore Weeden's analysis of Mark remains an essential antidote to the sort of triumphalism others have sometimes found in the gospel: if nothing else, Weeden helps establish how Mark was forged above all in response to an insoluble social conflict, and that whatever description of the various factions anybody might settle on, the immediate followers of Jesus are sure to be counted first among the ideologues to the extent they looked to him as a glorious miracle worker and man of power who may have come to an untimely end but whose swift return was supposed to set matters soon aright. This critical celebration of the disciples' contamination by the wrong kind of expectation is, as Weeden suggests (though without quite spelling it out), primarily a *dramatic effect*,[30] following in particular from the gospel's generically tragic conclusion. The followers completely repudiate Jesus (14:10–72) and are in turn abandoned by him. At the end it is a group of women—women!—who discover the empty tomb and then, for all the gospel says, fail to follow the angels' instructions or inform the others of Jesus' resurrection, but tremble, rather, "and were amazed, nor said anything to any man, for they were afraid" (Mk 16:8b). Here ends the gospel according to Mark.[31]

"With Easter Morning, Jesus is absent!"[32] The significance of this exclamation for the aesthetics of Antichrist lies in how Weeden links it not just to the gospel's original ending but also to the apocalyptic speech of Jesus, according to which "he will not be present again until his return at the end of the epoch of world history and the collapse of the cosmos. Anyone claiming that he is present before that is a *beguiler* [13:21ff.]" (op. cit.; my emphasis). Pursued to its utmost this logic leads, I think, to the argument that Mark's own devotion to resuscitating the Lord's presence cannot

29. Bilezikian, *Liberated Gospel* (n. 25), p. 142.

30. Theodore J. Weeden, *Mark: Traditions in Conflict* (Philadelphia: Fortress, 1971), p. 17 and passim.

31. At least in the best witnesses. For discussion and bibliography of the textual issues, see C. S. Mann, *Mark: A New Translation with Introduction and Commentary*, AB 27 (New York: Doubleday, 1986), pp. 159–62 and 677–79.

32. Weeden, *Mark: Traditions in Conflict*, p. 111.

escape the judgment day of its own performance. The earliest audiences of the final oracle would have seen *objectively occurring* what the Lord "himself" had prophesied—if not exactly the arrival of the Kingdom, then at least the Lord's mimetic reduplication as its negative herald: a pseudo-Christ literally appearing in his name and standing in his place, reciting the same proclamations of the Kingdom's near arrival and by the mimetic emptiness of the proclamation paradoxically affirming the ultimate reliability of Christ's prior predictions, even while renewing their deferral. The apocalyptic speech of Mark 13 is thus at once its own vindication and self-defeat. It formally defies what its content posits, granted the further, impossible provision that total defiance alone can fulfill the gospel's real promise. The beauty of Christ's apocalyptic discourse arises, in other words, from the way the performance itself represents the nearest instance of the end it proclaims for the simple reason that it can make proclamations only so long as the end has not come. The gospel is as close as you are going to get, until you get the real thing, which is not yet. Meanwhile the asymptotic approximation of this ersatz performance to authentic salvation seals off the gospel's self-movement from any possible surcease, its immanent dilemmas sublimated for good into a revolutionary and new "Aristotelian" unity. Heaven may never come. But in that case the show never ends.

The Gospel Truth

The peculiar suitability of such dramatic contrivances to matters divine had long been defended in the Greek-speaking world. A fragment from an Aeschylean drama—lost to us but known, perhaps, to the audience of Mark—could almost act proleptically as a gloss on the drama of Antichrist: "A god," it says, "does not abstain from righteous deceit."[33] The implication is that any god who refrains from lying has set an arbitrary limit to his godhead and so diminished it. A real god, by contrast, could afford to indulge in a whole panoply of anthropomorphic maneuvering, even so far as to countenance his own impersonation in the theater, presumably. Had the Greek divinities appeared anywhere else, barring Homer, with greater brilliance?

The counterargument implied by this fragment is fully preserved as the centerpiece of Plato's *Republic*. According to Socrates the gods do, in fact, abstain from deceit, righteous or otherwise (e.g., *Repub.* 381D–382C;

---

33. *Tragicorum Fragmenta Graecorum*, vol. 3, ed. Stegan Radt (Göttingen: Vandenhoeck & Ruprecht), p. 394, fr. 301.

LCL vol. 11). The same cannot be said for poets like Homer, or Aeschylus, who should therefore be banished before poisoning the youth any further with false tales.[34] In reality the city of Athens had condemned *Socrates* for defaming the gods and misleading the young; the resemblance between his philosophy's infraction and the supposed transgression that Plato has him attribute to poets helps underscore how little Plato managed to do without poetry's stock in trade. The philosopher kings remaining after poetry's exile, for instance, would nevertheless reserve for themselves the exercise of so-called noble lies as long as these worked toward the city's moral edification,[35] and the same exemption notoriously extends to Plato's own philosophy: the ban on literary fabrication, specifically on the myths of drama, actually seems to license him to manipulate fiction all the more readily toward his own approved ends. Plato's animus against poets could in fact be said to indemnify his radical dependence on the dialogue form, which by his own admission "works entirely through mimesis" (*Repub.* 294C; ibid.). In his case of course the aim was paradoxically to move the audience away from this traditional, artistic vehicle for truth, so that even if Platonic philosophy as a whole could be classed as a form of closet drama, his philosophy meant to raise itself above Greek theater by dismissing *all other* kinds of drama as useless myth. *The Republic*'s own parable of the cave and myth of Er conform instead to *higher* mythologies, ones that mimetically "liken the false to the true as far as possible and so make it useful" (*Repub.* 382D; ibid.).[36]

Some influential theologians would eventually define the truth of scripture against dramatic fiction through a related form of hypocrisy— a theatrical term I use, here and throughout, as a technical designation for the specific brand of feigning that pretends to repudiate whatever

34. Cf. the criticism of poets offered by Herodotus 2.53 (LCL), as well as the fragments from Heraclitus and Xenophanes quoted and discussed in Ernst Robert Curtius, *European Literature and the Latin Middle Ages*, trans. Willard R. Trask (New York: Pantheon, 1953), pp. 204–5. For an introduction to this ancient aesthetic debate, see Christopher Gill and T. P. Wiseman, eds., *Lies and Fiction in the Ancient World* (Austin: University of Texas Press, 1993).

35. On the noble lie, see *Repub.* 382C–D, 389B–D, 414B, 459D (LCL vol. 11).

36. For a bibliography on Plato's relation to drama, see James A. Arieti, *Interpreting Plato: The Dialogues as Drama* (Savage, Md.: Rowan & Littlefield Publishers, 1991), p. 12 n. 5, with further references spread over pp. 231–46. See also Jonas Barish, *The Anti-Theatrical Prejudice* (Berkeley: University of California Press, 1981), pp. 5–37, and Ramona A. Naddaff, *Exiling the Poets: The Production of Censorship in Plato's Republic* (Chicago: University of Chicago Press, 2002).

mimetic practice it most depends on.[37] Greatly aiding the theologians' case was the letter to Titus,[38] a forged testimonial against falsehood that explicitly adapts to the Christian cause this Platonic notion of a true fiction. Posing as Paul, someone purports to address the church on Crete. The address consists, authentically enough, of a polemical diatribe against a group of false teachers or "counterfeiters" (Ti 1:16) who had infiltrated the church with an unwelcome devotion to "Jewish myths" (1:14). "These people must be silenced," writes Paul's stand-in, "since they are upsetting whole families by teaching for the sake of filthy lucre what they have no right to teach. One of them, a prophet of their own, said: 'Cretans are always liars....' This is a true witness" (1:11–13a). We will have to come back in a later chapter to the persistent connection, heavily emphasized by the medieval Antichrist, between false teaching, incorrect myths, and "filthy lucre," a traditional rendering that dates, like so much of our biblical language, from Tyndale. The multiple layers of feigning here are for the moment sufficiently complex. There are masks within masks: for we face in Titus a canonical document written by an impostor who claims to speak for the God "that never lies" (1:2), who accuses some Christians on Crete of an excessive devotion to myth, and who then, as *proof* of their duplicity, quotes "one of their own," the philosopher-poet Epimenides.[39]

37. *Hypokritēs* in classical Greek means "actor" (e.g., *Poetics* 18, [14]56a; LCL vol. 23); in the NT it means "hypocrite" (Mt 6:2; 23:13ff.). These Matthean instances, plus the LXX rendering of Job 34:40 and 36:13, are the only pejorative uses of the word given by L&S. A. Lukyn Williams, *Talmudic Judaism and Christianity* (London: Society for Promoting Christian Knowledge, 1933), pp. 67ff., argues that the term was not always negative among Greek-speaking Jews.

38. Rejected as spurious already by Marcion, according to Tertullian, *Adv. Marc.* 5.21 (CCSL 1¹:725; ANF 3:473); it was likely written later in order to combat Marcion's influence and that of others like him: so Bauer, *Orthodoxy and Heresy* (n. 9), p. 226: "As its answer to the heretical Apostle of the epistles to Laodicea and Alexandria, 'forged in the name of Paul' (*Pauli nomine finctae*, Muratorian Canon, lines 64ff.) the church raised up the Paul of orthodoxy by using the same means" (i.e., that of forgery); hence the Pastorals. A number of scholars still accept their authenticity, however. For a detailed discussion that decides against Pauline authorship specifically of Titus, with a bibliography of the whole debate, see David G. Meade, *Pseudonymity and Canon: An Investigation into the Relationship of Authorship and Authority in Jewish and Earliest Christian Tradition* (Grand Rapids: Eerdmans, 1987), pp. 118ff. I give more references below in connection with 2 Peter and 2 Thessalonians.

39. On Epimenides, see Diogenes Laertius, *Lives* 1.10.109–15 (LCL vol. 1), and Aristotle, *Rhetoric* 3.17.10 (LCL vol. 22). The attribution to him of the quotation in Titus is traditional and seems to originate with Clement of Alexandria. (See the quotation from Clement in the following paragraph.) Cf. Socrates of Constantinople, *Hist. eccl.* 3.16.24 (SC 493:314–17; NPNF II, 2:88), and Jerome, *Comm. in Titum* 1.12 (CCSL 77c:28), whence the identification enters the wider Middle Ages, e.g., the Gloss (PL 114:639C).

A Cretan, he paradoxically proclaims all Cretans liars. This is true, concludes Pseudo-Paul.[40]

Later readers who wanted to demonstrate the full compatibility between Graeco-Roman letters and the Christian Word, despite the antagonism of their truth claims, could always thereafter turn to the liar of Titus[41]: "Do you see how he ["Paul"] grants a measure of truth even to the prophets of Greece," notes Clement of Alexandria, "and is not ashamed, while discoursing for the edification of some and the shaming of others, to make use of Greek poems?"[42] The potential for "Paul" to shame himself in shaming others inevitably arose from the way he castigated Cretan or Jewish myths as a form of counterfeit even while those same myths were raised, *by means of the castigation*, to the level of Holy Writ. The ruse differs little from what one sees in Plato's thoroughly pagan *Republic*, where the highest truths also find expression through the "right" kind of fiction, which exists, if at all, only as a glorified species of that otherwise depraved genus, the lies of poets. Finally, all poetry, dramatic or otherwise, could be made on this model to speak the truth, against itself, and this self-denial then counted as "philosophy" or "theology" rather than as an immanent moment in the paradoxical self-constitution of what Aristotle called the "nameless" art (*Poetics* 1, [14]47B; LCL vol. 23) and we call literature.

Even as the author of Titus was writing Paul more deeply into the pagan tradition—and thereby proving Paul's superiority to it—other Graeco-

40. For context and a fascinating discussion, see Heinrich Kraft, "Die Paradoxie in der Bibel und bei den Griechen als Voraussetzung für die Entfaltung der Glaubenslehren," in *Das Paradox: Eine Herausforderung des abendländischen Denkens*, ed. Paul Geyer and Roland Hagenbüchle (Tübingen: Stauffenburg, 1992), pp. 247–72 (260–61 on Titus).

41. Would-be humanists could likewise turn to Acts 17:28, where Paul points out to the Athenians that aspects of his special revelation had preceded his arrival in the proclamations of certain Greek poets. Cf. his allusion to Euripides or Menander (1 Cor. 15:33); for discussion see Robert Renehan, "Classical Greek Quotations in the New Testament," in *The Heritage of the Early Church*, ed. David Neiman and Margaret Schatkin (Rome: Pontificale Institutum Studiorum Orientalium, 1973), pp. 17–46, and Robert M. Grant, "Early Christianity and Greek Comic Poetry," *Classical Philology* 60 (1965): 157–63. For the classicism of the Fathers, see E. A. Quinn, "St. Jerome as Humanist," in *A Monument to St. Jerome*, ed. Francis X. Murphy (New York: Sheed & Ward, 1952), pp. 201–32 and E. K. Rand, *The Founders of the Middle Ages* (Cambridge: Harvard University Press, 1928), pp. 35ff. Along with Christianity's debt to the classics comes an enormous anxiety of influence. Hence Jerome's dream of appearing before the holy seat and finding himself judged there a Ciceronian instead of a Christian (*Ep.* 22.30 [PL 22:415–16])—or rather "overly devoted to pagan books," as John of Salisbury later put it in *Policraticus* 2.17 (CC, Continuatio Mediaevalis, 118:104); trans. Joseph B. Pike (Minneapolis: University of Minnesota Press, 1938), pp. 86–87.

42. *Strom.* 1.59.3–4 (GCS 15, Clemens Werke 2:37–38; trans. John Ferguson, FC 85:66; quoting 1 Cor. 15:32–33).

Roman writers were similarly updating their inheritance; on the topic of literature's truthful lying, Plutarch in particular rewards comparison. A near contemporary of the epistle to Titus, a keen critic of classical drama and, as chance would have it, a major source for plots on the Renaissance stage after its so-called secularization, Plutarch says the way to derive maximum spiritual benefit from the theater is to concentrate during the performance on the proverbial wisdom that "poets tell many lies," most of all concerning the gods.[43] While it is by definition impossible to find "any poetic composition without myth or without falsehood" (*De aud. poet.* 16C; op. cit.), for Plutarch this does not mean that dramatic poetry has *no* relation to truth, only that "poetry is not greatly concerned with the truth, and that the truth about these matters, even for those who have made it their sole business to search out and understand the verities, is exceedingly hard to track down and hard to get hold of" (*De aud. poet.* 17E; ibid.). In fact, for all his criticisms, Plutarch "still recognizes in fiction the right and main allure of poetry over and against 'reality, which tolerates no change.'"[44] Dramatic poetry, removed from the "actuality" of "clashing deeds" by an almost ontological distance—since "a tale [*logos*] is but a picture [*eikon*] and an image [*eidōlon*] of actuality, and myth but a picture and image of a tale" (*De gloria Atheniensium* 348A–B; in *Moralia*, LCL vol. 4)—manages for that very reason to resemble the truths that are, by Platonic convention, *beyond* actual reality. (One almost gets the feeling from Plutarch that the whole of theater's compromised virtue arises from its mythological distance from the social conflicts it manages to sublimate in the fiction of "dialogue.") In the Platonic system, the great threat and value of myth—which Plutarch defines following his master as "a false tale resembling a true one" (*De gloria Atheniensium* 348A; ibid.)—is that even if myth cannot *be* the truth it merely resembles, by virtue of that same differential it cannot be wholly false either if it is to remain at all *like* the truth.

Precisely that definition of myth is the one to make its way into the larger world of Neoplatonic literary criticism and from there into the medieval

---

43. *De audiendis poetis* 16A, in *Plutarch's Moralia* (LCL vol. 1). For an exceedingly useful introduction to Plutarch with an appendix giving summaries of the various essays collected in the Loeb *Moralia*, with their precise location throughout its many volumes cited by Latin, Greek, and English titles, see Robert Lamberton, *Plutarch* (New Haven: Yale University Press, 2001). In Plutarch's discussions of poetry, myth, and drama one should bear in mind the Socratic dictum that the highest purpose of dramatic poetry is the making of myth: see *Phaedo* 611B (LCL vol. 1).

44. Karl Borinski, *Die Antike in Poetik und Kunsttheorie: Von Ausgang des klassischen Altertums bis auf Goethe und Wilhelm von Humboldt*, 2 vols. (Leipzig: Dieterich, 1914), 1:2.

exegetical tradition, as well as the modern.[45] Origen, for example, relied heavily on the pagan understanding of myth as "a false image that [nonetheless] portrays a truth"[46] in order to rescue scripture's veracity from the manifest appearance of fraudulence that his pagan opponents were so fond of laughing at (*C. Celsum* 2.55–60, 4.36). Naturally in the course of any scriptural interpretation, as Robert Grant brilliantly demonstrates, Origen

> does not use the prejudicial terms "myth" and "fiction." Instead he sub-stitutes the words "enigma" and "parable," since they are to be found in scripture itself. We know that these words are the equivalents of "myth" and "fiction" because Origen's definitions of them, provided in his *Commentary on Proverbs*, are identical with the Greek definitions of the ordinary terms. We might suppose that Origen's conception was different from that of the rhetoricians because he insists on the hidden meaning to be found in "enigma" and "parable," but the rhetoricians too claimed *that "myth" contains an image of some truth.*[47]

Such conformity to the wider traditions of Greek thinking would soon enough lead to the accusation that Origen had been "blinded by Greek culture,"[48] a charge from which he has yet to escape even today, and may never. In effect his impeachment as an antichristian exegete and the subsequent apologies made on his behalf stage nothing short of a debate over the whole definition and possibility of "pure" Christianity, which is to say, of a Christianity free from the grandeur it borrows from human

45. Ironically under the name of "demythologization." See for example Rudolph Bult-mann, *Jesus Christ and Mythology* (New York: Charles Scribner's Sons, 1958), according to whom the Bible's patently mythological distortions, to the right sort of reader, themselves convey a kind of truth (e.g., p. 18). The kinship of this way of reading with hermeneutics of a very old sort was not lost on the man whose book could probably be credited with fathering the modern procedure: see David Friedrich Strauss, *The Life of Jesus Critically Examined*, ed. Peter C. Hodgson, trans. George Eliot (1846; repr., Philadelphia: Fortress, 1972), esp. p. 65.

46. Quoted from Greek rhetoricians in connection with Origen by Robert Grant, *The Earliest Lives of Jesus* (New York: Harper and Brothers, 1961), pp. 40–46, 119–22. On the more general topic of the relations between pagan and Christian literary criticism, see also by Grant, *Heresy and Criticism: The Search for Authenticity in Early Christian Literature* (Westminster: John Knox Press, 1993), esp. pp. 100ff. on Origen, and Henry Chadwick, *Antike Schriftauslegung: Pagane und christliche Allegorese Activa und Passiva im antiken Umgang mit der Bibel* (Berlin: de Gruyter, 1998).

47. Grant, *Earliest Lives*, p. 66; my emphasis.

48. *Panarion haer.* 64.72.9 (GCS 31, Epiphanius Werke 2:523); trans. Frank Williams, *The Panarion of Epiphanius of Salamis*, 2 vols. (Leiden: Brill, 1987–94), 2:207.

(and therefore idolatrous) artifice, let alone what it openly borrows from paganism.[49] If even Henri de Lubac, one of Origen's great Catholic apologists, is willing to concede that by means of the allegorical method Origen "discovers a role for classical aesthetics in expressing the Christian history of salvation,"[50] we might do well to ask whether this discovery was ever forgotten by later Fathers, putatively more orthodox, who would condemn him for it. We will explore soon enough the nature of their condemnation in greater detail; suffice it for now to say that Greek culture and classical aesthetics play as strong a role in their expressions as in Origen's for the simple reason that this cultural aesthetic plays a major role in Christian *scripture*, which was, after all, *written in* Greek—even their "Hebrew" Bible.[51]

Compare, for instance, the Synoptic apocalypse with two more of Plutarch's dialogues. These all clearly share, in the words of David Aune, "the common Greco-Roman literary pattern of an introductory peripatetic dialogue which leads to a seated dialogue set in full view of a temple."[52] What's more, the question under debate in Plutarch explicitly concerns the *literary form* taken by the prophecies then issuing from this temple—in particular how their belletristic character contributes as much to counterfeit posturing as to divine revelation. Recently, we are told, the Delphic oracle has switched from verse to prose, leading people to assume one of two things, according to Sarapion, the poet: "either that the prophetic priestess does not come near to the region where the godhead is, or else the spirit has been completely quenched and her powers have

---

49. A point made with exceptional clarity by Henry Chadwick, *Early Christian Thought and the Classical Tradition: Studies in Justin, Clement, and Origen* (New York: Oxford University Press, 1966), esp. pp. 95–123 on Origen. See also next note.

50. Henri de Lubac, *Scripture in the Tradition*, trans. Luke O'Neill (New York: Crossroad Publishing, 2000), p. 4. In one of the original works from which *Scripture in the Tradition* has been partially excerpted, Lubac presents, and attempts to answer, the wide range of scholarly "griefs contre Origène" which more or less parrot those made earlier by the Fathers. See his *Histoire et Esprit: L'intelligence de l'Écriture d'après Origène* (Paris: Aubier, 1950), pp. 14ff. It will be clear in everything that follows, if it isn't already, that I do not share Lubac's enthusiasm, here and throughout his corpus, for demonstrating the ultimate superiority of Paul, Origen, or any other Christian exegete over his pagan, specifically Platonic forbears (cf., e.g., *ME* 2:99ff.). This commonplace maneuver has always seemed to me to cheapen unnecessarily the full complexity of pagan philosophy and literature. On Origen's debt to Platonism specifically, see Chadwick, *Early Christian Thought* (n. 49), esp. p. 122.

51. On the Platonizing tendency of the LXX, see Morton Smith, "The Image of God," *Bulletin of the John Rhylands Library* 40 (1958): 473–512, esp. 474; I deal with some details of this translation in chapter 3.

52. Aune, *Prophecy in Early Christianity* (n. 15), p. 186.

forsaken her" (*De pythiae oraculis* 402B–C; in *Moralia*, LCL vol. 5).[53] The disappearance of the oracle's poetic meter and diction, in other words, seems tantamount to the disappearance of the godhead itself. God is dead without poetry—assuming the gods weren't dying off in fact, as scandalously suggested in another of the Delphic dialogues quoted at length by later Christians to demonstrate Christ's conquest of pagan antiquity.[54] Another speaker named Theon (possibly a mask for Plutarch, who was himself a priest at Delphi and no doubt had opinions on the matter) counters Sarapion with a different viewpoint: in the old days, he grants, yes, oracles had been without question a form of poetry, and for an obvious reason: "The *hoi polloi*, imputing to the hidden meaning of divinity what was not familiar or common, but expressed altogether indirectly and through circumlocution, were struck by it with awe and reverence" (ibid., 407A). This says, in effect, poetry is the opium of the masses. Without its mystifications the oracular utterances from Delphi would not have seemed sufficiently delphic; clarity does not impress the populace. Yet as people grew more accustomed to such grandiloquence and artificiality, "they blamed the poetic language with which the oracles were clothed, not only for obstructing the understanding of these in their true meaning and for combining vagueness and obscurity with the communication, but already they were coming to look with suspicion upon metaphors, riddles [*ainigmata*], and ambiguous statements, feeling that these were secluded nooks of refuge devised for furtive withdrawal and retreat for the one whose prophecy fails" (ibid., 407A–B). As if that were not enough, poetry had fallen into even deeper disrepute on account of a tribe of wandering soothsayers who lounged around shrines and exercised their gift for verses by prophesying extemporaneously, much to the delight of servants and women, "who are most enticed by verse and a poetic vocabulary. This, then, is not the least among the reasons why poetry, by apparently lending herself to the service

53. Cf. Pseudo-Justin, *Cohortatio ad Graecos* 37.2–3, where he justifies the Sibyl's poor verses with the argument that, speaking extemporaneously, unlike poets she could hardly pause to scan her words and then correct the meter. For text and a German translation, along with citations of the same idea in other ancient writers (including Plutarch), see Ps.-Justin (Markell von Ankyra?), *Ad Graecos de vera religione (bisher "Cohortatio ad Graecos"): Einleitung und Kommentar*, ed. Christoph Riedweg (Basel: Friedrich Reinhardt, 1994), pp. 517–18 (commentary), pp. 580–81 (Greek), and pp. 618–19 (German).

54. *De defectu oraculorum* 419B–D (in *Moralia*, LCL vol. 5). Quoted by Theodoret, *Graecarum affectionum curatio*, 10.6, 8, and 10 (SC 57.2:362–64), and Eusebius, *Praeparatio evangelica* 5.16–17 (GCS 43.1, Eusebius Werke 8.1:252–56); trans. Edwin Hamilton Gifford, *Preparation for the Gospel*, 2 vols. (Oxford: Clarendon Press, 1903), 1:204–7.

of tricksters, mountebanks and false prophets, lost all standing with truth" (ibid., 407C).

Christians had to reckon from the very beginning with the sort of complaint issued here in Plutarch to the extent that their scriptural drama, filled with miraculous events that a lot of people found impossible to credit, featured as its explicit *hero* a wandering enigma; though no poet per se, he certainly spoke in a similarly riddling manner, through parable, and seemed to die as a result of promulgating dangerous fictions regarding the nature of divinity.[55] Celsus for one classed Jesus exactly the way one of Plutarch's characters might have, had Plutarch heard of Jesus. He considered him just one of many crackpots roving Palestine and pretending through sheer rhetoric "to be moved as if giving some oracular utterance. It is an ordinary and common custom for each one to say: 'I am God (or a son of God, or a divine Spirit). And I have come. Already the world is being destroyed. But I wish to save you. And you shall see me returning again with heavenly power. Blessed is he who has worshiped me now!" (*C. Celsum* 7.9). To this objection could be added the criticism of "Celsus' Jew"— one of the characters in his book against Christianity, which, indeed, took the form of a dramatic dialogue (e.g., *C. Celsum* 1.28); according to him there were a thousand other swindlers able to "convince simple hearers, whom they exploit by deceit," yet Christians certainly would not worship any of *them*. Christian hypocrisy as a consequence was palpable: "Do you think that the stories of these others are the myths [*mythous*] which they appear to be, and yet that the catastrophic ending of your tragedy [*katastrophēn tou dramatos*] is to be regarded as noble and convincing?" (*C. Celsum* 2.55). At the heart of this controversy, which was to bend Christian theology permanently toward it, appears then a question genetically related to those explored in Plutarch's dialogues: whether the resurrection and all the other "signs and wonders" that Jesus presented as evidence of his divinity were ultimately akin to poetry and the most perverse kind of theater for being at bottom more fiction than fact, show without substance, performance without any real action and signifying nothing. Nothing, that is, unless the significance were to appear in the sinister beauty of

---

55. Jesus' relation to other Graeco-Roman and Jewish miracle workers has inspired a tremendous outpouring from twentieth-century scholars under the rubric of the so-called divine man tradition. For discussion and references, see, e.g., Paul J. Achtemeier, "Gospel Miracle Tradition and the Divine Man," *Interpretation* 26 (1972): 174–97, and David Flusser, "Jesus and Judaism: Jewish Perspectives," in *Eusebius, Christianity, and Judaism*, ed. Harold W. Attridge and Gohei Hata (Detroit: Wayne State University Press, 1992), pp. 80–109, esp. pp. 82–88.

the performance as such, the deceptive allure of its faux consolations, its half-broken promise of a more lasting happiness.

Christ as Antichrist

Any apologist who wanted to counter the sort of complaint given voice by Plutarch or Celsus had in scripture both a secret weapon and a worse opponent, since identical blasphemies make a critical appearance there, too, but as an integral aspect of its revelatory power. The voices opposing Christianity, enfolded in its founding texts, clearly make the disdain of the secular or non-Christian world a fundamental part of the Christian outlook; the secret of its universalism, its celebrated embrace of "otherness," boils down at least partly to its reliance on the drama of being despised. The scriptural accusations against Christ are in other words indispensable to his proffer of love, which becomes all the more generous— all the more divine—the more hatefully it was once declined. If anything the gospels tragically *intensify* Pharisaical or "Jewish" skepticism; in this way they both recuperate the historical opposition to Jesus and further sacralize him by means of it. So that even in the absence of Celsus or Porphyry or the emperor Julian (to name only those opponents whose writings were not completely obliterated by subsequent Christian triumph), the worst objections against Jesus had been already preserved in scripture as an object of *worship*. Without this founding blasphemy there would be no exaltation, no glory without this tribulation.

Christ's enemies are explicitly shown again and again trapped in an oddly reassuring worry: not simply that his charitable miracles are fake, but that fakery of such a grand variety goes well beyond the prowess of a mortal con man and so maybe derives after all from a genuine spiritual authority—obviously not the one Jesus *claims* as his "father" (whatever that means), but rather the master of all sham imitators and "the father of all lies" (Jn 8:44), Satan. The exorcisms of Jesus were among the most challenging of his feats for the Pharisees to interpret because it was here that his divine status had been publicly proclaimed by demons (e.g., Mt 8:29; Mk 1:24, 34, 3:11, 5:7; Lk 4:41, 8:28). Were these devils not prone by definition to uttering falsehoods? If Jesus is casting them out, the Pharisees argue, obviously he does so by means of other devils (Mt 9:34, 12:24; Mk 3:22; Lk 11:14). His parabolic response that Satan's house could not stand if divided against itself hardly clarifies things, since according to a traditional interpretation we'll later explore at length, it was exactly Satan's desolation and the dispersal of his chattels that Jesus was supposed to accomplish. Elsewhere in fact he claims to have seen Satan's destruction (Mk 3:27; Lk 10:18). The house had *already* fallen. Should this not have confirmed their suspicions that Jesus really did represent some sort of internal division within the devil's familial ranks, his very incarnation, as it were, on earth? Why speak so parabolically and deceptively in the first place?

That last question, if no other, receives in scripture a direct answer. According to his own confession, Jesus uses parables in order to *prevent* the repentance he elsewhere demands: "For those outside, everything comes in parables, in order that 'they may indeed look, but not perceive, and may indeed listen, but not understand; *so that they may not turn again and be forgiven*'" (Mk 4:11b–12; Isa. 6:9–11; my emphasis). Likewise in the other gospels, when confronted by the Pharisees, Jesus preaches against forgiveness, against the extension of "Christian" mercy to anyone who might doubt his miracles. It is here we find, on Jesus' own lips, the notorious doctrine of an *unforgivable* sin (Mt 12:31–32 and parallels), "the main proof text for the doctrine of eternal punishment."[56] It is here, in the words of no less an authority than the great and inspiring Ulrich Luz, that Matthew transforms the love of God, which supposedly "shines forth in Jesus' miracles[,] into its opposite" (Luz 2:212). It is here, in short, that the gospels themselves most succeed in transforming Christ into an Antichrist.

That transformation was explored exegetically long before Luz by Origen. You should consider carefully, he advises, what Paul says about the apocalyptic "man of sin," in particular how he will appear "'in all power and signs and lying wonders and with all deceit of unrighteousness' (2 Thess. 2:9) . . . imitating all miracles, even those of truth." Origen goes on:

> And just as the enchanters and magicians of the Egyptians [Exod 7:11], though inferior to the man of sin and the son of perdition, imitated certain powers, both the signs and wonders of truth, doing lying wonders so that the true ones might not be believed, so I think the man of sin will imitate signs and powers. And perhaps, also, the Pharisees (if not, I wonder, the Sadducees too) suspected these things because of the prophecies concerning him, when they tested Jesus by asking that he show them a sign from heaven. (*Comm. in Matt.* 12.2 [GCS 40, Origenes Werke 10:71; ANF 10:450 = *KEM* 1:160])

---

56. Hermann Olshausen, *Biblical Commentary on the New Testament*, vol. 1 (New York: Sheldon, 1863), p. 411, quoted by Luz 2:208, who gives further references and a synopsis of the traditional interpretations.

The first thing to note here is Origen's use of Old Testament history as a negative typology for the coming of Antichrist: just as the historical activities of Moses foreordain those of Christ, so too do the activities of his opponents, in this case the magicians of Egypt, anticipate the coming of Antichrist. The second thing to stress is how this typological genealogy, supposedly parallel to Christ's, unexpectedly short-circuits. In the eyes of the Pharisees (if not, Origen wonders, also the Sadducees) Christ *himself* appears to fulfill the historical foreshadowing of Antichrist when he, too, seems like a belated but even more frightening instance of Egyptian sorcery. Had Jesus not spent a portion of his youth in Egypt (Mt 2:13–15), perhaps receiving there training in its magical arts? According to Origen, as according later to Marlowe, the Jews were *rightly* skeptical of Christ's claims to divinity because Antichrist would make exactly the same claim, with exactly the same miraculous feats to back it up. In fact the lack of differentiation between them makes it impossible to tell in this passage whether "the prophecies concerning *him*" refers to Jesus or Antichrist. The pronoun's antecedent can be no more decided than the object of prophecy.

This fundamental lack of differentiation pushes Origen into a kind of self-criticism; no sooner has he admitted the intolerable proximity between Christ and his opposite than Origen backtracks for fear that "someone" might accuse him of excusing or defending the Jews.[57] He has just shown that according to 2 Thessalonians, Antichrist will imitate "*all* miracles, even those of *the truth*." Now in response to this mysterious, internal antagonist, Origen would withhold by fiat the miracles of Jesus from the economy of mimesis:

> If anyone supposes that we have given an occasion of defense to the Pharisees and Sadducees . . . let him know that we can plausibly say that they were drawn away to the end that they might not believe in the *paradoxois* of Jesus [i.e., his miracles], yet not that they might be forgiven [their unbelief], since they did not look to the words of the prophets which were being fulfilled in the acts of Jesus, which an evil power was not at all capable of imitating. (*Comm. in Matt.* 12.2 [GCS 40, Origenes Werke 10:72; ANF 10:450–51 = *KEM* 1:160])

57. For a brief commentary on Origen's relation to Judaism (and another translation of the passage under discussion), see *KEM*, esp. 1:160 n. 3. Further analysis in *The Westminster Handbook to Origen*, ed. John Anthony McGuckin (Louisville: Westminster John Knox Press, 2004), s.v. "Judaism," pp. 135–40. One might compare Rufinus' accusation, during the controversy over Origen, that Jerome's attachment to the Hebrew Bible was secretly a form of Judaizing. See *Apologia* 2.36–41 (CCSL 20:111–16).

Who exactly is this imaginary person conjured out of thin air by Origen to accuse him of heterodoxy or incoherence? Who else but the internalized voice of Origen's real-world opponents, which is to say, a version now of Origen *himself*—that intellectual hybrid and symbol of all Christian thought, the apologist whose defensiveness, in collaboration with scripture, will keep every accusation against Christ alive long after the initial antagonists have all died out. The same antichristian blasphemies are woven into the fabric of even the most orthodox thought, which could not otherwise *be* orthodox;[58] they contribute to its dramatic tension, which is to say, to its inner dialectic. Both medieval drama and scholastic disputation will consequently thrive on contradiction and revel in paradox, in the *quaestiones* which Origen tellingly likens "to the dialogues of the ancient Greeks."[59] Marlowe's *Dr. Faustus*, combining both Christian drama and disputation in the figure of a longing scholar, will speak for this internal linkage at the moment of its historic loss.

Long before that it was Jesus who had the Faustian appearance.[60] Origen means of course to defend him from the charge that he demonically affects his godhead, yet in mounting a defense Origen can only deepen his guilt: by whom, exactly, were the Pharisees and Sadducees "drawn away to the end that they might not believe in the miracles of Jesus" nor be *forgiven* their unbelief? According to the rest of the passage from 2 Thessalonians partially quoted by Origen, it is *God* who will "send strong delusion, that they shall believe a lie, that they all may be condemned" (2 Thess. 2:11–12a). It would seem that Paul and Origen together wind up arguing, in defense of Christianity, that the godhead made incarnate by Christ encourages faith in *lies,* just like the devil, so as to lead some people to their eternal damnation. Perhaps he might lead others to salvation by the same fraudulent means?

---

58. Cf. Werner, *Formation of Christian Dogma* (n. 12), p. 307.

59. *ME* 1:56, where Lubac catalogues at length the medieval worry that scholastic dispute only served to voice "impious questions, raised by the devil" (1:57, quoting Leo the Great), or that "'modern dialecticians'...all too often 'distress the house of God with their counterfeit meanings'" (1:62; quoting Hugh Metel); how could dialectic be an "excellent weapon against heresy" if heretics themselves "always have recourse to these kinds of 'dialectical questions'" (1:63; quoting Bruno of Segni)?

60. Cf. Flusser, "Jesus and Judaism" (n. 55), p. 82: "According to Matt 12:29 and Luke 11:15, Jesus' critics accused him of being a kind of Dr. Faustus, with the demon Beelzebub as his Mephistopheles." The connection between Faustus and Christ has also been made by K. Schmidt, "Die Stellung der Evangelien in der allgemeinen Literaturgeschichte," in *Eucharisterion,* Festschrift for Hermann Gunkel, 2 vols. (Göttingen: Vandenhoeck & Ruprecht, 1923), 2:51ff.; I will make it again in the final chapter on Marlowe.

These questions could only be encouraged by Jesus' apparent fulfillment, along with more positive predictions, of the Deuteronomic admo-
nition against false prophets: "If a prophet arises among you,...and gives
you a sign or wonder, and that sign or wonder which he tells you comes
to pass and if he says, 'Let us go after strange gods,' which you have not
known...you shall not listen to the words of that prophet...for the Lord
your God is tempting you" (13:1–3). Some fundamental characteristics
of Jesus' career come to light in this passage and, by ramification, a dim
outline of the Antichrists who, by imitating him, would exonerate his min-
istry.[61] Here are the obligatory signs and wonders, the temptation to fall
away from traditional religion, the explicit declaration that at some level
God himself, utterly sovereign, is always the most cunning tempter—and
finally, the refusal of merely historical fulfillment as a guarantor of truth.
Do not listen to the soothsayer whose portents actually come to pass! The
devil always lies, most of all when his words prove correct. Or as Origen
would come to put it in one of his most penetrating and honest commentaries: "I am sure that whether [the devil] deceives or tells the truth,
he traps me. For his truth also entraps" (*Hom. in Jer.* 20.4.3 [SC 238:270;
trans. John Clark Smith, FC 97:230]). By the same logic, God invariably
tells the highest truths, no matter how demonic his deceptive allurements
or the trials he inflicts, *sub contrario*, on his steadfast believers. "May God
alone deceive me!" (ibid.), Origen implores more than once: "Let us pray
to be deceived by God! Only let the Serpent not deceive us!" (*Hom. in Jer.*
20.3.5 [ibid., 266, 228]).[62] Righteous deceit, indeed....

The Sign of Jonah

"'The true and real God,'" writes Luz—again from his learned and
vast commentary on Matthew—"exercises 'in his deeds no greater power'

---

61. Cf. Deut. 18:9–22. Lars Hartman, *Prophecy Interpreted: The Formation of Some Jewish
Apocalyptic Texts and of the Eschatological Discourse of Mark 13 Par.* (Lund: Gleerup, 1966),
pp. 155ff., thinks that the allusions to Deuteronomy and Daniel in the Synoptic Apocalypse
suggest the existence of a coherent midrash joining them, now lost, but known also to Paul
and evidenced in his letters to the Thessalonians, both of which Hartman accepts as authentic (pp. 178–205, 235–52). Meeks, *The Prophet-King* (n. 4), pp. 47–57, considers these
Deuteronomic passages regarding false prophets central to the later development of the
figures of both Antichrist and Christ (cf. Jn 7:15–24).

62. For an illuminating commentary on these sermons, one that situates them in the
context of Plato's useful lies while (as usual) trying to free them from that context, see Henri
de Lubac, "'Tu m'as Trompé, Seigneur': Le commentaire de Origène sur Jérémie 20,7," in
Recherches dans la Foi: Trois études sur Origène, saint Anselme et la philosophie chrétienne (Paris:
Beauchesne, 1979), pp. 9–78.

than the Jewish exorcists also do. The Jesus story is an ambiguous story and by no means a clear revelation of the deity of God. Our text betrays this, so to speak, not intentionally but between the lines."[63] Such between-the-lines betrayal of a meaning deeper than any intention is essentially what Jameson describes as a text's *unconscious.* Being textual, therefore objective or "cultural" rather than personally subjective and limited to a single author, this consists not so much of libidinal conflict as of social contradiction. We have already seen the considerable depth and overde-termination of one specific contradiction at the heart of Christianity in what Luz calls the "aporia" (op. cit.) of Jesus' exchange with the Phari-sees, that is, the total impossibility of arriving at any consensus on the true source of his miraculous works, whether demonic or divinely influenced, or stemming rather from the madness of Jesus (Mk 3:21) or from the subsequent scribbling of delusional converts. There would be as a conse-quence no settling of accounts between Judaism and Christianity. These two peoples stand opposed to each other "in a real contradiction," as Lu-bac writes, using words of major import to Jameson's work. Yet they are op-posed, Lubac means to reassure us, "only once they have come to coexist, the first [people] not having wished to disappear on the arrival of the one for which its whole task was to prepare, because it had not understood that it was merely the means of getting ready for it" (*ME* 2:54). Stubborn Jews. As Lubac well knew, and otherwise wished to avert, there were ways besides exegesis to encourage their disappearance.

Judeo-Christian relations were made all the more aporetic as the scrip-tural impasse between Jesus and the Pharisees culminates in a bewilder-ing reference to the strangest of Hebrew prophets: when asked for yet a further, more conclusive sign in addition to his healings—as though a sign could ever be conclusive—Jesus refuses to give the scribes and Pharisees anything at all, save for "the sign of Jonah" (Mt 12:39, 16:4; Lk 11:29). Initially no one seems to have known what this meant. If Mark knew of the reference, he omits all mention. Matthew copes with it as best he can, but a little hysterically. He repeats the remark about Jonah twice, leaving it in one case unexplained (16:1–4) and in the other inventing a compensatory connection between Jonah's three-day sojourn in the whale and the Son of Man's descent, for the same duration, into the belly of the earth

---

63. Luz 2:212, quoting Athanasius a propos Mt 12:27—"If I by Beelzebub cast out devils, by whom do your children cast them out?"—traditionally understood as a concession to the Pharisees in acknowledgment that their children, too, can cast out devils, same as Jesus, in which case his exorcisms obviously do not constitute proof of divinity.

(Mt 12:40). Matthew then in the next verse elaborates on a completely different explanation (overcompensating now), this one found also in Luke: "The men of Nineveh shall rise in judgment with this generation, and shall condemn it: because they repented at the preaching of Jonah; and behold, one greater than Jonah is here" (Mt 12:41; Lk 11:32). Despite the simultaneous absence and plurality of explanation put forward by the gospels, the real verdict here was clear enough to later interpreters: just as Jonah, a Jewish prophet, saved the people of Nineveh—that is, a gentile city traditionally hostile to the Jews—so too would the message preached by Jesus, one greater than Jonah, save a non-Jewish church and allow Christians, in turn, to condemn "the scribes and Pharisees," which meant the Jews as a people.[64]

The emphasis of this interpretation on God's abandonment of the Jews so long as they *remain* Jewish only formulates the old aporia anew, however, to the extent that Jesus' "preaching of repentance" on the occasion with the Pharisees most closely resembles Jonah's in that Jonah does not preach repentance, either.[65] Unlike any of the other Hebrew prophets, major or minor, his prophecy consists of a single sentence (in all senses of the word): "Yet forty days and Nineveh shall be overthrown!" (Jon. 3:4)—or sooner, for readers of the Septuagint, which gives the city a mere "three days." Not one of the story's subsequent retellings expands Jonah's mandate to include a message of repentance. You will not hear a word of it in Josephus (*Jewish Antiquities* 9.205–214; LCL vol. 6); nor in the Greek *Lives of the Prophets* (1st century CE, Palestine);[66] nor in the targum attributed to the disciple of Hillel, Jonathan ben Uzziel;[67] nor in the midrashic

---

64. E.g., Hilary, *In Matt.* 12.20 (SC 254:288). The Gloss on the Jonah passage in Mt and the verses following assure the Jews that they need not despair as there is still time to convert (PL 114:128B), though they are otherwise, *qua* Jews, thoroughly condemned (cf. on Luke cols. 292Aff.).

65. E. P. Sanders makes a compelling case that the historical Jesus was actually not much concerned with repentance—hence the real horror at his teaching, which offered sinners antinomian access to the Kingdom whether they repented or not. The message of repentance was then later attributed to him by less radical adherents, Luke especially. So, for example, where Mark and Matthew report that Jesus "came to call sinners" (Mk 1:17; Mt 9:13), Luke adds the words "unto repentance." See Sanders, *Jesus and Judaism* (Philadelphia: Fortress, 1985), pp. 106–13, 175, 203–5, 255, 271, 301, and then the restatement of his position in *Historical Figure of Jesus* (n. 19), pp. 230–37.

66. *The Lives of the Prophets: Greek Text and Translation*, ed. and trans. Charles C. Torrey (Philadelphia: Society of Biblical Literature and Exegesis, 1946), pp. 27–28, 41–42.

67. *The Aramaic Version of Jonah*, ed. and trans. Étan Levine (Jerusalem: Jerusalem Academic Press, 1975).

tradition;[68] and not in the Pseudo-Philonic *On Jonah*, whose prophecy further instructs the people to spend their final few days "without joy or hope of any future."[69] For all their internal discrepancy these Jewish witnesses agree on one thing, and for once, Christians agreed: "Jonah did not announce mercy," says Augustine, "but coming wrath" (*Serm.* 361.20 [PL 39:1610; *WSA* III/10:238]). Everybody dies. God has spoken through his prophet.

Good thing God's prophets lie. According to the midrashic tradition, Jonah's first commission had once been to preach destruction against Jerusalem, and yet there, too, "the doom did not come to pass" (at least for the time being); "among the Israelites Jonah was, therefore, known as 'the false prophet.'"[70] When his doom against Nineveh likewise fails to transpire, according to the *Lives of the Prophets* he refuses to return to his own land but instead takes his mother and settles in shame among the foreigners of Tyre: "In this way I will remove my reproach," he says, "that I lied in my prophecy against the great city of Nineveh."[71] He lied, it turns out, because in response to his prophecy of total annihilation, the people of Nineveh came to repent despite all. Worse, God *too* then repented of the "evil he had intended" (Jon. 3:10), his prophecy notwithstanding. Thus Nineveh escaped its doom, and the prophet who doomed them under direct inspiration from God was (once again) proven wrong.

This puts Jonah in a famously paradoxical position.[72] In delivering his prediction he guarantees it will not come to pass. That is, the repentance

---

68. Louis Ginzberg, *The Legends of the Jews*, trans. Henrietta Szold, 7 vols. (Baltimore: Johns Hopkins University Press, 1998), 4:246–53; notes in 6:348–52. Further references to Jonah in the early literature have been collected by Yves-Marie Duval, *Le Livre de Jonas dans la littérature chrétienne grecque et latine: Sources et influence du commentaire sur Jonas de saint Jérôme*, 2 vols. (Paris: Études augustiniennes, 1973), 1:115–272, and by Yvonne Sherwood, *A Biblical Text and Its Afterlives: The Survival of Jonah in Western Culture* (Cambridge: Cambridge University Press, 2000), who gives a full bibliography. See in particular Elias Bickerman, "Les deux erreurs du prophète Jonas," *Revue d'histoire et de philosophie religieuses* 45.2 (1965): 232–64, a tremendous piece of scholarship to which I am much indebted. Revised and partially translated (sadly omitting the magnificent notes) in the first chapter of his *Four Strange Books of the Bible: Jonah, Daniel, Koheleth, and Esther* (New York: Schocken, 1967).

69. *Drei hellenistisch-jüdische Predigten: Ps.-Philon, "Über Jona," "Über Simson," und "Über die Gottesbezeichnung, wohltätig verzehrendes Feuer,"* trans. Folker Siegert (Tübingen: Mohr 1980), 1:9–50; here p. 11 (§19). Based on the Armenian translation of a lost Greek original in *The Pseudo-Philonic De Jona*, ed. H. Lewy (London: Christophers, 1936).

70. Ginzberg, *Legends of the Jews* (n. 68), 4:247.

71. *Lives of the Prophets* (n. 66), p. 41.

72. See Kraft, "Paradoxie in der Bibel" (n. 40), pp. 254–58, on Jonah and the prophets specifically.

and forgiveness of Nineveh—pointedly excluded from Jonah's oracle—is *inspired by this exclusion.* "I knew you would do this!" Jerome imagines Jonah telling God in the wake of Nineveh's salvation. "I was not ignorant that you are merciful, for that very reason I did not want to proclaim that you are severe and cruel!" (*In Jonam* 4.2–3 [SC 43:105]). Hence Jonah's flight to Tharsis and his death wish on the boat when he asked the sailors to throw him overboard: death alone, he thought, could resolve his irresolvable conundrum: "If I were to say that you are compassionate and merciful and forgive evil," Jerome further imagines him saying, "no one would repent"—in which case, of course, God would *not* be compassionate or merciful or forgiving; his mercy in the story of Jonah is completely conditional on the people's ostensibly *futile* regret. And yet, as Jerome's implacable Jonah continues, "if I proclaim that you are savage and strictly a judge, I would know this is not in your nature. Therefore, stuck in this ambiguous position, I preferred to flee rather than to deceive [potential] penitents with leniency, or to preach that you are something you are not" (ibid.). Jonah's hard options are entirely clear. Either by preaching a merciful God to deceive people into believing they will *not* be punished and thereby assure they *will* be punished, or spare them the punishment through a reverse deception, by presenting them with a figure of God that makes of him something far less than God—a figure that is, in fact, a conventional image of the devil. Either Jonah preaches God's mercy, in which case God will have none; or he preaches God-as-the-devil, *in which case alone God saves.* Either God the merciless destroyer or God the purveyor of demonic yet nonetheless salvific fictions.

With a little help from the techniques of allegoresis invented by pagan literary critics it was possible to show how the fiction of Nineveh's destruction, as with the fabrications of scripture in general, articulated spiritual truths that could not otherwise be realized. According to Pseudo-Philo, the prophecy actually *was* fulfilled in the "overthrow" of the city's *wicked way of life.*[73] God thus destroyed the Ninevehans' lesser selves. Only considered at the literal or "carnal" level does Jonah "seem to have said something false," explains Augustine (*Serm.* 361.20 [PL 39:1610; WSA III/10:238]). Considered spiritually, apparent fictions such as these convey the truth of salvation; hence the effectiveness of the overall "fiction" of the Jonah story as such, not to mention Christ's later reprise of his escapades: swallowed

---

73. *Drei hellenistisch-jüdische Predigten* (n. 69), 1:43 (§193–96); as Siegert notes, the reading was aided by the ambiguous wording of the prophecy in both Greek and Hebrew.

by a whale, then vomited out, safe on dry land? Dead on the cross, then alive in the flesh but passing through walls? It was the task of the serious interpreter to see within the reported facts of sacred history a saving alternative to all facticity—one that was completely unspeakable, however, outside these sacred happenings. Stories like Jonah's or the miracles of Christ are a kind of rhetorical fabrication after all—not because they never happened, but because the miracles themselves, which actually occurred, were otherwise impossible and therefore signified, under an apparent falsehood, the true nature of their unknown, alien, and hidden Lord. Scripture appears as a fraud only because history itself has been likewise forged by God, "the creator and fashioner [*fictor*] of everything" (Jerome, *Comm. in Zach.* 3.11.12–13 [CCSL 76a:857]). The word *fictor* here is difficult to translate without losing the word's affinity to *fiction*, and with it the especially powerful Latin connotation of deception: so, for example, when Virgil calls Ulysses a "fictor fandi" (*Aeneid* 9.602; LCL vol. 2), it falls somewhere between calling him a liar and a poet—a fitting ambiguity in that Ulysses himself narrates the most spectacular and dubious of his fabulous encounters in the *Odyssey*. So too, in Christian usage, does God "utter" the fantastic but factual events recorded in scripture. Thus the same word Homer uses of his devious hero in the opening line of the *Odyssey*—"polytropic"—the writer of Hebrews uses in the opening line of his letter to describe the way God communicates.

What makes pagan ridicule of the Jonah story's implausibility itself so ridiculous, according to Augustine, is that pagans nonetheless "believe in their own literature," no matter how extraordinary—for example, the story in Herodotus about Arion being saved from drowning by a dolphin. And yet, Augustine boasts, "that story of ours about the prophet Jonah is more incredible [*incredibilius*], obviously more incredible because more miraculous [*mirabilius*] and more miraculous because full of more power" (*De civ. dei* 1.14; LCL vol. 1). His apology responds to the charge that Christians worship unbelievable literature, in other words, by *conceding the point*: Christian books, Augustine argues, far outstrip all others in that nothing could be *more incredible* than the Bible, which was for that reason the greatest possible foundation for the greatest possible faith. Anyone who did not regard Christ's death and resurrection as the marvelous stuff of an unreal fiction was hardly going to accept those events as evidence of an all-surpassing godhead, for whom nothing is impossible (Lk 1:37). "What are the miracles of God," asks a medieval sermon ascribed to Augustine, "if *not* those things which are impossible for humans?" (PL 39:2110; my emphasis). Sacred history therefore *has* to present a contrafactual appearance, that in its very impossibility it might testify to a godly omnipotence.[74] That is why Christianity could no more do away with all claim to historicity than with the apparent fiction of its history. To achieve the effect of divine revelation *in* history requires holding the two in permanent dialectical suspension. "Considered from the outside," writes Pseudo-Dionysius of the Bible, "isn't it chock full of incredible and fictive fables?"[75] Yet it is only "through fabulous deeds—miracles and signs and incredible [*paradoxois*] powers," as Eusebius writes, that the Logos of God, "who is invisible to many," can reveal itself while still preserving its transcendence.[76]

From this perspective, it is the sheer force of *dis*belief in the face of outlandish happenings like Jonah's whale and the resurrection of Jesus that *converts* so many to a position of faith in Christ. Tertullian's most famous pronouncement makes the point all too plainly: "The Son of God died; it is completely believable, because it is absurd. And though buried, he rose again. It is certain, because impossible" (*De carne Christi* 5.4 [CCSL 1²:881; ANF 3:525]).[77] Or as Lubac would come to put it, in conversion

74. Cf. the sarcastic view of Celsus that a more suitable scriptural personage to have worshipped "would have been Jonah with his gourd... or those of whom stories yet more incredible [τερατωδέστεροι] than these are told" (*C. Celsum* 7.53). Celsus thinks Christians are fools not for putting their trust in literary fabrications but for choosing a hero whose predecessors were even more fabulous, in the literal sense of being sufficiently distinguished as to have a fable written about them. His point is that Jonah makes a better God than Christ because his book makes for a better *story* than anything in the New Testament.

75. *Ep.* 9 (PG 3:1104C); trans. Colm Luibheid, *Pseudo-Dionysius: The Complete Works* (New York: Paulist Press, 1987), p. 281.

76. *De laudibus Constantini* 14 (PG 20:1413A); trans. H. A. Drake, *In Praise of Constantine: An Historical Study and New Translation of Eusebius' Tricennial Orations* (Berkeley: University of California Press, 1975), p. 117. Cf. Cyril's use of τερατουργία (wonder-working) in one and the same treatise to refer to both Old Testament miracles and others' *false* wonders: *De adoratione in spiritu et veritate* 2 and 6, respectively (PG 68:252C and 469D). On account of its miracles, the emperor Julian calls Christian scripture a "monstrous tale" (τερατολογίαν); see *Against the Galilaeans* 398 in *The Works of the Emperor Julian* (LCL vol. 3). Origin concedes that although reports of the Lord's "prodigious miracles" (τεράστιοι δυνάμεις) may have been able to convince some of Jesus' contemporaries, "after many years they did not preserve their impressive nature and are now considered to be myths" (*Comm. in Joh.* 2, §204 [SC 120:346; trans. Ronald E. Heine, FC 80:150]). More than one modern commentator has found the regular appearance throughout the New Testament of the word τέρας (miracle) "disconcertingly pagan"; see, e.g., C. F. D. Moule, "The Vocabulary of Miracle," in *Miracles: Cambridge Studies in Their Philosophy and History*, ed. C. F. D. Moule (London: A. R. Mowbray, 1965), p. 235. I will have more to say about this contest between Christian miracle and pagan magic, with more citations, in the next and last chapters.

77. There have been a lot of attempts to tame this extreme formulation. For some further commentary, see Eric Osborn, *Tertullian, First Theologian of the West* (Cambridge: Cambridge University Press, 1997), pp. 48–64. Cf. Augustine, *Enn. in Ps.* 148.8: "It is more incredible that the eternal has died than that mortal creatures will live eternally. And yet we hold what is more incredible" (CCSL 40:2170; WSA III/20:482).

to the Christian religion, "a unique movement is involved; *beginning with initial incredulity*, it ascends by faith to the very summits of a spiritual life which does not have its term here below."[78] Some allegorists of concern to Lubac should allow us, I think, to put the case a little more strongly; for they seem to have enjoyed a spiritual life which had *only* its "term" here below, which had on earth *nothing but* the rhetoric and appearance of spirituality even when that drama took "historical" form, as in the life of Christ. This follows, as Origen explains, from the radical discrepancy between the degradation of every appearance and God's utter transcendence of all sensible limits, or in other words from the fact of his radically "alien nature," such that any term predicated of God is actually a "homonym" of the divine truth to which it applies.[79] God's "deceit" or "anger" or "repentance" shares with the human equivalent no more than, say, the Good shares with "goods"; no more than *traditio*, meaning Christian tradition, has to do with the *traditio* of Judas' betrayal, or the "price" of Christ's blood has to do with the price of thirty silver pieces—to glance briefly at some other homonyms (examined in detail later) without which scripture would be unable to communicate the incommunicable. "What is called anger" in God, Origen writes, "has something alien and different from all the anger of him who is angry, for it is the wrath of the One...who wishes to convert the one reproved through the reproof" (*Hom. in Jer.* 20.1.1 [SC 238:252; trans. John Clark Smith, FC 97:222]). According to Origen's theory the words used of God share nothing with what they normally convey other than their *sound* and actually signify something else entirely, as, for example, in God's "anger" against Nineveh, which betokened "mercy" but only if pronounced there as "anger." So that to the catalogue of rhetorical stratagems essential to the appearance of divinity as already given by Plutarch in his treatise on divine proclamations—their inherently "poetic" formality, their metaphors, riddles, and circumlocution—we should perhaps also make, on the authority of Origen, a more specifically Judeo-Christian addition: the pun.[80] It is on this level of purely aesthetic, strictly formal overlap with our fallen terminology that the revelation of grace to human sensibilities, according to Origen, has to take place.

---

78. Lubac, *Scripture in the Tradition* (n. 50), p. 22; my emphasis.
79. A sentiment articulated more recently by Kenneth Burke, *The Rhetoric of Religion: Studies in Logology* (Berkeley: University of California Press, 1970), p. 22.
80. Was it not through this particular rhetorical flourish that Christ founded his church (Mt 16:18)? In any case, the midrashic tradition also uses the pun as a fundamental hermeneutic device. See Gerald L. Bruns, *Hermeneutics: Ancient and Modern* (New Haven: Yale University Press, 1992), p. 110.

How deeply Origen's authority would eventually be questioned was, so to speak, prefigured in advance by his start as a second Hippolytus, the allegedly schismatic antipope and author of our treatise on Antichrist, whose very name, according to Prudentius, would dictate his final demise in a fateful pun: "torn apart" (*lytus*) by "horses" (*hippo-*).[81] Origen also wound up in the devil's camp, though in this case there's no big debate over the reality of his conviction, no legend of a subsequent reconciliation, and even clearer indication how his doom helped preserve his ideas. Given Origen's underlying importance to the present study, his story is worth briefly recounting. Banished from Alexandria after falling afoul of a bishop and forbidden to teach, he was then replaced as head of the catechetical school with one of his former catechumens, Heracles. "He was indebted to Origen for the best of what he was and knew," writes Walter Bauer; "nevertheless, he abandoned him and took sides against him. Indeed, when Origen later returned once more to Egypt, Heracles excommunicated him anew and repeated the charge of unecclesiastical teaching."[82] Origen found a more welcoming home among believers in Palestine—at least until the Romans tortured and broke him for being in the end all too authentic a Christian.

Heracles would not be the last authority to repudiate this particular well-spring of scriptural learning. By the fifth century Origen's writings stood at the center of a major controversy in which the two primary factions—Jerome and his (formerly) close friend Rufinus—each stood accused of Origenism, by then a well-known if still somewhat unofficial heresy.[83] Rufinus took the apologetic and ultimately losing position: Origen's ideas were at bottom orthodox, he argued, but his works themselves had been contaminated by scribal interpolation and bad translation—including the translation made by Jerome.[84] According to Rufinus, it was Jerome, not Origen, who had been blinded by pagan culture, as Jerome's continual quotations from Cicero, Virgil, and Horace more than sufficed to

81. See above n. 8. For how Hippolytus inspired Origen to emulate him, see Jerome, *De vir. ill.* 61.2–3 (PL 23:673A; trans. Halton, FC 100:88).

82. Bauer, *Orthodoxy and Heresy* (n. 9), p. 54. For a fuller discussion of Origen's fate, see Hermann J. Vogt, "Warum wurde Origenes zum Häretiker erklärt?" in *Origeniana Quarta*, ed. Lothar Lies (Innsbruck: Tyrolia, 1987), pp. 78–99.

83. Origen was not formally condemned till the Council of Constantinople (553). My account in this paragraph relies heavily on Elizabeth A. Clark, *The Origenist Controversy: The Cultural Construction of an Early Christian Debate* (Princeton: Princeton University Press, 1992).

84. *De adulteratione librorum Origenis* 1–2, 6–9, 14–16 (CCSL 20:7–8, 10–14, 16–17).

demonstrate (*Apologia* 2.6, 7, 9, 11 [CCSL 20:87–89, 90–92]). Jerome's retaliation takes a curious form. On the one hand, he begins increasingly to attack "the teachings of past, long-dead heretics, a practice that undoubtedly serves to advertise his own orthodoxy";[85] and chief among the advertisements is his newfound abhorrence of Origen's errors. On the other hand, as proof of his freedom from these errors he again and again encourages readers to comb through his earlier works in search of unorthodox, Origenist opinions when those very same works were shot through from start to finish with Origenist teachings.[86] He actively *directs* people, in other words, to his Origenist opinions even while condemning Origen. What can possibly explain this?

Condemnation saves! Without the flamboyant and strategic shock at Origen's errors, Jerome would not have been able to perpetuate his readings of scripture in an "orthodox" fashion; without the disdain, Jerome's constant use of Origen's teachings would have led his own books into heresy. Jerome outlines Origen's "specific" misconceptions so that his *other* interpretations can appear, to later readers, error free; and of course by specifically articulating certain errors for all of posterity, Jerome ensures their preservation, too. So, for example, in his Jonah commentary Jerome explicitly rejects the Origenist view that the king of Nineveh signifies Satan and will one day find repentance and be forgiven,[87] a doctrine known as *apokatastasis* and in direct conflict with, among other things, the unforgiving stance of the scriptural Jesus vis-à-vis the Pharisees, not to mention Jesus' stated hope that those "on the outside" might *never* repent. (When Faustus fulfills Jesus' wish and fails to repent, he recurs to this doctrine as proof of his all-surpassing sinfulness: "The serpent that tempted Eve may be saved," he claims, "but not Faustus" [5.2.15–16; A-text].) At the same time Jerome adopts the coup de grâce of Origen's interpretation, namely, that in the story of Jonah, "God threatens the people [sc. with death] *so that* they will repent" (*In Jonam* 3.10 [SC 43:102]), a reading then incorporated wholesale into the medieval Gloss.[88] Another Origenist

---

85. Clark, *Origenist Controversy*, p. 125.

86. Ibid., p. 122. See also Pierre Courcelle, *Late Latin Writers and Their Greek Sources*, trans. Harry Wedeck (Cambridge: Harvard University Press, 1969), pp. 100–13.

87. *In Jonam* 3.6–9 (SC 43:97). See *Westminster Handbook to Origen* (n. 57), s.v. "Apokatastasis," pp. 59–62.

88. Cf. Origen, *Hom. in Jer.* 1.1.1 (SC 232:196; trans. John Clark Smith, FC 97:3), quoted above. Also Duval, *Livre de Jonas* (n. 68), 1:191–211 on Jerome's debt to Origen and 2:562ff. for the subsequent influence of Jerome's (Origenist) Jonah. For the version in the Gloss (not reproduced in PL), see *Biblia Latina cum Glossa Ordinaria: Facsimile Reprint of the Editio Princeps Adolph Rusch of Strassburg 1480/81*, 4 vols. (Turnhout: Brepols, 1992), 3:402.

interpretation, transmitted via Jerome's reading of Jonah and later essential to medieval atonement theory, will greatly occupy medieval English drama: it takes Jonah's sojourn in the belly of a whale as a prefiguration of Christ's *descensus ad infernos* when at last he really would divide Satan's house against itself, triggering its collapse, *by posing as a sinful man* and so baiting the trap for the great satanic Leviathan.[89] This theology of deception will eventually help endow the appearance of evil, above all its artificial cultivation by medieval dramatists, with an aura of sanctity, as though from this one source especially might flow an untrammeled grace. "It is no wonder that men, although righteous, nevertheless on occasion dissimulate," writes Jerome elsewhere, "when even our Lord himself, though having no sin, nor sinful flesh, assumed a likeness of sinful flesh" (*Comm. in Galatas* 1.2.11–13 [PL 26:364D]). Salvation occurs, on this model, through Christ's willingness to costume himself as a fleshy sinner, that is, "to take on" the sins of the world the way paid actors would later assume the malignant costume of Marlovian villainy.

Salvation through Antichrist

After Christ, no figure more than Antichrist epitomizes the secret godliness of even the worst-seeming heresies, errors, and other seductive deceptions, insofar as he acts on God's behalf *by means of* an oppositional mimesis. In the end Antichrist's lies and his miraculous spectacles were to be *equally* historical and fictitious, prophetic and mendacious, false and yet somehow true, for with him the ersatz (however impotent in itself) would signal at last the imminent appearance of the genuine. At bottom a simulacrum—an actor, almost—Antichrist was to create what every Christian artist already performed as a matter of course: a second-order mimetic recapitulation of the divine-in-history whose secondary status, even its potential desecration, spoke most truly for the unrepresentable godhead by virtue of its non-identity. Were these simulacra to become the holy things they resembled, they would violate their promise of transcendence

---

89. Jerome, *In Jonam* 2.11 (SC 43:92); citing Job 3:8 LXX. Duval, *Livre de Jonas* (n. 68), pp. 201–3 observes that Origen precedes Jerome in connecting these verses. See Origen, *De oratione* 13.4, cf. 16.3 (PG 11:458B, 470C; trans. John J. O'Meara [Westminster, Md.: Newman Press, 1954], pp. 51–52, 62) and *Hom. in Lev.* 8.3.4 (SC 287:18; trans. Gary Wayne Barkley, FC 83:157). Also *Comm. in Rom.* 5.10.10–12 (PG 14:1051A–52B; trans. Thomas P. Scheck, FC 103:372–74); that last one is a central passage (along with *Comm. in Matt.* 16.8 [GCS 40, Origenes Werke 10:498–501; *KEM* 2:179]) in Origen's theory of "the devil's deception" by Christ. On its role in English drama, see chapter 3.

by rendering it immediate. Even the Holy itself had never come so close and could not—at least not unless the laws of creation were to draw to an end with the second coming of Christ.

That might take awhile. "Where is the promise of his coming?" asks the apostle Peter (2 Pet. 3:4) in demonstration of the scoffing he expects the church to endure when the final days are at last upon it; the question would have sounded very much like the doubt to which a lot of its members were already subject—hence the need for Peter to silence their skepticism by giving it voice: "For, from the day the fathers fell asleep," he says people might say, "all has remained just as from the beginning of creation" (2 Pet. 3:4). By impersonating a naysayer the writer would hope to reassure believers that Christ's coming was no "cleverly devised myth" (1:16), as the "false prophets" (2:1) among them were presumably asserting, yet the status of 2 Peter tells a more complicated story: the ventriloquy through which he voices the complaints of Christ's enemies is no more nor less an impersonation than when he speaks *in propria persona* about the coming judgment since, as with all the pseudepigraphical epistles in the New Testament, "Peter" himself is in this instance equally impersonated.[90] The early church knew this.[91] We know it. "We know full well," writes Norbert Brox, "of a patristic tradition that allowed lies, deception, and clever deceit under precisely specified conditions.... One has to say in advance that this tradition referred to no lesser a personage than Plato."[92]

---

90. Jerome H. Neyrey, *2 Peter, Jude*, AB 37c (New York: Doubleday, 1993), p. 111.

91. Eusebius acknowledges its spuriousness but admits "as it appeared useful to many, it has been studied with the other scriptures" (*Hist. eccl.* 3.3.1, cf. 3.25.3 [LCL vol. 1]). Jerome refers to it as the epistle "which is *attributed* to the apostle Peter [*nomine Petri Apostoli inscribitur*]" (*Ep.* 140.8 [PL 22:1172D]). Elsewhere he accepts it as genuine, though noting "it is denied by many to be his, on account of the dissonance of its style with the first [epistle]" (*De vir. ill.* 1.3 [PL 23:609A; trans. Halton, FC 100:5]). He explains in a letter to Hedibia that the discrepancy might be due to Peter's "interpreter" (*Ep.* 120.11 [PL 22:1002]), following the ancient idea that Peter did not speak Greek. For quotations from all the ancient testimony on 2 Peter's very dubious authenticity, see Charles Bigg, *The Epistles of St. Peter and St. Jude* (New York: Scribner's Sons, 1909), pp. 199–211.

92. Norbert Brox, *Falsche Verfasserangaben: Zur Erklärung der frühchristlichen Pseudepigraphie* (Stuttgart: KBW, 1975), p. 82. Similarly Bruce M. Metzger, "Literary Forgeries and Canonical Pseudepigrapha," *Journal of Biblical Literature* 91.1 (1972): 3–24; here 19. For more on the noble lie as it filters into the writings of the Fathers, see Franz Schindler, "Die Lüge in der patristischen Literatur," in *Beiträge zur Geschichte des christlichen Altertums und der Byzantinischen Literatur*, ed. Albert Michael Koeniger et al. (1922; repr., Amsterdam: Editions Rodophi, 1969), pp. 421–33; it will be clear from the following chapter that one cannot claim, with Schindler, that the Fathers' various justifications for lying end with Augustine; it is Augustine, rather, who places a certain *divine* mendacity at the heart of scripture—and history.

Had Christians never adapted Plato, and by this means helped elevate to the status of scripture the same kind of myth they claimed to reject, the religion could not have survived its historical mishaps.

That, at least, has been the kindest justification for the very real possibility that 2 Thessalonians, with its warnings against the "man of sin" (traditionally taken as a reference to Antichrist), is the pseudonymous invention of someone, like the writer of Titus, only purporting to be Paul.[93] Already by the time of 2 Peter, Christians were having to admit that the genuine letters of their "beloved brother Paul" had become "hard to understand" and were therefore increasingly subject to malevolent misconstruction (3:15–16). In particular they had difficulty grasping what Paul had meant in his first (and maybe only) letter to the Thessalonians when he expressed his conviction that the return of the Lord would come before his own death, "like a thief in the night."[94] His conviction was of course supposed to conform to Jesus' own reassurances that "some standing here…will not taste death before they see that the kingdom of God has come with power" (Mt 16:28; Mk 9:1; Lk 9:27; cf. Jn 21:22–23);[95] but the conformity with Christ's own message was exactly the problem. Such predictions rang to some increasingly hollow because the fathers of their religion had all tasted death and fallen asleep, yet nothing changed. History had belied revelation. To rectify matters (certain scholars have thought) someone forged a *second* letter to the Thessalonians in order to *put off* the second coming. If this supposition is right, then what Paul's impersonator offers there, in place of the second coming and almost as its compensatory replacement, is the eventual advent of an imposture even more grand than Christ's first coming had seemed to his enemies, but now in the person of Antichrist. Naturally believers would have to wait for Antichrist, too, though "Paul" does not leave them comfortless; in the meantime he offers yet another impersonation—as it were, an Anti-Paul—in the person behind this very letter. As proof that the letter is *not* a forgery coming merely "*as if* it were from us" (2:2)—that is, as if from Paul's genuine circle—the

93. Against the authenticity of 2 Thess. see Wolfgang Trilling, *Untersuchungen zum zweiten Thessalonicherbrief* (Leipzig: St. Benno, 1972), and, more recently, Maarten J. J. Menken, *2 Thessalonians* (New York: Routledge, 1994), pp. 27–43.

94. 1 Thess. 5:2, 4. The comparison between the coming Kingdom and a thief occurs also in Mt 24:43; Lk 12:39; Rev. 3:3, and will be of some interest to us later. For the argument that Paul's death, contradicting his expectation of the Kingdom, inspired the forgery of 2 Thess., see Menken, *2 Thessalonians*, p. 28.

95. For a riveting discussion of the parallels, see Sanders, *Historical Figure of Jesus* (n. 19), pp. 179–84.

writer offers to his readers the master stroke of Paul's personal signature. And so the letter ends: "I, Paul, write this greeting with my own hand. This is the mark in every letter of mine; it is the way I write" (3:17). The stress on authenticity alone should be enough to raise doubts. Even if a lie, it is not, however, without a deep truth; for had not Paul already repudiated every notion of an authentic self in the ultimate act of Christian playacting so as to win all the more converts? "To Jews I became like a Jew...to those under the law, like one under the law...to those without the law, like one without the law...I became to the weak as though I were weak, to win the weak; I became all things to all people that by all means I might save some" (1 Cor. 9:20–22).

When Paul lamented that he had become a spectacle (*theatron*) to the world, to angels and men (1 Cor. 4:9), later students of his thought, starting with Ambrose, took him to be looking ahead to the marketplace execution, in the final days, of Enoch and Elias by Antichrist.[96] And this recapitulation of the persecutions inflicted on Paul (himself once a persecutor) opened the way for the final release, provided only you were sufficiently trained in typological thinking to discern in the Antichrist the One he anticipated in the negative—to intuit the final truth, in other words, within the lies that announced its arrival. Thus the beauty of the Christian *theatron*, where the apparent absence of divine protection or worse, the seeming license of demonic mimicry to parody the divine, actually promotes faith in a coming fulfillment. "For God would never have created any human, much less angels, whose future wickedness he foreknew," Augustine writes, "unless he had equally known to what uses he could put them on behalf of the good, thereby adorning the course of ages like a most beautiful poem set off with antithesis" (*De civ. dei* 11.18; LCL vol. 3). God's artistry requires contraposition; history therefore requires darkness: "Just as the opposition of contraries bestows beauty upon language, then, so is the beauty of this world composed by the opposition of contraries, arranged, as it were, by an eloquence not of words, but of things" (ibid.). Consider the catastrophes suffered by Job as a sign of God's approval and the riches he afterwards reaped in recompense for his gorgeous laments. You learn from him how the goodness of godhead is hedged about with shadows and deception as a matter of course. As long as history lasts, divinity shall be like this: mediated by tragedy and the monstrous, by Leviathan

---

96. See, for example, Ambrose, *Comm. in 1 Cor.* 4.9 (PL 17:215D–16B); Rabanus Maurus, *Enn. in 1 Cor.* 4.9 (PL 112:47C–D), repeating Ambrose verbatim, as does the Gloss (PL 114:526A–B). See also Bruno the Carthusian, *Exp. in 1 Cor.* 4.9 (PL 153:143C–D).

and Behemoth, forgeries and farce, the godawful swirl of the whirlwind, the cross, and Antichrist. The Lord has approved this sort of temporal interference in an act of sublime artistry, or cunning—love, maybe. What better proof of divinity than to sustain a swarm of parasites without hardship or impatience, even to the point of crucifixion? Adversity becomes him.

CHAPTER 1

Lying Likenesses

Typology and the Medieval *Miracula*

> For a long time the religious imagination does not at all want to be-
> lieve in the identity of the god and an image: the image is supposed
> to let the numen of the deity appear—in some mysterious, not fully
> comprehensible way—as active here, as locally bound. The oldest im-
> age of divinity is supposed to reveal and at the same time conceal the
> god—to intimate, but not expose him to view.
> —FRIEDRICH NIETZSCHE

Imago in Evangelio

Despite a lot of variation in the commentaries, from the earliest of
them onward Antichrist was frequently recognized as the supreme adversary and herald of the final days in part by his *resemblance* to the true Christ.
"For the deceiver," writes Hippolytus, "seeks to liken himself in all things
to the Son of God" (*Antichrist* 6 [GCS 1:7–8; ANF 5:206]). Born among Jews,
he would send his apostles to the nations and convert multitudes through
the working of miracles. He would claim to be the messiah and "sit in
the temple of God, leading astray those who worship him as if he were
Christ" (Irenaeus, *Adv. haer.* 5.25.4 [SC 153:320; ANF 5:554]; 2 Thess. 2:4).
Practically everyone, even the most stiff-necked, would readily accept his
divinity. And why not? He had the miracles to prove it. He was exactly like
Christ, except he surpassed Christ, in that fewer people would suspect him
of demonism. It was as though the early gentile church—thwarted by the
Roman state, torn by internal faction, faced with the constant rebuke of
the parent religion whose spiritual prerogatives it had usurped—found
itself gripped by the nightmare of *another* Jesus, this time one who more

plainly fulfilled the messianic promise. Not only would the Antichrist of Hippolytus perform all the wonders Jesus had, for example; he would also go about "helping widows, protecting orphans, loving everyone, [and] bringing the contentious to charitable accord" (*De consummatione mundi* 23 [PG 10:925C–D]).[1] Such easy deliverance, real Christians insisted, had to be false. Whoever actually managed to deliver the Jews and return them to their homeland, whoever persuaded secular authority to kneel, whoever could propel Christianity from an obscure splinter group to a world power only *appeared* to fulfill God's covenants. In fact, the impotent dead man Christians worshiped at great cost, whose *parousia* seemed increasingly remote the closer it got—he was the genuine article and would one day return at last, infinitely empowered by his endless delay.

The church's eventual triumph over its traditional enemies—pagan Rome, Judaism—seemed by the late Middle Ages like an ugly failure to a few committed members, and in arguing this point they turned the old polemics against Antichrist to new use. The strange reversals that would occur under his reign had long been chronicled in sermon and song as that *furor ultimus* when holiness would pour from hell, falsehood pretend to truth, evil appear good:

> Now harlotry for mirth is held
> And vertues tornen in-to vice
> And Symonye hat chirches solde,
> And lawe is waxen Couetyse.[2]

Medieval and early modern dissenters accordingly found in Antichrist a ready explanation for how the worldly success of their faith actually signified the worst. Major heretics following Wyclif, and all the Protestants, drew the inevitable inference that if Christ and Antichrist were practically indistinguishable, if the "mystery of iniquity was *already* at work" (2 Thess. 2:7),

---

1. Possible dates for this homily range from the mid-fourth to the early ninth century. For further discussion, see Bernard McGinn, *Antichrist: Two Thousand Years of the Human Fascination with Evil* (New York: Columbia University Press, 2000), pp. 71–74, esp. n. 66.

2. Carleton Brown, ed., *Religious Lyrics of the XIVth Century* (Oxford: Clarendon Press, 1924), p. 129. "Furor ultimus" is a phrase from Bernard of Cluny, *De contemptu mundi: A Bitter Satirical Poem of 3000 Lines upon the Morals of the XIIth Century*, ed. H. C. Hoskier (London: B. Quaritch, 1929), p. 77. These and many other references to the transvaluations of apocalypse are collected by Joseph R. Keller, "The Triumph of Vice: A Formal Approach to the Medieval Complaint against the Times," *Annuale Mediaevale* 10 (1969): 120–37. See also Stuart Clark, *Thinking with Demons: The Idea of Witchcraft in Early Modern Europe* (Oxford: Clarendon Press, 1997), pp. 43–93, and those he cites, esp. p. 66 n. 97.

then maybe Antichrist had already come, and they were living out the final days under the delusion of his transvaluations, such that everything people unwittingly accepted as official Christianity—the episcopacy, the sacraments, the Vulgate, the supremacy of the pope—all these were in fact Antichristianity.[3] Virtue had turned to vice, law to covetousness, high office to simony. Idols had replaced the only true icon, which was the Word of scripture. Countless tracts appeared in England over the course of the sixteenth and seventeenth centuries proving through algebraic permutation of the number 666 (Dan. 13:18) that the pope was Antichrist—a position adopted, albeit unofficially, by the Church of England.[4] In response the Douai-Rheims commentators allowed that this number did indeed encode the name of Antichrist, just as "the ineffable name of God was among the Iewes expressed by a certaine number of 4 characters," but, they pointed out, no pope as yet had a name that really added up. The same could not be said of Luther, after some orthographic adjustments to reflect his name's authentic spelling "in the Alman tongue," yet even so, the commentators reverently decline to press the omen. To press further would deprive the Revelation of the ominous penumbra that, paradoxically, their clarifications had to uphold. To push on would only reduce their commentary to the same level of crass radicalism it was intended to combat. These are more refined exegetes. They judge not rashly God's secrets. To them, Antichrist's name remains hidden, "for certaine knowledge thereof no mortal man can haue vvithout an expresse reuelation." And the fact of the matter was, you hardly needed express revelation when dealing with so obvious an accessory to apocalypse as Martin Luther: "He is vndoubtedly one of Antichrists precursors," they conclude at last, "but not Antichrist him self" (Rev. 13:17–18, annotations).

As old as the earliest Christian faction and of equal use to subsequent competitors, this polemical gambit of discerning in rivals the imminent appearance of Antichrist displays in microcosm the whole of that figure's remarkable character. First, it establishes a parallel between his inscrutability and the radical hiddenness of a God that was unknown "among the Jews" save for the intermediary sign of an unspeakable name, and then later known among Christians only through Christ, whose life and death and afterlife presented difficulties every bit as enigmatic as the Tetragrammaton.

3. For a study of the use to which Luther and his followers put the myth, see Volker Leppin, *Antichrist und Jüngster Tag: Das Profil apokalyptischer Flugschriftenpublizistik im deutschen Luthertum 1548–1618* (Gütersloh: Gütersloher Verlagshaus, 1999).
4. See Christopher Hill, *Antichrist in Seventeenth-Century England* (London: Verso, 1990).

Second, there is the way this label of "Antichrist" (or libel, rather) implicitly acknowledges a resemblance between accuser and accused, so that even when directed at a group wholly repugnant to the truly faithful, the accusation itself confesses a secret affinity—the profound affinity between "true faith" and the bastardized, mimetic equivalent without which the chosen could not discern their election. If Antichrist's primary distinction is his lack of distinction from Christ, it follows that his "precursors" will be hard to discern from those who pursue the more benign, and highly recommended, *imitatio Christi.* Thus the late and seminal challenge of that ultimate *falsus frater,* Martin Luther. He may have been a heretical maniac, but to a lot of people he still seemed pretty devout. He looked like an Augustinian monk. That was the calamity.

Note, however, that the Douai-Rheims identification of Luther with Antichrist serves ultimately as a means of *differentiation.* He cannot really *be* Antichrist any more than he can be the good, Christ-like Augustinian that he equally resembles. He is "not Antichrist *him self*" but rather a premature anticipation. You see now Luther's real abjection: neither the holy man he pretends to be nor the true Pretender, he is merely the precursor to a precursor. This brings to light yet another critical ingredient to the myth of Antichrist, "surely the quintessence of oppositional representation in Western religion."[5] The basic idea is that resemblance can join no two things without offsetting a difference. And the difference is prophetic. Antichrist, coming in the likeness of Christ, heralds the real second coming insofar as he is *not* Christ. By the same logic, the coming of Antichrist can be foretold in the existence of all those who act just like him but are not he himself. The ultimate impostor has scores of imitators. These amount to a typological series parallel to Christ's own, stretching throughout all history. Just as Job was a type of Christ, Barabbas was a type of the Antichrist, and so on. Through some uncanny trick of the eye, however, at the furthest horizon these two parallel genealogies converge on a single point. Finally everything will culminate in the return of Christ. Both his official typological imitators and the antichristian impostors together predict what they themselves, as mere precursors, by definition fail to *be.*

It is here in their prophetic failure, however, that all of Christ's mimetic opponents paradoxically come closest to occupying the office that forever exceeds them, insofar as the person of Jesus likewise promised more than the events of his life really delivered. If his life (or death) alone had

---

5. Clark, *Thinking with Demons* (n. 2), p. 61.

sufficed, there would be no need for a *second* coming, and no promise of a "triumphant" Christ completely different from the Crucified, if also somehow the same. Christ at his first coming thus counts as his *own* typological precursor. Only some sort of "figure" can have saved the world *already*. Were a dim futurity not to suffuse the New Testament as much as the Old, at the anagogical level, Christ's strange arrival and stranger departure would have come and gone without predicting any ultimate consequence. "Here is the shadow, here the image," writes Ambrose under the influence of Origen, "there the truth. The shadow is in the law, the image in the gospel, the truth in heaven" (*De officiis* 1.48.239).[6] Or as John Chrysostom reportedly put it, the Old Testament is actually "a type of a type, and the New a type of reality," where "reality" as such "belongs to the age to come."[7] The "real" events composing Christ's life, this says, are meaningful chiefly as a prelude to events as yet unrecorded but nonetheless impossibly figured in the records we have. "It would seem necessary, then," Lubac emphasizes, "to conceive the New Testament as truth with respect to the Old, but as mere 'image' with respect to the ultimate reality still to come."[8] It would seem, in other words, that no matter how ingenious the exegete, he is left in the end with images and words— "mere representations"—to flesh out the Lord's present absence until the day of his return. "The most basic piety should hold to this inevitable dilemma," writes Jean-Luc Marion in a recent radicalization of Lubac's insight. "Either the Holy maintains itself as such, in which case it refuses itself to every visible spectacle, and the holiness of God remains without either image or visage; or the image that delivers the Holy to the visible simply abandons it as a victim to the torments of its executioners—and

6. PL 16:94A; NPNF II, 10:40; but see the better Latin text with a more recent translation and notes by Ivor J. Davidson, *De Officiis*, 2 vols. (Oxford: Oxford University Press, 2001), 1:254–55 and 2:664–66, where he gives further references on the debt to Origen and, more distantly, Plato. Cf. Heb. 10:1–2.

7. From an otherwise unidentified work quoted by John of Damascus, *De imag. orat.* 1.53; repeated at 2.49 and 3.51 (PG 94:1272A etc.); trans. Andrew Louth, *Three Treatises on the Divine Images* (Crestwood, N.Y.: St. Vladimer's Seminary Press, 2003), p. 49.

8. *ME* 2:182. Throughout this work one finds eloquent testimony to the endless deferrals of Christian fulfillment: "So however high anagogy leads, it always leaves something to look for and always with greater fervor, because it still does not uncover the Face of God" (*ME* 2:193; cf. pp. 197, 179, 160). According to Christoph Schönborn, *God's Human Face: The Christ Icon*, trans. Lothar Krauth (San Francisco: Ignatius Press, 1994), "An entire current of spiritual and theological Christian tradition can be assigned to this tendency" (53), that is, the tendency to see even the events of the New Testament "merely as 'shadows of spiritual realities'" and then to interpret its "'fulfillment' passages…as predictions of the good things [yet] to come in the world" (51).

the image ... fills out the role of an obscene blasphemy. Either the invisible or the impostor."[9]

The image of Christ's historical presence as presented by the gospels and transmitted thereafter through religious iconography such as drama, though officially fuller than the figurations that came in the Old Testament, can in other words never be divested of this scandalous inadequacy—the scandal of being *no less* an image, no less an anticipatory stand-in, lest the biblical Jesus fail to represent the promise of a future infinitely *better* than gospel history. In the next section I want further to explore first how typological readers insist on the representative or "imaginary" significance of biblical events by interpreting them *as images* of something more sacred yet to come, and then second, how this mimetic deferral risks transforming the whole of scripture into a kind of fantasy or artistic deception—a species, that is, of Satan's original, failed aspiration to "be like God." That aspiration, as we'll see in a section on York's Creation, not only sets all recorded history in motion but also articulates the one goal medieval drama most wants to aim for.

Of course major episodes of the Bible hardly required a typological transformation in order to rise above the appearance of being merely historical. The essential historicity that typology presupposes at its first and most basic level (before arguing for a higher, more refined significance) in places looks obviously impossible, and has to look impossible, if sacred history itself is going to signify the presence of divinity. After all the historical Jesus can appear "as the image, seal, adumbration, and reflection of his archetype," Gregory of Nyssa says, only "through the thaumaturgy [*thaumatopoiïas*] of his actions" (*Homilia in diem natalem Christi*; PG 46:1141B). What makes Jesus the ultimate "type" of divinity, according to this, is the very thing that will characterize Antichrist (we'll look eventually at his appearance in the Chester cycle), the very thing from which medieval drama as a whole takes one of its names: the ability to perform miracles. The "thaumatopoetics" celebrated in Christ had long been attributed to precisely the kind of charlatan that any number of antitheatricalists such as Augustine or Gerhoch of Reichersberg saw on stage in the theater. Before finishing this chapter with a look at some dramatic events in Beverley,

9. Jean-Luc Marion, *The Crossing of the Visible*, trans. James K. A. Smith (Stanford: Stanford University Press, 2004), p. 67. He goes on to argue as persuasively, I think, as one possibly can that icons manage to escape the "mimetic rivalry" inherent to idolatry because they are "types" rather than mimetic figurations. I have been enlightened and challenged by his subtle argument; in what follows I will try to show that typology, too, remains trapped by—and thrives on—the dilemmas of mimesis.

we'll return to York to consider its culmination in the trial and crucifixion of Jesus on the charge that the miracles supposedly proving his divine nature were themselves nothing but histrionic mimicry.

Where typology manages to salvage a certain romantic integrity from sacred history by aestheticizing its mishaps, I want to say, the theory of miracles defends in turn the stuff of Greek romance and mythology, whenever it happens in Christian scripture, as being in fact strictly historical. A miracle, by common definition, proved that for God all things were possible (Mt 19:26 and parallels). At certain critical junctures he made the impossible actually happen. What anywhere else would have to be dismissed as a perverse mirage (e.g., resurrection) or the wild lie of imaginative writers (e.g., virgin birth) is in the case of biblical miracles accepted as testimony to the boundlessness of the sacred. Taken together the type and the miracle thus balance the historicity of scripture against its apparent contrafactuality: sacred events may then be witnessed after all as a sequence in which *the fictive really happens,* just as an actor actually steps on stage even if he is not in fact the Christ he portrays.

The Typological Image

Typos means literally an impression, as in wax or a coin. Taken at face value the term suggests that the precursors of Christ (and even Christ's first appearance) anticipate fulfillment the way an empty indentation bears the image of its absent seal. To form the name of this higher counterpart one need only add to "type" the amphibolous prefix *anti-*, which means literally "opposed to" but also "instead of"[10] and thus provides the abstract grammatical analogue to the unity of opposites achieved more

---

10. *A Greek-English Lexicon of the New Testament and Other Early Christian Literature,* ed. Frederick William Danker, 3rd ed. (Chicago: University of Chicago Press, 2000), s.v. ἀντί. This tends to bleed into the Latin homonym, *ante,* as for example in the Chester play of "Antechrist." Augustine has to spell it out so as to avoid confusion: Antichrist, he wrote, is so called on account of his opposition and not just his immediate priority to Christ (*In ep. Joh.* 3.4 [SC 75:190–92; NPNF 7:476–77]). Repeated by Isidore of Seville (PL 82:316B), Rabanus Maurus (PL 111:427D–428A), and Martin of Leon (PL 209:264A), among others. The French still say "Antéchrist," Augustine be damned, and I suspect this tradition has led André Grabar to adopt "antetype" as the term for Old Testament prefigurations of New Testament "types" in his important *Christian Iconography: A Study of Its Origins* (Princeton: Princeton University Press, 1968), pp. 140–46 and passim. James J. Paxson, "A Theory of Biblical Typology in the Middle Ages," *Exemplaria* 3.2 (October 1991): 359–83, demonstrates that this variety of prefixes "inhibits taxonomical clarification" even while contributing "to the dynamics of typological invention, particularly in the medieval drama" (369).

concretely in ancient technologies of mechanical reproduction;[11] a type, that is, reproduces its antitype "identically," but *in reverse.*

Paul's use of this terminology in an openly hermeneutic sense, where Adam appears as a "type of Christ" (Rom. 5:14), simply applies its mechanical version of likeness, exact but reversed, to history. For Paul it is as though God's Word, having first been pressed on creation, was then removed, leaving behind in human affairs an inverted image of the grand design. This fallen world, real enough to us but insubstantial compared to the uncircumscribed God whose form it somehow bears, yawns for fulfillment like a hollow vessel. It gives a backward shape to all that it lacks. Its vacancy is God-shaped. Hence for Paul, Adam possesses a prophetic likeness to Christ by virtue of a reversed anticipation: what Adam has lost, Christ will regain; "the first man was from the earth, a man of dust; the second is from heaven" (1 Cor. 15:47). The initiator of sin models in advance the man of grace: "For as by a man came death, by a man has come also the resurrection of the dead. For as in Adam all die, so also in Christ shall all be made alive" (1 Cor. 15:21–22).[12]

Generalizing from here, I suspect we are meant to view the current world "as through a looking-glass, enigmatically" (1 Cor. 13:12).[13] Historical existence, though disastrous in itself, foreshadows redemption through the determinant emptiness of a mirror image or typological impression. Insofar as history works like either, occurrences closely resemble the eschatological events they foretell but for a sharp reversal. What today you hold in your left hand, tomorrow will be on the right. What today seems sinister is only the mirror image of tomorrow's rectification. Today a crucifixion, tomorrow eternal life. For a typological likeness to function as a

11. Eric Auerbach, "Figura," in *Scenes from the Drama of European Literature* (Minneapolis: University of Minnesota Press, 1984), p. 15, mentions the relation of type to impression, but not the inversion this implies, though he elsewhere comments on the deceptiveness of typological images, which amounts almost to the same thing (pp. 44–47). For the inversion specifically, see Leonhard Goppelt, *Typos: The Typological Interpretation of the Old Testament in the New,* trans. Donald H. Madvig (Grand Rapids: Eerdmans, 1982), pp. 129ff., and P. Bloch, "Typologie," in *Lexikon der christlichen Ikonographie,* vol. 4 (Rome: Herder, 1972), p. 395. My thinking on the topic of seals and impressions has been greatly influenced by Margreta de Grazia, "Imprints: Shakespeare, Gutenberg and Descartes," in *Alternative Shakespeares,* ed. Terence Hawkes, vol. 2 (London: Routledge, 1996), pp. 2:63–94.

12. Cf. Rom. 5:12–21. For further commentary, see Paul Ricoeur, *The Symbolism of Evil,* trans. Emerson Buchanan (Boston: Beacon Press, 1967), pp. 232–78. On the relation of Paul's "Adamology" to his and others' conception of the Antichrist, see McGinn, *Antichrist* (n. 1), pp. 33–56.

13. In what follows I am close to the thinking of Rudolf Bultmann, *History and Eschatology* (Edinburgh: University Press, 1957), pp. 40–41.

means of prognostication, it *has* to contain this oppositional or negative aspect. Otherwise the likeness could not prophesy. It would automatically fulfill in its own untroubled identity the conditions to come. It would reconcile heaven with earth prematurely, in the present, and you could look forward at best to things as they are: a carpenter's son predictably crucified in politico-religious retaliation for proclaiming his Kingdom, whose corpse was then stolen but freakishly reappeared incognito. The typological vision sees in the historical grounds of the church something else: not an executed magician and the traumatized delusions of his followers but the historical resurrection of a real miracle worker and the Son of God, "hidden" however in the sign of the cross, in the cold emptiness of a stone tomb, and clouded over by the fantastic enigmas of his post mortem appearance. For the typologist, events like these only serve to proclaim his *parousia* all the more forcefully. They clap for the second coming like tongueless bells.

In effect, typological thinkers have to take sacred history in all its banality and error as the promise of a future recapitulation whose coming will render the horrific meandering of the past somehow *artistic*. This is to say, for them, scripture records events that cannot be exactly what they purport to be if the typologist is to find any transcendent truth in them beyond their historical content. Scripture cannot record mere events. Instead, the manifest confusions of its history must be the cunning of God's art, and only by means of this supreme aestheticism are the events recorded by scripture raised *beyond* the concrete historical processes through which alone the sacred can be meaningfully expressed to a time-bound humanity. "The type is a manifestation of things to be expected," writes Basil the Great, "giving advance, demonstrative indication of what is going to happen *by means of imitation*" (*De spirit.* 14.31 [PG 32:121C; NPNF II, 8:19]). According to the typological model, history can have an end, in all senses of the word, only if events figure or mimetically *represent* their own fulfillment. As with Antichrist, here too everything rests on the representation's inadequacy: there were those who looked at historical imitations such as Moses and judged the coming reality of Christ unnecessary for having been already achieved in its foreshadowing; these people, Basil says, do not grasp how "the difference between these things is as great as that between dream and reality, between shadows or images and substantial existence" (*De spirit.* 14.32 [ibid., 125A; 20]). For him, history offers salvation the way any species of mimetic art offers its pleasures: as an insubstantial or fallen reflection which gives some negative indication of a reality, more essential than itself, that has otherwise failed to appear. It is the same for

Augustine: what fascinates him, according to Peter Brown, is not so much history in itself but history considered as "the language of God, distant and opaque as a liturgy. It is the significance of this language, suddenly uncovered in the appearance of Christ among men, that poured meaning into a small part at least of this disquieting inanity: 'the centuries of past history would have rolled by like empty jars, if Christ had not been foretold by means of them.' "[14] What the empty jars predict, however, is simply one further, more hopeful form of emptiness: Christ's tomb. Thankfully this too is a simulacrum. It represents the day, as yet unrealized, when every tomb will gape.

At the same time, in refusing to fulfill immediately what they promise, sacred events threaten to promote, instead of prophecy, a lie. The classic definition of a "type" as the mimetic representation (in history) of a future truth can never be entirely disentangled from the conventional understanding of demonic deception: "a lie always imitates the truth," explains Jerome, "for unless it were to have some semblance of virtue, it would not be able to deceive the innocent" (*In Jer.* 4.61.2 [CCSL 74:228]).[15] What else was the life of Christ, typologically understood, *except* a series of semblances in anticipation of a future fulfillment that Christ proved unable as yet to deliver? Or as Augustine asks, what does it mean that the messiah who appeared on the road to Emmaus following his death "*feigned* as though to walk farther with his disciples" (*C. mend.* 13.28 [CSEL 41:508; NPNF 3:494]; Lk 24:28)? Why did the disciples fail at first to recognize him? Is the substantial semblance of godhead a disguised dissembler? And for that matter, why, during Jesus' lifetime, when he openly proclaimed his divine status, did he so often pretend not to know what a God-on-earth, by Augustine's lights, would most certainly have known? Why does he ask of the woman reaching after his hem, "Who touched me?" (Lk 8:45). Either these historical details recorded by scripture matter, or they do not. "Do we suppose these things have no meaning?" asks Augustine, speaking of another, equally impenetrable scriptural detail. "I can suppose no such thing" (*Tract. in Joh.* 120.8 [CCSL 36:663; trans. John W. Rettig, FC 92:54]). His incredulity joins a chorus of faithful theologians united in the anxiety that if scripture has nothing more to it than the plain historical sense, scripture tends toward barbarism. Worse, if Jesus truly embodies God without omission or shortcoming (Col. 2:9) and the facts of Jesus'

14. Peter Brown, *Augustine of Hippo: A Biography* (Berkeley: University of California Press, 1967), p. 318; quoting *Tract. in Joh.* 9.6 (CCSL 36:94; trans. Rettig, FC 78:200).

15. Cf. Augustine, *Sol.* 2.10 and 2.30, where nothing is false "except by some imitation of the true" (CSEL 89:57, 87; NPNF 7:550, 557).

life are true as reported, God is a liar. He knows who grasps at his hem, always.

As handed down from Hippolytus and Irenaeus to Origen, from Ambrose to Augustine and onward, the most elementary task of typological hermeneutics has always been to unveil a "spiritual" meaning underlying those passages of scripture that seem to teach falsehood or "perversion" when interpreted *ad litteram* (*Conf.* 6.4.6).[16] In the feigning of Christ, for example, the hermeneutic eye discerns more than a mendacious feint. "As if everything feigned [*fingitur*] were a lie!" Augustine reasons, "when so many things may be truly feigned for the sake of signifying one thing by another" (*C. mend.* 13.28 [CSEL 41:508; NPNF 3:494]).[17] The woman at Jesus' hem, he explains, was a *type* of the gentile nations, on the Old Testament model. After all, the psalmist had predicted, "A people whom I have not known shall serve me" (Ps 18:43; *C. mend.* 13.27 [ibid.]). And lo, Christ did not know that woman, either. So too when the Lord, costumed as a stranger in the wake of his dismal end, feigned to go farther with his disciples. This theatrical fiction according to Augustine is temporal, momentary, and necessary; under the aspect of eternity it signifies the ultimate truth, that Christ will go with them beyond the very heavens (*C. mend.* 13.28 [ibid.]). But not till later. In the meantime—the vast interim of non-apocalyptic eschatology—you have to make do with the world as it is, granted the further provision that the world as it is, is secretly a stage.

Augustine can borrow from the vocabulary of ancient aesthetics to rescue Christian history, I think, because that discourse first taught him to value literary fiction as a special kind of revelator. Augustine savors, for

---

16. Cf. Eric Osborn, *Irenaeus of Lyons* (Cambridge: Cambridge University Press, 2001), p. 182: "One principle of exegesis…is that what appears scandalous in scripture should not be rejected, because God put it there and he has higher standards than we have. It should be seen as part of the total economy, and discerned as a type. This point was taken up by Origen, who claimed that God placed offensive material in the text of scripture so that readers would look beyond the literal to the spiritual sense."

17. Cf. *Serm.* 89 (PL 38:553–58; *WSA* III/3:439–46), which addresses the same issues and passages from scripture, esp. §6: "So whatever is said figuratively is, in some sense, feigned [*modo fingitur*]." Also *Sol.* 2.16 (CSEL 89:65–66; NPNF 7:552); *De doct. christ.* 1.36.40 (CCSL 32:29; *WSA* I/11:124); and Isidore of Seville, *Etym.* 1.40 (PL 82:122). Further discussion in Brian Stock, *Augustine the Reader: Meditation, Self-Knowledge, and the Ethics of Interpretation* (Cambridge: Belknap Press of Harvard University Press, 1996), pp. 134–35. Edmund Reiss, "Ambiguous Signs and Authorial Deceptions in Fourteenth-Century Fictions," in *Sign, Sentence, Discourse: Language in Medieval Thought and Literature*, ed. Julian N. Wasserman and Lois Roney (Syracuse: Syracuse University Press, 1989), pp. 113–37: "According to Augustine, feigned narratives like fables may give true significations. Of this sort are the fictions of late medieval writers, which, while purporting to deceive, actually serve to teach wisdom" (124).

example, the same paradox of representation that Plato and Plutarch describe in their definition of myth as a false tale resembling the truth.[18] In his *Soliloquies*—the first of his works he wrote as a Christian, and one whose title incidentally coined a new word of considerable importance to the history of theater—Augustine does not systematically discriminate among the mimetic arts any more than other ancient authorities had, since for Augustine the truth of poetry, drama, painting, and sculpture, if not also their unity, resides in their fictiveness: how, he asks, could Roscius, the famous actor, "be a true tragedian, were he not willing to be a false Hector, a false Andromache, a false Hercules, and innumerable others?" What had Roscius to do with Hecuba, or Hecuba with him? "Or how would the picture [of a horse] be true, if the horse were not false? how would the mirror-image of a man be true, if the man [in the mirror] were not false?" (*Sol.* 2.18 [CSEL 89:69; NPNF 7:553]). Unless the image as such were in some sense *unreal*, it could not be a *true likeness*. But of what exactly does this nebulous "truth" consist? The temptation for uncultured ancients must have been to say that it consists of obedience or loyalty, that is, the "troth" of similitude to its original; in short, its refusal to deviate from the slavish law of replication. Yet deviate it must, and radically, as Augustine points out with relish: replicas fulfill their own mandate only so long as they are not what they imitate. "And this alone is of use for their truth, that they are otherwise false. For which reason they in no way attain what they either want or ought to be, if they escape being false" (ibid.). Images become what they are by *not* becoming whatever it is that they profess to be.

At these remarks Augustine's fictional self—irony of ironies—can only "marvel" (*miror*). We'll see the same language of miracle again in his descriptions of the theater, and precisely this terminology will come to apply, in time, to the sacred drama or *miracula* of England. For that application to work, however, a crucial modification in classical aesthetics had to be made and that is what Augustine accomplishes here, by first intensifying the paradox of representational truth already noted by Plutarch and others, and then *transferring* it to Holy Writ, as though the events it records had themselves been penned by God, the *supreme author* [*summus auctor*].[19]

---

18. See introduction, pp. 19–20.

19. For the commonplace of God as author or artist (*artifex*), see Ernst Robert Curtius, *European Literature and the Latin Middle Ages*, trans. Willard R. Trask (New York: Pantheon, 1953), pp. 544–46. For Augustine specifically, see Brown, *Augustine of Hippo* (n. 14), pp. 259ff. and 318. Also Robert J. O'Connell, *Images of Conversion in St. Augustine's "Confessions"* (New York: Fordham University Press, 1996), pp. 171–72: "In one of Augustine's favorite metaphors, the temporal universe constitutes a universal poem, a *carmen*

This sublime, aesthetic aspect of God-in-history licenses the typologist to extract—from the incoherence and brute meaninglessness of all that merely happens—the promise of an event to come which will justify all this apparent nonsense.[20] For him, scriptural history takes the first step toward the redemption of historical existence by failing to be equated wholly with it. Any scriptural fact is closer to a contrafactual image of some higher, transcendent reality than it is to the history such transcendence means one day to salvage. Augustine explicitly argues that great writers like Horace regularly tell the truth through fiction, so why not God, who is greater (*C. mend.* 13.28 [CSEL 41:508; NPNF 3:494])? If poetry and drama were to reflect, without the least mediation, all that is or has been, literature would have no claim to a meaning more profound than what has thus far existed. Of course, conceived as mimesis, literature does nothing more than imitate existence, however much it exaggerates. What saves it from endless recapitulation of the past and present is the same thing that allows a mimetic truth to emerge from patent fictiveness: the simple, paradoxical fact that any representation cannot be that which it purports to be.[21] Otherwise it would cease to represent. It would simply *be,* and like all postlapsarian existence, it would be wrong.

Ad Imaginem in the York Cycle

The triune nature of the English mystery cycle—fictive drama, historical fact, and the truth beyond history—in knotting together such incompatible elements cultivated of necessity a whole theodicy of mimesis. The first problem was to explain the presence of evil in advance of human

---

universitatis, into which the master-artist introduces each word and syllable and letter at precisely the appropriate point." For a later Augustinian's rehearsal of this aesthetic view of the universe, see Gerhoch of Reichersberg (e.g., PL 193:1224C, 194:964), whose views on theater will become important to my argument presently. For Augustine's aesthetics more fully considered, see Robert J. O'Connell, *Art and the Christian Intelligence in St. Augustine* (Cambridge: Harvard University Press, 1978), and Carol Harrison, *Beauty and Revelation in the Thought of Saint Augustine* (Oxford: Clarendon Press, 1992).

20. *ME* 2:201: "Allegory fulfills history by giving it sense." My point in what follows is close to Rüdiger Bittner's argument, "Augustine's Philosophy of History," in *The Augustinian Tradition,* ed. Gareth B. Matthews (Berkeley: University of California Press, 1999), pp. 345–60, esp. the remark "Augustine's 'historia' is not 'history,' it is 'story'" (345).

21. Cf. John of Damascus, *De imag. orat.* 1.9 (PG 94:1240C; trans. Louth [n. 7], p. 25): "An image is a likeness depicting an archetype, but having a certain difference from it," and *De imag. orat* 3.16 (ibid., 1337A–B; 95): "An image is therefore a likeness and a pattern and impression [*ektypōma*] of something…the image is one thing and what it depicts is another."

disobedience. The plays followed various theologians in piecing together, from the barest of scriptural hints, the Fall's prehistory, that is, the narrative of evil's development *prior* to evil's existence.[22] Humanity's decline, it had long been established, was best explained by another preceding it of an altogether higher magnitude, of an altogether different temporal order. This displacement of the problem from earth into heaven of course risked causing an infinite regress, each Fall requiring some Fall previous to it that would make sin first possible in an otherwise perfect universe, and so on ad infinitum it seemed, unless there be found some aspect of the prelapsarian cosmos, not evil in itself, that nonetheless occasioned the lapse. The dramatists and the theologians both found that aspect in similitude.

"I will ascend to heaven," said the Star of the Morning. "I will make myself like the Most High" (Isa. 14:12–14). The regress traditionally stops here, in the first appearance of evil not as evil but as God's *likeness*. (The Devil, as René Girard has said, is "totally mimetic.")[23] Isaiah hardly explained why Lucifer resolved to make himself like the Most High in the first place, however, and therefore left open the possibility of yet a further recess of evil that first caused his hubris. Of all the extant cycles York alone posits this ur-occasion for the devil's illicit similitude. Here, it is God's intended kinship with the flesh of his creation by way of the Incarnation that both prompts Lucifer's fall *and* follows from it as the happiest consequence.[24] Lucifer meditates on God's resolve to be made incarnate, then imagines—fatal speculation!—that his own form, fair and bright, would be more suitable for a being such as God.

> The Godhede þat I sawe so cleere,
> And parsayued þat he shuld take kynde,
> of a degree
> That he had wrought, and I dedygned [was offended]
> Þat aungell kynde shuld it noʒt be. (*York* 5.3–7)

22. A good introduction to this labyrinth of theological speculation, for those interested in English literature, is J. M. Evans, "*Paradise Lost" and the Genesis Tradition* (Oxford: Clarendon Press, 1968). The writers of the York cycle, with which I deal here, had access to a wide range of theological learning in the libraries of the Augustinian Friary and St. Mary's Abbey. See Alexandra F. Johnston, "The York Cycle and the Libraries of York," in *The Church and Learning in Later Medieval Society: Essays in Honour of R. B. Dobson*, ed. Caroline M. Barron and Jenny Stratford (Donington: Shaun Tyas, 2002), pp. 355–70.

23. René Girard, *I See Satan Fall Like Lightning*, trans. James G. Williams (Maryknoll, N.Y.: Orbis Books, 2001), p. 42. For a critique of Girard, see below n. 47 and chapter 3, n. 35.

24. Rosemary Woolf, *The English Mystery Plays* (Berkeley: University of California Press, 1972), p. 116, calls the idea of Incarnation preceding the Fall "Franciscan" and is followed in this by Michael O'Connell, *The Idolatrous Eye: Iconoclasm and Theater in Early-Modern*

God's timeless resolution to "take kynde" of a lesser degree, in both opening the way for Lucifer's original resentment and delivering humanity from the consequence of that resentment, closes the circuit in on itself, allowing evil no further origin or end other than God's own intentions—which in and of themselves of course cannot have been evil. Disgusted that God could conceive of making himself into something less than himself—and so much less even than Lucifer—Lucifer decides to make his lesser self more like God: "I sall be lyke vnto hym þat es hyeste on heghte" (*York* 1.91). His fall, then, consists of little more than this false inference: that a gradient exists between likenesses to the unequaled; that he, of an airy substance, stood *closer* to heaven than those created from earth. He failed to appreciate that what is like God, whether the angelic "merour of [his] mighte" or that "skylfull beeste" made after the divine image (*York* 1.34; 3.22), serves the holy grandeur best in not being sufficiently like it. "Between creator and creature," resolved the Fourth Lateran Council, "so great a likeness [*similitudo*] cannot be noted without the necessity of noting a greater dissimilarity between them."[25]

The council's reasoning gives the official imprimatur to an ancient sentiment stretching back through a twelfth-century vogue ultimately to Plato's *Statesman* (273d; LCL vol. 8). That dialogue explores how all sublunary reality threatens to dissolve, by sheer force of its chaotic materiality, into "an ocean of unlikeness" unless God directly ordains its motions in a manner consummate with his own harmonious being. In one strain of the textual tradition *topon* appears in place of *ponton*, producing, instead of "ocean," a "region" of unlikeness. That is the word adopted by Plotinus and passed on by him to later Christians through Augustine, in whom the phrase takes a turn somewhat foreign to Platonic tradition.[26] Whereas for Plotinus dissimilitude acts as a barrier—the barrier of "sinful" materiality

---

England (New York: Oxford University Press, 2000), pp. 79–80. Actually the idea has a more diffuse genesis. See Georges Florovsky, "*Cur Deus Homo?* The Motive of the Incarnation," in *Creation and Redemption* (Belmont, Mass.: Nordland, 1976), 3:163–70.

25. Latin and trans. in *Decrees of the Ecumenical Councils*, ed. Norman P. Tanner, 2 vols. (Washington D.C.: Georgetown University Press, 1990), 1:232.

26. See Étienne Gilson, "*Regio dissimilitudinis* de Platon à saint Bernard de Clairvaux," *Medieval Studies* 9 (1947): 108–30. For more medieval instances of the phrase, see Pierre Courcelle, "Traditions néo-platoniciennes et traditions chrétiennes de la région de dissemblance," appended to his *Recherches sur les "Confessions" de saint Augustin*, 2nd ed. (Paris: E. de Boccard, 1968), further supplemented by "Treize textes nouveaux sur la 'région de dissemblance,'" *Revue d'études augustiniennes* 16 (1970): 271–81. For the importance of this "region" to Dante, and a fine analysis of its function, see John Freccero, *Dante: The Poetics of Conversion* (Cambridge: Harvard University Press, 1986), pp. 1–28.

itself (*Enneads* 1.8.13; LCL)—in Augustine the barring difference *motivates communion*. While reading "Platonic books," Augustine sees a light completely unlike the light of day, "not that but another, exceedingly different from all such lights," whose radiance blinds him into insight: "You raised me up so that I could see there was something to see and that I who saw was not yet [*ut... et nondum me esse viderem*]...and I found that I was far from you in a land of unlikeness" (*Conf.* 7.10.16.). The passage, which is tricky to translate, has invited a lot of commentary.[27] It seems to suggest that the farther he strays into the land of unlikeness, increasingly cognizant of unlikeness as an inherent difference between creator and creation (as well as a difference inhering within himself), the *closer* he gets to God. That is, the discernment of a certain ineradicable, "ontological dissimilitude"[28] *intensifies* his hunger to approach the divinity, even while he "cannot yet eat" (*Conf.* 7.17.23). Dissimilitude occasions the approach, which properly speaking is infinite because never complete outside of the Incarnation and Eucharist. Plotinus' land of unlikeness thus turns out, in the Augustinian account, to be a silent, empty waste where God's call to the starving resounds most loudly: "I am the food of full-grown men" (*Conf.* 7.10.16). It is the same remote place where the Prodigal Son winds up just before going home to feast (Lk 15:13), with the added condition that in Augustine one can never return; having been made originally *after* the image of God (*ad imaginem*), humanity stands at a permanent, constitutive distance from its divine essence (cf. *De trin.* 7.6.12 [CCSL 50:266; *WSA* I/5:231]). A believer has endlessly to *repeat* the ritual of communion because the body of Christ cannot satiate once and for all the hunger for union with God, which Christ alone incorporates. The conundrum of Augustine's faith is to know this but anyway to hope the differential might one day be erased. Gerhoch of Reichersberg—a twelfth-century Augustinian, major commentator on Antichrist, and, as we'll see, a critic of church drama—puts it this way: "Created after the image of God, still I lack similitude as long as I live in the land of unlikeness." *Ergo*, without any reason for hoping that he might come any closer to God—any reason other than his own present unlikeness—Gerhoch resolves to move closer: "*Therefore* I will

---

27. References and discussion in James J. O'Donnell, *Augustine: Confessions*, 3 vols. (Oxford: Clarendon Press, 1992), 2:443–44.

28. See A. Solignac, "Notes Complémentaires" to *Les Confessions*, trans. E. Tréhorel and G. Bouissou (Paris: Desclée de Brouwer, 1962), p. 691 n. 26. For the places in Augustine's works where dissimilitude operates less dialectically as the "distance" caused by sin, see Cornelius P. Mayer, *Die Zeichen in der geistigen Entwicklung und in der Theologie des jungen Augustinus*, 2 vols. (Würzburg: Augustinus-Verlag, 1974), 1:147 and 350–52.

arise and go to my father... I will arise and surpass everything that disjoins me from him and makes me dissimilar" (PL 193:1408B–D).[29]

In the hope of rising and overcoming *everything* that separates creature from creator, of becoming entirely like him who has no equal, there is more than an echo of the old satanic seductions. For as it happens Augustine's ontological dissimilarity, inherent in all images of the divine outside of Christ, also explains how creatures such as Adam and Eve, already made in the image of God, could ever find the subsequent offer of becoming "like God" at all tempting. Unless being in the image and likeness of God of necessity opens up some massive incongruity which an even closer similarity might seem to correct, Satan's offer to Eve would have no meaning. (Nor would the later promises of Christ.) The serpent's temptation to become a "goddis" and "pere to hym [God] in all-kyn thynge" (*York* 5.70–71) works only if she already intuits that her initial likeness is at best a *second-best* reflection. Though sufficient to have stood, humanity fell prey to the basic tendency of all representation; failing of its very nature to be that which it purports to be, such images as ourselves long to live up to our founding pretense: "Does your image in the mirror not look as though it wants to be you yourself, but is therefore false, because it isn't?" Augustine asks. "What about pictures or other such resemblances and everything of that sort made by artists? Do they not strive to be the thing in whose likeness [*similitudinem*] they have been made?" (*Sol.* 2.17 [CSEL 89:66–67; NPNF 7:553]). Whenever humans try to achieve union with the entity in whose image they have been made, it is a usurpation like Satan's and false, *unless* the union occurs materially and sacramentally through the body of Christ, in whom there is "such congruence, and prime equality, and prime likeness, differing in nothing, and in no way unequal, and in no part unlike, but answering identically to him whose image he is" (*De trin.* 6.10.11 [CCSL 50:241; WSA I/5:213]).[30] Christ acts as humanity's mediator insofar

---

29. Cf. Thomas à Kempis [?], *The Imitation of Christ: A New Reading of the 1441 Latin Autograph Manuscript*, trans. William C. Creasy (Macon, Ga.: Mercer University Press, 1989), p. 3: "Anyone who wishes to understand Christ's words and to savor them fully should strive to become like him in every way"—becoming in the process, as it were, an Antichrist. See also the Middle English version, *De Imitatione Christi*, ed. John K. Ingram, EETS e.s. 63 (London, 1893), p. 2: "For who euere wol understonde þe wordes of crist pleinly and sauerly, he must studie to conforme all his lif to his lyf."

30. Further citations from Augustine on this point are given by Gilson, "*Regio dissimilitudinis*" (n. 26), p. 126 n. 11. For a much more detailed discussion of how exactly Christ, as the image *and* equal of God, restores man to his own *unequal* similitude, see Gerhart B. Ladner, *The Idea of Reform: Its Impact on Christian Thought and Action in the Age of the Fathers* (Cambridge: Harvard University Press, 1959), chapter 5, esp. pp. 153–203: "Man will always have less than that perfect resemblance or equality to God which exists only in Christ" (196).

as he is the sole permissible instance of "that unspeakable embrace, as it were, between Father and image" (ibid.). The same embrace that for Augustine is "unspeakable" (*ineffabilis*) to York's Satan is so ghastly it prompts his own mimetic insurrection. "He who has seen me has seen the Father," Christ says (Jn 14:9). This, for Satan, is the founding blasphemy of what Augustine calls "the divine art" (ibid.).

Christ as the sole "image of the invisible God" (Col. 1:15) which manages to defy the otherwise constitutive differential between original and replica was an idea as indispensable to the development of orthodox Trinitarian thinking as to the later justification of icons.[31] Neither could be entirely justified without Satan as a scapegoat: the reconciliation-through-likeness that Christ supposedly allows for can seem conceptually permissible, that is (given its foundation in an iconoclastic, Hebraic monotheism), only to the extent that the sacrilege of God's self-replication in Christ has been displaced onto some other mimetic equivalent and is there condemned as a "mere" reflection. Or in other words the conceptual precondition for Christ's saving likeness to God is the damnation of Satan, in his place, for the same imitation.

The centrality of likeness to York clearly grows from an ancient theological dependence on and difficulty with concepts of representation, and yet the drama manages both to widen the scope of the dilemma and to offer a novel solution by means of its form. Drama could realize the central mystery of Christian mimesis even more fully than other kinds of critical exegesis because the plays themselves were explicitly mimetic: as with Christ and Satan, the plays also presented an image of God, then imitated Christ and Satan, too—plus their typological envoys. Folded into the series of sacred emulations that the drama itself had to emulate, the plays gave immediate flesh to the *miracula* of revelation. While partly accounting for the drama's success, this self-referential "immediacy" accounts also for its demise, since emulating the sacred left it invariably open to the condemnation Satan suffered for his desecrations, which the drama also emulated; that condemnation then helps explain in turn, however, English drama's persistence beyond the grave of the Tudor Reformation. Condemnation once again saves. So long as drama formally employed the mimetic hubris traditionally charged to Satan, it could continue to sit on the left hand of an inscrutable God, its sacred character still intact but changed now that divinity had officially decamped from the stage.

31. A point made with exhaustive thoroughness by Schönborn, *God's Human Face* (n. 8).

Miracula

The similarity of Antichrist's miracles and those of his minions to the miracles of Christ and his saints recapitulates at the end of history the mimetic crisis with which it began. Jeremiah predicts, for example, along with the coming messiah, the coming of false prophets who will ensnare all they can "in their lying and in their miracles" (Jer. 23:32; Douai-Rheims). Of course this and other Hebrew admonitions (e.g., Deut. 13:1–3) originally fomented suspicion against the first Christians, without which New Testament narrative would lack a fundamental plotline—the plot against Jesus. According to Jerome's influential gloss, however, it is not so much Jesus whose miracles look suspiciously false but subsequent liars who will increasingly appear ever more godlike. Immediately following his comment on Jeremiah that *every* lie imitates the truth or else it could not persuade the innocent (see above p. 52; the medieval Gloss disseminates this viewpoint pretty widely [PL 114:39B 43B]), Jerome then looks ahead to the dastardly miraclers still awaiting their turn: "The Lord warns of these sorts of leaders who are to come…who seduce his people with their lies and bedazzlement and miracles. For they promise great and incredible and prodigious things, so that they may mislead the wretched" (*In Jer.* 4.61.3 [CCSL 74:228]). Just as Christ had promised heaven to the wretched and dazzled them with healings, so too would every Antichrist exhibit the same stunning power. Rabanus Maurus repeats Jerome verbatim on the miraculous powers of these end-time opponents (*Exp. super Jer.* 9.23 [PL 111:987C]) while adding new warnings: "Nothing will be more dangerous than the final persecution that is predicted to come through Antichrist" (*Exp. super Jer.* 19.3 [PL 111:1219A]), he says, partly because of Antichrist's violence but equally on account of his winning marvels. "Antichrist will deceive through miracles," Maurus states again elsewhere (*Alleg. in univ. script.*, s.v. "Sternutatio" [PL 112:1053B]). Following the testimony of the gospels' apocalypse, nearly everyone came to agree that by way of these miracles Antichrist would mislead "if possible even the elect."[32]

Innocent III consequently worried that the miraculous deeds required of candidates for sainthood might be the work of a devil intent on fooling the church. He cited in support of this fear Satan's power to transform

---

32. Mk 13:22 and parallels. Aquinas collects the teachings of the Fathers on this verse in his *Catena aurea*. See *The Sunday Sermons of the Great Fathers*, trans. M. F. Toal, 4 vols. (San Francisco: Ignatius Press, 2000), 4:336–37. "If possible" is a strange qualification. The Genevan gloss tries to clarify by stating categorically that "Antichrist hathe not power ouer the elect" (Rev. 13:8; 1560, side note m). Even so, he reportedly might: that is why they have to spell it out.

himself back into an angel of light (2 Cor. 12:14) and warned of the many reprobates who "accomplish good works, that they may be seen by men. Indeed they positively gleam with miracles, whose lives are otherwise disgraceful in terms of merit" (*Ep.* 530 [PL 214:483D]). Since the mere working of miracles could never suffice as grounds for canonization, Innocent required more quotidian evidence that the miracle worker had led a virtuous life (though this, too, could be presumably faked). Innocent's skepticism, so far as it goes, in a way anticipates the empiricism of Bacon, who, centuries later under different conditions but for similar reasons, dismissed the "Miracles wrought by Martyrs, Hermits, or Monkes of the desert, and other holy men." Such frauds, Bacon wrote, had been tolerated for too long as harmless stories or "diuine poesies," when in fact they were "impostures of the Cleargie, illusions of spirits, and badges of Antichrist."[33] Miracles, for Bacon as for Innocent—though the unlikeliest of bedfellows—were just too easily *staged*. Not incidentally the two of them also shared an aversion to performance: "It is not good," warned Bacon, "to stay too long in the Theatre" (75–76), while Innocent condemned *ludi theatrales* outright (PL 215:1070C).[34]

Both would have to concede, however, that miracles, even and especially those of Antichrist, no matter how illusory, ultimately had some higher revelatory function. That concession necessarily follows from the common argument that Satan, though fallen, always accomplishes the will of God, just as Antichrist faithfully anticipates the second coming. Hence the weird aestheticism of demonic trickery: in falsely imitating the good and thereby bastardizing it, the devil unwittingly enacts, for real, the spectacle of God's ingenuity. Boccaccio, for one, is able by means of this logic to make a very strong case for the redemptive power of merely pretending, above all when the impostor's ruses are almost satanically cagey. Such cunning proves to the first narrator of *The Decameron* the surpassing righteousness of God, who might accomplish, among his other "marvelous works," Innocent III's worst fear—*real* deliverance via the intercession of a canonized *sinner*: "Our regard for Him . . . is all the greater when, the human eye being quite unable to penetrate the secrets of divine intelligence, common opinion deceives us and perhaps we appoint as our advocate in his Majestic presence one who has been cast by Him into

33. *The Advancement of Learning,* ed. Michael Kiernan (Oxford: Clarendon Press, 2000), p. 26.

34. We do not really know of what these *ludi* consisted. See E. K. Chambers, *The Mediaeval Stage,* 2 vols. (London: Oxford University Press, 1903), 1:279 and 2:99–103; Woolf, *English Mystery Plays* (n. 24), pp. 79–81; and Lawrence Clopper, whom I discuss below.

eternal exile....Yet He...answers those who pray to him exactly as if the advocate were blessed in His sight."[35] The narrator goes on to relate how this one deeply irreligious man, Ciappelletto—"perhaps the worst man ever born" (71) and almost, as it were, a kind of Antichrist—managed to dupe a pious friar with a false deathbed confession, and was thereafter venerated for a series of miracles by those whose faith his duplicity strengthened. "Successful in his deception, and apparently damned because of it," writes Edmund Reiss, Ciappelletto "becomes through his deception an agent for good."[36] Only the worst man alive could testify so well to God's total omnipotence and absolute charity, whereby deliverance may arrive via the most damnable media: fallen history, demonic impersonation, miraculous lies, and by implication aesthetic fabrications like Boccaccio's own.[37]

Lawrence Clopper has nevertheless singled out the word *miraculum* in support of the argument that heretofore classic statements of medieval antitheatricalism, such as *A Tretise of Miraclis Pleyinge*, do not target the dramatic staging of miracles in religious drama after all, but rather secular games, church ales, wrestling matches, mimed routines, and other crude antics performed on Sundays or religious holidays in defiance of proper decorum. *Miraculum*, he says, had been continuously used after Jerome as a synonym for "terrifying" and "stupefying" spectacles. This supposedly older sense of the word "differs radically from that of Medieval Latin *miraculum* (a supernatural event brought about by the intervention of God or his agents)."[38] since this particular denotation implies nothing supernatural and could therefore refer to entertainments that had little to do with the pious re-creation through drama of manifestly religious events. Clopper concludes that medieval legislation against *miracula* does not give any solid evidence for a generalized anxiety around dramatic representation in and of itself, much less for antipathy to the representation of specific miracles (which we know were usually welcome within the confines of the church, as *repraesentatio*), but reflects fear of something closer to *play*: "Miraclis and steraclis involved illusions—not dramatic illusion but tricks

35. Boccaccio, *The Decameron*, trans. G. H. McWilliam (Harmondsworth: Penguin, 1972), p. 69.

36. Reiss, "Ambiguous Signs" (n. 17), p. 122.

37. See Guido Almansi, *The Writer as Liar: Narrative Technique in "The Decameron"* (London: Routledge and Kegan Paul, 1975), pp. 24–55, a reading that in places supports my own.

38. Lawrence Clopper, *Drama, Play, and Game: English Festive Culture in the Medieval and Early Modern Periods* (Chicago: University of Chicago Press, 2001), p. 76.

intended to delight and amuse people and that, in many cases, led people to devalue the truth of God's miracles" (106).

I am no more sure how Clopper manages to distinguish dramatic illusion from tricks intended to delight and amuse people than I understand how Jerome's use of the term *miraculum* for a demonic prodigy can "differ radically" from the usual sense of the term—an act of God or his agents—when God oversees Satan's whole entourage of silly tricksters. Their monstrous spectacles unwittingly formed as much a part of the divine plan as God's less roundabout interventions, and in any case even a supposedly benevolent intrusion of the absolute godhead into the finite concerns of humanity has not always seemed heaven-sent. Ask the quaking shepherds. "Be not afraid" (Lk 2:10) announces Christ's birth because the awesome glory of God overhead at first appeared awful. "We give the name nature to the usual common course of nature," Augustine explains, "and whatever God does contrary to this, we call prodigies or miracles [*magnalia uel mirabilia*] "(*C. Faustum* 26.3 [CSEL 25:731; NPNF 4:321–22]). According to this a miracle or "marvel" makes God's complete sovereignty over the world's known regulations manifest *in* the known world. What could be more spooky and unsettling? More to the point, what report of it could escape the appearance of fiction? That is why Augustine says that "the multitude of those miracles [*miraculorum*] . . . are called monsters, signs, portents, or prodigies [*monstra, ostenta, portenta, prodigia*]" (*De civ. dei* 21.8.5; LCL vol. 7) without drawing any rigorous distinction between them.[39] Between God's good marvels and a demonic or merely ostensible suspension of the laws of possibility there were in the final analysis only subtle distinctions to make. Being "signs," miraculous events needed interpreting, and the interpretation aimed to disclose whatever inscrutable future the present monstrosity seemed to herald as a creepy "portent." So for example in the *Acts of Peter*, to which some detailed analysis will be given later, Simon Peter ruins Simon Magus by means of a *magnum et mirabile monstrum*,[40] then himself suffers crucifixion, but claims while on the cross that in reality this is yet another miraculous triumph.

The ambiguity and fraudulence, if not outright demonism, of any miraculous happening clearly caused the primitive church a lot of trouble, and the problem was by no means solved by the time of the Middle Ages,

39. Cf. *De civ. dei* 12.14 (LCL vol. 4) for another passing equation of *miracula* with *monstra*.

40. *Acta Apostolorum Apocrypha*, ed. R. A. Lipsius and M. Bonnet, vol. 1 (Leipzig: Hermannum Mendelssohn, 1891), p. 56; I quote the editors' emendation of the MS, which a scribe (anxious about *monstrum?*) has garbled.

or after.[41] Hadn't Jesus followed Jeremiah in warning of the "prodigies" to be enacted by the pseudo-Christs and false prophets that would follow him (Mt 24:24)? "O light and truth," exclaimed the incorrigible Celsus, "with his own voice he explicitly confesses, as even you [Christians] have recorded, that there will come among you others also who employ similar miracles, wicked men and sorcerers.... Is it not a miserable argument to infer from the same works that he is a god while they are sorcerers?" (*C. Celsum* 2.49). Eventually a large apologetical literature grew up in response to questions like this,[42] which scripture also voices as an essential part of its message. Such questions could therefore never be fully silenced or extirpated without eliminating the true revelation of God along with them. Jesus' miraculous works *had* to look monstrous, in the literal sense that he claimed by their means to de*monstr*ate his godliness.[43] What could be more satanic than that? What could be more fictive? Yet at the same time, by what other means could the real godhead appear? His intervention in history by definition had to seem preternatural, or worse, *contra naturam*. It is from there a short step to the contrafactuals of medieval drama.

Salvaging the Audience, or Christ as Antichrist Redux

That *prodigia* could mean both "portentous marvels" as well as "monstrous crimes"[44] speaks directly to the Christian dialectic of salvation, which

41. For the beginnings, see Anton Fridrichsen, *The Problem of Miracle in Primitive Christianity*, trans. Roy A. Harrisville and John S. Hanson (Minneapolis: Augsburg, 1972), and Harold Remus, *Pagan-Christian Conflict over Miracle in the Second Century* (Cambridge, Mass.: Philadelphia Patristic Foundation, 1983). For the Middles Ages, Benedicta Ward, *Miracles and the Medieval Mind: Theory, Record, Event, 1000–1215* (Philadelphia: University of Pennsylvania Press, 1987), and Michael Goodich, "Miracles and Disbelief in the Late Middle Ages," *Mediaevistik* 1 (1988): 23–38; for the Renaissance, Bernhard Bron, *Das Wunder: Das theologische Wunderverständnis im Horizont des neuzeitlichen Natur-und Geschichtsbegriffs* (Göttingen: Vandenhoeck & Ruprecht, 1975); for the Enlightenment, Colin Brown, *Miracles and the Critical Mind* (Grand Rapids: Eerdmans, 1984).

42. See elsewhere in *C. Celsum* 1.6, 28, 38, 46, 68; 2.14, 32, 44, 48–53, 55–56; 4.36. Also Justin, *1 Apol.* 30ff. (PG 6:373Bff.; ANF 1:172ff. and 233); *Dial.* 69 (PG 6:640A; ANF 1:233); Arnobius, *Adv. gentes* 1.43ff. (PL 5:773A; ANF 6:425ff.); Ignatius, *Ep. ad Eph.* 19 (ANF 1:57); Tertullian, *Adv. Marc.* 3.3 (CCSL 1¹:510–11; ANF 3:322–23); Lactantius, *Div. instit.* 4.15.1 and 5.3 (SC 377:130, 204:140–46; ANF 7:114–16, 138–39).

43. See Robert Mills, "Jesus as Monster," in *The Monstrous Middle Ages*, ed. Bettina Bildhauer and Robert Mills (Toronto: University of Toronto Press, 2003), pp. 28–54. On God's monstrosity more generally, see David Williams, *Deformed Discourse: The Function of the Monster in Mediaeval Thought and Literature* (Exeter: Exeter University Press, 1996), esp. pp. 93ff. (John Scotus Eriugena) and pp. 133ff. (Pseudo-Dionysius).

44. *A Latin Dictionary*, ed. Charlton T. Lewis and Charles Short (London: Oxford University Press, 1980), s.v. "prodigium."

succeeds, as by an internal negative, by means of the violent outrage directed *against* Christ's miracles. Without the scandal and apparent criminality
of Christ's divine acts, there could be no crucifixion, and without the crucifixion, no redemption. Christ dies on the cross, in other words, because
he appeared to the authorities as an Antichrist—a peasant who with all
the hubris in the world claimed to be the son of God then tried to prove
it with his magical skills. Or at least so it would appear in the medieval
miracle plays,[45] where Christ is tried—in full compliance with the divine
plan to save humanity from worldly injustice *by means of* that injustice—
as a blasphemous, satanic juggler capable of "meruaylles and mirakills"
(*York* 36.93) but for all that unable to save himself from the cross (so the
high priests suppose) because his "mirakills" are lies. "He sclaunderes þe
Godhed and greues vs all," charges Annas, "Wherfore he is wele worthy to
be dede" (*York* 29.302–3). From their perspective, Jesus displays a typically
demonic arrogance in claiming to *be* God, then backing up his "lowde
lesyngis" (*York* 29.271, 387) with utterly specious, seemingly "wondirfull
werkis" (*York* 29.34):

> Yha, thurgh his fantome and falshed and fendes-craft
> He has wroght many wondir where he walked full wyde,
> Wherfore, my lorde, it wer leeffull his liffe were hym rafte.
> (*York* 30.298–300)

The word "leeffull" has to sustain an almost mind-breaking paradox,
namely, that the exercise of worldly justice in the execution of an innocent man is *in fact* the fulfillment of God's own "lawfulness"; demanding
blood restitution from a bankrupt humanity, the divinity accepts it from
Jesus on humanity's behalf in a quasi-illicit act of vicarious substitution
that passes for mercy.

According to R. H. Nicholson's thorough and illuminating account of
the York Trials, this dynamic paradox finally explodes outward against the
injustice of the medieval legal process: "In sequence the plays demonstrate the judiciary at work, and it is a recognizably English judiciary," he
writes; "the action of these plays is such as to put earthly society on trial *in
fact*."[46] Would that the final words were true. The plays' judgments against
medieval society, such as they were, were without effect. They implicated

45. Cf. Martin Stevens, *Four Middle English Mystery Cycles: Textual, Contextual, and Critical
Interpretations* (Princeton: Princeton University Press, 1987), p. 207.
46. R. H. Nicholson, "The Trial of Christ the Sorcerer in the York Cycle," *Journal of Medieval and Renaissance Studies* 16.2 (1986): 125–69; here 162. I have inverted the order of the
sentences and added emphasis.

no one "in fact," only in faith. That is because the plays were make-believe (in every sense), and everyone knew it. Their worldly impotence, in contrast to the real powers that regulated the plays, was the whole source of their aesthetic and spiritual enticement since here you could look on the brutal inadequacy of the medieval judiciary (thinly veiled)—or for that matter on the brutality of medieval society as a whole—and for once take pleasure in its shortcomings. Of course it was also possible to enjoy the brutality of justice gone awry in real time, quite independent of its staged representation, so long as you stood at a distance whenever the law's savagery seized on a displeasing neighbor. But only in the drama could you enjoy the injustice *and* maintain your Christian innocence, because here there *was no* injustice, simply its insubstantial representation. That is the genuine, strictly formal miracle of any so-called miracle play: you are, in the experience of it, objectively innocent of the hideous happenings that it gloriously fails, as a mere depiction, to realize in fact. This aesthetic guarantee of a certain aloofness from whatever "happens" on stage (because the worst of it is not actually happening) formally resolves and, in the resolution, promulgates at a more refined level the doctrinal, miraculous "crux" of the plays: namely, that the blood of Christ guarantees the viewers' innocence regardless of the pleasure they may have normally taken in real atrocity. Here for once the enjoyment of cruelty could not redound to anyone's moral discredit because there was no cruelty, only its festive appearance. Drama, like the Mass but unlike, say, the crusades, could have all the gruesome thrill of bloodshed, only without any shedding of blood.

I want to stress this because even the most brilliant, consequential critics of medieval drama such as V. A. Kolve and Sarah Beckwith, or a theorist of Christianity as insightful as René Girard, have sometimes wanted to overlook the hilarity of crucifixion in a neo-Aristotelian attempt to measure the plays by "the horror and pity with which we respond to the action."[47] It could almost go without saying that this "we" whose response supposedly corroborates a critic's own sentiment(ality) and which would rescue

---

47. V. A. Kolve, *The Play Called Corpus Christi* (Stanford: Stanford University Press, 1966), p. 179; cf. René Girard, *I See Satan* (n. 23), p. 37: "When the spectators are satiated with that violence that Aristotle calls 'cathartic'—*whether real or imaginary it matters little*—they all return peaceably to their homes to sleep the sleep of the just." I have underscored the phrase that illustrates one of Girard's regular oversights. Whether violence is real or imaginary makes all the difference in the world, above all to the victims; when the violence is imaginary, there *aren't* any victims, not really, and the sleep of the spectators is in that case far closer to real innocence.

it from subjectivism is as fictive as the events on stage. We all know this.[48] People love plays, they hate plays, during the same play they make conflicting judgments, they daydream and sleep. We know they're there, the play addresses them; we, in some sense, are they. But we are not the play, and the play's the thing that matters, precisely because it implies, above and beyond our myriad, incoherent responses, some other, more ideal audience, even as this ideal collectivity has no existence outside of its objective textual implication and is invariably betrayed by the built-in limitations of any *actual* audience.[49]

To overlook this point, to locate the playtext's audience outside the text in some actual collection of putatively like-thinking people unwilling to laugh at Christ's suffering, is to shortchange the drama, which evidently strove on behalf of a universal church structured by the *Word* and its "comic" capacity for sustained torment. The easiest way to substitute an actual audience for the social plenipotentiary of the textual object that hoped to stand in for this Word is to speak too quickly of genuine affect rather than the literary forms that inspire its affectation. Sarah Beckwith grasps with unprecedented acuity how the plays would conjure a "sacramental community" out of the real community's internal fractures and constitutive antagonism, yet still she succumbs to Kolve's audience-based reading of the passion. She sees it as "agonizingly extended," "brutal," an "excruciating, almost endless interval" that asks the audience to "*bear a terrible witness* as we ourselves are addressed as participants at the scene of crucifixion."[50] Hardly. First of all, the crucifixion is the highest

48. Or at least Sarah Beckwith knows it: see her *Signifying God: Social Relation and Symbolic Act in the York Corpus Christi Plays* (Chicago: University of Chicago Press, 2001), p. xv n. 2. I am going to quibble with her reading of the crucifixion in a second, but this book has had a major influence on my reading of York.

49. Cf. Adorno's remarks on the primacy of text over performance in *AT* 153–54, 190, 415; trans. 100, 125, 279, respectively. Also, on different grounds, Harry Berger Jr., "Text against Performance in Shakespeare: The Example of *Macbeth*," *Genre* 15.2–3 (1982): 49–79, and "Text against Performance: The Gloucester Family Romance," in *Shakespeare's "Rough Magic": Renaissance Essays in Honor of C. L. Barber*, ed. Peter Erickson and Coppélia Kahn (Newark: University of Delaware Press, 1985), pp. 210–29. It is significant that one of Berger's best critics can save audience-based reading only by "re-assembl[ing] critically... theatrical experiences that are neither specifically [his] own, nor (for the most part) directly attributable to historically specific individuals or audiences." From Thomas Cartelli, *Marlowe, Shakespeare, and the Economy of Theatrical Experience* (Philadelphia: University of Pennsylvania Press, 1991), p. xiii. "One means of compensating for the silence of the absent playgoer," Cartelli later acknowledges, "is to indicate how the kinds of responses we delegate to guesswork may have been prompted by both explicit and implicit directives *in the playtexts* that survive them" (39; my emphasis).

50. Beckwith, *Signifying God* (n. 48), p. 70. She echoes Kolve pretty closely again on p. 138.

cause for *joy*, and no one enjoyed it more than Christ, in whom we—whoever we are—are supposed to find our real collectivity: "According to the blessed Hilary," writes Luther, "it filled [Christ] with the greatest joy to suffer the greatest pain. For thus it is that 'God is wonderful in his saints' [Ps 68:35], so that he causes them, at the very time they are suffering the greatest pains, also to experience the greatest joys."[51] Second, the agony of Christ's "death" *on stage* and the "terror" or "pity" it inspires are as far from real agony, terror, and pity as an actual execution is from a farcical reenactment. Christ's pathetic appeal to the audience does not collapse the aesthetic distance between his spectators and the events on stage but *presupposes* it; his words are more like an apostrophe to an absence than a direct address, in that they posit a "redeemed" audience as separate from the real audience as the actor is from Christ himself or as the church visible is from the true elect. These separations are the source of his appeal's enormous pathos and give the one justification for your taking pleasure in it. Christ's death here confers on the invisible, select few a blithe immunity to sin in return for their enjoyment so long as they believe with all their faith that Christ will rise again. And rise again he will, have no fear—as soon as he reaches the next station.

When audiences really did act as "participants" in the crucifixion, it was not with the reluctant, agonized guilt described by Beckwith and others, but with the enthusiastic bloodlust dramatized by the soldiers, and the scene moved quickly from a staged representation of persecution to its licensed enactment on the sad sack unlucky enough to find himself in the "role" of Christ; here the playacting all too quickly turned real.[52] These genuinely "participatory" and genuinely violent games are far less interesting than the cycle plays for the simple reason that they never formally achieve any momentary or apparent release from the guilt-nexus of history; such a release, most of all when merely apparent, is in the final analysis probably the lone best promise of Christianity, though it has been largely unrealized outside the frail aesthetic practices that themselves constitute the

51. *Lectures on Romans* 9.2 (WA 56:389; *LW* 25:379), citing Hilary, *De trin.* 10.45 (PL 10:379A; trans. Stephen McKenna, FC 25:432–33).

52. Siegfried Wenzel, "*Somer Game* and Sermon References to a Corpus Christi Play," *Modern Philology* 86.3 (1989): 274–83. My point here and in following sections is, I think, somewhat at odds with Jody Enders, *Death by Drama and Other Medieval Urban Legends* (Chicago: University of Chicago Press, 2002); she seems to take any breakdown (however imaginary or accidental) between reality and performance as broadly constitutive of medieval theater. I want to emphasize, by contrast, what I see as the more essential and normative divergence between them, without which there could be no occasion for the (potential) *exceptions* of such interest to Enders.

promise—precisely by not realizing it. Too many historicist critics of medieval drama too often want people to respond to plays like the Crucifixion *as though they were not play*. To be sure, the antitheatricalism implied by this approach is also implied by the plays themselves, which on some deep level claim to be more than play, and more than illusion. But they fulfill that claim only as an illusion.

Kolve understood this even if he could not abide by his understanding when it came to the passion: "The particular order that this game sought to create was not only aesthetic, but historically true: it sought to pattern human experience, to give to the history of men an order that would reveal its meaning. Play and game thus creates a world within the real world, and the dramatist relates the two worlds meaningfully to each other. But the two need never be mistaken or confused."[53] To this he might have added that the order-in-history created by the plays—an order that seemed to transcend mere aesthetics—was itself the highest effect of that aesthetic. Kolve then gives an extended account of the role that "religious laughter" plays in medieval drama, but he cannot bring himself to acknowledge the comedy of the crucifixion, even while he himself explains that from the Christian point of view, "God is in control, the evil and demonic behave stupidly because that is their nature, and the proper reaction to this example of the rightness of things is laughter" (140). In the passion plays, the same sort of laughter—both at and *with* the torturers—does not preclude pity or terror, the so-called tragic emotions, but rather acknowledges the distance between those feelings as inspired by play and what it means to experience them in earnest, a difference so radical as almost to prohibit our calling them by the same names. The terror inspired by medieval theater is wholly artificial, far closer to the campy fun of a horror flick than to real trauma.

This artificiality may give new meaning to the classic Marlovian allegation that religion exists to keep men in awe (*CM* 221, 227). People have assumed he meant it as criticism, but for a playwright who put enormous stock in awesome spectacles, there may well be an element of professional admiration. Fear of the Lord is the beginning of wisdom,[54] rather than paralysis, because religious terror is no less refined than what happened in Marlowe's theater: as Kant puts it in his aesthetics, "the righteous man

---

53. Kolve, *Play Called Corpus Christi* (n. 47), p. 20.
54. A constant biblical refrain. See, for a few examples, Ps 19:9, 34:11, 111:10; Prov. 1:7, 9:10, 15:33, 31:30; Job 28:28. Note that according to prophecy Christ will "*delight* in the fear of the Lord" (Isa. 11:3).

fears God *without being afraid of him*"[55] in a manner akin to the way he responds to any sublime thing. With medieval *miracula*, as we'll see also in Marlowe, it was a clearly a small step from the terror of the sublime to a ludicrous carnival. "The *tortores* play with Christ," writes Kolve, "but we must not forget that Christ is playing too.... They do not know what we know as audience, that they are playing essential roles in a divine game" (200–201). That is why their heartless buffoonery makes for such great comedy, in the full Dantean sense of the word. "The persistence of their sacrilegious cruelty," says Leo the Great, "*helped* the Savior's work" (*Serm.* 60.3 [PL 54:344C; FC 93:262]; my emphasis). If Christ hadn't suffered "interminably," all humanity would be damned for eternity. His loss is the audience's gain, and in any case he doesn't lose a thing. Why shouldn't they laugh themselves limp?

The answer—this usually goes unsaid—is that active assent to this aesthetico-theological moment embraces a God who playfully sanctifies torture and seems for that reason at least as savage as the human agents who unknowingly carry out his acts or who directly profit from them in an un-earned windfall of eternal reward. This is, in other words, the deity as devil or Antigod: "How cruel and wicked it seems," writes Peter Abelard, repeat-ing an ancient sentiment, "that anyone should demand the blood of an in-nocent person as the price for anything, or that it should in any way please him that an innocent man should be slain—still less that God should con-sider the death of his Son so agreeable that by it he should be reconciled to the whole world!"[56] Abelard's horror at the normative theology of atone-ment, which shaped every medieval cycle, compelled him to work up an alternative to Anselm's satisfaction theory. In the miracle plays, however, the norm for once could satisfy *by means of* its terrifying, diabolical appear-ance, because here it was openly restricted to appearance. The terrors of the Christian God became on stage as nowhere else simply terrific.

---

55. "So fürchtet der Tugendhafte Gott, ohne sich vor ihm zu fürchten." Immanuel Kant, *Kritik der Urteilskraft* §28, ed. Wilhelm Weischedel (Frankfurt am Main: Suhrkamp Taschen-buch, 1957), p. 184; trans. Werner S. Pluhar (Indianapolis: Hackett, 1987), p. 120.

56. Peter Abelard, "Exposition of the Epistle to the Romans," in *A Scholastic Miscel-lany: Anselm to Ockham*, trans. and ed. Eugene Fairweather (New York: Macmillan, 1970), pp. 282–83. Cf. the objection in *C. Celsum* 8.41 (i.e., "What father is so ruthless?"), a concern shared by Gregory of Nazianzus, *Or.* 45.22 (PG 36:653A–B; NPNF II, 7:431). Erasmus raises a related objection to the teachings of Wyclif and Luther: "Who will be able to bring him-self to love God with all his heart when he created hell seething with eternal torments in order to punish his own misdeeds in his victims as though he took delight in human torments?" From *Luther and Erasmus: Free Will and Salvation*, trans. E. Gordon Rupp et al. (Philadelphia: Westminster Press, 1969), p. 41.

Antichrist and Antitheatricalism

Whatever *miracula* meant in the Middle Ages—whether acts of God, his angels, or the devil, a dramatic reenactment of these events, or some other spectacle wild enough to seem out of this world—we may be assured of one thing. God himself never appeared in any of them. Atheists, Augustine, and Aquinas are united on this point. "A miracle," writes Aquinas, "is so called if it is altogether wondrous, i.e. having its cause *hidden absolutely and from everyone.*"[57] Needless to say, for him, the hidden cause is God. The virtue of a miracle is to let you *see* that he is hidden. His hiddenness then expresses how inexpressible his essence actually is;[58] it makes the darkness visible. God's specific intention with miracles, according to a formulation by Augustine, is in other words "to signify and show himself *without his own substance, whereby he is, itself appearing,* which is completely unchangeable and more inwardly and secretly sublime than all the spirits that he has created" (*De trin.* 3.4.10 [CCSL 50:137; *WSA* I/5:133]; my emphasis). Some of those inferior spirits, both angels and demons, act instead as his vicarious agents in the execution of miracles and thus manage to reveal God without exposing his substance to the human gaze.[59] That is the borrowed source of all their brilliance.

Now, if you want to visit a place where you are likely to see God "exhibited" in this mediated fashion as spectacularly as possible, a place where, in *miracula,* God's own agents and under his license "truly reveal themselves to human eyes" (*De civ. dei* 2.25, LCL vol. 1), Augustine recommends the theater as much as the church, though his recommendation of the theater, to be sure, usually comes in reverse. It is the power of his loathing that bespeaks the old urge to go. At one point he contradicts those who argue that the devil cannot conceivably accomplish true miracles by pointing out that humans themselves do it all the time *on stage:* "If earthly bodies, having been modified by several arts and exercises, exhibit such miracles in theatrical spectacles [*spectaculis theatricis tanta miracula*] that those people who did not witness them would

---

57. *Summa th.* I, Q. 105, art. 7, resp. Text and trans. in *Summa Theologiae: Latin Text and English Translation, Introductions, Notes, Appendices and Glossaries,* 61 vols. ([Cambridge?]: Blackfriars; New York: McGraw-Hill, 1964–81), 14:84–85; my emphasis.

58. Cf. *Summa contra gentiles* 3.102.2. Original in *La Somma contro i Gentile,* ed. P. Tito Sante Centi (Bologna: Edizioni Studio Domenicano, 2001), 2:390; trans. Vernon Bourke, (London: University of Notre Dame Press, 1975), 3²:83. Also Hilary, *De trin.* 3.6 (CCSL 62:77; trans. McKenna, FC 25:69).

59. For commentary and further citations from Augustine, see Eugene TeSelle, *Augustine, the Theologian* (New York: Herder and Herder, 1970), pp. 219–23.

hardly believe the report, why would it be difficult for the devil and his angels with their airy bodies... to do what astonishes mere flesh?" (*De trin.* 4.11.14 [CCSL 50:179; *WSA* I/5:162]). Mortals are right to marvel. In these demonic works they witness as much of God's naked power on earth as they are going to, so long as history lasts. Augustine does not thereby erase the distinction between the deceptions of demonic stage tricks and the wonder of angelic miracles, any more than he fails to acknowledge the superiority of God's name when written in gold as opposed to black ink; gold far surpasses black, but nonetheless regardless of color the characters still signify *the same thing*, without actually presenting it (*De trin.* 3.9.20 [ibid., 148; 139]). The written name of God, after all, is not God. In the case of nefarious spirits, who take that name on themselves through their God-given power to delight, something like fake gilt, rather than ink, rivals the true gold. Their theatrical evil, says Augustine, "would not accomplish the business of deception, were they not occasionally to transform themselves into angels of light, as we know from scripture" (*De civ. dei* 2.26; LCL vol. 1).

"For Augustine," writes Jonas Barish, "the theater has played the role of a false temple, or anti-temple, standing in mocking antithesis to the true temple, masquerading indeed *as* the true temple, with its own antipriests and antirituals, inhabited by demons, devoted to the Devil, and dedicated to the overthrow of humanity."[60] This dedication, however bad, redounds to the greater glory of God by inadvertently strengthening a number of humans it had meant to damn—among them Augustine himself. Devoted early on to *theatrica spectacula* (*Conf.* 3.2), he turned when converted toward the opposed, though similar, spectacle of God. His devotion to the theater in the *Confessions* clearly prefigures, in typological fashion, his coming devotion to the church. His love for the church *fulfills* his enjoyment of the theater. And why shouldn't the one act as an opposed representative of the other? So long as the City of God remains historical and time-bound, it is entangled and mixed (*perplexae et permixtae*) with the Devil's City. There will always be Christians who murmur against God, one day crowding the theaters, other days the church, making no fast distinction. Augustine may condemn the theater, but he realizes he has no business condemning the people in it. On the final day, he admits, some who relish its demonic *miracula* will be saved, while some who witness the Eucharist in the church will be damned (*De civ. dei* 1.35; LCL

60. Jonas Barish, *The Antitheatrical Prejudice* (Berkeley: University of California Press, 1981), pp. 63–64.

vol. 1). The pagan players who mimicked Christian ritual,[61] that is, might perhaps turn out to have performed those rites *more effectively* than the church. There's just no telling.

Augustine's doctrine of the mixed church posed serious challenges to Gerhoch of Reichersberg, a twelfth-century Augustinian who authored a tome on Antichrist. "For in the present church, corporal cohabitation of evil people with the good does not permit one to know who is truly in the unity of the church" (*Comm. in Ps.* 1.14.1 [PL 193:821C]), he wrote, or rather quoted word for word from Gilbert of Poitiers.[62] Still Gerhoch longed to know—to know and to drive Antichrist from the pews through unstinting critique of his secret cohort. The cohort included Gilbert of Poitiers, whom Gerhoch attacked with the ferocity of an inquisitor—despite, or perhaps because of, his heavy reliance on Gilbert's Psalm commentary in his own scholarship. It is almost as if Gerhoch contained the confused multitude of the mixed church within himself, in the form of his former influences, and polemic against them was his central means of self-overcoming. To the extent that he had been taken in by secular philosophers as a young man, for example, "so he repudiated them all the more with the zealotry of a convert";[63] he spurned the dialectic in which he had been trained and used dialectics to do it. Although his calls for reform resembled the same radical demands made by Arnold of Brescia, he attacked Arnold as the epitome of unreason. It is probably no surprise that Gerhoch's offensives against him, as Horst Rauh writes, nonetheless "resonate with secret sympathy" (460).

His attack on church drama harbors the same dirty secret. Like his patron saint Augustine, Gerhoch too had fallen victim to the satanic ruse of theatrical spectacle when young; as master of the scholars and doctors at the Augsburg cathedral (ca. 1117 to ca. 1120), he oversaw the staging of liturgical plays, to which he was then regrettably devoted (*Comm. in Ps.*

61. William Beare, *The Roman Stage: A Short History of Latin Drama in the Time of the Republic* (London: Methuen, 1950), p. 232. Allardyce Nicoll, *Masks, Mimes and Miracles: Studies in the Popular Theatre* (New York: Cooper Square, 1963), pp. 120–23.

62. For Gerhoch's full borrowings from Gilbert, see Damien van den Eynde, *L'Œuvre littéraire de Géroch de Reichersberg* (Rome: Apud Pontificium Athenaeum Antonianum, 1957), pp. 358–96; here 363. A very similar passage appears also in Peter Lombard's *Comm. in Ps. Davidicos*, Ps 14 (PL 191:167B–C). For Gerhoch on Augustine's doctrine of the two cities, see Erich Meuthen, *Kirche und Heilsgeschichte bei Gerhoh von Reichersberg* (Leiden: Brill, 1959), pp. 26–29. And cf. Peter Classen, *Gerhoch von Reichersberg: Eine Biographie* (Wiesbaden: Franz Steiner, 1960), pp. 141ff.

63. Horst Dieter Rauh, *Das Bild des Antichrist im Mittelalter: Von Tyconius zum deutschen Symbolismus*, 2nd ed. (Münster: Aschendorff, 1979), p. 421.

133.3 [PL 194:890–91]).[64] Again, this misplaced devotion resembles as though by negative prefiguration a mature dedication to church ritual. Gerhoch himself acknowledges that resemblance in frequently likening the church and all its workings to one gigantic theater. Of the Lord's Eucharist he apostrophizes, "I see in this, your table, a sublime miracle, a sublime spectacle" (*Comm. in Ps.* 22.5 [PL 193:1051]). And yet nevertheless, in his study of Antichrist, he condemns those priests who "transform the churches themselves, that is, the houses of preaching, into theaters, and fill them with the farcical spectacle of plays" (*De investigatione Antichristi* 1.5).[65] Probably in every instance where Gerhoch makes use of a damnable theatrical vocabulary in order to praise the church, he means to *oppose* its ritual to mere drama, and the opposition is the same as Antichrist's; it occurs in the likeness. The same church that inspires him inspires his contempt.

Composed again after the first version was lost, Gerhoch's *De investigatione Antichristi* crowns the long career of an old polemical warrior.[66] Only his magnum opus, an expansive commentary on the sixty-fourth Psalm, rivals the *Investigatione* for the scope of its ambition. The two share a great deal: their polemical topicality, their typological rigor, and most important, the antichristian aesthetic implicit in their eschatology. Gerhoch gives a good indication of that aesthetic when, in the course of his Psalm commentary, he digresses into an exegesis of some enigmatic verses from Revelation where an angel pours his bowl over the Euphrates, drying its waters, and three foul demons "making signs" emerge separately from the mouth of the dragon, the beast, and the false prophet (Rev. 16:12–14). "Signs" as usual carries a force similar to "miracles" or "wonders," with which biblical writers frequently pair it. In fact every post-Wycliffite English Bible

---

64. Karl F. Morrison, "The Church as Play: Gerhoch of Reichersberg's Call for Reform," in *Popes, Teachers, and Canon Law in the Middle Ages*, ed. James Ross Sweeney and Stanley Chodorow (Ithaca: Cornell University Press, 1989), pp. 114–44: "Like Augustine, Gerhoch retained, even after conversion, patterns of thought and expression borrowed from the theater" (134). See also Morrison, *"I am You": The Hermeneutics of Empathy in Western Literature, Theology, and Art* (Princeton: Princeton University Press, 1988), pp. 217–18: "To be sure, Gerhoch occasionally expressed his affinity to the theater in denials.... These denials, however, did nothing to conceal the degree to which theatrical play marked Gerhoch's thought and work."

65. Text in *Monumenta Germaniae Historica, Libelli de lite imperatorum et pontificum saeculis XI. et XII. conscripti*, 3 vols. (Hannover: Impensis Bibliopolii Hahniani, 1891–97), 3:315–16, and *DMC* 2:524–25.

66. For a brief synopsis of the events surrounding the composition of *De investigatione* (and each of Gerhoch's works), see van den Eynde, *L'Œuvre littéraire de Géroch* (n. 62), pp. 121–22 and 131–39. For an exhaustive look, Classen, *Gerhoch von Reichersberg* (n. 62).

through to the Authorized Version (excepting Douai-Rheims) translates the Greek word for "signs" (*semeia*) in this verse *as* "miracles." The two terms had become interchangeable on the (Augustinian) grounds that, since God does not immediately appear in miracles anyway, they have to be *interpreted*, same as every other scriptural hieroglyph.[67]

And so Gerhoch, a skilled hand at typological decipherment, sets to work. For one thing, he finds in the wonders of Revelation an opportunity to denounce all competing interpreters of scripture, especially the allegorists like himself, who "stand out among the false prophets, for prophesying according to their own hearts" (*Comm. in Ps.* 64 §141).[68] He attacks poetry, philosophy, and magic for taking inspiration from "the muse," that is, Satan. Pagan writers working in divers genres—"the eloquent Greeks and the well-spoken Latin grammarians, rhetoricians, dialecticians, not to mention the tragic, comic and satirical poets"—share with bad interpreters of scripture the same liability, which, it turns out, is the liability of Antichrist. They all speak "many lying fictions intermixed with certain expressions of the truth" (*Comm. in Ps.* 64 §139 [op. cit., 480]). Like the river Euphrates, which once flowed purely from paradise but now runs polluted across the land, so too have their voices poured into the "sea of this world" in such a way as to promote "miraculous exaltations, although the Lord has not yet appeared in the marvelous depths, nor would the testimony of him be credible to a demented and bewitched world of so many liars, whom as many waters of Babylon have intoxicated" (ibid.).

According to Gerhoch, then, antiquity's whole literary output and much current writing (besides his own) contain at best lying fictions modeled on the truth so as to *seem* genuine. The Lord has not appeared in the writings of Gerhoch's adversaries, but even if he had appeared there, as he presumably does in scripture, his "testimony" would be no more "credible" than it is to Christ's opponents in the Bible. Once Christ returns in glory, however, all the pagan and heretical rhetoricians who have denied him on account of his apparent fraudulence will have their literary efforts exposed by the truth of scripture's scandals, the truth of Christ's foolishness. In fact, just this exposure has been already foretold by the rhetoricians' *own* fictions. For Gerhoch as for all who have imbibed the lesson of Antichrist, even non-Christian literary efforts *already anticipate* the truth that will repudiate them, since it is precisely the truth of scripture which they themselves hold

67. Cf. Ward, *Miracles and the Medieval Mind* (n. 41), pp. 8 and 24–25.
68. The best text for this portion of the Latin is in *Monumenta Germaniae Historica* (n. 65), 3:481.

captive "in lies, inspired by evil spirits, so that in their lies a great likeness to truth and an image of the good might be found" (*Comm. in Ps.* 64 §142 [PL 194:97B]). Since the truth of Christ appears fictive from humanity's only possible vantage point, an image and likeness of its coming exists on earth *already* in every human fiction, above all in the dazzling and "inspirational" effects of pagan writers.

Too bad for the priests who dare to stage the coming of Antichrist. Theatrical lies, of necessity imitating the truth, in fact do achieve through their imitation some mediated affinity to the divine, yet the affinity in this case is horrifying. What you see when you look on stage is, to be sure, God at work; but it is God in the process of selecting for damnation his anti-elect. Recently, Gerhoch reports, one of the actors playing a corpse revived by Antichrist wound up dead for real within a week. When performing their play, Gerhoch argues, "they do not, as they think, stage an imaginary simulacrum but in truth...fulfill, for their own part, the mystery of iniquity itself. Why wouldn't the devil appropriate for himself, in earnest, things presented in a play [*ludicrum*] of vanity, just as even Lord Jesus converted into a serious matter the mockery [*ludibria*] he suffered in his passion before Pilate and the Jews?" (*De investigatione Antichristi* 1.5 [op. cit.; see n. 65]). As was the historical farce of Christ's passion, so now is the emptiness of playing Antichrist: according to this, the drama of Antichrist, in its inanity, is *all too true*—a device of the Lord, working by way of his opposite, to visit affliction on his opponents. In the play, "kingly matters, the majestic sublimity of the divinity, of priests and prophets, are ridiculed, but he himself, who is the truth, has used their ridicule in earnestness of truth" (ibid.).

If Gerhoch lauds the crucified God and condemns his mocking adversaries, this does not signal a less "devotional" attitude toward the mockers; they equally express, in ways they do not expect, the worst aspects of God's infinite mystery: namely, how in the final days he will send to some "strong delusion, that they should believe a lie: that they all might be damned who believed not the truth, but had pleasure in unrighteousness" (2 Thess. 11–12). As to the exact timing of those final days, Gerhoch pointedly refuses to say; then again, he did not have to, since the signs were everywhere: the Investiture controversy, the calamitous defeat of the second crusade, the corrupt opulence of the church, the existence, in Gerhoch's lifetime, of no fewer than eleven antipopes. (Evidently it had become a regular feature of papal legitimacy to designate some *other* pope as the *illegitimate* head of the church.) Gerhoch took from these troubles the same assurance he took from the abomination of dramatic spectacle; ultimately God himself had his hand on the ropes. History was his theater, where he disclosed his eternal truth in temporal deviations from that truth. Even the worst deviations could therefore be read as clandestine purveyors of hope.[69] Gerhoch's hope was no doubt at its greatest wherever he liked to affect the greatest shock.

One should keep Augustine and Gerhoch in mind when considering other, equally dialectical outbreaks of antitheatrical fervor.[70] After all, a theology predicated on a three-personed God could hardly produce a straightforward denunciation of playacting when its God never appeared, except as impersonated.[71] Truth be told, subsequent *defenses* of iconography make relatively weak claims for the power of images in comparison to the fears of iconoclasts.[72] According to *A Tretise of Miraclis Pleyinge*, for example, medieval defenders of theater argued that their sacred imagery might educate an audience, excite its devotion, convert the doubtful, and so on. At worst, drama provided beleaguered humans with a modicum of recreation. For the antitheatrical writer of the *Tretise*, by contrast, this kind of recreation had the potential to become re-*creation*, the usurpation of amazing activities reserved for God: "Therfore in siche miraclis pleyinge the devel is most plesid, as the dyvel is best payid to disceive men in the

---

69. Rauh, *Bild des Antichrist* (n. 63), p. 465: "Gerhoch inquires into the role of evil in sacred history and in the world and like Rupert of Deutz grasps it dialectically: the evil of the *corpus diaboli* calls out for the Redemption" (cf. 469). This ability to derive comfort and hope not just in defiance of but directly *from* calamity is generally characteristic of an eschatological outlook. Cf. Morton Bloomfield, "Piers Plowman as a Fourteenth-Century Apocalypse," in *Interpretations of Piers Plowman*, ed. Edward Vasta (Notre Dame: University of Notre Dame Press, 1968), pp. 339–554: "The very presence of Antichrist is, to thinkers like Langland, actually evidence for the imminence of renewal and fundamentally a hopeful sign" (345–46). Cf. Clark, *Thinking with Demons* (n. 2), p. 348: "Whether as a prelude to Doomsday or to a New Jerusalem within history, they [disastrous contemporary events] were the climax of the universal dualisms of good and evil, true and false, Christ and Antichrist, and, for that very reason, held the promise of imminent deliverance by divine agency." Jeffrey Helterman, *Symbolic Action in the Plays of the Wakefield Master* (Athens: University of Georgia Press, 1981), p. 127: "The rage of Antichrist contains hidden consolation for man, since its growth marks its imminent cessation."

70. Cf. Ritchie Kendall, *The Drama of Dissent: The Radical Poetics of Nonconformity, 1380–1590* (Chapel Hill: University of North Carolina Press, 1986), esp. pp. 8 and 118 on the iconoclast's attraction to theater.

71. Tertullian's adoption of the word for theater mask (*persona*) to describe the divisions internal to an otherwise unitary godhead probably preserves an aspect of the drama he formerly loved but claimed to repudiate. For a brilliant discussion of this much-debated term, see Carl Andresen, "Zur Entstehung und Geschichte des trinitarischen Personbegriffes," *Zeitschrift für die Neutestamentliche Wissenschaft und die Kunde der älteren Kirche* 52 (1961): 1–39. Also Alois Grillmeier, *Jesus der Christus im Glauben der Kirche: Von der Apostolischen Zeit bis zum Konzil von Chalcedon (451)*, 3rd ed. (Freiburg: Herder, 1990), 1:251. I intend to write more on this topic elsewhere soon.

72. See Cartelli, *Marlowe, Shakespeare* (n. 49), p. 13, and those he cites.

licnesse of that thing in whiche by God men weren convertid biforhond and in whiche the devel was tenyd [grieved] byfornhond."[73] That is, God *himself* used to convert people through the playing of miracles (or some activity a lot like it), much to Satan's grievance. But nowadays Satan is pleased to win people back to hell under the "licnesse" of God's own methods. Since Christ "doth now no miraclis for us," say the drama enthusiasts, "pleye we therefore his olde." And yet of course the dramatists add many lies "so colowrably that the puple gife as myche credense to hem as to the trwthe" (111). Theater appears so awful, in other words, *because* it appears so godly, even while this appearance in fact "reversith" (passim) the godliness it imitates. That is why staged miracles are "ginnys [snares] of the devel to cacchen men to byleve of Antichrist." Priests are supposed to be "the ginne of God to cacchen men and to holden men in the bileve of Crist" (99), but in playing miracles outside the Mass, they threaten to transform the liturgy into its exact opposite or, more frighteningly, to expose its true essence as inherently a form of antichristian theater.[74]

The Chester Antichrist

"Antichrist," writes David Mills, "represents the [Chester] cycle itself, which replicates God's signs ostensibly for the edification of the audience, but also exploits their 'marvellous' quality, their effectiveness as dramatic material, for its own artistic ends, diverting us from their transcendental truth."[75] I want to qualify this important remark with the observation that throughout the history of the church, similar diversions have largely *constituted* its "transcendental truth"; more strongly, that the figure of Antichrist encouraged premodern believers to see Christian transcendence as itself an effect of artistic representation, more stunning in proportion to the representation's actual vacuity. If Augustine could find no radical difference between God's true acts and the titillating artifice of theater, I don't suppose we have much hope of telling them apart either, especially

---

73. *A Tretise of Miraclis Pleyinge*, ed. Clifford Davidson (Kalamazoo: Medieval Institute Publications, Western Michigan University, 1993), p. 112.

74. That the Mass was sheer theater is a frequent complaint among Protestant reformers. See for example William Prynne, *Histrio-mastix* (London, 1633), pp. 112–14, where he quotes for corroboration the comparison to classical tragedy made by Honorius Augustodunensis, another medieval scholar of Antichrist whom the next chapter will examine.

75. "The Chester Cycle," in *The Cambridge Companion to Medieval English Theatre*, ed. Richard Beadle (Cambridge: Cambridge University Press, 1994), p. 132. See also Kolve's analogy between Satan's attempt to imitate God and the cycle plays as a whole in *Play Called Corpus Christi* (n. 48), p. 9.

if the stage really *is* demon-inspired. Medieval drama at its most demonic, at its most bawdy and grotesque, at its most slapstick and retrograde, still hoped to participate in genuine revelation. At its most demonically theatrical, it *was* revelation, as close, in fact, as an audience was ever likely to come outside of the Mass, which also had its share of antichristian prestidigitation, above all in the "revelation" of God's real presence as nothing more impressive than a piece of bread. Now *that* is an amusing trick!

Chester's Antichrist discovers to his detriment the close kinship, hence fierce animosity, between the host's revelatory non-revelation and his own gimmicks. In the course of the play Enoch presents the true God, against his false surrogate, as precisely what cannot be staged:

> The poyntes of thy privitie
> any yearthlye man to see
> ys impossible, as thinkes mee,
> for any worldelye wight. (*Chester* 23.257–60)

And yet the cycle itself has repeatedly put God on view as though it *were* possible for earthly men to see him. This particular play will leave room for that possibility, despite God's indescribable "privitie," by showing how the theater's demonic imposture providentially *fails* to describe him:

> Your saviour nowe in your sight
> here may you saffelye see.
> Messias, Christ, and most of might,
> that in the lawe was you beheight,
> all mankind to joye to dight
> ys commen, for I am hee. (*Chester* 23.11–16)

This fellow then proceeds to work various miracles as a sign of his authenticity. He raises the dead and himself undergoes resurrection. He sends the Holy Spirit to his followers, who rejoice with gratitude: "A, God! A, lord mycle of might! / This holye ghoost is in me pight!" (197–98). The only thing divine about their inspiration, really, lies in the subsequent discovery of Antichrist's deception. Their mistaken conviction regarding his divinity ultimately does work to manifest God, in other words, but only in the *discrediting* of God's negative semblance. There are several signs of Antichrist's impending unmasking: "Christ" seems strangely intent this time around on rescuing the Jews from their servitude rather than abandoning them like the last. Also, in a debate with Enoch and Elias, he denies the Trinity. At first none of this suffices to raise the suspicions of the worldly powers, so deeply enthralled are they to the drama of his miracles. What trumps his claims to righteousness, finally, is the Eucharist. In a scene unique among Antichrist plays,[76] Elias blesses a piece of bread in the name of each member of the Trinity and offers it to the dead whom Antichrist supposedly revived. "Alas, put that bread out of my sight!" cries the first corpse, his miraculous reanimation now exposed as a form of demonic possession:

> To looke on hit I am not light.
> That prynt that ys uppon hit pight,
> hit puttes me to great feere. (*Chester* 23:577–80)

The "prynt" on the bread, though probably the sign of the cross, could have been any number of impressions characterizing the medieval host, which by then was stamped, like a coin (more on that in the next chapter). This sign, the type on the face of the sacrament, while it overturns the "false" appearance of Antichrist, counterintuitively *confirms* him, with all of his illusions and lies and fakery, as the genuine typological precursor to an imminent second coming. It glances as well at the original raison d'être of most of the cycle plays, the great Feast of Corpus Christi and doctrine of real presence, in which a trivial material increment laid claim to the highest spiritualism for having been imperceptibly saturated with the condemned blood of God.

It takes a dialectician of supreme talent working within this framework to prevent the history of the Eucharist from collapsing into nightmare, the endless repetition of past events, each as horrifying and fraudulent as the last: the miracle of Passover (a massacre), its recapitulation in the Last Supper (a death sentence), the reprise of that sad meal at Mass (a sacrifice), the mock consecration in Chester's play of the Antichrist (a lie). All these performances were supposed to intimate a coming revelation that, for once, would not conclude in betrayal. Of them all, the drama had the least reliable authority in spiritual matters; yet given the unreliability of

---

76. For plot summaries of the others, see Klaus Aichele, *Das Antichristdrama des Mittelalters, der Reformation und Gegenreformation* (The Hague: Martinus Nijhoff, 1974). For commentary on this moment in Chester and an interesting description of its reception history, see Richard K. Emmerson, "Contextualizing Performance: The Reception of the Chester Antichrist," *Journal of Medieval and Early Modern Studies* 29.1 (Winter 1999): 89–119. I don't see that any play's meaning can be restricted as narrowly as Emmerson thinks to the medieval history of its reception, however (mainly because the history of its reception obviously includes *us*), nor that historicism must repudiate formalist and aesthetic categories, as Emmerson seems to. For further remarks of mine on this topic, see "The Promise of History," *Shakespeare Studies* 30 (2002): 43–46.

real spiritual authority, this refusal to *be* the Eucharist it presented seems almost like a corrective insubordination. The play's belated, second-order imitation rises above the bad repetitions from which it sprang on account of its being, by comparison, so frivolous—and so funny.[77] By replaying the Eucharist in the midst of Antichrist's life of faked emulations, the Chester play would redeem through laughter the real Eucharist, whose efficacy was no less questionable, from its own bad faith. The drama, as *actual* drama rather than mere theater masquerading as a serious liturgy, could then play Christ to the Antichristianity already embedded in the pompous solemnity of the Mass.

The Anagogical Promise of Art

We do not know how the vernacular drama developed outside the liturgy to which it sometimes referred and which it hoped, through allusion and the occasional emulation, to extend into the secular world. The earliest mention in England of a play taking place outside the church involves some miraculous events in thirteenth-century Beverley; while not dealing directly with Antichrist, these events may be illuminated by him, and I want to conclude this chapter by looking at the episode rather carefully. A large crowd gathered before the church of Saint John, we are told, "led there by different impulses, some on account of mere pleasure, or from wonder, others for the holy purpose of arousing their devotion."[78] The chronicler says they had come to see a *repraesentatio* of the Lord's resurrection, performed by actors in masks through words and gestures (*verbis et actu*). Then in the course of the drama a group of boys climb into the vaults of the church in order to get a better view of the players—either by virtue of the height, the chronicler supposes, or by gazing through holes in the glass windows. Afraid that the boys might intentionally break the windows to see all the better, some angry sextons chase them "beyond the great cross," when suddenly a stone comes loose from its mortar and a boy plunges to the ground, where he lies "in utter semblance of death [*mortuo simillimus*]" (*DMC* 2:540). As usual a likeness this exact promises by its very nature the complete opposite, and behold, the boy revives.

77. See Leslie Howard Martin, "Comic Eschatology in the Chester Coming of Antichrist," *Comparative Drama* 5.3 (1971): 163–76; for a "moral defense" of the play that would lessen its comedy, see Peter W. Travis, *Dramatic Design in the Chester Cycle* (Chicago: University of Chicago Press, 1982), pp. 228ff., esp. pp. 235–36.

78. Latin in *DMC* 2:539–40. For an exhaustive treatment of the document (and a translation), see Patricia Badir, "Representations of the Resurrection at Beverley Minster circa 1208: Chronicle, Play, Miracle," *Theatre Survey* 38.1 (1997): 9–41.

Somehow Lawrence Clopper has determined that the drama going on outside the church and occasioning these incredible events was neither a resurrection play nor in any way conducive to genuine religious admiration. In his words the play "not only [was] false but deprived those outside of seeing the *repraesentatio* of the resurrection within"[79]—the fall and revival of the boy. The medieval chronicler of these events, on the contrary, explains that God wished through the revival of the boy "to give testimony to the *truth* which was then being played in the representation of the resurrection" *outside* the church (*DMC* 2:540). According to the narrator's account, the drama outside the church, far from being a false diversion, in fact gave rise to an even *more* miraculous revelation of the truth of its contents—more miraculous because the revival of the boy was not only a representation of Christ's resurrection but also *real*: "Thus it happened that those whose presence at the representation outside the church was prevented by the size of the crowd saw a more marvelous proof of the resurrection inside; and not only of the resurrection, but also of the Lord's passion" (ibid.). The chronicler approves of the *repraesentatio* outside the church, however subordinate it may be to the main plot, because he sees its instrumental value as the lure that brings the boy to the heights of his fortunate fall. The chronicler does not condemn the players for being the least proximate to the holy (this is obvious), but rather analyzes with a cold, scientific eye the wisdom of a God who allows the serpent of staged illusion to induct believers into his mysteries. In short, the miracle staged outside the church by actors is staged as *reality* within it by God. God, according to this account, is the ultimate director, history his mise-en-scène.

Where it takes a whole aesthetics to explain how an artificial, palpably fake reenactment of the resurrection could draw one closer to the truth of events past and to come precisely because it had been *fabricated* toward this end, to make the same interpretive leap with regard to real events requires the special science of typological analysis. To the untrained modern viewer of the events at Beverley, it may seem that a witless kid, hooked on visual stimulants, escaped by chance having his skull cracked. The narrator, however, could still discern beneath this lucky event the recapitulation of biblical history, and in the recapitulation, presumably, the promise of future redemption. To him, the received narrative of sacred miracles, through its contrafactuality, could work in tandem with outright fictions

79. Lawrence Clopper, "*Miracula* and *The Tretise of Miraclis Pleyinge*," *Speculum* 65.4 (1990): 878–905; here 886–87.

like the miracle play to extract from historical events something more than history had ever really offered:

> The stone falling from the wall without the [touch of a human] hand plainly indicates the Lord's incarnation from a virgin without the intervention of a man: the fall of both, stone and boy, signified his passion, as man and God. The stone broken by its fall, however, was a type of the ram slain; and the youth a type of Isaac, who remained unharmed. And in like manner, as the fall [*ruina*] was a sign of his passion according to his humanity, so the miraculous raising was a sign of his resurrection according to his divinity. (ibid.)

You can see here with special clarity how typological allegoresis "explains" one incredible event—that fall and resurrection of the boy—with reference to a master code that is equally unbelievable. Were the master code any less fantastic, if it seemed any less fictive, it would promise nothing beyond the bald facts of dying in their myriad historical forms. To the chronicler's eyes, long trained no doubt on icons of the crucified, a dead youth is not dead in fact so long as he seems the very picture of death (*mortuo simillimus*). Here representation's lack of authenticity in comparison to what it represents *recommends* it as a vehicle for the revelation of all that surpasses actuality. The apparent falsehood of sacred history, the played reenactment of the resurrection, and the boy's own simulacrum of death all express the same sublime truth. It is their glaring non-correspondence to things as they normally are that puts them in dialogue with God.

According to Augustine, those who scoff at the mysteries of faith because of their patent contrivance—that is, "the humanity assumed by the eternal, all powerful, changeless son of God and that he was born of a virgin, and all the other miracles of this history" (*De quant.* 33.76 [CSEL 89:224; trans. Ludwig Schopp et al., FC 4:142]—must have an equally difficult time getting their minds around the far less complex but equally mysterious process of aesthetic rendering, for example, the process whereby a painter transforms a real person into an identical simulacrum that could not be more different from the original insofar as the painting is *unreal* (ibid.). Augustine knows by contrast that the picture can be a "true" rendering of a man only to the extent that it presents a "false" man, and that this "miracle" inheres in every representation. On stage specifically, he wrote shortly after his conversion, "a kind of marvel is born, which still no one doubts to be so" (*Sol.* 2.18 [CSEL 89:68; NPNF 7:553]). The miracle consists of this: simply that staged things, and mimetic artifacts more generally, "are in certain respects true, by virtue of the very fact that they are in certain respects false" (ibid.). The miraculous aspect of aesthetic experience, whereby false, unreal images are rightly taken to intimate via their unreality a form of truth, contains the same typological conversion whereby historical events of dubious significance are sublimed into the stuff of faith, except that even the unconverted can accept the aesthetic version without contest: "No one doubts it." Where only the faithful see truth in the events of sacred history, and in its miracles especially, everyone can find a quasi-transcendental truth in the *greater* vacuity of secular art, though it is supposedly "inferior in proportion to its emptiness" (*Sol.* 2.12 [CSEL 89:61; NPNF 7:551]). The miracle of classical drama, Augustine seems to suggest, operates just like any historical miracle of the Christian faith, except that it works without faith.

All this begins to suggest that straight entertainment in the Middle Ages could seem to imitate the divine so long as it involved a certain "miraculous" effect. Maybe a *miraculum* on occasion was as nondramatic as Clopper thinks all *miracula* were, and as secular as a juggling act. In that case, we might ask, how secular was a juggling act, and to what extent did every religious performance depend on exactly this same shtick? Why, for instance, is there a jongleur carved in relief atop a column and capital at Bayeux cathedral? The answer probably lies in the ape to which he is chained, apes being the symbol of mimetic behavior par excellence and therefore linked "to another class of representations deemed undesirable by the Church: mimes and actors."[80] This will become important when we get to Marlowe's alleged charge that both Moses and Paul were jugglers, too. From very early on the word "juggler" encompassed the tricksy, entertaining buffoon as well as the black magician enthralled to the satanic arts that could not help but ape God's own thaumaturgy. The more his juggling seemed "wonderful," either because it defied the laws of the humanly possible or else involved some hidden act of legerdemain, the more his ability to depart from the actual by means of his art seemed like an act of God.

"The unity and indivisibility of belief and unbelief," writes Johan Huizinga, "the indissoluble connection between sacred seriousness and pretense or 'fun,' are best understood in the concept of play."[81] If nowhere else, that is true of medieval and early modern playing, where the more spectacular

---

80. Michael Camille, *The Gothic Idol: Ideology and Image-Making in Medieval Art* (Cambridge: Cambridge University Press, 1989), p. 14 n. 19.

81. Johan Huizinga, *Homo Ludens: A Study of the Play Element in Culture* (Boston: Beacon Press, 1950), p. 24; quoted and discussed in *AT* 472; trans. 318.

and affecting a performance, the more it seemed to encroach on, or speak for, God's own prerogatives. The shenanigans that wowed an audience, the intervention of God in history via his aerial powers—*both* could count as *miracula* because both inspired a thrilling blend of admiration and serious doubt about their authenticity. Performances that did not specifically involve scriptural absurdities could still achieve, through nothing more than their own gargantuan pretense or sham substance, the same divine magic as the Christian faith. The magic in fact was never magic. Not even in church. Where it seemed so, that was an art. Only when transcendence was artificially and materially performed, whether "acted," sculpted, sung, or written out, only then could people sense some promise of impending freedom from the burdensome weight of time-bound existence. The performances themselves were of course completely embedded in history. Through the representation and restructuring of historical elements, however, players and priests enacted on occasion something of more than historical interest. This more constitutes the anagogical promise of art, even the secular. "Whether the promise is deception—that," writes Adorno, "is the enigma" (*AT* 193; trans. 127).

CHAPTER 2

Blood Money

Antichristian Economics and the Drama of the Sacraments

God loves a cheerful giver.

SAINT PAUL

The Root of All Evil

Prior to Christian scripture redemption in Greek meant to free by cash payment. The way we might redeem an old heirloom from hock, money back then could purchase human life. It freed prisoners of war, for example, or convicts. In the case of temple slaves, you had to pay the gods—or, what comes down to the same, the temple priests. Redemption meant you bought the person *back*.[1]

Christianity introduces just a couple of novelties into this usage. First, those in need of manumission now include the unimprisoned and free-

---

1. See the entries for λύτρον-ἀπολύτρωσις by F. Büchsel in *Theological Dictionary of the New Testament*, trans. and ed. Geoffry W. Bromiley, 10 vols. (Grand Rapids: Eerdmans, 1964–76), 4:340–51. Paul J. Achtemeier, *1 Peter: A Commentary on First Peter*, Hermeneia (Minneapolis: Fortress, 1996), p. 127, provides a helpful synopsis on the prehistory: in the LXX this cluster of terms covers "redemption of property by paying its value to the present holder [Lev. 24:26, 33, 48–49]; the retribution for faults committed [Exod. 21:30]; the ransom of the firstborn [Exod. 13:12–13; Num. 3:44–51, 18:15–17]; and the 'atonement price' (half-shekel paid by every Israelite [Exod. 30:12–16]). The term is also used to describe the deliverance of Israel by God from its bondage and exile, in which case the price is normally not mentioned [Exod. 6:6; Deut. 7:8; cf. Isa. 44:22–23, 51:11, 52:3]." For fuller treatment, see Bernd Janowski, "Auslösung des verwirkten Lebens: Zur Geschichte und Struktur der biblischen Lösegeldvorstellung," *Zeitschrift für Theologie und Kirche* 79 (1982): 25–59.

born. Birth itself, irrespective of any social determinant, is condemnation enough. Life as such has become the universal life sentence. This sounds grim, maybe, but the new outlook promised great relief. Slavery, imprisonment, guilt—these imply clear remedies, whereas the quotidian limitation of a finite existence by itself does not. So long as you are only imprisoned, you can, in exchange for freedom, pay damages or ransom. You can bribe the judge. You have only to know what sort of payment the judge accepts. That is the second Christian novelty. According to scripture, God accepts restitution, same as in any Greek religion—only not in cash and not from you. Christ alone provides the necessary "ransom" (*lutron*; Mt 20:28; Mk 10:45).[2] And Christ pays your debt in blood.

Judaism had offered at best a single biblical instance "in which sacrificial blood is said to be a ransom for human life" (Lev. 17:11),[3] but with the advent of Christ, God's economics would henceforth conform more strictly to an old rabbinic dictum than had the rabbis: "There is no remission without bloodshed" (Heb. 9:22).[4] Without the crucifixion, in other words, there is no redemption. In Paul's sublime understatement, "You are bought at a price" (1 Cor. 6:20, 7:23). By this he presumably meant a price beyond all cost, since to make payments in exchange for salvation of course you cannot be rich enough. You are bought, rather, at the price of blood, though this does not mean you can bleed enough, either. On the contrary, the church of God has to be "purchased with his own blood" (Acts 20:28b).[5] With *God's* blood. That oxymoron caused some scribes to

2. More fully, "ransom for [*anti*] many." Cf. 1 Tim. 2:6, where *antilutron* is used synonymously with *lutron*. I deal with the word *anti* as a preposition connected to fiscal exchange in the next chapter. "That they had been ransomed," writes Peter H. Davids, "is found in all strata of the early church" (*The First Epistle of Peter* [Grand Rapids: Eerdmans, 1990], p. 71); he then gives a convenient list of instances in the NT. For an overview of the ransom motif specifically in Paul, see Wilfrid Haubeck, *Loskauf durch Christus: Herkunft, Gestalt, und Bedeutung des paulinischen Loskaufmotivs* (Giessen: Brunnen, 1985). There are scattered pagan instances of the same idea; see, for example, the citation in Martin Hengel, *The Atonement: The Origins of the Doctrine in the New Testament* (Philadelphia: Fortress, 1981), p. 24.

3. Baruch J. Schwartz, "The Prohibitions Concerning the 'Eating' of Blood in Leviticus 17," in *Priesthood and Cult in Ancient Israel*, ed. Gary A. Anderson and Saul M. Olyan (Sheffield: Sheffield Academic Press, 1991), pp. 34–66, here 56.

4. For the rabbinic and biblical background to this verse, see Robert J. Daly, *Christian Sacrifice: The Judaeo-Christian Background before Origen* (Washington, D.C.: Catholic University of America Press, 1978), p. 96; on blood rites more generally, pp. 87–117.

5. In translating περιεποιήσατο as "purchased," I follow every English Bible from Wyclif to the King James, though this tradition has since fallen into doubt. "The verb is often taken to mean simply *to acquire* [as at 1 Tim. 3:13]....Its meaning in the OT and NT seems to be prevailingly 'save alive,' or 'rescue from destruction.'" From C. K. Barrett, *A Critical and Exegetical Commentary on the Acts of the Apostles*, 2 vols. (Edinburgh: T & T Clark, 1998), 2:976.

prevaricate, apparently, and in a lot of manuscripts the God who bleeds has been softened to "the Lord."[6] The change requires in manuscript the alteration of just a single letter yet eliminates the sole direct allusion to the divinity of Jesus in the whole Book of Acts.[7] It leaves intact his blood payment, however, and that is the main thing, whether Acts is Patripassian or not. The point to take is that redemption comes exclusively "through his blood...according to the riches of his grace" (Eph. 1:7; cf. Col. 1:14). Owing to the crucifixion, a person could now cash in his time on earth for a new kind of death: that fantastic, insuperable contradiction, *eternal life.*

Later commentators who were called upon to elucidate the idea of Christ's blood as God's chosen currency found themselves having to differentiate it from, while simultaneously likening it to, worldly lucre. Tertullian for example rebukes persecuted Christians for attempting to escape by paying off their tormentors in cash rather than suffering bodily harm and rendering to God's demonic proxies what he, as the ultimate source of all affliction, has obviously demanded. "How unworthy of God and his will," Tertullian complains, "that you try to redeem with mere money a man who has been ransomed by the blood of Christ!" (*De fuga* 12.2 [CCSL 1²:1150; trans. Edwin A. Quain, FC 40:299]). A Christian faced with death by persecution may be momentarily "saved by money," but this salvation is strictly temporal and will be reversed in eternity, since a man who can afford such unholy deliverance is "rich in opposition to God. Christ, by contrast, became rich for him in blood" (*De fuga* 12.5 [ibid., 1151; 301]). To escape through temporal bribes from the suffering mandated by God may seem like a "gratuitous redemption [*redemptio gratuita*]" (*De fuga* 12.1 [ibid., 1149; 298]), but make no mistake: this is the opposite of redemption by grace. Redemption by grace alleviates affliction through Christ's blood payment and nothing else. If you want remission of sin, Tertullian explains, God must receive the due remittance in this, "his own image and coin, inscribed with his own name," just as Caesar gets paid in his. "So what do I owe God, as I owe Caesar money," Tertullian asks, "but the blood which his own Son shed for me?" (*De fuga* 12.10 [ibid., 1153; 303]).

6. For a defense of the interpretation I put forward here, see C. Devine, "The Blood of God," *Catholic Biblical Quarterly* 9 (1947): 381–408. For a briefer, more general synopsis of the textual issues surrounding this verse, see *TC* 425–27; also Bart D. Ehrman, *The Orthodox Corruption of Scripture: The Effect of Early Christological Controversies on the Text of the New Testament* (Oxford: Oxford University Press, 1993), pp. 87–88.

7. What the 1587 Geneva calls "a notable sentence for Christes Godhead" (note h), borrowing from Calvin's own gloss, *The Acts of the Apostles*, trans. John W. Fraser and W. J. C. McDonald, 2 vols. (Grand Rapids: Eerdmans, 1965–66), 2:184.

Anyone who tries to make payment in cash will hear the words of Peter as spoken to that colossal figure of the medieval Antichrist, Simon Magus: "Let your money go with you to destruction, for you reckoned that the grace of God was obtainable for a price" (*De fuga* 12.4 [ibid., 1151; 300]).[8]

I linger on these passages from Tertullian because they seem to me crisply illustrative of how money and Christ's blood find their respective values in the wider traditions of Christianity through a consistent kind of antithesis. Consider 1 Peter: "You were not ransomed with perishable things, as silver and gold...but with the costly blood of Christ" (1.18–19). Normally, gold and silver would act as "costly" repositories of more perishable values because unlike blood *they don't perish.* Christ did. Yet according to this verse his dying accomplished among other miracles a radical transvaluation, such that God's blood now borrows from money its most winning predicate, "costly," and foists onto gold and silver the misfortune of God's mortality. Money here perishes *in place of* Christ. It takes on his humanity that he might gain the transgenerational, quasi-immortal perpetuity of wealth.[9] Arguably this contrafactual exchange of predicates between blood and money accounts for the otherwise needless comparison between them in the first place, what one puzzled commentator has called "the almost trivial negative detail that [God] does not pay in depreciable coin."[10] Without the negative likeness of Christ's blood to money—that ugly repository of human social value—there would be no intelligible expression of a value that transcends all intelligibility. The sacrifice of Jesus, though a payment of sorts, pays off a debt that silver and gold could never match. It satisfies the Infinite.

Why then do so many Christian writers compare the process of salvation to commercial trade without any explicit negation whatsoever, as if it were, after all, a matter of plain economics? Heaven, though supposedly hard for a rich man to enter, frequently resembles in Christian writing nothing so much as an invaluable pearl or some other precious commodity

---

8. Citing Acts 8:20; for Simon Magus as Antichrist, see the final section of chapter 4.

9. The association of money with immortality is ancient and probably stems from the practical necessity that whatever passes for cash be durable. See Richard Seaford, *Money and the Early Greek Mind: Homer, Philosophy, Tragedy* (Cambridge: Cambridge University Press, 2004), p. 31. Norman O. Brown, *Life against Death: The Psychoanalytic Meaning of History* (New York: Viking, 1959), p. 286 and passim; Ernest Becker, *Escape from Evil* (New York: Free Press, 1975), pp. 73–90.

10. Norbert Brox, *Der Erste Petrusbrief* (Zürich: Benziger, 1979), p. 81, to whom I owe the inspired translation of φθαρτός as *wertschwundanfällig,* which I in turn have rendered as "depreciable." It had not occurred to me that this strange phrase—literally "mortal money"—might be hiding the problem of inflation.

that a person with sufficient resources might acquire, if not through direct transfer, then through a more roundabout investment strategy known to the usurer as credit and the believer as "faith." Had not Christ himself in the parable of the talents implicitly sanctified the earning of interest as a real-world avenue to grace? "You wicked and slothful servant," says the master of the parable (presumably speaking on behalf of the Lord to his less profitable followers). "You knew that I reap where I have not sowed, and gather where I have not winnowed? Then you ought to have invested my money with the bankers, and at my coming I should have received what was my own with interest" (Mt 25:26–27).[11] Christ's teaching in this case is either obscene or a hermetic way of communicating the purity of heaven by means of an obscene terminology. Orthodox commentators go with the latter possibility. For them money serves in the Bible as an allegory or type, and the lucre in Christ's story actually signifies *lucrum spiritale*.[12] About the value of this, of course we know very little, save that it is exactly like money, only totally different.

In other words even the strongest of parallels between salvation and economic profits could help illustrate, with a little typological adjustment, Christ's *aversion* to cash transactions. Hence the rhetorical and dramatic effectiveness of stressing the likeness—which is to say, of stressing the *difference*. "Behold," writes Augustine, "the kingdom of heaven is set before you for purchase, along with the auction and sale of faith!" Unlike at any normal auction or sale, however, here "you buy gratis, if you recognize the free grace [*gratam gratiam*] which is offered to you. You spend nothing; nevertheless, what you acquire is great" (*Serm.* 216.3 [PL 38:1078; *WSA* III/6:168]). Even positive comparisons between spiritual commodities and worldly commerce can in this way ultimately work to elevate the spiritual *beyond* anything available on the common market; and the comparison could then serve, from this point of elevation, to marshal a critique of all money-based economics. "Your money is unsound," warns Augustine's

---

11. For a comprehensive and efficient introduction to the *Wirkungsgeschichte* of the parable, see Luz 3:250–62. For its place in medieval drama, V. A. Kolve, "*Everyman* and the Parable of the Talents," in *Medieval English Drama: Essays Critical and Contextual*, ed. Jerome Taylor and Alan H. Nelson (Chicago: University of Chicago Press, 1972), pp. 316–40, and Victor I. Scherb, "The Parable of the Talents in *The Castle of Perseverance*," *English Language Notes* 28.1 (1990): 20–25.

12. The phrase frequently occurs in the writings of Gregory the Great though does not necessarily originate there; in any case he used it as a rebuke of the servant who failed to seek "spiritual profit" when he buried his talent; see *XL hom. in ev.* 9.1 (CCSL 141:59); trans. David Hurst, *Forty Gospel Homilies* (Kalamazoo: Cistercian Publications, 1990), pp. 123, 128. Gregory is followed in this by Bede, Rabanus Maurus, and others.

teacher, Ambrose. "The money in your purse is not good." Why? Because Christ *himself* "is your money, *he* is your price" (*De Jos.* 9.50 [PL 14:662C–D; trans. Michael P. McHugh, FC 65:222]). It is as though the language of money best expresses the inestimable value of God's gifts, even as any such expression fails to equal the surpassing value of what it says and is therefore condemned for the presumption.

Behold Antichrist's most insidious tool for the capture of souls: money—the abject, crudely material, opposed equivalent of Christ's sublime worth; the continual, negative representative of his sacrifice, whose representation threatens at every step to usurp its prototype, and yet whose very usurpation functions as the surest augury of a final rectification. We have seen Antichrist, remarked Luther contemptuously at dinner, "how he spreads his money around" (*Tischreden* 4063 [WAtr 4:108]). It had by then become a standard element of the legend that whomever he could not conquer through miraculous deceit and terror he would "subjugate with avarice,"[13] giving "to those who believe in him plenty of gold and silver."[14] His persuasiveness in other words would depend a great deal on his grotesque yet spectacular and winning literalization of scripture's fiscal metaphors for grace. Luther's claim to have seen this spectacle with his own eyes does not, for once, refer to the rampant commercialism of a corrupt church, but rather in this case to the popular dramas or *spectacula ludorum* so inspired by it as to feature scenes like the one at Chester where Antichrist opens his money bags in parody of God's real gifts to come (*Chester* 23.50ff.).[15] Here more than anywhere else in that play the total failure of Antichrist to realize on earth the celestial munificence he would claim for himself is not exactly failure—or parody. His phony charity rather anticipates the divine *charitas* by presenting an overly literal

13. Jerome, *Comm. in Dan.* 11.37–39 (CCSL 75a:928); trans. Gleason L. Archer Jr., *Jerome's Commentary on Daniel* (Grand Rapids: Baker Book House, 1958), p. 139.

14. Adso, *Lib. de Antichristo* (PL 101:1294B); text also in *DMC* 2:498; trans. Bernard McGinn, *Apocalyptic Spirituality* (New York: Paulist Press, 1979), pp. 89–96; here 92. Adso is following a remark from Jerome's Daniel commentary (above note) which will be further disseminated in *Jacobi a Voragine Legenda Aurea*, ed. Th. Graesse, 2nd ed. (Leipzig, 1862), p. 8; trans. William Granger Ryan, *The Golden Legend: Readings on the Saints*, 2 vols. (Princeton: Princeton University Press, 1993), 1:9. For others' connections between Antichrist and money, see Horst Dieter Rauh, *Das Bild des Antichrist im Mittelalter: Von Tyconius zum deutschen Symbolismus*, 2nd ed. (Münster: Aschendorff, 1979), pp. 461–62, and also p. 253: "Money is the instrument that opens the way for him [Antichrist] into the hearts of the powerful. Behind this stands a critique of the martial nobility's avarice, profligacy, and love of ostentation."

15. Cf. the gift-giving in *Ludus de Antichristo;* original in *DMC* 2:371–87; trans. John Wright, *The Play of Antichrist* (Toronto: Pontifical Institute of Mediaeval Studies, 1967), e.g., lines 217–44.

image of it in lieu of its immediate realization. God's "real" gifts—always deferred—will according to the words of scripture look very much the same as the theatrical Antichrist's material offerings, yet without being any more reducible to a material reward than the subject of a painting can be reduced to swirls of paint—although painting does, nonetheless, credibly stand in for the real thing as its mimetic equivalent. So too could money, the ultimate antichristian equivalence, function as a prescient, fallen image of God's body in the absence of any such body, its illicit substitute yet most promising representative.

So promising, in fact, that at some point in the Middle Ages it started to look to plenty of people as though maybe they could receive the all-surpassing bounty of heaven in exchange for the very things heaven surpassed. Did the Mass not celebrate the *admirabile commercium* whereby God "received" human nature in the person of Christ so as to "give" humanity his divine undying?[16] The miracle of redemption as such allowed immortality to be purchased by *death*: "What a trade! [*qualia commercia*]," Augustine had preached. "No one would trade death for life!" (*Serm.* 80.5 [PL 38:496–97; *WSA* III/3:353–54]).[17] No one would, but Christ our "merchant" (as Augustine calls him) did anyway; if the rituals of his church could facilitate the same asymmetry, why not use the Mass as an opportunity to get a vast return on a comparatively minor offering, a prayer, for instance, or a Mass penny? Why not both? Through a happy quirk of Middle English, the *Lay Folks Mass Book* need not bother, when explaining the Offertory, to distinguish "paying" from "pleasing" God:

> Offer wheþur þe luste,
> How þou schuld pray, I wold þou wyste.
> And whyl þou stondus, I rede þou say,
> As is wrytun, god to pay...[18]

16. For the full history, see Martin Herz, *Sacrum Commercium: Eine begriffsgeschichtliche Studie zur Theologie der römischen Liturgiesprache* (Munich: Kommissionsverlag Karl Zink, 1958), esp. pp. 210–20 on the role of Christ's blood as a monetary instrument. Also next note.

17. The translator Edmund Hill notes that "this conceit of envisaging the incarnation as a commercial transaction finds its way into the liturgy of Christmas time." He compares *Serm.* 121.5 (SC 116:230–32; *WSA* III/4:236); see also *Serm.* 130.2 (PL 38:726; *WSA* III/4:311), *Enn. in Ps.* 102.6 (CCSL 40:1456; *WSA* III/19:85) and 147.16 (PL 37:1925; *WSA* III/20:458). The language derives in part from 2 Cor. 8:9: "For you know the grace of our Lord Jesus Christ, that though he was rich, yet for your sakes he became poor, so that by his poverty you might become rich."

18. *The Lay Folks Mass Book*, ed. Thomas Frederick Simmons, EETS o.s. 71 (1879; repr., London: Oxford University Press, 1968), p. 23; E-text. D alone of all the texts has "pray" where the others have "pay" or "pey."

In this instance the overlapping meanings of the word "pay" must have seemed perfectly apt: paying God literally, you managed also to pay in the higher sense (now obsolete) of "placating" him.[19] The wrath of God, satisfied with money! The generosity lay not in the gift but in God's willingness to receive it.

Of course there were limits. An Offertory procession in Germany that ended with people depositing their goods directly on the high altar drew fire from a scrupulous priest of the early sixteenth century, just prior to Luther's eruption but with a less ambitious objective. "The faithful," he insisted, "ought not lay their money on the Communion cloth."[20] Presumably for him this superimposition threatened to wash away the theological niceties by which Christian thinkers had long preserved the sacrament and money in an *opposed* likeness. The whole beauty of Eucharistic exchange was that it took the "form" of commerce, while the commodities traded in it were those that could never freely circulate—the bloody flesh of Christ and all this brought: posthumous happiness, the true health of eternal life. That was why, strictly speaking, the beneficiaries of this ritualized commerce could not take full possession of anything purchased at the altar until after death—notwithstanding the crass guarantees of more immediate benefits like those offered by a Middle English treatise on "the Manner and Mede of the Mass":

> Of sinnes hit wol make þe to sese,
> And þi catel also encrese
> Of seluer in þi Cofre.[21]

Ideally the point of investing in the Mass was that it made you poorer in goods and therefore richer in *intangible* assets. That was the true allure of the ritual, and it served to justify a lot of people's lives, which by their own admission teetered otherwise on the brink of total meaninglessness: "The fleeting light of life is worth nothing," wrote a monk of St. Gallen in

---

19. From *pacare*. Cf. the final lines of Simmons, *Lay Folks Mass Book*, "and of alle þo prayers þat here are prayde, / pray I to god that he be payde" (B-text; lines 616–17). The word here means "satisfy" (see also p. 244n.).

20. Quoted in Josef A. Jungmann, *The Mass of the Roman Rite: Its Origins and Development (Missarum Sollemnia)*, trans. Francis A. Brunner, 2 vols. (New York: Benziger, 1951–55), 2:16 n. 81. Cf. Simmons, *Lay Folks Mass Book*, p. 233 n. 2 and 235 n. 1.

21. From the Vernon MS, Bodeleian, in Simmons, *Lay Folks Mass Book*, p. 142.

the eighth century, "unless one can use present goods to buy everlasting ones."[22]

Apologies for equating spiritual transactions with straightforward commerce seem rarely so straightforward. Even according to this, present goods—and presumably money above all—are themselves worthless, unless they can take on some worth *beyond* the present world. Maybe they can't, but such sublimity appeared anyway in the ritualized commerce of the church as one of its central, constitutive utopias. The *admirabile commercium* so happily celebrated throughout medieval Christianity even as the Mass increasingly mirrored commerce of a less than admirable sort could always be admired for "mirroring" in the strict sense: on some inherent level it opposed what it extolled. The increasing lack of distinction between commerce and Christian practice, easily accommodated if not also encouraged by scripture's own fiscal discourse and subsequent doctrine, found itself in other words perpetually contested by that discourse, which would locate in money the expression of a value impervious to monetary exchange. The novel forms of vernacular drama—some semi-professionalized, some sponsored by trade guilds—that increasingly supplemented and in places competed with the ritual performances through which the church augmented its revenues could therefore apologize for the church's total collapse into worldly commercialism (and for the drama's supporting role in it) even as these same rituals and dramas themselves brought to bear on church finance a radical critique. By making the fetishistic allure and utopian premise of monetary trade completely central to the performance of late medieval Christianity in England, both ritual and drama laid the essential groundwork, I want to argue, for the commercial aesthetics of the London stage. Marlowe in particular helped preserve through his heroes' reverence for wealth, we'll eventually see, the half-fraudulent promise formerly reserved to churchly commerce.

Through it all, from sacred to secular, there persists the figure of Antichrist—as, for example, in the person of Herod, that "early Faustus"[23] and

22. Quoted in Arnold Angenendt et al., "Counting Piety in the Early and High Middle Ages," in *Ordering Medieval Society: Perspectives on Intellectual and Practical Modes of Shaping Social Relations*, ed. Bernhard Jussen, trans. Pamela Selwyn (Philadelphia: University of Pennsylvania Press, 2001), p. 37.

23. David Staines, "To Out-Herod Herod: The Development of a Dramatic Character," *Comparative Drama* 10 (1976): 29–53; here 50.

one of Antichrist's finer incarnations.[24] An unconscious imitator of the God he opposes, Towneley's Magnus Herodes unwittingly proclaims the birth of Christ by virtue of his proleptic usurpation of the Christ child's fabulous titles, "kyng of kyngys" and "Chefe lord of lordyngys" (*Towneley* 16.53, 55).[25] When Herod first hears the "rumore" of a rival claimant to his throne, of course he rants, he rages, and then, in keeping with his antichristian lineage (and in parody of the Offertory),[26] he dangles before his followers overwhelming material benefits in recompense for their obedience; to the mercenary soldiers who will carry out the massacre of the innocents, Herod promises a "drope" of his "good grace," that is, "Markys, rentys, and powndys, / Greatt castels and groundys" (*Towneley* 16.385–88). Naturally Herod's payments will never materialize. Onstage alone at the close of the play, imagining his infant foe has been vanquished, the Towneley king addresses the audience with his final antichristian gloat, the solitary example of a medieval Herod remaining still sovereign as his pageant ends:

> Draw therfor nerehande,
> Both of burgh and of towne:
> Markys, ilkon [everyone], a thowsande,
> When I am bowne [ready],
> Shall ye haue.
> I shal be full fayn
> To gyf that I sayn;

24. Herod's identification with Antichrist is a commonplace of medieval exegesis: for a few examples, see Bede, *In Luc. exp.* 1.2 (PL 92:333D–334A); Rabanus Maurus, *De universo* 4.1 (PL 111:83D); Honorius, *Speculum ecclesiae* (PL 172:839A–B); Gerhoch of Reichersberg, *Comm. in Ps.* 1.18 (PL 193:906A); and Hildegard of Bingen, *Liber divinorum operum simplicis hominis* 3.10 (PL 197:1015D). Various critics have commented on the relation between Antichrist and the Herods of the liturgical and cycle drama. See Theo Stemmler, *Liturgische Feiern und Geistliche Spiele* (Tübingen: Max Niemeyer, 1970), pp. 255–85; summarized and translated in "Typological Transfer in Liturgical Offices and Religious Plays of the Middle Ages," *Studies in the Literary Imagination* 8 (1975): 123–43, specifically 138ff. Also Rosemary Woolf, *The English Mystery Plays* (Berkeley: University of California Press, 1972), pp. 202–4; Thomas P. Campbell, "Eschatology and the Nativity in the English Mystery Plays," *American Benedictine Review* 27 (1976): 297–320; here 312–17. On Wakefield in particular, see Charles Eliott, "Language and Theme in the Towneley Magnus Herodes," *Mediaeval Studies* 30 (1968): 351–53; John Gardner, *The Construction of the Wakefield Cycle* (Carbondale: Southern Illinois University Press, 1974), pp. 98–103 (Herod as "parody" of God/Christ); Jeffrey Helterman, *Symbolic Action in the Plays of the Wakefield Master* (Athens: University of Georgia Press, 1981), chapter 6, "Herod as Antichrist."

25. The editor notes that these phrases "are used to describe Christ's majesty in Rev. xvii.14 and xix.16" (*Towneley* vol. 2:523) and that a later epithet for Herod, "all-weldand" (line 421), is "generally used of God (e.g. at 3/714)" (2:527).

26. See Helterman, *Symbolic Action* (n. 24), pp. 132–36.

Wate when I com agayn,
And then may ye craue [ask for it]. (*Towneley* 16.668–76)

Then may ye crave, indeed! This parting promise to "com agayn" with his "thowsande markys," never fulfilled, only seals more firmly the bond between him and his divine nemesis. Far from discrediting Herod's grandiose sense of entitlement, he earns it here most of all, as Christ, too, according to Ambrose, "invites his people with promises and invites them with presents" (*De Jos.* 13.77 [PL 14:669C; trans. McHugh, FC 65:233])—a remark brought vividly to life, I think, by the Towneley Judgment (adapted from York), where even Jesus' "final" appearance is openly a *deferral* of his bodily appearance in the heavenly afterlife: "All mans-kynde *ther* shall it se," he says, not *here* (*Towneley* 30.130). Actually the manuscript does continue the cycle beyond its final apocalypse, though admittedly neither of these two supplementary documents stages the true Kingdom of God in all its glorified fullness. How could they? Instead the manuscript ends at last with a fragmentary poem or soliloquy, of unknown provenance, in the despairing voice of Judas, the disciple who tried to realize Christ's worth in the present, for once, by selling him for thirty silver pieces.

That sale above all else in the Bible ensures the continued centrality of money to the Christian hope for "redemption," though it depends, like any sale, on an ethereal negativity already inherent to monetary exchange, with or without Christ. Money had always been by definition the deferred possession of some objective plenty it could represent only *in potentia*; the quasi-spiritual "common denominator"[27] of all things, money achieves its ultimate value the way Herod's gifts do: by virtue of its *failure* to realize materially, in and of itself, its real worth. Otherwise there would be no reason to give money away in exchange for something different. As we're about to see in *Everyman*, in the cycles' presentation of Judas, in descriptions of the Offertory, in Croxton and in *Mankind*, the singular ability of money to picture God's grace wins it pride of place among the various mimetic usurpations

27. I borrow this phrase from an illuminating passage on the relation of money to God in Georg Simmel, *The Philosophy of Money*, ed. David Frisby, 2nd ed. (London: Routledge, 1990), p. 236. The association between money and divinity is very old and very persistent. For the primitive origins, see William H. Desmonde, *Magic, Myth, and Money: The Origin of Money in Religious Ritual* (Glencoe, Ill.: Free Press, 1962), and those he cites; also Russell W. Belk and Melanie Wallendorf, "The Sacred Meanings of Money," *Journal of Economic Psychology* 11 (1990): 35–67. For the persistence of the money-God link in medieval art, see Michael Camille, *The Gothic Idol: Ideology and Image-Making in Medieval Art* (Cambridge: Cambridge University Press, 1989), pp. 258–71, and Dominic Janes, *God and Gold in Late Antiquity* (Cambridge: Cambridge University Press, 1998).

of his grandeur, eerily similar to the real godhead, yet utterly opposed, save for the de facto promise occasioned by all of God's most formidable opponents. Money on the medieval stage has about it, that is, an oddly alluring, inverted glamour, as though among all transgressions the love of lucre could especially foreshadow humanity's hoped-for deliverance; as though the daily degradation of divinity by the material exchanges that underwrote or openly constituted the most sacred rites of the medieval church still managed to further Christ's celestial cause, not because crass materialism was, at bottom, really good, but rather because it was evil, if evil on the model of Judas' sale and therefore, from an Augustinian perspective, beautifully self-correcting—the ironic, aesthetic means by which a transcendent God appeared immanent in but still unsullied by the worst side of history.

Blinde Rekenynge (*Everyman*)

The way Everyman's devotion to earthly riches prefigures his impending spiritual windfall is almost paradigmatic for the rest of medieval drama. According to God's opening lament, humans have grown, in direct proportion to their "worldly prosperyte" (24), oblivious of his "blode rede" (30).[28] They live comfortably now, without fear, superstition, or regret, and find all their happiness, such as it is, in what's immediately present; no memory of their creation, nor any attendant obligation to their creator and savior, exists to trouble the apparent permanence of their secular bounty. Everyman possesses, rather than any recollection of the divine, his collected wealth instead, and this tangible monument would appear to secure his truest self from temporal assault far better than some supposedly deeper affinity between his "soul" and the vacuity of spirit. What could be a greater preservative of and memorial to the value of a man than his own personal hoard?

God's difficulty will be to recall to humans, by means of this wealth, his own radically alien form of exchange, which circumscribes and surpasses their pathetic commerce. A difficult task, since at the moment the seeming omnipotence of their material abundance blinds them to his superior powers—and more than blinds them: "In worldely ryches," God complains, "is all theyr mynde" (27). Humanity's mind is not too much *on* their money; their money has become the exclusive repository of all their

---

28. All quotations from the play are taken from *Everyman*, ed. A. C. Cawley (Manchester: Manchester University Press, 1961), and are keyed to line numbers.

higher cognitive faculties, as though (to borrow from Nietzsche) setting prices, determining values, contriving equivalences constituted thinking as such.[29] To ponder, to meditate—the highest forms of human ratiocination present to *Everyman*'s God at best a degraded species of his own mighty "rekenynge," a fallen way of balancing accounts under the delusion that calculations of this sort might somehow count as "thought." For the God of *Everyman*, this fall into the oblivion of commercial equivalence erases the one aspect of humanity that had promised to elevate humans above animals: "Veryly they will become moche worse than beestes, / For now one wolde by enuy another vp ete" (49–50).

I think we're meant to see in this particular form of beastliness, however, the negative imprint of Everyman's impending moral domestication: in place of cannibalism, those who "by enuy another vp ete" must learn by charity to consume God's crucified flesh. In fact each of Everyman's many sins seems to find its corrective in an identical opposite, that is, in an opposite virtue for which a particular sin provides the necessary precondition, a virtue which sin itself could therefore be said to prefigure. So for example Everyman's thoroughgoing fixation on the accumulation of wealth will correct itself in alms, that is, in an act of generosity whose magnanimity his selfish expropriation alone makes possible. Likewise, in the play's most important reversal, a *divine* reckoning takes over for Everyman's trivial sales receipts. Thus Everyman's fixation on calculating expenses ironically foreshadows the day when he will himself enter into an even grander, more dangerous settlement with the absolute Banker.

To initiate these substitutions God need only send to Everyman, grown fat at the expense of Everyone Else, his famished messenger, Dethe. God answers humanity's devotion to riches, in other words, by reasserting his alternate, anti-economy of deliverance, which is the same as worldly commerce, but true, because God traffics exclusively in blood. Heretofore humans have treated their money as the highest good; now they will be counted in the eyes of the Highest as *themselves* a form of currency: "Therfore I wyll, in all the haste, / Haue a rekenynge of euery mannes persone" (45–46). The body of the "persone" whom God would audit is actually, as it turns out, a *corpor*ation, its "soul" nothing more than the abstractions on a balance sheet. While Everyman's mind is in his money, his soul is in the "boke of counte" that he will carry with him to the grave (104). Confronted

---

29. Friedrich Nietzsche, *On the Genealogy of Morals* 2.8, trans. Walter Kaufmann (New York: Vintage, 1989). More recently, see Angenendt et al., "Counting Piety" (n. 22), esp. pp. 15–54.

by this traditional ledger (which he has trouble reading), Everyman finally learns what his riches really amount to: a negative asset. The more money he has on earth, the more penitential suffering he owes in heaven's economy of blood. Conversely, the more wealth he gives away on earth by means of his last will and testament, the more he will profit from Christ's own testamentary bequest. "Sell all you have and distribute unto the poor, and you shall have *treasure in heaven!*" (Mt 19:21; Mk 10:21; Lk 18:22). So counsels the divine "testator" (Heb. 9:17).

It takes awhile for Everyman to grasp the inverse relation. When first confronted by Dethe he imagines the best expedient would be to pay him off directly: "of my good wyl I gyue the, yf thou wyl be kynde" (121). This is not, however, the kind of payment unkind Dethe has been licensed to accept:

> Eueryman, it may not be, by no waye.
> I set not by golde, syluer, nor rychesse,
> Ne by pope / emperour / kynge / duke, ne prynces.
> For, and I wolde receyue gyftes grete,
> All the worlde I myght gete;
> But my custome is clene contrary. (124–29)

Were Dethe to accept monetary payments, he could "gete" the whole world; instead he refuses bribes of this sort, for which reason he is going to "gete" the whole world in another sense: its entire population from beggar to king will be his equal fodder. There is only one possible escape from this absolute dominion, only one possible asset that any man could offer in return for eternal life. Instead of his "good" (by which Everyman means "goods"), he must offer its "clene contrary" or mirror image: God's "Good" (which, as we know, means blood).

The play's blocking realizes the transition from good to Good with typical literalism: here the universal individual probably progresses from one side of life's stage, where Goods are heaped and impotent, to the other side, where Good Deeds lie—equally low and corrupted but capable of rejuvenation by a systematic undertaking of the sacraments.[30] In the wake of crucifixion, if humans want to enrich their store of Good Deeds, they need only "participate" physically in the divine bloodshed: "But rejoice, inasmuch as ye are partakers of Christ's sufferings!" (1 Pet. 4:13).

---

30. G. A. Lester, ed., *Three Late Medieval Morality Plays* (New York: Norton, 1981), p. xxix, proposes this staging and sees the conversion from Goods to Good as the "center" of the play, in all senses.

Toward this end Confession shows Everyman the scourge, whose "knottes" are "paynful and harde, within" (576), and explains that to endure a good whipping is to "remember thy Sauyour was scourged for the" (563). Recollection of Christ's suffering in the sacrament of penance is coded, so to speak, as the material act of re-membering Christ's agony in one's own limbs at a time when the higher cognitive faculties have given over the task of memorialization to the pursuit of cruder profits.[31] While money overtakes Everyman's oblivious mind, in other words, its opposite—Christ's blood—colonizes his body so as physically to re-mind him which sort of currency *really* counts. "Thus I bequeth you in the handes of our Sauyour," says Knowledge, handing him the whip:

> Now may you make your rekenynge sure.
> *Eueryman*: In the name of the Holy Trynyte,
> My body sore punysshed shall be:
> Take this, body, for the synne of the flesshe! (609–13)

Everyman becomes a bequest to Christ sufficient to satisfy his spiritual debt only when his blood and flesh have been baptized by self-flagellation and thereby transformed into a memorial for and species of Christ's "payment." As Everyman whips his body, every drop of blood, participating in Christ's suffering, replenishes his spiritual account. He becomes "partynere, / By the meanes of his passyon" (602–3) to that "ghostly treasure...raunsomer and redemer" (589), Christ. At last Everyman will have something far more effective than worldly wealth with which to barter down Dethe. Now that raw coin has been transformed to God's blood by way of the sacraments, the godhead is ready to bargain.

This transformation is paradoxically assured in advance, if also constantly jeopardized, because it would convert "Goods" into the one thing they already appear to be, "Good." In fact throughout the play the same term, "Good," serves in Everyman's vocabulary as both a substantive for his wealth—"my Good" (e.g., 121)—and the approbative modifier of the penitential "Good Dedes" that will save him when bedewed with the blood of Christ. For Everyman to find his way to heaven he has to moralize two meanings in this one Word. And to do that—to make sense of how commercial "good" could ever appear as its opposite, Good—Everyman turns, predictably, to the language of antichristian myth. In the dead

---

31. For the play's interest in memory, see David Mills, "The Theaters of *Everyman*," in *From Page to Performance: Essays in Early English Drama*, ed. John A. Alford (East Lansing: Michigan State University Press, 1995), pp. 127–49, specifically p. 143.

center of the play, when he finds himself equidistant between the two mirror poles of Good(s) and (the) Good, he dresses his money in all the old
satanic attributes—a false deceiver laying his traps for humanity, and none
more sinister than money's apparent *virtue.*

> O false Good! cursed thou be,
> Thou traytour to God, that hast deceyued me
> And caught me in thy snare! (451–53)

Of course money's ersatz show of goodness, though damnable in itself,
pictures as closely as any earthly representation ever can the invaluable
virtues of Christ. In thinking his goods were good, Everyman erred, but
he erred in exactly the right way. He fell into redemption's best enabling
condition, commerce, and his fall in this way testified from the beginning
to the play's happy end. Commerce is Everyman's *felix culpa.*

In the end Everyman actually succeeds, from one perspective, in buying
his way out of mortality, only he does it by giving his "thousande poundes"
not to Dethe but rather to a far more concrete entity: when he wills his
money away in preparation for the Eucharist, half is earmarked for alms;
"the other halfe styll shall remayne / In queth, to be retourned there it
ought to be" (701–2). In both cases where it ought to be bequeathed, one
gathers, is *to the church,*[32] ideally so that the church could redistribute these
goods on Everyman's behalf in return for providing him the sacraments
before death, and by extension, the sacraments' eternal benefits. There is
a reason the play mentions this exchange so obliquely; it is the same reason the Eucharist, which Everyman has effectively just bought, remains off
stage while in its place Knowledge delivers to the audience a mini-homily
against the sin of simony:

> Whan Iesu hanged on the crosse with grete smarte,
> There he gaue out of his blessyd herte
> The same sacrament, in grete tourment;
> He solde them not to vs, that Lorde omnipotent.
> Therfore Saynt Peter the apostell dothe saye
> That Iesus curse hath all they,
> Whiche God theyr Sauyor do by or sell,
> Or they for ony money do take or tell. (751–58)

My sense is that this polemical outburst against "synfull preestes" (759)
marks the final attempt of the play, not without desperation, to secure the

---

32. As noted in passing by Kolve, "*Everyman* and the Parable of the Talents" (n. 11), p. 332.

opposition of money and Christ's blood for a church that had come to depend as never before on a certain commensurability between them— whether in the Offertory, tithes, the trade in relics, Mass stipends, or the indulgence—such that payment to the church effectively constituted its most central rite.[33] The threat this posed of an absolute vendibility is the play's central crux, the real social contradiction to which it would provide the impossible symbolic resolution—impossible because at best the play could offer, as reconciliation, an image of the problem, which was the Mass itself. The dramatic solution of *Everyman* is *not* to offer it, to give, in place of this commercialized consecration, a denunciation of its wrongful performance, which it pointedly keeps in the wings.[34]

A similar denunciation occurs in *Jacke Uplande* and is noteworthy for its willingness to name the one disciple of Christ whom *Everyman* puts, along with the performance of Mass and the specific recipient of Everyman's wealth, under a kind of erasure: "Freer, when thou receivest a penie / for to say a masse," Jack points out,

> and if thou sellest Gods bodie, other [i.e., or] thy prayer;
> then it is very simonie,
> and art become a chapman worse than Judas,
> that sold it for thirtie pence.[35]

We find explicitly named here the one person to whom most belongs the epithet "traytor to God," which Everyman has transferred instead to his Goods— the one person, of crucial prominence elsewhere on the medieval stage,

33. On the Offertory, see the section of this chapter after next; on the Mass stipend, see Jungmann, *Mass of the Roman Rite* (n. 20), 2:14–25; Thomas N. Tentler, *Sin and Confession on the Eve of the Reformation* (Princeton: Princeton University Press, 1977), pp. 71–72; on the indulgence, Nikolaus Paulus, *Geschichte des Ablasses im Mittelalter vom Ursprunge bis zur Mitte des 14. Jahrhunderts*, 3 vols. (Paderborn: F. Schöningh, 1922–23). These monetary practices of the church were part and parcel of a larger historical shift toward a profit economy. For that, see Marc Bloch, *Feudal Society*, trans. L. A. Manyon (1961; repr., London: Routledge, 1989); R. S. Lopez, *The Commercial Revolution in the Middle Ages, 950–1350* (Cambridge: Cambridge University Press, 1976), and Lester K. Little, *Religious Poverty and the Profit Economy in Medieval Europe* (Ithaca: Cornell University Press, 1978).

34. Nicholas Maltman, "Meaning and Art in the Croxton *Play of the Sacrament*," *ELH* 41.2 (1974): 149–64, notes p. 159 the medieval convention whereby the words of absolution are not pronounced on stage. See also on this point Mary Philippa Coogan, *An Interpretation of the Moral Play, "Mankind"* (Washington, D.C.: Catholic University of America Press, 1947), pp. 15–16.

35. *Jacke Uplande*, quoted in Simmons, *Lay Folks Mass Book* (n. 18), p. 240. A more recent edition gives a different wording: see *Jack Upland*, in *Six Ecclesiastical Satires*, ed. James Dean (Kalamazoo: Medieval Institute Publications, Western Michigan University, 1991), pp. 127–28.

who makes the Mass and its offer of spiritual redemption possible in the first place through precisely what *Everyman* condemns: the sale of Christ. Where the play has tried to draw the starkest contrast between money and God, that is, it finds itself compelled to refigure and displace the "historical" fact that the sacrament flows from Christ's heart only after Christ's life has been sold by one of Antichrist's more notorious and consequential members, Judas Iscariot.

Judas Superstar

"Bludmoney" comes to English thanks to Miles Coverdale, though he himself did not, as it were, coin the term. That we owe to Martin Luther. We get it from him only because Coverdale could not actually read the original scriptures he was supposed to translate; his German though was solid, so he turned to Luther (among others) for help in creating what would become the first complete printed Bible in English (1535). As a consequence the translation shows throughout a penchant for the compound nouns of German idiom.[36] "Bludmoney" specifically derives from Luther's demotic *Blutgeld*, perhaps the finest fulfillment of Luther's own ambition to render the Bible in the language spoken by "the common man in the marketplace" (*Sendbrief vom Dolmetschen* [WA 30.2:637; *LW* 35:189]).

Much else in Coverdale's edition was borrowed from Tyndale, who had gone the way of his earlier Bible, was declared heretical, then likewise burned. Curiously Coverdale would come to amend Tyndale in places by setting aside his predecessor's acute sense of the Greek in favor of a direct translation from Luther's *German*, even though Tyndale himself had died for his Lutheran bias. Further purification was obviously in order, and in the case of "bludmoney," no major English Bible for the coming three centuries chose to promulgate Coverdale's second-order innovation. Yet it has become since the late nineteenth century a standard idiom and is listed today in the most recent, authoritative lexicon of New Testament Greek as the preferred rendering, should subsequent translators with a shaky command of the Koine find themselves like Coverdale at a complete loss for words when faced with Judas' antichristian purchase.[37]

36. David Daniell, *The Bible in English: Its History and Influence* (New Haven: Yale University Press, 2003), p. 181, notes the preponderance of Teutonic compounds in Coverdale's Bible but does not list among them "bludmoney."

37. *A Greek-English Lexicon of the New Testament and Other Early Christian Literature*, ed. Frederick William Danker, 3rd ed. (Chicago: University of Chicago Press, 2000), s.v. τιμή, p. 1005.

The original Greek means literally "price of blood" (*timē haimatos*) and occurs just once, in reference to the thirty silver pieces for which Judas handed over Christ (Mt 27:6). This more literal translation (standard in every sixteenth-century English Bible except Coverdale's) gives an especially clear picture of the way that Judas' wages strangely resemble God's preferred currency—the "pricey blood" (*timiōi haimati*) of Christ that scripture elsewhere *opposes* to pieces of silver (1 Pet. 1:18). The Latin of the Vulgate succeeded in preserving the linguistic proximity of these two diametric opponents, blood and money, by giving *pretium sanguinis* for Judas' blood money and *pretiosus sanguis* for Christ's. The proximity in Latin is so close that among the church Fathers and later schoolmen Judas' "price of blood" and Christ's "pricey blood" eventually became interchangeable[38]—or perhaps exchangeable, on the model of Judas' own salvific substitution. "The world," writes Ambrose, "is bought by Christ at the price of blood [*pretio sanguinis*]" (*Exp. Lucam* 10.96 [CCSL 14:373]). Presumably Ambrose is referring here to the quote unquote cost of salvation, what Innocent III would later describe as the "*inestimable* price of the blood of Jesus Christ [*inaestimabile pretium sanguinis*]" (PL 216:274B, 289B). But as Ambrose and Innocent both well knew, the sole scriptural instance of this phrase, "the price of blood," far from remaining "inestimable," explicitly stipulates the paltry figure of thirty silver pieces. Why then have both these authorities assigned to Christ's priceless blood the dismissive epithet that Jewish priests gave to Judas' finite asking price?

It would seem that God's grace can exceed all possible estimation only if some estimate has first been made, then magnificently surpassed. Without this disgraceful "price of blood," what has no possible equivalent on account of its otherworldly magnitude might equal a void. The scanty number of Judas' coins, as an especially *inadequate* representation of Christ's true worth, could illustrate his unfathomable value better than some closer approximation—say, "infinite riches"—because their inadequacy

---

38. See for a few noteworthy examples (by no means all of them) Jerome, *Comm. in Matt.* 4.27.6 (SC 259:276); Augustine, *In Joh.* 13.16 (PL 35:1500), *Serm.* 5.2 (PL 38:54; WSA III/1:217), *Serm.* 71.2.4 (PL 38:446; WSA III/3:248), *De catechizandis rudibus* 1.14.21 (CCSL 46:145; trans. Joseph P. Christopher [Westminster, Md.: Newman Bookshop, 1952], p. 47), and *Contra ep. Parm.* 1.7.12 (PL 43:42); Bruno the Carthusian, *Exp. in Rom.* 3.23 (PL 153:41A) and *Exp. in Cor.* 1.91 (PL 153:132A); Peter Lombard, *Comm. in Ps.*, Ps 26:11 (PL 191:266A) and Ps 61:14 (664A–B and passim); Gerhoch of Reicherberg (quoting honorius augustodunensis), *Comm. aur. in Ps. et Cant.*, pars tertia, on Ps 33:23 (PL 193:1334C), though the phrase "pretio sanguinis" is omitted from the text in *Opera inedita*, ed. Damiani ac Odulphi van den Eynde and Angelini Rijmersdael (Rome: Apud Ponificium Athenaeum Antonianum, 1956), 2:305.

invited radical supplementation in a way that grander comparisons did not. One could therefore affirm the sickening equation of the thirty silver pieces so as to shadow forth, in the appalling inappropriateness of the affirmation, Christ's overwhelming worth: "He *ought* to be compared to such a price!" says a sarcastic sermon dubiously ascribed to Augustine, "—he, whom nothing can equal!" (*Serm.* 150.3 [PL 39:2038]). The more outrageously meager the commercial price, the more clearly Christ's passion could transcend all commerce. Hence the appropriate impropriety or double applicability of *pretium sanguinis* in the Latin tradition to *both* Judas' pathetically finite "price of blood" *and* the infinite value of Christ's pricey suffering. Latin theologians following Ambrose could speak of these together in the same breath, using the same *phrase* even, because at this one scriptural node the finite and the infinite had made impossible, ironic contact. The sale of Christ marked the point where the divine had touched the earthly world as a tangent glances off a sphere—which is to say, without entering into it. Judas' "price of blood," standing on the outer perimeter of worldly exchange, by means of this extremity could indicate some purer, spiritual traffic *external* to all known trade.

Thus its beauty. Here the "representational" function of money, its implicit adequacy to whatever it buys, openly crosses over into an aesthetic discourse, for example, when Zechariah specifically prophesies these thirty silver pieces as a "beautiful" or, in Wyclif's double entendre, a "fair price" (*decorum pretium* [11:13]). Presumably the thirty silver pieces are "fair" because they serve to express an otherworldly love that without fiscal impropriety could have no earthly utterance, but this took some explaining, given the ugly unfairness of Christ's sale and death. Zechariah "doubtless calls the price beautiful with the heaviest irony," says Rupert of Deutz, "since it is not beautiful. Who exactly would be strong enough to weigh a thing of this kind or express it worthily?" (*In Zach.* 4.11 [PL 168:788B]).[39] Who indeed but God's own prophet, speaking in God's voice? The word "beautiful," as drastically insufficient as the thirty silver pieces it predicates when compared with the "worth" of the sacrifice that the price pretends to match, conveys that worth nonetheless so long as it is read *negatively*, that is, with "heaviest irony." Such irony itself then covertly expresses an otherwise inexpressible beauty. If the innocent Christ had not been betrayed for

---

39. Cf. Jerome, *Comm. in Zach.* 3.11.12–13 (CCSL 76a:857), for whom the "beauty" of the price is an instance of God's derisive pantomime: "hoc autem pressius est legendum cum irrisione et subsannatione dicentis." See also Luther: "This is irony. He is saying, as it were... 'Is it not a beautiful sum, for which he buys me?'" (*Praelect. in proph. minores,* Sacharja 11:13 [WA 13:650; *LW* 20:124]).

this "beautiful sum," if he had not been obscenely reduced to a market price and unjustly condemned, the divine justice could not have accepted his life as payment on behalf of humankind when no possible money could ever suffice *except* blood money. "Ironically" the thirty silver pieces are the *most* beautiful sum, the sum of all sums, though their (in)ability to encapsulate the whole worth of the godhead automatically appears, within the confines of this backwards world, as a monstrous, antichristian impropriety. Without glorious monstrosity of this sort a transcendent godhead could never appear or intervene in human affairs at all;[40] that is the secret of God's aesthetics, the artful mode of divine self-expression made manifest in history. His beauty incorporates even the greatest ugliness.

"Then the Lord said to me," Zechariah says of his thirty shekels of silver, "'Caste it awei to a makere of ymagis'" (Wyclif) or rather "to the statuarie" (Douai-Rheims), or as all the other sixteenth-century versions have, "unto the potter," which is what the Hebrew says. At least in some manuscripts. Others, differing by a single letter, say "treasury" instead, and the discrepancy may ultimately explain, in a way no longer available to us, the fate of Judas' blood money in Matthew's account, where the thirty silver pieces, cast at the feet of the priests, are then withheld from the "treasury" and go instead to buy the potter's field.[41] And so was fulfilled, Matthew explains, "that which was spoken by the prophet...Jeremiah" (Mt 27:9). Jeremiah! Perhaps, opined the Geneva commentators, the misattribution was the "printers fault" (ibid.; 1587, side note e). Obviously he meant Zechariah. In any event, his point was secure regardless of the prophecy's specific wording or source, and it was the same point made by every Christian typologist when faced with the apparent incoherence or savagery or stupidity or outright fictiveness of scripture, namely, that the appearance of godlessness could indicate the hand of God at work insofar as such appearances had been foretold by prophecies (or prophetic events) which, at the time, looked equally absurd. As we've seen, typological hermeneutics had been almost explicitly designed to sublate the apparent crudities of sacred history into the fulfillment of a prior and greater prophetic emptiness, so that everything worked to the good no matter how awful or vain events like the sale and subsequent death of God might seem on their surface, much less the random detail thereafter about the purchase of the potter's field. Or rather, all this was *only* surface, and surface indicates depth, like two mirrors' infinite regress: the New facing

---

40. On sacred monstrosity, see above, pp. 64–65.

41. See Carol L. Meyers and Eric M. Meyers, *Zechariah 9–14: A New Translation with Introduction and Commentary*, AB 25c (New York: Doubleday, 1993), pp. 277–78.

the Old, marvelously flat, but for all that capturing between them an un-ending visual stretch. Judas' treachery was *more* than treachery because it repeated typologically an earlier, historical betrayal and so demonstrated that some divine principle had structurally orchestrated the whole narra-tive toward a meaningful end—an end that would be made all the more harmonious by such momentary dissonance. Judah, too, had tellingly conspired with his brothers to sell Joseph into slavery (Gen. 37:26–28); did this not contribute to their later rescue from famine, when, though a slave, Joseph counseled the pharaoh to husband the resources of Egypt? Had not Joseph's fate prefigured the world's coming salvation from sin *through the workings of sin itself?*[42]

"Consider the usefulness of heretics," Augustine more than once urged his congregants; "their usefulness, that is, with respect to the designs of God, who makes a good use even of people who are bad....Just as with Judas; what great good he did! By the Lord's passion all nations are saved!" (*Serm.* 51.11).[43] Augustine's exaltation of Judas exemplifies his apprecia-tion for heretics for two reasons: first, because Judas' "heresy" established the church and second, because Augustine's enthusiastic acknowledgment of that fact puts to new use an old heretical argument. According to some earlier groups known as Iscariots or Cainites, Judas did indeed deserve our utmost thanks. By the Lord's passion all nations are saved! Judas was the

---

42. "In the patriarch Joseph was a type of Christ," wrote Ambrose. "Joseph was sold, Jesus Christ was bought; the one to slavery, the other to die" (*De spirit.* 3.17.123–24 [PL 16:608A; trans. Roy J. Deferrari, FC 44:198]). Many others adopt this typology, and Ambrose himself expanded on it greatly elsewhere (see the end of this note). Jerome, *Comm. in Matt.* 4.26.16 (PL 26:200C), stresses that the Septuagint got the kind of coin wrong, and that according to the "true Hebrew" Joseph had actually been sold for twenty silver pieces not twenty pieces of gold, "since it would not be possible for a servant to be more costly than the Lord." Repeated by Rabanus Maurus, *Comm. in Matt.* 8.26.3 (PL 107:1102D); Paschasius Radbertus, *Exp. in Matt.* 7.26 (PL 120:885D); Zacharias Chrysopolitanus, *De concordia evan-gelistarum* 4.153 (PL 186:493A). See also Gregory the Great's brief remark that Joseph's be-ing sold figured the sale of Jesus (*XL hom. in ev.* 29.6 [PL 76:1217A]), included by Aquinas in the *Catena aurea*, trans. M. F. Toal as *The Sunday Sermons of the Great Fathers*, 4 vols. (San Francisco: Ignatius Press, 2000), 2:429; and Rupert of Deutz, *In opus de gloria et honore filii hominis* 10 (PL 168:1539ff.). Luz suggests that the typological reading might explain why in a Christian addition to the *Testament of Gad* (2.3), which deals with the sale of Joseph, the price has been raised from twenty to thirty shekels (3:347 n. 27). Ambrose explains all the discrepancies as follows: "Therefore we find that Joseph was bought for twenty gold pieces by one account, for twenty-five by another, and thirty by another, because Christ is not valued at the same price by all men. To some he is worth less, to others more. The faith of the buyer determines the increase in price" (*De Jos.* 3.14 [PL 14:678C; trans. McHugh, FC 65:196–97]).

43. Original in *Revue Bénédictine* 91 (1981): 23–45; here 29–30; also in PL 38:339, though punctuated as a question rather than an exclamation. Trans. WSA III/3:26.

mastermind who arranged this. They even had a *Gospel of Judas* as proof of his righteousness.[44] Though it was lost until quite recently, something of that gospel's bias had already filtered into the canonical Bible: Judas alone of the disciples belongs to the tribe of Judah and descends from David as the messiah was supposed to according to prophecy and as Jesus strangely does not, on account of his bizarrely mixed paternity (Mt 2:6). Jesus himself goes to some lengths to single Judas out among the Twelve as of special significance, and none but Judas was permitted a kiss. Jesus may have trusted Peter to act as a foundation for his church, but to Judas he entrusted something far more important—its treasury (Jn 12:7, 13:29).[45] Given scripture's predilection for fiscal terminology when representing the mechanics of redemption, this special association between Judas and money seems in its way to figure Judas as the more consequential, though secret, champion of grace.

And sure enough, according to the Iscariots, Judas "alone grasped the truth," then acted on his inspired knowledge and "completed the mystery of betrayal."[46] Judas, they allegedly said, understood that Jesus was a complete fraud—in effect, an Antichrist—who "wanted to subvert the truth" and was betrayed by Judas for that reason, "so that the truth could not be subverted."[47] Or alternately, others of the sect were said to have proposed, if Jesus really was the redeemer, born to die, then Judas realized that the worldly authorities would have preferred nothing better than to *prevent* the crucifixion and thereby thwart humanity's salvation. In the latter case Judas outfoxed them by selling Jesus directly to the high priests, "so that salvation through the suffering of Christ could not be delayed" (op. cit.). Either way Judas stood at the center of salvation's labyrinth; it was he who held the keys, he who ensured, where Jesus could not, that humanity would have a chance at surviving death. He acted, so to speak, as the messiah's messiah.

Those advocating the deification of Judas lost out in the end, but their defeat could be secured only by incorporating their interpretation into a new orthodoxy. Augustine's later, countervailing exaltation of Judas of course no longer directly promotes the idea that he deserves the reverence

---

44. See *The Gospel of Judas: From Codex Tchacos*, ed. Rodolphe Kasser et al. (Washington, D.C.: National Geographic Society, 2006).

45. Cf. Erasmus, *Paraphrase on John*, trans. Jane E. Phillips (Toronto: University of Toronto Press, 1991), pp. 164–65: "Jesus...seemed in some fashion to prefer [Judas] to the others (since the common cash-box had been entrusted to him)."

46. Irenaeus, *Adv. haer* 1.31.1 (SC 264:386; ANF 5:102). Discussed by Hans-Josef Klauck, *Judas—ein Jünger des Herrn* (Freiburg: Herder, 1987), pp. 19–20.

47. Pseudo-Tertullian, *Adv. omn. haer.* 2.6 (CCSL 1²:1404; ANF 3:651).

due to Jesus, but, more complexly, that Judas earned with his betrayal a necessary yet limited and ironic appreciation as the tainted, economic instrument of humanity's spiritual deliverance. As a matter of fact, the same bizarre sanctification that slowly accrued over the course of the Middle Ages to the wood of the cross, the nails, the side-piercing spear, and other instruments of Christ's torture (the so-called *arma Christi*) accrued also to the head and lips of Judas.[48] Anyone who wanted a theological explanation for this hugely negative form of piety could find a good one in Augustine:

> If we consider only the action of handing Christ over [*traditio Christi*]... Judas did the same thing as God the Father; for of the Father it is written that *he did not spare even his own Son, but handed him over [tradidit] for us all* [Rom. 8:32]. Judas also did the same things as Christ our Lord did himself, for of Christ it is written that *he loved us, and handed himself over [tradidit] for us as an offering and sacrifice to God for a sweet fragrance*, and again *Christ loved the church, and handed himself over [tradidit] for her* [Eph. 5:2, 25]. And yet we give thanks to God the Father...we give thanks to the Son...but we loathe Judas, through whose act God has bestowed on us so great a gift (*Enn. in Ps.* 93.28, v. 23 [CCSL 39:1328; *WSA* III/18:406]).[49]

The precise "act" committed by this unexpected Trinity—God, Jesus, and Judas—entails some major complications in translation, especially since Augustine is mainly quoting from scripture. The convention in English has always been to render the biblical verb as "betray" whenever it has

48. For the lips of Judas included in medieval reliquaries, see Arnold Angenendt, *Heilige und Reliquien: Die Geschichte ihres Kultes vom frühen Christentum bis zur Gegenwart* (Munich: Beck, 1994), pp. 215–16. For other devotional objects named after Judas, such as the so-called Judas candle, "a wooden imitation of a candle used at Easter to support the true paschal candle," see Wayland D. Hand, *A Dictionary of Words and Idioms Associated with Judas Iscariot: A Compilation Based Mainly on Material Found in Germanic Languages* (Berkeley: University of California Press, 1942), p. 321; cf. "Judas cross" and "Judas cup" (323). For a theological justification of the veneration paid to the *arma Christi*, see John of Damascus, *De imag. orat.* 2.19: "If I venerate and reverence, as the cause of my salvation, the cross and the lance and the reed and the sponge, with which the deicide Jews insulted my Lord and killed him, shall I not venerate the images of the sufferings of Christ?" (PG 94:1305A–B); trans. Andrew Louth, *Three Treatises on the Divine Images* (Crestwood, N.Y.: St. Vladimir's Seminary Press, 2003), p. 75. Cf. 3.34.

49. See also *Tract. in Joh.* 61–62 (CCSL 36:480–85; trans. John W. Rettig, FC 90:33–41). And cf. the seminal, if problematic, analysis of Karl Barth, *Church Dogmatics*, ed. G. W. Bromiley and T. F. Torrance, 4 vols. (Edinburgh: T & T Clark, 1960–61), 2.2:501: "The more profoundly and comprehensively we attempt to formulate the sin and guilt of Judas, the more nearly his will and deed approach what neither he himself willed and did...—the more nearly his will and deed approach what God willed and did in this matter, the divine handing-over which here took place."

Judas as the subject but "hand over" or "deliver" when God or Christ is the agent; *tradere*, after all, can mean either. Yet Augustine pointedly refuses in this passage to make any differentiation between the actions of Judas and God as worded by scripture, and most English Bibles in any case claim to be translating not from Latin but from Greek, which calls Judas a "betrayer" just once (Lk 6:16; *prodotēs*). According to the Greek *verb* that Luke and the other evangelists invariably use for his action, however, he never "betrays" anyone. Rather, he does the same thing as God the Father: he "delivers" (*paradidomi*).[50] The Greek in other words upholds Augustine's insistence that Judas, though a "betrayer," ultimately accomplishes with his actions something other than betrayal, if something which nonetheless *requires* for its completion this act of treachery. That requirement only comes more into the foreground when the Greek is translated into Augustine's Latin: now, on account of the verb *tradere* (which means "to betray" as much as "hand over"), even the actions of *God* imply a necessary iniquity; he too, in the Vulgate, could be said to have "betrayed" (*tradidit*) his own son. In the final sentence quoted from Augustine above, one sees how Judas answers for this iniquity, so that God may be thanked. The Latin Judas, in a passage like this, atones for Christ's double-cross.

Arguably the "handing over" or "betrayal" of Christ (*traditio*) provides the archetypal model for the whole of Christian *tradition* as ritually constituted by the Latin Mass for subsequent generations. No less an authority than Paul teaches the real followers of Jesus (in contradistinction to Paul's opponents) to legitimate the Christian community by *repeating* what happened to Christ. I am going to capitalize on the full versatility of the Latin in the following translation in order to show just how closely intertwined in the Middle Ages were meanings that we now tend to separate: "For I have received from the Lord," writes Paul (of the Vulgate), "that which also I delivered [*tradidi*] to you, that the Lord Jesus, the same night in which he was betrayed [*tradebatur*], took bread: and when he had given thanks, he broke it, and said, Take, eat: this is my body, which will be handed over for you [*tradetur*]" (1 Cor. 11:23–24). Post-Reformation readers have been fixated on the words "this is my body," but the real curiosity

---

50. See William Klassen, *Judas: Betrayer or Friend of Jesus?* (Minneapolis: Fortress, 1996), pp. 22–23, 41–61. According to him, "Not one ancient Greek text has so far surfaced in which παραδίδωμι (paradidomi) means 'betray' or has the connotation of treachery" (p. 46). A more comprehensive discussion of the verbs used for "handing over" in biblical literature is Wiard Popkes, *Christus Traditus: Eine Untersuchung zum Begriff der Dahingabe im Neuen Testament* (Zürich: Zwingli Verlag, 1967).

is the clause that follows, which has no known Greek parallel.[51] It is as though the word *tradere* exerted so irresistible a pull on Latin copyists and commentators that they could not help but insert it into Paul's account of the earliest Mass. Paul then hands down what Judas handed over: the betrayal of their mutual master. As we'll see in the final chapter, Paul was also devoted to destroying Christ's sect but then likewise conformed to its cause despite himself. How fitting to see him here advocate (in Latin) the continual iteration of Christ's persecution by authorities and intimates alike as the most certain means of establishing and communicating the heart of Christian "tradition." In this passage the transmission of Christ's message—which is to say, of the crucified Christ himself, since that *is* the message (cf. 1 Cor. 2:2)—takes Judas' betrayal for its paradigm on the irrefragable theologico-linguistic grounds that his betrayal was no more perfidious, ultimately, than Christ's death was absolutely terminal; these calamities are just the prelude to deliverance.

This of course could only make Judas seem all the more devoted a Christian, were it not for the repeated assertions in scripture that he was in fact a "devil" (Jn 6:70); or possessed (Lk 22:3; Jn 13:1, 27); or worse, a member of Antichrist, with whom he shares the epithet "son of perdition" (Jn 17:12; 2 Thess. 2:3).[52] Judas' apparent preeminence among the other disciples and his initial shows of piety made him like Lucifer in the circle of God's angelic supporters: first among equals and therefore the first to fall by becoming too godlike, yet likewise in his fall securing, happily, the full aftereffect of the Incarnation—namely, human redemption. Once again a member of Antichrist seems good precisely where he most opposes

51. The Greek ms. tradition produces several variants of Christ's words as reported by Paul here—just not the one adopted by the Vulgate. The original wording was probably "this is my body for you," but then the awkwardness of "body for you" (τὸ σῶμα τὸ ὑπὲρ ὑμῶν) led to the addition of various participial phrases: *which is broken* for you (κλώμενον, θρυπτόμενον) or, through assimilation of Lk 22:19, *which is given* for you (διδόμενον). See *TC* 496. The variants in the Latin tradition, by contrast, frequently involve some version of *tradere*: "my body, which will be handed over for you," "which I will hand over," and so on. The full range can be seen on-line: *Vetus Latina Database* (Turnout: Brepols, 2002).

52. The link between Judas and Antichrist is further developed among the Fathers: see, for example, Ambrose, *De patriarchis* 7.32–34 (PL 14:717C–18C; trans. Michael P. McHugh, FC 65:260–1); Gregory the Great, *Moralia* 29.7.15, on Job 38:15 (CCSL 143b:1443; trans. J. Bliss [Oxford, 1844–50], 3^1:311); for some medieval instances, see the remark attributed to Bede (PL 93:754D), plus the interesting commentary of Archbishop Hincmar of Rheims (845–882), *De praedestinatione dissertatio posterior* (PL 125:432C), who at one point calls him "Judas Antichrist" (ibid.; 463C), and Bruno Astensis, *Exp. in Apocal.* 2.7 (PL 165:642C). On the iconographic association of Judas with Satan and its relation to drama, see Patrick J. Collins, *The N-Town Plays and Medieval Picture Cycles* (Kalamazoo: Medieval Institute Publications, Western Michigan University, 1979), p. 13.

God, even if that opposed likeness in the last instance actually does represent the will of God. You have to understand that the devotion enacted by Judas "represents" Christian obedience the way paintings represent a subject: by not being it.

Better yet, Judas' loyalty to Christ is "just an act" in the strictly theatrical sense, which presupposes the formal absence of genuine action, lest drama dissolve the one element—representation—through which alone it differentiates itself from the normal and unredeemed course of events. Medieval drama—itself a simulacrum with a tenuous connection to the higher themes that it hoped to duplicate—obviously profited from mounting the spectacle of God's own willingness to use even the most sinister feigning as a temporary means to his timeless ends. On stage Judas' deception, like that of his contemporary stage villain Antichrist, was a way of inscribing within the theater the hopeful promise of its own dissimulation. Judas' historic role in human salvation especially conveyed the potential of theater since his fake devotion had greater and better consequences than the other disciples' authentic belief. Just as Antichrist does unwitting, aesthetic homage to the one he precedes by staging him in advance of his coming and acting therefore as the ironic guarantor of his arrival, so too had Judas' imitation of loyalty to Christ kept faith with the divine mission by means of his *inauthenticity*, his *feigned* discipleship. With Judas before them, audiences had a cheating villain in whom to delight was a form of dialectical reverence already well established by higher church authorities. What great good Judas did! In projecting a false image of piety Judas inadvertently produced a form of dissimulation that spoke more *truly* than his actual, debased motives or the others' comparatively impotent loyalty. Judas's intrigue could for that reason win an audience's enthusiasm and applause even while officially receiving their hatred and "horror." To disapprove and enjoy in this case were one and the same. To feel mortified was to be thoroughly gratified.

The playwrights cultivated Judas' appeal by having him literally appeal to the audience in his own direct speech, a formal device that would later become a mainstay among the dissembling villains of the commercial stage.[53] In all the cycles Judas comes forward to plot revenge and openly explains the discrepancy between his pious appearance and real

53. *York Mystery Plays*, ed. Richard Beadle and Pamela King (Oxford: Oxford University Press, 1984), p. 125, describes Judas as "a very early example of a familiar type of English stage villain." A number of Shakespeareans take Judas as an early example of the tragic *hero*, whether villainous or not. See, for example and further citations, Roy W. Battenhouse, *Shakespearean Tragedy: Its Art and Its Christian Premises* (Bloomington: Indiana University

intentions: "Now cowntyrfetyd I haue a prevy treson."[54] The distance between the counterfeit of discipleship and the reality of betrayal provided
an objective correlative for the appalled approval his speech could inspire among audience members, and automatically did, to the extent that
they could not help but look forward, in the literal sense, to the moment
of betrayal toward which the whole cycle was ineluctably hurtling; if they
wanted, they could look forward to it in a more figurative and problematic sense, too, because Judas' betrayal of Christ was going to wind up
fulfilling his otherwise empty loyalty. The betrayal *realizes*, for once, his
pretended devotion. Judas gives voice to that Mephistophelean spirit who
always negates, who even while trying for evil invariably accomplishes the
good; through whose *persona* and his human No, God ventriloquizes the
divine Yes.

In the cycles, the primary act of counterfeit that Judas had to explain,
besides his ostensible loyalty to Christ, was his show of solidarity for the
poor when Christ allowed his body to be anointed by Mary with lavish oils
in the house of Simon:

> I sayd it was worthy to sell
> Thre hundreth pens in oure present,
> For to parte poore men emell [to divide among poor men];
> Bot will ye se wherby I ment? (Towneley 20.294–97)

Everybody already knew exactly what Judas, an icon for clandestine
greed, had "ment" when he tried to one-up Christ with his more-
charitable-than-thou posturing vis-à-vis the poor. But this somewhat
redundant explanation nonetheless cultivates the kind of suspense that
occurs, as it were, in messianic time, where the coming is assured but,
since always delayed, always in need of further proclaiming. Naturally a
person was supposed to loathe Judas' deception in this matter, but you
could crave to hear the actor's reprise of his scheming again this year,
because Judas' antics were, as everybody knew, all to the good and worth

---

Press, 1969), pp. 94–102, 226–27. Both Marlowe and Shakespeare might have seen Judas
on stage firsthand; there are payments for instruments involved with his hanging as late as
1578: see R. W. Ingram, ed., *Coventry*, Records of Early English Drama (REED) (Toronto:
University of Toronto Press, 1981), p. 289. For more about the influence of Judas on later
drama, see Sybil Truchet, *Le théâtre médiéval en Angleterre et son influence sur l'œuvre de Marlowe,
Kyd et Lyly: Contribution à l'étude du drama pré-Shakespearien*, 2 vols. (Lille: Atelier reproduction des thèses, Université de Lille III, 1980), 1:139–54, 276, 280.
54. *The N-Town Play: Cotton MS Vespasian D.8*, ed. Stephen Spector, EETS s.s. 11–12,
(Oxford: Oxford University Press, 1991), 1:274 (play 27, line 269).

longing for. After all, Judas saw to it that the ultimate spiritual wealth *could be* shared among poor men—in the form of Christ's betrayed and broken body, though this result was not what Judas "ment" when he merely *pretended* to act on behalf of the poor; he had in fact a purpose wholly at odds with his projected image of piety, but the counterfeit spoke more truly than the reality of Judas' personal intent; thus the other great pleasure of his "confession" to the audience: it confesses more than he knows.

> The tent parte, truly to tell,
> To take to me was myne intent,
> For of the tresure that to vs fell,
> The tent parte euer with me went;
> And if iii hundreth be right told,
> The tent parte is euen thryrty;
> Right so he shal be sold;
> Say if ye will hym by. (*Towneley* 20.298–305)

What Judas intends to do by selling Christ, we learn here and in the other cycles (cf. *York* 26.127ff.; *Chester* 14.289–96), is to recoup his customary share of the money given for poor relief. According to a widespread medieval legend, it had been Judas' custom while managing the treasury to withhold exactly 10 percent of the disciples' overall take, like a private tithe to the church of himself. He feels entitled to thirty of the three hundred denarii that Mary spent on oils because this is what he would have received had she donated it to the poor box rather than wasting it on Christ. To recover his losses, Judas wants to sell Christ for exactly that amount. Thus the notorious thirty silver pieces, with their collateral, negative capacity to "illustrate" for once the ever elusive worth of Christ.

Here in Towneley, Pilate and the high priests remain on stage while Judas talks (they have explicitly asked him why he intends to sell Christ, and this is his response), but he almost certainly directs his words to the audience, as he clearly does in the other cycles where a version of this speech occurs as a soliloquy. What's unique in Towneley is the brief impression at the very end that Judas might be trying to sell Christ *to the audience.* "Right so he shalbe sold; / Say if ye will hym by." Officially the "ye" in question addresses Pilate and the priests, but if he has just spent the last however many lines talking to the audience in front of him, they might well have felt partially included in his final sales pitch. Surely no one in the audience volunteered to take him up on his offer, but the moment could have been a dramatic and tense one, because so tempting. If it was possible to hate Judas but to cheer for him all the same, could you not offer up a handful of filthy lucre in the hope of seeing it transmogrified on stage, during the coming scenes of bloody sacrifice, into something far more valuable and ultimately beyond any possible purchase outside this theatrical transfer? That transformation seemed to happen all the time when the Offertory procession at Mass preceded transubstantiation, so why not here preceding the theatrical spectacle of the passion? Why not here above all, where the whole operation, the gigantic and unfathomable mechanics of salvation, could finally be grasped as the highest and truest effect of Christianity's own inherent commercial aesthetic?

The Offertory as Price of Admission

The semi-liturgical donations by means of which the earliest congregations supplied their Mass with its necessary stage props soon generated more property than was strictly requisite.[55] Once Christians began to call the bread and wine "oblations" and to see in them a way of participating, more or less directly, in Christ's own sacrificial offering, they laid at the altar more provisions than they could consume of his body and blood. Certain people improved on bread and wine, bringing grapes in season, vinegar, birds, flowers, honey, milk, ears of wheat, vegetables, lamp oil, candles, incense, plus deeds of ownership for the expedient contribution of immovables. Some of this could be used in the service. The rest was in places repeatedly banned from the altar, but given the repetition of regulative decrees, apparently you could not keep these people down. At some point their supererogation took on a monetary function: from the leftover surplus of goods the priests culled a share in payment for their service while the rest went to the poor in alms. By the eleventh century, elaborate church-run operations were responsible for fashioning the host from unleavened dough according to a variety of technical requirements and so obviated the pretense that commoners could offer donations in kind. Now in place of the traditional bread and wine, "pregnant signs" of Christ's sacrifice, people offered hard cash.[56] Their hope was that this, too, could be made acceptable to God through some special

55. For the history of the Offertory, see Jungmann, *Mass of the Roman Rite* (n. 20), 2:1–26; Rupert Berger, *Die Wendung "Offerre Pro" in der römischen Liturgie* (Münster: Aschendorff, 1965), pp. 48ff.; Theodor Klauser, *A Short History of the Western Liturgy: An Account and Some Reflections*, trans. John Halliburton, 2nd ed. (Oxford: Oxford University Press, 1979), pp. 8, 65, 109–13; Dom Gregory Dix, *The Shape of the Liturgy* (Westminster: Dacre Press, 1945), pp. 110–25, and on the Anglican reforms, pp. 660–62; for the medieval English version(s), see Simmons, *Lay Folks Mass Book* (n. 18), pp. 228–44.

56. Giving bread and wine survived only on special occasions: see Jungmann, *Mass of the Roman Rite* (n. 20), 2:11–12; Simmons, *Lay Folks Mass Book* (n. 18), pp. 232 and 237–39.

transmogrification akin to consecration, an expectation encouraged by what had replaced the traditional bread loaf: the new wafers were not baked so much as minted, pressed into the shape of coins by the curiously named "singing irons." Especially once the real presence became official dogma, the Offertory and then the Mass stipends that superseded it save for great feast days must have seemed to require only a few further transmutations: instead of giving a loaf of bread to be directly changed in substance through the ordained agency of the priest, you gave the coins that through the de facto mystery of market exchange would be transformed at the moment of purchase first to flour, then through the laborious application of a special instrument into a coin-shaped wafer, then finally to God at the moment of consecration.[57]

For people excluded from consuming the body, the Offertory would be the only participation they were allowed in this central symbol—that and their ability to gaze on the bread when elevated during a quasi-theatrical moment that was likewise "marked," as Miri Rubin describes it, "with the stamp of an exchange. Petitions and requests were made at the elevation in a pandemonium of vernacular prayers and salutations, exchanging faith and acceptance of the host as God, for a large variety of benefits."[58] All along the figure of Judas was there to clarify how the increasingly bald commerce of the Mass furthered rather than maimed its divine purpose; or better, how divine purposes, maimed by commerce, were in that way best served. The *Lay Folks Mass Book*, for example, describes the Elevation much the way Rubin does, only in rhyme, and stressing, in place of "pandemonium," one demon in particular:

> And so þo leuacioun þou be-halde,
> for þat is he þat iudas salde.[59]

57. A point already made by E. C. R. Lamburn, *Behind Rite and Ceremony: An Historical Survey of Their Development in the English Church* (London: W. Knott & Son, 1961), p. 57, who is at pains to prevent the common "misapprehension," however, that people in the Offertory are paying off God.

58. Miri Rubin, *Corpus Christi: The Eucharist in Late Medieval Culture* (Cambridge: Cambridge University Press, 1991), p. 155. For more on the Elevation, as well as processions and their stress on visual participation (if not outright theatricality), see Charles Zika, "Hosts, Processions, and Pilgrimages: Controlling the Sacred in Fifteenth-Century Germany," *Past and Present* 118 (1998): 25–64, and Edouard Dumoutet, *Le désir de voir l'hostie et les origines de la dévotion au Saint-Sacrament* (Paris: Gabriel Beauchesne, 1926).

59. Simmons, *Lay Folks Mass Book* (n. 18), p. 38 (B-text). Cf. the earliest surviving Middle English ballad (thirteenth century), where Christ sends Judas on Holy Thursday to shop for the Last Supper: "Iudas, þou most to Iurselem, oure mete for to bugge [buy]" (line 3); text in *Fourteenth-Century Verse and Prose*, ed. Kenneth Sisam (Oxford: Clarendon Press, 1937), pp. 168–69. Why do you not eat? Christ asks his disciples at the ballad's conclusion, for "ic am iboust [bought] ant isold today for oure mete" (line 26).

Here in the Mass you could behold Christ only because Judas had sold
Christ. His exchange and your exchange through some divine mystery appeared united for an instant in the coin-like host. Honorius Augustodunensis—an enormously influential twelfth-century scholar with early ties
to Anselm's circle in Canterbury though later flourishing in Germany[60]—
explains that "the bread is shaped like a coin, because the bread of life,
Christ, was betrayed [*tradebatur*] in exchange for coins and is the true
coin that will be given in recompense to those laboring in the vineyard"
(*Gemma animae* 1.35 [PL 172:555; cf. 564D]). Judas' radically uneven exchange, in other words, both prefigured and made possible humanity's
acquisition of a heavenly reward in huge disproportion to their actual des-
erts; his greed, memorialized in the Mass by the shape of the host, functions in this reenactment as a negative presentment of the divine *charitas*
operative in heaven's wholly opposed but intimately related economic
system. Neither a real coin nor the unmediated presence of Christ's flesh
but rather a mimetic fiction for both, the host held two worlds together
in momentary reconciliation; and in this reconciliation—imaginary, un-
constrained by actuality, for that reason more potentially real than what
occurred outside the conjurer's circle of churchly ritual—a communi-
cant could glimpse how Judas' historical blood money made possible an
extrahistorical, eschatological reward that would be *eventually* given but
had not been delivered in its entirety yet and till then could not appear
more fully than in the refiguration of Christ's sacrifice: "Thus the image of
the Lord," Honorius further explains, "is pressed with letters in this bread,
since the image and name of the emperor is also written on a coin" (ibid.).
This monetary "image"—sometimes, as here, Christ's initials "pressed with
letters," sometimes the cross or more ornate emblems[61]—was maybe the
most significant of all God's "appearances," for through it "the image of
God is restored in us and our name marked down in the book of life"
(ibid.).[62] Through it, that is, we may achieve the welcome and eternal status of pure signature, returned once again to the prelapsarian state of a
total and pristine image, if only we ingest—visually, for most of us, and as

---

60. For a recent biography in English, see V. I. J. Flint, *Honorius Augustodunensis of Regensburg* (Brookfield, Vt.: Ashgate, 1995). Earlier works that I have consulted are Richard
W. Southern, *Saint Anselm and His Biographer: A Study of Monastic Life and Thought, 1059–
c. 1130* (Cambridge: Cambridge University Press, 1963), pp. 209–17; Joseph Anton Endres,
Honorius Augustodunensis: Beitrag zur Geschichte des geistigen Lebens im 12. Jahrhundert (Kemp-
ten: Verlag der Jos. Kösel'schen Buchhandlung, 1906).

61. See Jungmann, *Mass of the Roman Rite* (n. 20), 2:36–37.

62. Following Augustine, *Enn. in Ps.* 95.2 (CCSL 39:1332; *WSA* III/18:410–11).

an image—this small material husk, impressed with an empty and inverted figure of the divine Antitype.

As an "exegete of the hidden revelation,"[63] Honorius worked often enough with inversions of this sort in his writings on "Contrarius," a.k.a. the Antichrist. His widely read *Elucidarium* (a Latin catechism possibly written in England, eventually translated into Middle English and of considerable use to Lollard critics)[64] complains, for example, of the frequency with which priests in charge of the Mass, rather than obeying their true calling, "doon herof al þe contrarie"—"þat is to seie, [they] sellen alle þe sacramentes þat schulden freely be ȝouun, as crist comaundeþ, no masse syngeþ but for lucre & hope of grete auaunsementes of lordes or ladies." The master of the catechism fiercely condemns "suche vncleene preestis" as latter-day Judases—"traytours to crist" and like Judas "verray disciplis of antecrist" (*Eluc.* 1.29)[65]—yet as the days grew more latterly, such members of Antichrist had predictably proliferated, to the point where the anglicized Honorius has to admit that no one, least of all the episcopacy, could entirely escape the devil's taint: "þe hedes of hooly chirche ne her officeres neiþer ben cleer fro viciouse lyuyng" (*Eluc.* 1.31), his master says. And this was so primarily on account of the "grete possessiouns of temperaltees," which, like Everyman's bequest, "weren first graunted in help of hooly chirche to susteyne wiþ þe pore þat may no þing laboren" (ibid.). These temporalities had been so thoroughly appropriated to noncharitable ends that the master can think of nothing sufficiently powerful to amend the situation "but god him self; for þe neer [þe] eende of þe world, schal antecrist haue gretter & gretter clerkes & richer & richer clerkes, lordes, peeres to his disciples to be strong y nouȝ to mayntene al þis errour" (ibid.).

One gets the feeling Honorius is maybe exaggerating a little the extent of the church's commercialization so as to derive all the more comfort from it. In the end this purportedly metastatic commercialization of God's body—the universalization of Judas' criminal sale—offers the master of the catechism the same thing Honorius elsewhere sees in the coinage of the host, namely, an indication of the coming payback from "god him self." For the moment the lone best indication of God's continuing

63. Rauh, *Bild des Antichrist* (n. 14), p. 251.

64. See Flint, *Honorius Augustodunensis* (n. 60), pp. 101, 131.

65. *Die mittelenglische Version des Elucidariums des Honorius Augustodunensis*, ed. Friedrich Schmitt (Burghausen: W. Trinkl, 1909), p. 26. Loosely translating PL 172:1130A. The next passages quoted in this paragraph have no known Latin parallel and are cited by section number.

investment in human history would appear to be humanity's monetary investment in God. Honorius' discernment of thieves within the church carries with it an implicit hopefulness, for the thieves embody an anticipatory, mirror image of Christ himself—the "true Lucifer" (PL 172:1082A), as Honorius calls him in a treatise on the liturgy composed for the benefit of Canterbury's monks and fittingly titled *Speculum ecclesiae.* According to this, the real Christ, too, would arrive like "a thief in the night," yet that cataclysmic heist would herald the dawn of an eternal day bringing an end to the myriad and false expropriations made at present in Christ's name (ibid. and 1078C).

Till then it would seem that for every legitimate priest whose ritual utterance made the bread current, and flesh, somewhere else there lived a pardoner or a priestly merchant who under a similarly pious pretense made a killing instead. The trouble was telling them apart—not only because the opponents of legitimacy imitated their rivals, but also because their antichristian imitation played an indispensable role in the cosmic drama; here the villains, too, contributed in an ultimately salutary fashion to the overall, divinely sanctioned effect. Judas had sold Christ, and look what that brought us: the sacraments. If people now were selling them still, at least this served to maintain the church in the form it had taken since Judas first infiltrated and directly helped found it; according to Honorius, so long as priests "polluted...wiþ symonye" (*Eluc.* 30; cf. PL 172:1130A–C) are not in "*opyn* doome departed from hooly chirche," they retain the power to bind and unbind *just as Judas had,* for as long as he, too, "was wiþ þe apostelis & schewide him as a freend" (*Eluc.* 31; PL 172:1132C). In other words it is Judas' *show* of friendship, entirely deprived of substance, that preserves his power to accomplish the good despite his evil motives and that allows him to act as an efficacious agent of the church—even at the critical moment of the fatal, hypocritical kiss when Jesus renders Judas the compliment, withheld from every other disciple, of calling him "friend" (Mt 26:50).

In the end for Honorius it is *hypocrisy* that holds the temporal church together and hypocrisy that anticipates its rebirth into something far more pure: the "show of friendship" maintained by simoniacs and other sellers of Christ typologically conjures a nonexistent inclusivity or "catholicism" that will come into being only at the end of history, when, perhaps, these reprobates will attain the faith and friendly feeling they currently feign; or, barring that, will be cast into utter darkness and there secure the outermost limit of the bright circle comprising the truly elect—a limit as impossible to discern at any given moment as it was violently enforced.[66] This specter of a radical universality—wherein even enemies of Christ are included under show of friendship as efficacious agents in a program of salvation that may come in time to their own rescue—arguably corresponds to or even arises from the universality posited by their simoniacal exchanges; the Absolute itself thereby joins the abject things-of-this-world in an illicit, commercial equality. The greed of unclean priests, under the cover of charity, in other words enables and foreshadows the love of a God who is likewise willing to count himself among his fallen creations, to see himself treated as his creatures' equal in conformity with their demonic willingness, through the momentary, constitutive fiction of commercial exchange, to suspend even the most radical differences in the abstract equivalence of price.

These two related fictions—the simoniacal show of friendship and the equivalence posited in its most extreme form by the monetary exchange of simoniacs—define moreover even the *legitimate* rituals of the church, since they are themselves founded on Judas' hypocrisy and continue to replay it through the Offertory and other licensed exchanges, as well as through the material shape of the host, which commemorates Judas' coins. However much the sacraments could be said to "effect" the grace they signify, they necessarily continued to function nonetheless as "mere" signs, too, so long as the church invisible delayed its final embodiment. Such signs always operate through a certain "hypocritical" pretense. Because for Honorius, as for others, even if the sacraments could be said to realize their value in themselves, as with coinage their more sign-ificant aspect was the tantalizing deferral of the higher value they *promised*: "For just as the synagogue was a shadow and whatever those people accomplished was a shadow of the thing we now perform, *so too the sacraments and feasts of the church are shadows of a future glory....* Therefore when the light of eternal glory breaks, then the shadow of the sacraments vanishes, and present tribulation recedes."[67] The sacraments of the church are not only

---

66. Cf. Sarah Beckwith, "Ritual, Church, and Theatre: Medieval Dramas of the Sacred Body," in *Culture and History, 1350–1600: Essays on English Communities, Identities, and Writing*, ed. David Aers (Detroit: Wayne State University Press, 1992), pp. 65–89, esp. p. 72: "Defining the Christian community meant defining its enemies."

67. Honorius, *In cantica canticorum* 1.2.16–17 (PL 172:396B; my emphasis). He is following the commonplace of Ambrose (who himself follows Origen), *Umbra in lege, imago in evangelio, veritas in caelestibus*; see *De Officiis*, trans. Ivor J. Davidson, 2 vols. (Oxford: Oxford University Press, 2001), 1:254–55 and 2:664–66; I related this saying to typology in chapter 1, p. 47. It was applied to the Mass also by Amalarius—hence the controversy around his allegoresis; see the next note. Cf. John of Damascus, *De imag. orat.* 2.23 (PG 94:1309C; trans. Louth [n. 48], pp. 77–78).

"analogous" to the accomplishments of the Jews—consistently coded else-where in the period as a purely commercial achievement; the sacraments are equally hollow: shadows of some future substance that a more substan-tial realization could not so well "prefigure." Under the rubric of "present tribulation," then, Honorius could include not just the obstinacy of Jews and heretics or the hypocrisy of retrograde clerics—all those in need of conversion or reform—but the hypocrisy of the sacraments that would reform them, too.

In descriptions of church ritual Honorius especially justifies using the word hypocrisy to the extent that drama's shadowy hollowness, always somewhat illicit, for him stands united with the liturgy's inordinate power. "It is known," he writes in a well-thumbed, less well-analyzed passage, "that those who recited tragedies in theaters represented the actions of the pro-tagonists [*pugnantium*] by gestures before the people. In the same way our tragedian [*sic tragicus noster*, the celebrant] represents by his gestures in the theater of the church before the Christian people the struggle of Christ [*pugnam Christi*] and teaches them the victory of his redemption" (*Gemma animae* 1.83 [PL 172:570]).[68] How can this be? If the Mass ex-plicitly shows Christ locked in a *tragic* death struggle (with Antichrist), how does it manage to teach the *victory* of redemption? The answer lies, I think, in the peculiar, hopeful satisfaction which Christians derived from the reenactment of the meal that was both occasion and outcome of God's betrayal to criminal execution—a reenactment that subsequently made his spilled blood and broken flesh available for mass consumption. Hono-rius suggests that the Christian appreciation for this pageantry of blood-shed could be justified with reference to the ancients' delight in (pagan)

---

68. Cf. O. B. Hardison's discussion of Amalarius' allegorical reading of the Mass as dra-ma (an influence on Honorius' conception of the liturgy) in *Christian Rite and Christian Drama in the Middle Ages: Essays in the Origin and Early History of Modern Drama* (Baltimore: Johns Hopkins University Press, 1965), pp. 35–79; *DMC* 1:15–43; Rainer Warning, *The Am-bivalences of Medieval Religious Drama*, trans. Steven Rendall (Stanford: Stanford University Press, 2001), esp. pp. 27–46: "Judged by the standard of his understanding of the Eucharist, Amalarius' 'figures' remain shadowy evacuations of the *plenitudo sacramenti*, mere images of history rather than the continuation of its *fructus spiritualis*" (34–35). Also Sarah Beckwith's insightful remarks regarding the relation of ritual to drama in *Signifying God: Social Rela-tion and Symbolic Act in the York Corpus Christi Plays* (Chicago: University of Chicago Press, 2001), p. 28, along with her "Ritual, Church, and Theatre" (n. 66). See too John Wesley Harris, *Medieval Theatre in Context: An Introduction* (London: Routledge, 1992), pp. 23–46 and 73; T. P. Dolan, "The Mass as Performance Text," in *From Page to Performance: Essays in Early English Drama*, ed. John A. Alford (East Lansing: Michigan State University Press, 1995), pp. 13–24; Glynne Wickham, *The Medieval Theatre*, 3rd ed. (Cambridge: Cambridge University Press, 1987), pp. 11ff.

tragedy. So that one of the deeper mysteries of Christian soteriology—the religion's dependence on a commercialized, hemophilian ritual—has been displaced onto a prior and deeper *aesthetic* mystery: the notorious pleasures of tragedy, which had so tellingly agitated Augustine: "Why is it that a man wants to be sad there [in the theater] when he watches doleful and tragic things that he himself would not at all want to suffer? And yet, as a spectator, he *wants* sadness from them, and *this very sadness is his pleasure*" (*Conf.* 3.2.2; my emphasis).

What disgusts and "vehemently" attracts Augustine—*was ihn erregt,* Freud would say—is basically the same "show of friendship" that Judas had staged, only for Augustine it is the *spectator* who now displays an illusory compassion. Augustine concedes that his former commiseration with suffering stage characters sprang from a genuine "vein of friendship" and in fact constitutes a form of God's own *misericordia*; yet the absence of *any actual object* for this friendly feeling taints it with "impurity" (*Conf.* 3.2.3). That is to say, in the theater the feigning is not restricted to the actors, because the audience members also experience empty emotions—feelings of compassion without any object. Augustine could cleanse these emotions of impurity, I would argue, only by displacing the theatrical attraction of "another person's feigned and impersonated misery" (*Conf.* 3.2.4) *into Catholic ritual*, where the dramatic reprise of such calamitous events as Christ's apparent defeat, his sale and death, his nearly eternal war with Antichrist, could offer the same satisfaction that Augustine once got from watching the "fake" (*falsa*) disasters of classical tragedy, now without any guilt. The "impersonated misery" of the pagan stage became, after the fall of Rome and the demise of its theaters, the suffering of God in the person of Christ, as symbolized by priests, and openly led to the spectators' innocence. The radical contrafactuality of the staging worked if anything *better* in Christian ritual, because it was the *truth* of Christ's historical death: though dead, he lives; violated he remains inviolate; with blasphemy he is glorified and forgives the enjoyment of his suffering.[69]

By the twelfth century the liturgical reenactment of Holy Week—or "Judas Week," as some countries called it[70]—had grown to the point where

69. The pleasure of such contrafactuality was decidedly social; see John Bossy's interpretation in which the Mass's ritualized sacrifice binds people together insofar as its "ritual murder *takes the place of actual murder* and hence enables the population to live in peace" ("The Mass as a Social Institution, 1200–1700," *Past and Present* 100 [1983]: 29–61; here 50–51; my emphasis).

70. Hand, *Dictionary of Words and Idioms Associated with Judas Iscariot* (n. 48), s.v. "Judas Wednesday" (English), "Judasweek" (Dutch), "Judaswoche" (German): "According to popular belief, Holy Week is characterized by bad weather. Cf. ... *Judaswetter*" (p. 353).

the Mass's internalization of the dramatic form in opposition to whose emptiness Christian ritual had partly evolved was plain to Honorius, at least, and of a piece with the antichristian, theatrical aspect he saw in all of sacred history. As Horst Rauh writes: "What occurs here [during Holy Week] is neither historical accident nor the defeat of fictitious prophecy: it has to happen according to the strict law of the liturgy. The passion, standing under the signs of Antichrist, flows necessarily into the Easter events, into the triumph of Christ the King over Rex Tyrannus, into the rebirth of the church."[71] Let it be said that such necessity would presumably have to be conveyed by the "signs of Antichrist" themselves, however, since of course the triumph of Christ, the victory of redemption, and the rebirth of the church, though theoretically secure even at the time of the Fall, have yet to be realized in anything other than this liturgico-theatrical form. Which is to say they have not been realized. It was in some sense the whole purpose of the Mass to make the calamities of sacred history themselves appear as a pleasing if tragic interlude that would eventually be superseded by some future reality *in caelestibus* to which the tragedy referred but which seemed comic by comparison. Not coincidently, the Easter Mass is where we find the earliest dramatization of biblical history above and beyond the latent, somewhat shamefaced drama of the liturgy as such. Here in the trope of the *quem quaeritis* nothing more divine than a young man angelically clad needed to appear on stage to ask the Marys whom they sought, then to descant, soft and sweet, the Christian negative: *He is not here.*[72] The song prompted instant rejoicing, as the disappearance of his corpse signaled resurrection and at the same time justified his absence from the church in all but the likeness of icons, plus the dimmer, more critical likeness of the host, where you likewise could not see him.

Frankly this was in itself a great mercy. Otherwise you would have to look on that hardest kernel of the real presence, God's carved flesh and streaming blood, served up for the sustenance of his flock. "God feared," Cyril

71. Rauh, *Bild des Antichrist* (n. 14), p. 247.

72. His absence, according to historicists of the old school, signaled the resurrection of Western drama. See E. K. Chambers, *The Mediaeval Stage,* 2 vols. (Oxford: Oxford University Press, 1903): "In the Easter *Quem quaeritis* the liturgical drama was born" (2:10). For its supposed gradual development into the *Visitatio sepulchri,* see *DMC* 1:201–38; the narrative Karl Young gives there is much in dispute, but for an evaluation of the evidence that sides in his favor, see David A. Bjork, "On the Dissemination of *Quem quaeritis* and the *Visitatio sepulchri* and the Chronology of Their Early Sources," in *The Drama of the Middle Ages: Comparative and Critical Essays,* ed. Clifford Davidson et al. (New York: AMS, 1982), pp. 1–24. Some current scholars of Mark have begun to speculate that the gospel's abrupt ending was itself originally a liturgico-theatrical device inviting some kind of antiphonal response from the audience. See introduction, nn. 23–25.

of Alexandria freely admits, "that seeing actual flesh and blood placed on the holy tables of our churches would terrify us,"[73] so he allowed the bread and wine to stand in their place as a more pleasant, mimetic substitute. Cyril's explanation for this mimicry at the heart of the Mass was still current in the late Middle Ages; it received further elaboration, even. For example, when the student of Honorius' *Elucidarium* asks his master why the "likness of breed & wyne" remain unchanged *despite* transubstantiation, the master responds, "If þou siȝe in liknesse of fleisch & blood þat blessed sacrament, þou schuldest loþen & abhorren it to resseyue it into þi mouþ" (*Eluc.* 1.28; PL 172:1129C). Without the stage props, in other words, communicants would not be spared the reality of their communication, and instead of mere show they would have to contend with open cannibalism. It is hardly a stretch to say that the *appearance* of bread and wine, deprived of any corresponding substance (if the substance has indeed changed), *redeems* participants from the potential barbarism of Christianity; it creates in turn an occasion for the "more merijte" of faith, since according to Honorius' master it redounds entirely to your spiritual credit if you "wolt bileeue bi goostly vndirstondinge þat it [the bread] is oþer þing þan þou seest" (ibid.). This "other thing" (the mortal flesh of Christ) then leads to yet another thing, even more other: immortal life. You need only grasp inwardly that material appearances in the liturgy, however real, are also an *image* of the highest realities, just as playgoers, though seeing real actors, understand that the main point of looking is to witness the ghostly characters, not otherwise there, who are better, because imaginary, than anything that is.

The Miracle at Croxton

Not everyone had such faith. The "goostly vndirstondinge" that could look upon liturgical props as objective representations of other, more significant objects required constant shoring up. Where catechism and Mass had failed to instruct, there was fortunately the delight of

73. *Commentary upon the Gospel According to St. Luke,* Homily 142 (PG 72:905A–911C); trans. R. Payne Smith, 2 vols. (Oxford, 1859), 2:668. Ironically agreeing with an ancient critique, attributed to Porphyry, in response to Jn 6:53: "Unless you eat the flesh of the son of Man and drink his blood you have no life in you"; see Robert M. Berchman, *Porphyry against the Christians* (Leiden: Brill, 2005), pp. 202–3: "Truly this saying is not merely bestial and absurd—but it is more absurd than any absurdity, and more bestial than any beast's art—that a man should taste human flesh and drink the blood of the same tribe's members and race—and by doing so he should partake of eternal life.... It seems that neither Mark, nor Luke, nor even Matthew recorded this because they regarded the saying as indecent."

extraliturgical fiction. In connection with the growing emphasis on the real presence (which is to say, a growing emphasis on the *fictiveness* of the *actual* bread and wine as "mere likenesses"), Benedicta Ward notes "a flood of miracle stories that illustrated the 'reality' of the change. Such stories could even be called 'counter-miracles,' since they break through the miraculous surface of illusion to a representation of the substance that lies behind the unchanged appearance."[74] According to this casually profound description, the Eucharist's "miraculous surface of illusion" (!) gives rise to anti-miracles that would affirm the truth of transubstantiation by inverting it. That is, in order to *prove* that the bread and wine are merely appearance, and therefore signs of a miraculous, substantial transformation, the story of the anti-miracle claims, through an equally fictive appearance, to represent "the substance behind the unchanged appearance," as though a representation of substance were more substantial than the appearance. One illusion would here demonstrate the truth of another illusion, in other words, by pretending to puncture its illusions.

What better anti-miracle to supplement the dramatic miracle of the Mass than drama itself? What better way to re-theatricalize an event that risked losing its dramatic force?[75] That certainly looks like the purpose of the so-called Croxton *Play of the Sacrament*, with its oft-noted recapitulation of the liturgy[76] even while the opening banns summarize and assert the *historical* validity of the play "representyd now in yower syght" (10).[77] On comes Aristorius Mercator, a Christian merchant, with a traditional prayer that Christ "from shame...cure vs" and "Vnto hys en[d]lesse joye myghtly...

---

74. Benedicta Ward, *Miracles and the Medieval Mind: Theory, Record, Event, 1000–1215* (Philadelphia: University of Pennsylvania Press, 1982), p. 15.

75. Cf. Lynette R. Muir, "The Mass on the Medieval Stage," *Comparative Drama* 23 (1989–90): 314–30.

76. On the play's liturgical elements, see Maltman, "Meaning and Art in the Croxton *Play of the Sacrament*" (n. 34), and Andrew Sofer, *The Stage Life of Props* (Ann Arbor: University of Michigan Press, 2003), pp. 31–60. Croxton is the sole extant English adherent to the genre of host-miracles frequently dramatized on the continent, as for example *La Sainte Hostie*. For the dark side of a lot of these miracle stories, see Miri Rubin, *Gentile Tales: The Narrative Assault on Late Medieval Jews* (Philadelphia: University of Pennsylvania Press, 1994). Also Stephen Greenblatt and Catherine Gallagher, *Practicing New Historicism* (Chicago: University of Chicago Press, 2000), pp. 75–109. One particular example of a host-miracle—related by no less an authority on the real presence than Innocent III two years before the Fourth Lateran codified the doctrine—deserves careful reading. See Solomon Grayzel, *The Church and the Jews in the XIIIth Century: A Study of Their Relations during the Years 1198–1254, Based on the Papal Letters and the Conciliar Decrees of the Period*, rev. ed. (New York: Hermon, 1966), pp. 136ff.

77. All quotations from the play taken from *Non-Cycle Plays and Fragments*, ed. Norman Davis, EETS s.s. 1 (London: Oxford University Press, 1970), pp. 58–89; cited by line number.

restore vs" (83). Pure hypocrisy. A long inventory of all the lands where Aristorius' "merchaundyse renneth [i.e., travels]" (94) immediately follows, usurping his invocation to God. Without peer among rich men (85, 130), Aristorius imagines that his unsurpassed wealth, like Christ's blood, might purchase the whole world (88), and it is this satanic hubris (modeled more or less directly on the cycles' Herod)[78] that transforms him over the course of his opening monologue into a special antichristian image of Christ's geopolitical body, the *ecclesia universalis,* containing multitudes and extending as far as God's love.[79]

Though ostensibly peerless, Aristorius is of course not the only one to stand in place of God's body on the strength of his wealth. So too does Jonathas, the leader of the Jewish merchants, arrive on stage extolling the power of *his* God, "Machomet" (149), before he, too, turns to a catalogue of the riches with which that god has endowed his presumptive favorite. The worldly glory of both Jonathas and Aristorius clearly means to reflect in the negative the magnanimity of the Christian God; it will be the self-serving, explicit objective of the play—itself a sensuous reflection every bit as specious as the wealth of its characters—to demonstrate a powerful, prophetic beauty in this artificial transposition.

But first, Aristorius and Jonathas must bargain together. They need to settle the price at which the host will be sold, with Aristorius once more echoing the words of a cyclic counterpart, this time Judas[80]: "I sold yon same Jewys owr Lord full ryght / For couytyse of good, as a cursyd wyght!"

78. See David Lawton, "Sacrilege and Theatricality: The Croxton *Play of the Sacrament,*" *Journal of Medieval and Early Modern Studies* 33.2 (2003): 281–309; here 286.

79. For Christ's body as a model for society and the relation of this model to the cycle plays, see Mervyn James, "Ritual, Drama, and Social Body in the Late Medieval English Town," *Past and Present* 98 (1983): 3–29, and Sarah Beckwith, "Ritual, Theater, and Social Space in the York Corpus Christi Cycle," in *Bodies and Disciplines: Intersections of Literature and History in Fifteenth-Century England,* ed. Barbara A. Hanawalt and David Wallace (Minneapolis: University of Minnesota Press, 1996), pp. 63–86.

80. Ann Eljenholm Nichols, "The Croxton *Play of the Sacrament*: A Re-reading," *Comparative Drama* 22.2 (1988): 117–37; here 125. See also Stephen Spector, "Time, Space and Identity in the *Play of the Sacrament,*" in *The Stage as Mirror: Civic Theater in Late Medieval Europe,* ed. Alan E. Knight (Cambridge: D. S. Brewer, 1997), pp. 189–200; here 190, 194. My reading of Judas in the cycles will have already shown that I don't see the plays' anti-Judaism quite as straightforwardly as Spector does when he writes, "In psychoanalytic terms, the drama calls on the Christian community to project onto the Jew the qualities that it cannot tolerate in itself, and then to hate the Jew for having them" (191), a point given greater elaboration in his "Anti-Semitism and the English Mystery Plays," in *The Drama of the Middle Ages,* ed. Clifford Davidson et al. (New York: AMS, 1982), pp. 328–41. The drama had a rather more complex psychopathology, I think, since it projected onto Jews "intolerable" Christian qualities so that Christians might all the better *enjoy them.* For a fuller psychoanalytic account, see Slavoj Žižek's interpretation of anti-Semitism in *The Sublime Object of Ideology* (London: Verso, 1989), pp. 124–27.

(853–54). By "good" of course Aristorius means "goods," but the whole play, like *Everyman*, is predicated on the staged confusion between the two; again, the higher, moral Good finds expression only in and as a fallen economics.[81] By play's end the Christian as well as the Jewish merchants will have denounced their seemingly all-surpassing "good" in favor of a genuinely infinite "Good," access to which they gain the way all humanity has: through the fortunately sinful sale of Christ's flesh. "Here is an hundder pownd, neyther mor nor lasse," Jonathas finally offers after the initial bickering, "of dokettys good, I dar well saye" (315–16). The gratuitous reassurance that the coins are "good," following so closely on the overstated precision of his offer—one hundred pounds "neyther mor nor lasse"—raises the specter of counterfeit that will haunt the rest of the play: first, in the Jews' treatment of the host as though it were a fraudulent coin, and then second, in the artificiality of the "miracles" that arise from this mistreatment. These homologous forms of (potential) counterfeit take their cue, as false coinage itself does, from a certain radical substitution on which even a legitimate money economy depends: by "an hundder pownd" Jonathas means he can offer the "equivalent" of one hundred pounds *in weight* of sterling silver, even though the ducats he actually gives Aristorius weigh considerably less. What makes those (presumably gold) coins "equal" to one hundred pounds of silver—regardless of their weight or metallic composition—is the royal *type* impressed on the coins' surface. This alone certifies them as "good."

To accept that certification requires one of the more common varieties of secular belief: namely, faith in the legitimacy of the issuing mint, which at money's first genesis would have always been a temple; hence the derivation of the word from Juno Moneta (the admonisher), in whose sacred dwelling on the Capitoline Hill Roman money was coined (*O.E.D.* s.v. "money"). (Mary Douglas goes so far as to call money an "extreme form of ritual.")[82] Every participant in a cash economy has to *believe* that the divine (or royal) certification of money can ensure the coin

---

81. For the word "good" used in the sense of "goods," see lines 272, 286, 789, 854, 914, 917, and 991. Though not particularly interested in this term, Alexandra Reid-Schwartz explores the general "erosion of boundaries" between mercantilism and the Mass in her "Economies of Salvation: Commerce and the Eucharist in *The Profanation of the Host* and the Croxton *Play of the Sacrament*," *Comitatus: A Journal of Medieval and Renaissance Studies* 25 (1994): 1–20.

82. Mary Douglas, *Purity and Danger: An Analysis of Concepts of Pollution and Taboo* (1966; repr., London: Routledge, 2002), p. 86. Alternately religious ritual as such itself becomes in Western Christianity a special form of *money*.

a nebulous, complex, but legitimate correlation with its "real worth"; such faith is what staves off—and, wavering, helps cause—fluctuations in the currency's value. Long before the *Play of the Sacrament* sets about to mimic the Mass, then, its opening exchange between Aristorius and Jonathas already reproduces that rite's sine qua non: the de rigueur allowance that a piece of metal, so long as it is good and officially stamped, can serve as *more* than metal, that it can serve as *money*, and that this mysterious "more" inherent to currency might then allow it to stand in for almost anything else, even the Absolute sum of all things, provided you could find an unscrupulous merchant or priest willing to bargain. By further ramification, the absurdity of this or any other medieval play's pretense to represent the Absolute adequately while clearly failing to equal it—or even going to some lengths, as in Croxton, to fan the flames of dissimilarity—is at bottom no more or less absurd than counting a few ounces of coined gold as one hundred *pounds* in weight of sterling silver and then trading those coins in a fair and equal exchange for something radically different.

The pressing question in Croxton is whether the host essentially differs from the coins given for it; that is, whether the host, as David Lawton asks, "can entirely escape the instability of semiotic systems such as the economic, money theory, which accounts for the fact that money is both value in itself and a sign of a value that it actually is not."[83] Theologians since at least the thirteenth century (beginning, it seems, at Oxford) had probed this relation quite openly and held in the end that money took on value in precisely the same way that the sacraments contained or purveyed grace. They debated only whether value inhered *in* the sacrament and coinage—whether they made their values "incarnate"—or if real value could also, independent of their intrinsic worth, be *ascribed* to them by a superior power (God in the case of the sacraments; the king for coins). Here is Aquinas' summary of the conflict:

> Some say that... God ordains and, as it were, contracts that they who receive the sacraments at the same time receive grace from them, although the sacraments do nothing toward this end. And it is similar to the man who receives a leaden coin when a pact has been made such that whoever had one of the coins would have one hundred pounds from the king. This coin, however, does not give the hundred pounds, but the king alone does, by his acceptation. And because such a pact had not been made in the sacraments of the old law, that whoever participates in them receives

83. Lawton, "Sacrilege and Theater" (n. 78), p. 299.

grace, for that reason, they say, the sacraments do not confer grace, but rather have promised it.[84]

As William Courtenay has shown, a wide array of medieval monetary instruments underlay this comparison: there were promissory notes and substitute money like the leather coinage issued by Frederick II at Faenza in 1241; closer to home for sacramental theologians were the *méreaux*—a token coinage circulating as wages in monasteries and other religious organizations as well as royal households—and the charity tokens given to the poor, which were redeemable for food.[85] At the end of the day to be of any real worth all these tokens *had* to be redeemed for the value they symbolized. But so long as you believed in the continued wealth and trustworthiness of the issuing agency (whether church or crown), the day of redemption could be deferred indefinitely, and in the meantime it would have been possible (at least in theory) to trade the tokens on the strength of their promise, just as nations on the gold standard once traded paper money without cashing in.[86]

In the meantime all that materialized the promise was sheer representation: the king's face or some other impression stamped on an ingot as much to mark its value as that value's absence since the impression pointed elsewhere to the real source of wealth—the king's treasury or whatever the guarantee of that treasury allowed one to purchase. The invention of modern coinage—in sixth- or seventh-century Greece (BCE)— thus produced what Marc Shell calls "the first widely circulating 'publications' in human history"[87] and has been recently correlated by Richard Seaford in extraordinary detail with the explosion of Greek epic, metaphysics, and drama. He argues for a strong link between the Greek refusal to identify gods with their images and the "monetization of the cult"; since offerings were made to the gods through the *mediation* of an image, Seaford supposes, eventually it became possible to make the sacrifice, also, in a wholly symbolic, that is, monetary way. So, for example, instead of offering to the gods the traditional *pelanos* (a kind of cake), one might have offered the *image* of a cake fashioned from a more durable and precious

---

84. Latin quoted by William Courtenay, "The King and the Leaden Coin: The Economic Background of 'Sine Qua Non' Causality," *Traditio* 28 (1972): 185–209; here 186 n. 1. Cf. *Summa th.* IIIa q. 62 a 1.

85. Courtenay, "The King and the Leaden Coin," pp. 196–97.

86. Ibid., p. 200.

87. Marc Shell, *Money, Language, and Thought: Literary and Philosophical Economies from the Medieval to the Modern Era* (Baltimore: Johns Hopkins University Press, 1993), p. 171.

substance: "If so, then imitative (or symbolic) substitution prepared the way for monetary substitution: we pass from a cake to a non-perishable imitation of a cake, and from there to money, which—though it may still, as coinage, resemble the imitation of a round cake—has in fact left the particular use-value of the imitated cake well behind, for it has instead only the relatively general (and so abstract) quality of exchange-value."[88] And sure enough the Greek word for cake—*pelanos*—comes eventually to mean a monetary payment made to a temple. I suspect it is this abstract and "timeless" form of value—exchange-value—that provokes the Jews' desire in Croxton to prove once and for all the total fraudulence of any belief "on a cake" (200); they attribute this belief to Christians, though it is actually a version of the faith in monetary exchange which everyone shares.

As a number of critics have realized, the very test that the Jews devise to discredit the real presence—namely, by "torturing" the host—fully depends on the assumption that the host *is* Christ. The Jews' animosity, or better, their hostility, in other words amounts to a secret longing that the host *not* be a fraud. They express the iconoclast's clandestine desire that destruction might strengthen the image's aura. And it is precisely when Jonathas offers the final coup de grâce—the fifth of five wounds—by planting his dagger in the "myddys of thys prynt" in the host (467), making, as it were, an even deeper impression on it, that the play's strangest revelations begin to unfold:

> Now am I bold with batayle hym to bleyke,
> þe mydle part alle for to prene;
> A stowte stroke also for to stryke—
> In þe myddys yt shalbe sene!
> *Here þe Ost must blede.* (477–80 + SD)

Jonathas' unwitting prediction that "yt"—an unlocatable subject—"shalbe sene" when he lays his dagger in "þe middys of thys print" enters its first phase of fulfillment in the ensuing stage direction: the host begins to bleed. And so begins the cascade of miracles, each one more demonic and horrifying than the last—"What deuyll ys thys?" (481), "What deuyll ys herein?" (673, cf. 516)—until there finally comes the ultimate anti-miracle to travesty, and thereby fulfill, the awful miracle of the Mass: there comes at last the bloody appearance of Christ *himself*...

88. Seaford, *Money and the Early Greek Mind* (n. 9), p. 78.

Or rather, Christ's "ymage."[89] I do not think anyone has yet to explain successfully the enigmatic stage direction stipulating that this grand revelation must be *only* an "ymage," and I doubt anyone ever will, because part of its function is to intimate a truth that concealment alone can reveal. Maybe it is right that a boy actor would have spoken the lines attributed to this "ymage" (a common speculation), but one could hope the players might have found a way to honor more stringently the literal stage direction and assigned the speech to a talking picture—a two-dimensional puppet, as it were. What the Jews (and audience, too) are supposed to behold and see here is the full force of a conditional *question* regarding the status of Christ's own likeness. Here are the first lines attributed to "Christ":

> O mirabiles Judei, attendite et videte
> Si est dolor similis dolor meus. (717–18)[90]

When an "ymage" asks if there is any sorrow *like* what it pictures, I think the picture itself should look especially questionable. In this case there both is and is not such a likeness. There is a likeness in this very image, but as a mere likeness it is by definition inadequate, therefore dissimilar to the unparalleled suffering it purports to reveal—and so does represent, insofar as its parallel fails. The miracle of this impossible "dissemblant similitude"[91] arguably extends to the suffering Jews themselves, Jonathas above all, who in torturing the host, tortures himself and thus also becomes in his way an image of Christ. *O mirabiles Judei!* Stephen Spector has pointed out that this somewhat solecistic exclamation does not appear in the liturgy or in the scriptural passage from Lamentations which the image otherwise quotes.[92] The homage to these "miraculous Jews" is a purely dramatic interpolation, an unexpected exaltation of stage villains *as themselves* the repository of a marvelous revelation in their own monstrosity.

They will not remain monsters for long. So utterly appalled by the abomination of the image now lecturing them, they retreat to the bishop and unveil to him in the words of confession the equally "swemfull" (800)

---

89. On this, the so-called Image of Pity, see Richard L. Homan, "Devotional Themes in the Violence and Humor of the *Play of the Sacrament*," *Comparative Drama* 20 (1986): 327–40 (esp. 337–38), and Ann Nichols, "Croxton *Play*" (n. 80), pp. 127–30.

90. "O astounding Jews, take heed and see, / If there is sorrow like my sorrow." The editor emends "similis" to "sicut," which may make for more biblical Latin but places at a further distance the central question of similitude.

91. The phrase is from Georges Didi-Huberman, *Fra Angelico: Dissemblance and Figuration*, trans. Jane Marie Todd (Chicago: University of Chicago Press, 1995), p. 149.

92. Spector, "Time, Space and Identity" (n. 80), p. 196.

spectacle of their sins. The abominable image *is* their sin: the "Holy Sacrement," which "sheuyd them grette fauour" (50) by showing them their bleeding victim, drives them to the church, where they "shewyd ther lyues to a confesour" (52); both "shows" are the same, and they are what the audience will have also seen: that is, the revelation of Christ's wounds. Then comes one of the weirder moments in medieval drama. We could almost call it an anti-anti-miracle, the negation of the negation which produces some final, liturgical positive. The bishop prays, first, on behalf of the Jews, that they be cleansed of their sin; second, that *the horrific spectacle of the bleeding Christ be removed from everyone's sight*:

> O Jhesu, fili Dei,
> How thys paynfull passyon rancheth myn hart!
> Lord, I crye to the, *miserere mei*,
> From thys rufull syght þou wylt reuerte! (814–17)

The bishop is praying that the host revert *back* to the appearance of mere bread—despite the real presence having been made at last, for once, a real appearance in this image of the passion. Immediately at the end of his speech a stage direction answers his prayer: *Here shall þe im[a]ge change agayn into brede* (825 SD). (I think the players would have been wise, from a strictly theological perspective, to go for the big laugh by making the stage machinery as ham-handed and transparent as possible.) The purely accidental appearance of the bread in other words here *counters* and *redeems* the sudden, cataclysmic appearance of Christ's "actual" image, for now we see an even more distant representative of him—the host—which offers solace and hope only insofar as it does *not* reveal God. It is as though the very materiality of the sacrament, its fully accidental aspect, itself acted as a latent iconoclasm in suppressing the feigned appearance of the wounded God so as to produce an even more sublime revelation[93]—sublime because the host reveals God as he is not and thereby preserves what he is against the degradation of visual commerce: "The Sacrament so semly ys borne in syght," rejoices the bishop in the sacramental procession that ends the play. "I hope that God hath shewyd of hys grace!" (848–49). And what a show it has been! The very seem-liness of the host has established itself as an object of "semly" beauty

---

93. Michael Jones points out that we probably owe the preservation of the play, in a single manuscript (ca. 1520–40), to the interest it provoked among the newly *reformed*; see "Theatrical History in the Croxton *Play of the Sacrament*," *English Literary History* 66.2 (1999): 223–60, esp. 247ff.

insofar as it *conceals* the frightful aspect of Christ's awful countenance (itself a fake). Thus around the host congregates the "semely" (assembly) (3) that will be saved through its efficaciousness, a community of believers finally as nebulous and lacking in real substance as the dramatic object that charmed this church visible into half-being. Were the audience any more substantial a collectivity, any more genuine a "community," it would have no hope of harboring in itself the one group that ever really matters: the church invisible.[94]

Scholars debate whether the procession ending the play actually took its spectators into a nearby church; but if, as John Wasson holds, it did,[95] then they could have found there the traditional opportunity to participate more materially than drama as yet allowed, by means of the Offertory, in the creation of the Eucharistic collective that this particular drama so forcefully advocates. In the end that collective was mainly what the church collected, money the de facto consensus of otherwise fragmented communities. That the audience had *paid* for the liturgy best guaranteed the mysterious excess that they experienced during its dramatic proceedings, which was the excess of themselves cooperating in a collective dispossession. The surfeit could be interpreted either positively or negatively. It hardly matters. If certain priests, given over to "the practices of avarice, vanity, and spectacle,"[96] had transformed the church into a commercial theater, its commerce gave flesh to the myth of Antichrist, and its false appearances might therefore still serve the truest of ends. People like Gerhoch denounced what they worshipped. Others celebrated, gave what they could, and saw their money transformed, if not always to the social good of alms, then to something less instrumental and therefore one step closer to God's unworldly instruments: the utter gratuitousness of architecture and icons, costuming and song—the whole expensive pantomime, which if dedicated to anything, really, was dedicated to achieving the aesthetic

94. Cf. Lawton, "Sacrilege and Theatricality" (n. 78), p. 295: "There is no community in the play worth speaking of: in the words of Gertrude Stein, there's no *there* there."

95. John M. Wasson, "The English Church as Theatrical Space," in *A New History of Early English Drama*, ed. John D. Cox and David Scott Kastan (New York: Columbia University Press, 1997), pp. 25–38; here 31–32. For some other viewpoints, see Sofer, *The Stage Life of Props* (n. 76), pp. 46–49.

96. Gerhoch of Reichersberg, *De Investigatione Antichristi* 1.5; text in *Monumenta Germaniae Historica, Libelli de lite imperatorum et pontificum saeculis XI. et XII. conscripti*, 3 vols. (Hannover, 1897), 3:315. For his specific debts to Honorius, perhaps more important in connection with his antitheatricalism than is usually noted, see Peter Classen, *Gerhoch von Reichersberg: Eine Biographie* (Wiesbaden: Franz Steiner, 1960), pp. 50–51 and 433–34. For a more involved reading of his antitheatricalism, see chapter 1, pp. 74–79.

effects that promoted future collections;[97] these effects, in other words, secured the perpetuation of money's more promising existence as an element in Christ's struggle toward the radically different but still quasi-economic transaction of redemption. Lollards later on, and finally all the Protestants, were right to denounce major aspects of churchly ritual as so much thievery, but they were right to keep faith with it, too, in their conviction that if money now was God, if the idolized images that all this wealth was sponsoring stood in God's place, then "god him self" could not be too far away. So that the church's commercial aesthetic could be a deeply satisfying sign after all, even if the satisfaction some people took in the drama increasingly tended toward longing for its violent destruction. They lived out what Augustine once had preached: "that you may deserve to be what you are not," he told his congregants, "condemn what you are" (*Enn. in Ps.* 99.5 [CCSL 39:1395; *WSA* III/19:16]).

Coda: The Blood Money of *Mankind*

Mankind makes reference to every coin circulating in the mid-fifteenth century save for the angel, first minted in 1470 and showing Michael in combat with the antichristian Beast of Revelation. That date provides the closest thing we have to a *terminus ad quem* for the play's composition. The earliest possible date *a quo* comes from its mention of "red royals," presumably the so-called rose noble first issued in 1464–65.[98] This featured, on the one side, Edward IV in battle regalia sailing the ship of state under a flag whose monogram—"E"—signifies both him and his English kingdom.[99] Such double signification summed up the union that the Yorkists wanted. Now their money embodied it. The rose affixed to the ship's stern appears again on the obverse, where it has been superimposed on the sun and cross in reference to the Battle of Mortimer. Legend had it that the morning of the fight three suns appeared through the fog, then merged into one so as better to illuminate the victory of York.[100] Divine sanction for Edward's royal title was likewise

---

97. According to Bernard of Clairvaux, prospective donors eyes are intentionally "feasted with relics cased in gold, and their purse stings are loosened." Trans. in Caecilia Davis-Weyer, *Early Medieval Art, 300–1150: Sources and Documents* (Englewood Cliffs, N.J.: Prentice-Hall, 1971), p. 169.

98. D. C. Baker, "The Date of *Mankind*," *Philological Quarterly* 42 (1963): 90–91.

99. The ship also refers to English naval power. See Glyn Davies, *A History of Money* (Cardiff: University of Wales Press, 1994), p. 144.

100. Charles Oman, *The Coinage of England* (Oxford: Clarendon Press, 1931), p. 220.

suggested by the biblical legend running along the coin's edge: IHC AVT
TRANSIENS PER MEDIUM ILLORVM IBAT.[101] The words describe Jesus' narrow
escape from a group of Galileans enraged by his refusal to perform any
miracles—on the grounds, he says, that a prophet is never recognized
in his own country. In response to this insult the locals dragged him to
the edge of town with the intention of hurling him over a cliff, "but passing through the middle of them he went his way" (Lk 4:30). So too had
Edward passed through the adversity of his countrymen's unbelief in his
claim to the throne. He had been marked out by the higher power that
he refused to degrade through too full a display; he gave the faithful
nothing more than the brute fact of his own survival and his subsequent
power to determine the currency's value throughout the entire kingdom by embossing it with his image and biblical quotations of his own
choosing. That was miracle enough.

This, then, is the coin that the vices ask for in the earliest recorded instance of actors collecting money directly from an audience in exchange
for the performance. It comes at a crucial moment: Mercy has just exited
the stage, or been run off it, rather, by the three N's, each representing the
sins of the present: Nowadays, New Guise, and Nought. These would now
prepare the way for the appearance of an even more authoritative evil, "a
man wyth a hede þat ys of grett omnipotens" (461), who, we find out later,
"properly syngnyfyth the Fend of helle" (886).[102] Before cueing their chief
to enter, however, New Guise makes an announcement:

> We xall gaþer mony onto,
> Ellys þer xall no man hym se....
> *Nowadays:*...He ys a worschyppull man, sers, sauyng yowr reuerens.
> He louyth no grotys, nor pens of to pens.
> Gyf ws rede reyallys yf ȝe wyll se hys abhomynabull presens. (457–58, 463–65)

The novelty of this moment in theater history is at once intensified and
deeply compromised by its clear indebtedness to the Offertory of the
Mass, whose revelatory privileges the devils here borrow for themselves.
Before the audience can witness this "worschyppull man," it must do what
congregations had long done in church before the unveiling of another
kind of "presens," one which was equally "abhomynabull," insofar as the

---

101. George C. Brooke, *English Coins* (London: Methuen, 1932), p. 155.
102. All quotations from *Mankind* are cited by line from *The Macro Plays*, ed. Mark Ec-
cles, EETS o.s. 262 (London: Oxford University Press, 1969), pp. 154–84.

worshipful man *it* "revealed" was at the same time *ab homine*—that is, according to the traditional (and false) etymology, "away from man"— because *he* was divine and his flesh in this case looked like bread. That the devils specifically ask to see *red* royals has been explained in the secondary literature with reference to a "traditional epithet for gold,"[103] but in this quasi-liturgical context I think that epithet taps into a rather different tradition. Is it not the tradition of blood money? If in the Offertory you "be-halde...he þat iudas salde," surely you could hope to catch a glimpse here too, through the same theatrical transmogrification, of the man represented on the coin that you gave the players—not the kingly embodiment of the whole nation, I mean, but the King of Kings whose place the English crown occupied only *in vice* (hence Edward's biblical quotation). This at any rate is the identity that Titivillus claims for himself on arriving at last, after his minions collect their fee: "Ego sum dominancium dominus" (475), I am the Lord of Lords. An audience would know by this boast that he stood for everything *opposed* to the character of Mercy, who had just exited, while being somehow simultaneously at one with his prerogatives, because the two were in some sense united under God's absolute sovereignty. Here on stage that dialectic was made more concrete than in any possible conceptual theodicy since the actor who exits as Mercy returns, for a price and in a new guise, as the extravagantly masked Titivillus.[104] They are, as it were, two sides of the same coin.

Presumably an audience could have discerned Mercy's voice beneath the comic mask of Vice, just as people were supposed to see beneath the triumph of Antichrist his own impending doom, which was the triumph of Christ and could come only by way of this indirection. "Thus God hides his eternal mercy and kindness under eternal wrath; righteousness under iniquity," writes a late medieval Augustinian friar. "Therefore if by any means I could comprehend how this God can be merciful and just who displays so much wrath and iniquity, there would be no need of faith" (*De servo arbitrio* [WA 18:633; *LW* 33:62–63]). The friar, I'm afraid, is Luther. In his seminal conflict with the church he gives voice to the special appreciation for evil that will preserve medieval theater for the commercial stage; its divinity, as we'll see, is conspicuously absent and the villainy, to compensate, ever more greedy and flagrant. As William

---

103. Lester, *Three Late Medieval Morality Plays* (n. 30), p. 28. Cf. O.E.D., s.v. "ruddock."
104. A commonly supposed doubling; see, for example, David Bevington, *Medieval Drama* (Boston: Houghton Mifflin, 1975), p. 901.

Perkins writes in sixteenth-century England: "It is the principal art of a Christian to believe things invisible, to hope for things deferred, to love God when he shews himself to be an enemy and thus to persevere unto the end.... [For] all the works of God are done in contrary means."[105] In time the contrary was all that remained of the sacred in English drama. According to Perkins it was all there had ever been.

105. Quoted by Debora Shugar, *Habits of Thought in the English Renaissance: Religion, Politics, and the Dominant Culture* (Berkeley: University of California Press, 1990), p. 86, with a footnote to other passages of this sort in the works of English Protestants.

CHAPTER 3

Vicarious Criminal

Christ as Representative

The awareness that the symbolic communication with the deity
through sacrifice was not real must have been age-old.

—THEODOR ADORNO AND
MAX HORKHEIMER

Antigraphy (the Making of the Septuagint)

Legend has it the group of writings now loosely called the Septuagint first came into being when Ptolemy II Philadelphus (285–46 BCE)
resolved to place in his library at Alexandria every text then in existence.[1]
The story of his resolution became especially popular among later Christians for explaining how they had inherited a *Greek* Old Testament that
happened to be more readily compatible with Christ than was the Hebrew Bible. The Septuagint, it turns out, is the Bible that Jesus frequently
quotes, the Bible whose law and prophecies he best fulfills, the one that
contains, for example, the prediction of his impossible birth from a virgin, which in Hebrew does not exist. When, in the Chester cycle, a pious Jew named Simeon vainly tries to restore the original reading and so
remove that impossibility, we will see how he winds up underscoring not
only the essential contrafactuality of Christian scripture, but also the indis-
pensability, to true faith, of parabiblical literature: that is, all the belated

---

1. Whether there was any actual Ptolemaic involvement in the translation has been
much debated. For bibliography and discussion, see Gilles Dorival, Marguerite Harl, and
Olivier Munnich, *La Bible Grecque des Septante: Du judaïsme hellénistique au christianisme ancien*
(Paris: Cerf, 1988), pp. 72–78.

translations and elaborations, such as medieval drama, that would transmit the truths of scripture by altering it. The New Testament does this in its quotations from the Old, and medieval drama does it to the Bible as a whole—if not also to the apocrypha; the *Gospel of Nicodemus*, for instance (supposedly written by Simeon's two sons), gives us the episode of Christ's descent into hell, which is as central to the creed as to the cycles but hardly evident from the approved canon. The Christian scriptures from which medieval drama draws its authenticity are in certain respects no less parabiblical than the drama; more pointedly, the Christian Bible of the Middle Ages was itself already a belated attempt at replication which threatened to usurp the textual authorities it meant to preserve. A selective sketch of its genesis should provide some final parallels—in the case of Philadelphus, almost a prehistory—of the way Antichrist, too, displaces the Word that he replicates, before we arrive, in the next chapter, at Marlowe's debt to both the Antichrist myth and the Greek Old Testament.

To partisans of Philadelphus, the collection at Alexandria offered the best possible means of reflecting, if such a thing were possible, his unparalleled sovereignty. The third king of Egypt in succession from Alexander the Great but "the first truly 'absolutist' ruler in antiquity,"[2] he was practically out of this world according to ancient sources: "with respect to the virtues required to reign," Philo testifies, "he was the best of all—not only of his contemporaries but of all who ever lived before." The word "Philadelphian" was accordingly still proverbial, centuries after, for incredible extravagance (*De vita Mosis* 2.29–30 [LCL vol. 6]). The way the *Letter of Aristeas* tells it (though neither a letter nor written by Aristeas, its fictional narrator), hundreds of thousands of books had accumulated by the time the royal librarian ascertained which scroll might supplement them all so as to produce an all-surpassing collection, one whose inescapable finitude would contain in itself, so to speak, the infinite. This was the word of God. And not just any God, but the absolute divinity worshipped under differing names by Greek and Jew alike (§15–16), whose directives had been set down in writing by his chosen intermediary, Moses the lawgiver.[3]

2. Martin Hengel with the assistance of Roland Deines, *The Septuagint as Christian Scripture: Its Prehistory and the Problem of Its Canon*, trans. Mark E. Biddle (Edinburgh: T & T Clark, 2002), p. 75.

3. I have relied primarily on the Greek text, notes, and accompanying translation of Moses Hadas, *Aristeas to Philocrates* (New York: Harper & Brothers, 1951), with regular consultation of the philological notes in Henry G. Meecham, *The Letter of Aristeas* (Manchester: Manchester University Press, 1935), along with his own translation and commentary, *The Oldest Version of the Bible: "Aristeas" and Its Traditional Origin: A Study in Early Apologetic with Translation and Appendices* (London: Holburn, 1932), while cross-referencing the notes and

According to the *Letter*, no sooner had the king's library acquired the unadorned word of God than it proved insufficient. "The books of the Law of the Jews, among a few others, are wanting," explains Demetrius, the librarian, "for it happens that these are written in Hebrew characters and the Hebrew tongue" (§30). The Bible was absent, even when present, because no one of consequence could actually read it—least of all Philadelphus. Those who could were an anonymous group of experts, though their expertise in this case only let them discern lacunae. "According to the testimony of experts," Demetrius further relates, the manuscripts "have been copied somewhat carelessly and not as they should be, for they have not received royal providence" (§30).[4] Earlier transcriptions had in other words lacked what the Greek translation now stood to gain. If not exactly divine inspiration, this was the next best thing. For by "providence" Demetrius means, in plainer speech, the money "provided" by the king.

Philadelphus' enormous buying power was in this case all the more imperative given the absence of any translated excerpt from, or reference to, the contents of the Pentateuch anywhere among the library's other "writers and poets and the whole army of historians" (§31). The literati had refused en masse all mention "of the aforementioned books," Demetrius explains, "because the views [*theōrian*] therein are sacrosanct and holy, as Hecataeus of Abdera says" (§31). It would seem that anybody who

---

translation into French by André Pelletier (SC 89). The account of "Aristeas" (hereafter without the tiresome scare quotes) has a long afterlife: it gets retold in abbreviated form with otherwise minor modifications by Josephus, *Jewish Antiquities* 12.11–118 (LCL vol. 7); cf. 1.10–14 (LCL vol. 4), *Against Apion* 2.45–47 (LCL vol. 1), and with major modification by Philo, *De vita Mosis* 2.25–40 (LCL vol. 6), assuming Philo actually had Aristeas as one of his sources—a fact not altogether agreed upon. Barring Jerome (see below, n. 70), the church Fathers repeat, alter, and elaborate on the legend with great relish; see Heinrich Karpp, "'Prophet' oder 'Dolmetscher': Die Geltung der Septuaginta in der Alten Kirche," in *Festschrift für Günther Dehn*, ed. Wilhelm Schneemelcher (Neukirchen: Kreis Moers, 1957), pp. 103–17 (esp. 107ff.), and Pierre Benoit, "L'inspiration des Septante d'après les Pères," in *L'Homme devant Dieu: Mélanges offertes au Père Henri de Lubac*, 3 vols. (Paris: Aubier, 1963), 1:169–87.

4. Some philological intrigue here. The word translated as "copied" (σεσήμανται) means literally "indicated" and has occasioned a lot of debate. See R. J. H. Shutt, "The Letter of Aristeas," in *The Old Testament Pseudepigrapha*, ed. J. H. Charlesworth, 2 vols. (New York: Doubleday, 1985), 2:14 nn. e and f; also Oswyn Murray, "The Letter of Aristeas," in *Studi Ellenistici II: Biblioteca di studi antichi* 54 (Pisa: Giardini editori, 1987), p. 24 n. 29, where he sees the problem exacerbated by the *Letter's* systematic conflation of translation with transcription—both of which quickly overlap with "emendation" (i.e., διακριβοῦν). According to Murray this last term "is equivalent to the technical διορθοῦν" (24) of Alexandrian scholarship, on which see Rudolph Pfeiffer, *History of Classical Scholarship: From the Beginnings to the End of the Hellenistic Age* (Oxford: Clarendon Press, 1968), pp. 94, 110. More on this in a moment.

spoke of the Bible only affirmed its unspeakable character. (If anything the textual blemishes of the manuscripts seem to have helped preserve the purity of the Law by blocking its indiscriminate perusal. Thanks to scribal error the Law remained "flawless" [§31] to all but the faithless, who found it unreadable.) Its views (*theōrian*) could hardly be viewed (*theōrien*) on stage, either. As a final example of the Bible's holy ineffability, Demetrius relates the sad fate of the ironically named Theodectes ("acceptable to God"), who tried, once, to "introduce into a play something recorded in the Bible" (§316).[5] So divine (*theōrien*) a theology was simply not for the theater. Cataracts afflicted the poet forthwith. It was as though the hallowed intensity of the Hebrew scriptures could literally *blind* a practitioner of the spectacular arts. If only an authentic text might be established, and then somehow adequately translated, there could hardly be a more fitting illustration of so illustrious a king as Philadelphus, or a more demonstrative example of his unexampled accomplishments. His grandeur, like the Bible's, was indescribable. So was his wealth.

Thus there came into Greek a replica of the Bible allegedly composed with such exactitude that among Christians in particular it eventually displaced the Hebrew—not so much despite but rather *because* of its objective variance with that authoritative witness. (In time there also emerged a lot of resistance. Certain rabbis later rejected the Septuagint as an idol on par with the golden calf[6]—an anti-Bible, as it were, whose collateral purpose, even for Jewish apologists like Philo and Aristeas, had been to reflect the messianic pretensions of a worldly dictator.) The objective variance of the Septuagint with the Hebrew model(s) already in the royal library is precisely what proves to Aristeas, however, its superior status. Such is the premise underlying all textual criticism, then or since: the production of an authentic copy in every way identical to the original necessitates above all the production of a new edition to *stand in* for its

5. The first recorded instance of the word "book" (*biblos*) used for the Bible, according to Hadas, *Aristeas* (n. 3), pp. 223–25. Aristotle also mentions Theodectes: *Nicomachean Ethics* 1150b (LCL).

6. See the quotations from the Talmud in Natalio Fernández Marcos, *The Septuagint in Context: Introduction to the Greek Version of the Bible*, trans. Wilfred G. E. Watson (Leiden: Brill, 2000), p. 45; also Hadas, *Aristeas* (n. 3), pp. 80–81 and 117 n. 44. For the developing insistence on Hebrew as the *exclusive* language of revelation, see Sebastian Brock, "To Revise or Not to Revise: Attitudes to Jewish Biblical Translation," in *Septuagint, Scrolls and Cognate Writings: Papers Presented to the International Symposium on the Septuagint and Its Relation to the Dead Sea Scrolls and Other Writings (Manchester, 1990)*, ed. George J. Brooke and Barnabas Lindars (Atlanta: Scholars Press, 1992), pp. 301–38, esp. 320–24.

predecessors.[7] If an extant copy were sufficiently pristine to speak for
the original, there would be no need for textual editing—a need that in
ancient Alexandria was famously deep-felt; spurred by the vast number
of variants in authoritative texts such as Homer, the city's grammarians
began to collate the classics as never before. The genius of Aristeas was
to fuse this Alexandrine enthusiasm for emendation with the process of
biblical translation, so that the Septuagint appears in his account less a
subordinate replica than a superior *restoration* of its ultimately superfluous model.[8] Without the textual emendation inherent to the process of
translation as the *Letter* envisions it, there would *be* no original to speak
of. Demetrius can tell the king that the books of Moses "need to be with
you," even when the king already has them, because Demetrius knows
that the king cannot authentically possess them unless he acquires yet
another *copy*. Replication establishes authenticity. And the replica is authentic only insofar as it *differs*: that is why Demetrius thinks the sole text
suitable for an authority of the king's stature is a "copy" that has not been
copied *exactly* but *emended* (§31), rather. An ideological vision, to be sure,
but one that a history of irretrievable losses has come partly to endorse:
today scholars of the Hebrew Bible regularly concede, with forceful evidence from the Dead Sea Scrolls, that the Greek text in places could well
be older than the Masoretic and therefore on occasion a more authoritative witness to the earliest Hebrew than the Hebrew we now possess.[9]

So much for the autograph of Moses. And so much for its separatist
function: even the Decalogue's most distinctive trait vis-à-vis Alexandrian
paganism—namely the ban on worshipping idols, images, or any other human "invention" (§136)—contributes in the *Letter* to the complex rapproche-
ment of these opposed religions. "All the rest of mankind (excepting
ourselves)," the High Priest tells Aristeas on a trip to Jerusalem, "make
images from stone and wood and declare that these are likeness of those

---

7. For this point I am much indebted to Margreta de Grazia and Peter Stallybrass, for
example, "The Materiality of the Shakespearean Text," *Shakespeare Quarterly* 44.3 (1993):
255–83.

8. See Günther Zuntz, "Aristeas Studies 2: Aristeas and the Translation of the Torah," in
Studies in the Septuagint: Origins, Recensions, and Interpretations, ed. Sidney Jellicoe (New York:
KTAV, 1974), pp. 208–25, esp. 210–13; also Murray, "Letter of Aristeas" (n. 4), p. 24, and
then for the fullest, most persuasive account to date, Sylvie Honigman, *The Septuagint and
Homeric Scholarship in Alexandria* (London: Routledge, 2003), pp. 44ff., 119ff.

9. See Frank Moore Cross, *The Ancient Library of Qumrân*, 3rd ed. (Sheffield: Sheffield
Academic Press, 1995), pp. 128–42. For a more recent synopsis of the secondary literature
and some cautionary remarks about overhasty use of the LXX to edit the Masoretic Text,
see Marcos, *Septuagint in Context* (n. 6), pp. 70ff.

who have made some discovery beneficial to life, and these they worship" (§§134–35). The pagan gods that had up to then received so much adulation were according to this passage originally great men, such as Philadelphus, whose contributions to humanity had long ago become the subject of a far more idolatrous inventiveness—that of the poets and other writers, such as Aristeas. The stories of these "fabricators and mythmakers" (§137) amount, in the eyes of the High Priest, to the fraudulent apotheosis of people who merely "took things [already] in creation and recombined them...though they themselves did not make these things" (§136). Poetry, too, was at best a recombination of existing elements into some pseudo-novelty, so that in elevating creative types to the status of gods, the poets had absurdly "deified their equals," which in Greek is to say their own "likenesses" (*homoious*; §137). Human re-creation had in this way overtaken the Creator.

And yet the usurpation is not quite so "vain" (*kenov*; §136) as the High Priest makes out—or rather the emptiness of any made thing in comparison with the Unmade is here, as elsewhere, equally a point of contact (cf. Phil. 2:6). Again the priestly attack on idol worship hardly excludes all material support from Bible-based devotion but on the contrary mediates their collaboration—just as, in the *Letter*, the Mosaic code mediates between, and so reconciles, the very peoples it would separate. That is, the prohibitions in the Pentateuch against images (and countless other pagan activities) are explicitly designed, according to the High Priest, to function as "impregnable palisades and iron walls to prevent our mixing with any of the other peoples in any matter" (§139), yet it is precisely this text of prevention, once emended in translation, that will epitomize the utopia of Jewish-pagan cooperation as against their straight assimilation or the subsumption of one by the other.[10] Because in the end it is an extremely specialized Greek "invention"—the Septuagint—that alone enables "a Jew to remain a Jew and, *at the same time*, to belong to the elect society of the Greeks, the bearers of world culture."[11] Only by way of a Greek Bible can the Jewish population, otherwise enslaved in Egypt (along with the natives), participate *as Jews* in the perquisites of their cultural and political masters.[12]

10. See V. Tcherikover, "The Ideology of the Letter of Aristeas," in Jellicoe, *Studies in the Septuagint* (n. 8), pp. 181–207; Murray, "Letter of Aristeas" (n. 4), p. 17–18, 24; Honigman, *Septuagint* (n. 8), pp. 17–25 and passim.

11. Tcherikover, "Ideology of the Letter," p. 203; my emphasis.

12. This fantasy of reconciliation clearly depends on the exclusion of a native population. In this the *Letter* is a consummate text of occupation. Cf. Andrew W. Erskine, "Culture and Power in Ptolemaic Egypt: The Museum and the Library of Alexandria," *Greece and Rome* 42.1 (1995): 38–48, esp. 43.

As in the gospel of Mark, drama here too would reconcile biblical Judaism with its pagan superiors, inasmuch as the Bible cannot be staged according to the *Letter* but somehow anyway is: the edition-*qua*-translation that would legitimately claim to reveal the Jewish God to a non-Jewish king gets created, after all, through a clandestinely sanctioned *performance.* Aristeas implicitly draws here on the Jewish convention whereby the unpunctuated, unpointed Bible has to be vocalized in order to be read; as a result the text "in itself" never consists exclusively of the words on the page. On the page there are no words, but consonants only, and all too often these allow for interpretative conflict.[13] Only by *sounding out* the correct reading could scholars establish what the text "really" said. And in the mind of Aristeas what they established was nothing less than the right way to "perform" what the Law itself had prescribed.

So, if the Bible cannot be staged by the Greeks (recall the fate of Theodectes), that is only because its correct venue is the Temple at Jerusalem where its holiest rituals are to be *exclusively* realized. Only through this exclusion can Jerusalem include Athens: for all of Judaism's transcendence of pagan theatricalization, its holiest of cities nonetheless appears to the visiting Aristeas "like a theater" (§105), and later the Jewish elders go so far as to advise Philadelphus that in times of leisure it is best "to watch plays done with propriety and to set before one's eyes scenes from life performed with decency and restraint" (§284). Apparently the Jews' religion, too, had theater at its center—and therefore prohibited all competing dramatizations. In place of Aristotle's carefully regimented, theoretical decorums, we simply find instead some quasi-Mosaic regulations on what counts as "proper" drama (cf. §219).

Aristeas clearly wants to link this (partly fabricated) penchant for performance in the Jewish tradition to the enviable standards of Alexandrine scholarship, where any editorial enterprise similarly began by reading a text out loud (*anagnōsis*; §305). This sort of recital, according to Dionysius Thrax—a disciple of Aristarchus, the second-century librarian at Alexandria some years after the reign of Philadelphus and closer in time, for that reason, to the historical "Aristeas"—was not for the lackadaisical; it required above all that the scholar read "with dramatic expression" (*kath' hypokrisin*).[14] At Alexandria this specifically meant emending the text so as

13. Elias Bickerman, "The Septuagint as Translation," in *Studies in Jewish and Christian History,* pt. 1 (Leiden: Brill, 1976), pp. 167–200; here 191 n. 63.

14. Text given in William G. Rutherford, *A Chapter in the History of Annotation, Being Scholia Aristophanica III* (1905; repr., New York: Garland, 1987), p. 97 (English); p. 98 n. 2 (Greek). The relation between this account and that of Aristeas has been emphasized by

to *allow for* the dramatic expression that the grammarians axiomatically imagined had been the author's original creation. Every critic was consequently a hypocrite: no sooner had he repaired the copies of his predecessors through a performative *anagnōsis* than the copyists of this restored text "marred it by their own emendations."[15] To the hypokritical copyist, however, the true text could only be *salvaged* by continued corruption. Such corruption, for him, was renewal.

Aristeas gives in passing a fitting name to this hybrid process of performance, emendation, cultural reconciliation, and the recovery (through translation) of an otherwise inaccessible, utopian original: in one place at least he calls it *antigraphē* (§28a)—though that is not the word you will find in the paraphrase of the *Letter* by Josephus or the extracts of Eusebius, since both of them appear, indeed, to have emended their texts. Even more ironically, their reading has been adopted, sometimes without acknowledgment, by all three of the modern English editions, despite the *complete* unanimity of the manuscript tradition on the word *antigraphē*[16] and despite the fact that the word these editions substitute for it (*anagraphē*) does not quite fit the context.[17] *Antigraphē* unquestionably does: the term includes in its lexical range not only "transcript" and "copy" (in this case its denotative meaning) but also "a counter-reckoning of money paid or received" (L&S), which is just what the Greek Bible, for Aristeas, turns out to be: the transcript of a scholarly performance paid for by Philadelphus and the return receipt on his massive investment. A true "genius of

---

Arie van der Kooij, "Perspectives on the Septuagint: Who Are the Translators?" in *Perspectives in the Study of the Old Testament and Early Judaism*, ed. F. García Martínez and E. Noort (Leiden: Brill, 1998), pp. 214–29; here 222.

15. Elias Bickerman, "Some Notes on the Transmission of the Septuagint," in *Studies in Jewish and Christian History*, pt. 1 (n. 13), pp. 137–66; here 158.

16. See the text of H. St. J. Thackeray, appended to Henry Barclay Swete, *An Introduction to the Old Testament in Greek*, rev. Richard Rusden Ottley (1902; repr., New York: KTAV, 1968), p. 556, where he grants in his apparatus that all the mss., without exception, contain a different reading from the one he adopts, but he curiously fails, for all that, to put the reading he prints instead (taken from Josephus and Eusebius) in angular brackets as per his stated policy for "emendations of, or insertions introduced into, the reading of the MSS" (550). Hadas, who used Thackeray, as a result didn't notice the change and so failed anywhere to note it. Meecham likewise reproduces the text of Thackeray and so also omits *antigraphē*, but then includes an endnote on its meaning—"Here synonymous with μεταγραφή" (199)—despite there being in his own text no here here. Metagraphy, indeed! André Pelletier (SC 89:118) rightly relegates Josephus and Eusebius to the apparatus, as does Palvis Wendland, ed., *Aristeae ad Philocratem Epistula: Cum Ceteris de Origine Versionis LXX Interpretum Testimoniis* (Leipzig: Teubner, 1900).

17. See the explanation given by Zuntz, "Aristeas Studies 2" (n. 8), p. 211 n. 2.

fiscality,"[18] Philadelphus offers gifts to the Jews who in turn offer sacrifices in the Temple on his behalf, "that your affairs," the High Priest assures him, "might always turn out as you desire…and that the translation of the sacred Law might come about to your profit" (§45). In fact it is here in the dramatic commerce of aristocratic and religious offertories that we see the deepest and most phantasmatic reconciliation between Jew and Greek, as though in the *Letter* God were primarily a name for the common substrate of all human exchange, and by extension for the more various mechanisms of representative substitution on which sacrificial atonement, textual emendation, translation, and the mimesis of theater all depend.

Given the impotence of his in-house experts, Philadelphus has to invest heavily if he wants to find critics both intimately acquainted with Hebrew and sufficiently skillful in the art of *hypokrisis* to conjure, at last, the original Pentateuch from its less than perfect—or perfect but ambiguously silent—copies. Who else to ask but the Jews of Palestine? It is here that Aristeas, an adviser to Philadelphus, introduces himself into the story as the bearer of a fatal objection. On what conceivable grounds could anyone persuade these people to give Philadelphus an emended translation of the Bible, when more than a hundred thousand of them had been enslaved by his father, then used as currency to pay off his soldiers, to whom they still belonged as servants (§15)? His army owns half as many Jews as Philadelphus owns books! No sooner has Aristeas pointed out this impasse than a solution presents itself: Philadelphus will have to *redeem* (§20) the Hebrew people from their servitude. That is, for the current king of Egypt to read, in Greek, how Moses freed his people from a former king of Egypt, Philadelphus must first *enact* the narrative himself as though his actions had been already scripted, so to speak, by the prior events of sacred history—events that were therefore still open, like anything scripted, to dramatic improvement. In this case the emendation that is Philadelphus' next act—in the dramatic sense of the word— fulfills the Exodus narrative "typologically": he effects its *reversal*. This time around on hearing a plea for Jewish freedom, the king of Egypt immediately resolves, of an unhardened heart, to make "a thank-offering [*charistikon*] to God the Most High," who, he gladly acknowledges, "has preserved our kingdom in peace and with the mightiest glory throughout the inhabited world" (§37). The glory of Philadelphus, we learn, has all along been none other than the reflected glory of the Jewish God; his

---

18. M. Rostovtzeff, "Seleucid Babylonia: Bullae and Seals of Clay with Greek Inscriptions," *Yale Classical Studies* 3 (1932): 68; quoted by Hadas, *Aristeas* (n. 3), p. 114.

open recognition of that debt then accounts for why "God enabled [him] to become a means of salvation to large multitudes" (§21; cf. §18). Philadelphus, an anti-Pharaoh in contrast to his predecessor, simply manumits every Jewish slave in his jurisdiction by paying off, at huge expense, his own military.

This ungrudging gift of redemption, with all its godlike beneficence, has been obviously fabricated by the *Letter* to demonstrate Philadelphus' worthiness as a recipient of scripture. It helps in this regard that Philadelphus gives more than mere redemption actually takes: after commanding that a letter be written to Eleazar, the High Priest of Jerusalem, informing him of the slaves' liberation, Philadelphus then allocates of his own volition "fifty talents in weight and seventy talents of silver and a great quantity of [precious] stones" to be used "for the construction of bowls and goblets and a table and libation cups," and then adds "for sacrifices and other purposes...as much as a hundred talents of coined money" (§33). What makes this extravagance so interesting (to begin with) is that Philadelphus clearly intends with these gifts to *buy* his Bible—or rather, given the peculiar *do-ut-des* logic of aristocratic gift exchange, to trigger with his magnanimity the reciprocal "gift" of scripture. Philadelphus is "worthy" to receive scripture mainly because he is able to offer an incalculable wealth in exchange for it. And what makes his wealth "incalculable," for the chronicler Aristeas, is explicitly the secular "miracle" of mimetic art. Philadelphus does not give the stones and talents directly to the Jews but instead first sends them to the royal craftsmen with the command "to use the arts to the fullest, in all their scope" (§56). He thereby demonstrates in himself a piety of far greater consequence than faith in any god; he has, in short, "a knack for picturing the appearance of things" (§56). The point here is that his inbred aesthetic instinct, his eye for the *appearance* of his expenditure, itself elevates his payment above monetary or gift exchange and in such a way as to guarantee its *religious* worth. (It is, by the way, a similar love of "beauty" in opposition to the "charm of gold or any other treasure prized by the vainglorious" [§8] that qualifies Philocrates, the *Letter*'s putative addressee, as a suitable recipient.) Philadelphus gives not just gold and coins but gold coins further transformed and ornately wrought—partly *objets d'art* and partly, at the king's insistence, usable stage props in the Jews' own rituals of sacrifice.

"The artistry of the works" aids in the ultimate purpose of those rituals by remaining, despite Aristeas' lengthy descriptions, "totally indescribable" (§78). In this they make a fitting backdrop for the High Priest, whose costume is also "indescribable" (§97) and among whose ineffable vestments is an "inimitable mitre" (§98) fitted with gold plate on which the unspeakable "name of God" has been "engraved in relief [*ektypoun*]" (§98)—"typed," as it were, on the gold's surface. The total effect, Aristeas affirms, was that after witnessing the priest's performance "you might think you had come out of this world into another" (§99). Admittedly the Greek here is a little strange and follows a probable lacuna in the manuscript (itself something of an aperture to the indescribable), but the role of all the artifacts remains clear enough: essentially it is up to them to convey this "otherworldliness," in that the indescribable artistry of the craftsmen consists entirely of making the artifacts appear as though they haven't been crafted. Consequently "the overall effect of the spectacle was entirely beyond description, and even those who approached to view were unable to tear themselves away from the brilliance and delight in what they saw" (§77). The king's men created the face of the offertory table, for example, out of three different pieces, but so carefully dovetailed—so "marvelously contrived" (§67)—that the seams were "invisible and undiscoverable" (§71) and presented to viewers "an inimitable sight" (§67), not unlike the inimitable mitre bearing the unspeakable name of God. It was as though they stood before the Unmade.

The centrality of this table in the sublime ekphrasis of Aristeas is not accidental. "The most important sanctum except for the Ark,"[19] it was meant to display, as an offertory to the Lord every Sabbath, the fresh loaves of bread that were afterwards eaten by priests—and *only* by priests (Lev. 24:9; Mt 12:4).[20] So it is here that the "thank-offering" of Philadelphus will be finally transmuted into an offering acceptable to God, here that God will be bound to reciprocate and then reveal himself to the king in scripture, even if what those scriptures reveal is nothing other than the Exodean

19. Jacob Milgrom, *Leviticus 23–27: A New Translation with Introduction and Commentary*, AB 3b (New York: Doubleday, 2001), p. 2092.

20. That is, the "show bread," so called after Luther's *Schaubrot*, first brought into English by his advocate Tyndale and retained through to the AV (excepting Douai-Rheims). NRSV gives instead "bread of the presence," which is basically what the church Fathers took it to prefigure in type. See Jerome, *Ad Titum* 2.14 (CCSL 77c:54–55); John of Damascus, *De fide orth.* 4.13 (PG 94:1135–54; trans. Frederic H. Chase in *Writings*, FC 37:354–61); Cyril of Jerusalem, *Catechesis* 12.1 (PG 33:728A; trans. Leo P. McCauley and Anthony A. Stephenson, in *Works*, FC 61:228). All cited by the Douai-Rheims in a side note to Exod. 25:30 as proof that "Christ is really present in the B. Sacrament. For if there were bread in substance, it should not excel the figure; which is required in euerie thing prefigured"; that is, if the bread were not transubstantiated, it would be the *same* as its typological prefiguration, rather than its fulfillment. The "excess" of an antitype over its type is in this case literally the flesh of Christ.

narrative and ritual requirements that Philadelphus, in making the table, has already fulfilled. The table *is* the Septuagint—in the flesh, so to speak. Or better yet, the Septuagint in *gold*, for only in the Septuagint is the offertory table designed the way Philadelphus designs his: where the Hebrew stipulates that the table be "*overlaid* with gold" (Exod. 25:24, 37:11), the Greek "translation" emends the stipulation so that the gold now has to be *solid* (Exod. 25:22 [LXX]; §57). The table consummates Philadelphus' trade for the Bible, in other words, because Aristeas borrows his description of it directly *from* the translation for which it is traded. Even before getting his Greek Bible, Philadelphus thus has his craftsmen forge its advance embodiment. In exchange, seventy-two elders arrive in Alexandria from Jerusalem bearing a Hebrew Torah, on the basis of which they will make their real return gift, the translation. Even the Torah, however, is tellingly written in "gold" letters on "precious parchment" so "wonderfully worked" that the scroll (or maybe the letters) has been "imperceptibly joined together" (§176). Sound familiar? What we have here is quite a technical feat: the golden appearance of an *unmade* book, of an *unwritten* script, one that when translated will make yet another counterpart to Philadelphus' gifts, which likewise efface their human and political origin.

Or half efface, rather, since viewers can marvel at the seeming otherworldliness of such artifacts *only if they know full well* that the objects are really the product of human hands. Consider for example how the sculpted ivy and acanthus are wound about the table's legs "with such an abundance of skill and art as to approach reality without deviation, so that if a breath of wind moved, the leaves stirred in their place, everything having been modeled [or "typed"] on the pattern of reality" (§70). The quasi-religious wonder felt by the table's onlookers is inspired, on the one hand, by an artificiality or artistry all the more conspicuous the more natural its products appear; on the other, even as this "abundance" of artistic technique approximates, it also *exceeds* nature in such a way as to seem *super*natural. Key to this conversion from a purely idolatrous image to one of iconic excess is the firm knowledge of the viewers that what they are seeing is not actually real: where the representation appears, through sheer technique, to be *more* than representation, this effect only confirms the mimetic "preeminence" that would instantly evaporate if the leaves (for example) ever became, even for an instant, real leaves. If the leaves moving in the breeze were real, they would hardly mesmerize with their "invisible" artifice. The artistry appears all the more the less it appears—or as Kant once put it, "Nature proved beautiful when it wore the appearance of art; and art can only be termed beautiful, where we are conscious of its being art, while yet it has the appearance of nature."²¹ On this, the *Letter* suggests a materialist gloss: the surpassing, transcendent value of mimetic beauty exists only so long as the representation cannot be equated with immediate, time-bound existence because only in such representations is "reality" (whether natural or social) freed through fiction from the domination from which it would, in turn, free its audience.²² You might think you had come out of the real world into another.

Is not the whole of the *Letter* an extended exercise in the same techniques of escapist realism that Aristeas celebrates in the artworks of Philadelphus? Only, instead of making the narrative appear "natural," the whole of Aristeas' artifice has been directed toward making it seem *historical.* Hence his regular inclusion of his sources in the form of *antigrapha*— that is, allegedly verbatim copies of strictly historical documents, official letters, and the like (§§21, 28, passim).²³ The *antigraphon* means to authenticate what would otherwise seem a patent fabrication, yet this added effect of "authenticity" only heightens the wonder of readers who know in their hearts he has made it all up: "I suppose that everyone likely to get

---

21. Immanuel Kant, *Kritik der Urteilskraft*, §45, ed. Wilhelm Weischedel (Frankfurt am Main: Suhrkamp Taschenbuch, 1957), p. 241; trans. Werner S. Pluhar (Indianapolis: Hackett, 1987), p. 174. These considerations are inextricably bound up with a certain "as if" that allows for the apprehension of one thing as another even while maintaining their difference. For the role of this figure in Kant, see Herman Parret, ed., *Kants Ästhetik* (Berlin: de Gruyter, 1997), pp. 219ff. More generally, Hans Vaihinger, *The Philosophy of "As If": A System of the Theoretical, Practical and Religious Fictions of Mankind*, trans. C. K. Ogden (1911; repr., London: Routledge & Kegan Paul, 1968); Wolfgang Iser, *The Fictive and Imaginary: Charting Literary Anthropology* (Baltimore: Johns Hopkins University Press, 1993), pp. 13–17; Slavoj Žižek, *The Sublime Object of Ideology* (London: Verso, 1990), pp. 33ff.; Catherine Gallagher and Stephen Greenblatt, *Practicing New Historicism* (Chicago: University of Chicago Press, 2000), pp. 168–69, esp. n. 5. This issue runs very deeply throughout Christian theology, beginning with the God of Paul, who "calls nonbeings *as if* [ὡς] they were beings" (Rom. 4:17). Belief in such a God, for Paul, should then result in a comportment vis-à-vis the world that is at once apocalyptic and deeply aesthetic, insofar as he would have his followers treat facts, here in the meantime, "as if" they were a fanciful drama: "The time is short.... [T]hose who have wives should be as if [ὡς μή] they had none, and those who weep as if they wept not, and those who rejoice as if they did not rejoice, and those who buy as if they had no goods, and those who use the world as if they were making no use of it. For the figure [σχῆμα] of this world is passing away" (1 Cor. 7:29–31). See also the discussion of the Christian "as if" in Jean-Luc Marion, *God without Being: Hors-Texte*, trans. Thomas A. Carlson (Chicago: University of Chicago Press, 1991), pp. 88ff. and 126–32; Hent de Vries, *Philosophy and the Turn to Religion* (Baltimore; Johns Hopkins University Press, 1999), pp. 199–203.

22. For the full theoretical reticulation of this idea, see *AT*, esp. the paired chapters on Natural and Art Beauty, pp. 97–154; trans. 61–100.

23. For more on these, see Werner Schmidt, *Untersuchungen zur Fälschung historischer Dokumente bei Pseudo-Aristaios* (Bonn: Dr. Rudolph Habelt, 1986).

hold of this account," Aristeas admits toward the end, "will find it incredible" (§296). His admission probably expresses at bottom a certain self-satisfaction in his own literary accomplishment. After all, he has managed through the fiction of the *Letter* to unite Judaism, symbolically at least, not only with Alexandrian textual criticism but with pagan drama as well, while at the same time acting as a witness to the higher truths of God almighty. Outlandish, otherworldly—same difference.

Christ and Vicarious Substitution

The evangelist to whom tradition has dubiously ascribed the name of Paul's companion Luke (Philem. 1:24; Col. 4:14) likely modeled key aspects of his gospel on the *Letter of Aristeas*.[24] A fitting homage, given Luke's debt to the Septuagint, which moreover left its mark not just on him, writes Henry Barclay Swete, but "on every part of the New Testament."[25] In fact, as Swete goes on to emphasize, "it is not too much to say that in its literary form and expression the New Testament would have been a widely different book had it been written by authors who knew the Old Testament only in the original, or who knew it in a Greek version other than that of the LXX" (op. cit.). Until recently few scholars made any systematic attempt to absorb the full implications of Swete's observation.[26] This would have meant accepting fundamentally that the Protestant Old Testament (or in other words the Hebrew Bible of the early medieval rabbinate) is *not* the primary Bible of Christianity—at least, not the Christianity of the New Testament, or of the Fathers, and certainly not of the Middle Ages. On the contrary: the various Greek translations and Latin renderings, numbing in their variety and only haphazardly standardized

24. See Sidney Jellicoe, "St. Luke and the Letter of Aristeas," *Journal of Biblical Literature* 80 (1961):149–55, and idem, "St. Luke and the Seventy(-two)," *New Testament Studies* 6.4 (1960): 319–21.

25. Swete, *Introduction to the Old Testament in Greek* (n. 16), p. 404. On Luke specifically, see Fearghus Ó Fearghail, "The Imitation of the Septuagint in Luke's Infancy Narrative," *Proceedings of the Irish Biblical Association* 12 (1989):58–78; also (the aptly named) Luke Timothy Johnson, *The Writings of the New Testament: An Interpretation*, rev. ed. (Minneapolis: Fortress, 1999), pp. 217, 226.

26. Such attempts include Jennifer M. Dines, *The Septuagint*, ed. Michael A. Knibb (London: T & T Clark, 2004), esp. pp. 142–43. Morgens Müller, *The First Bible of the Church: A Plea for the Septuagint* (Sheffield: Sheffield Academic Press, 1996); see also Marcos, *Septuagint in Context* (n. 6), pp. 320–37; Dorival et al., *Bible Grecque* (n. 1), pp. 274–88; Karen H. Jobes and Moisés Silva, *Invitation to the Septuagint* (Grand Rapids: Baker Academic, 2000), pp. 183–205; finally R. Timothy McLay, *The Use of the Septuagint in New Testament Research* (Grand Rapids: Eerdmans, 2003).

by the plethora of versions that would eventually pass for "Jerome's" Vulgate, all of which to some extent *retain* the Septuagint-based Old Latin Jerome had been commissioned to replace[27]—these are the primitive, patristic, and medieval scriptures, to the average Christian no more or less authentic compared to their allegedly univocal origin than the other apocryphal legends, pseudo-gospels, and dramatic reenactments that circulated with minimal hindrance throughout the Middle Ages.

The consequences of that license are enormous, and enormously complex. Among other things it confirms that for the better part of Christian history—all of it, anyway, that we've so far experienced—there has been no single, authentic Bible, only a multitude of competing versions whose incompatibility is a primary motive behind the search for some singular corrective that yet another revision of scripture, yet another new edition, might someday recapture. The tellingly named "New" Testament itself epitomizes the proliferation of novel scriptures toward the end of unifying and finishing an ongoing set of originals: this seminal addendum would perfect a speciously singular "Bible" by *adding to* an already interminable series of textual fissures. (Recall that the New Testament contains in itself no fewer than four recapitulations of its central saving narrative, and that the irreconcilable discrepancies among the retellings have themselves inspired an unthinkable load of further additions in the form of exegesis and criticism.) One particular textual mystery neatly illustrates the constitutive plurality of Christian scripture: more often than not whenever Jesus "himself" quotes the Bible, his quotations demonstrably stem from the Septuagint—even in Matthew, where the evangelist is fully capable of reproducing the non-Hellenized versions that would have been closer, presumably, to what Jesus really cited.[28] In other words the Christ

---

27. For a compact overview of the ms. families of the medieval Vulgate, see J. K. Elliott, "The Translations of the New Testament into Latin: The Old Latin and the Vulgate," in *Aufstieg und Niedergang der Römischen Welt: Geschichte und Kultur Roms im Spiegel der neueren Forschung*, pt. 2, ed. Hildegard Temporini (Berlin: de Gruyter, 1972–), 26.1:198–245, with an appendix on the Old Testament. The hybridity of the Vulgate has four main sources: (1) Jerome himself appears for some reason to have revised little of the New Testament beyond the gospels (221); (2) his retranslation of the Old Testament was in places based on the LXX (as was the Old Latin), not the Hebrew—for example, the version of the Psalms that Coverdale translates, whence it enters the Book of Common Prayer, is Jerome's revision of the Old Latin against the LXX of Origen's Hexapla, *not* a translation of the Hebrew Psalms (240); (3) "compromises between the new and the old text meant that many of Jerome's manuscripts were contaminated with familiar Old Latin readings" (222); (4) Successive attempts at correction then introduced fresh contaminations (222).

28. See Richard N. Longenecker, *Biblical Exegesis in the Apostolic Period*, 2nd ed. (Grand Rapids: Eerdmans, 1999), pp. 45–50. For a detailed discussion of Matthew in particular,

of the gospels shows an even more consistent preference for the Septuagint than the evangelists themselves, on whom its influence was nonetheless extremely pronounced. (And in any case—this cannot be stressed too much—when quoting the Hebrew Bible, aside from a few exceptions, the New Testament "quotes" it *in Greek*,[29] which is to say, the quotations automatically introduce a major difference, on par with that of the Septuagint, whether they reproduce the Septuagint's specific wording or not.) As a consequence, what Christ actually fulfills is rather like a *new* Old Testament. By citing the scriptures, but citing them in Greek, the figure of Jesus rewrites the scriptures; in this way he expresses their ultimate but alterior truth—Himself—or at any rate the truth he plans to have on his final return, whose narration will likely require a new New Testament, if the making of books does not altogether end with it.

Historically the truth of Christian scripture has been that of antithesis: not only the upside-down beatitudes where the last shall be first and the neediest will someday inherit the earth but also, more dialectically, in Christ's affirmation of Mosaic law at the point of its nullification. "Do not think that I have come to abolish the law or the prophets," he says in the Sermon on the Mount. "I have come not to abolish but to fulfill" (Mt 5:17). The reassurance probably comes in the negative because his program had been confused with pure abolition by some of his most committed (Pauline or proto-Marcionite) followers, who were at the time competing with Matthew's message—to say nothing of the competition mounted by Christ's enemies. Speaking for the latter centuries later, Celsus complains that the New Testament's God plainly "forgot the commands which he had given to Moses," for in Jesus he appears to "condemn his own Laws, and change his mind, and send his messenger for the opposite purpose" (*C. Celsum* 7.25). The charge might have stung Christians more if the whole of their scriptural allegoresis, from Origen on, had not taken such opposition as an essential *confirmation* of the "fulfillment" offered by Christ. He did not offer fulfillment in any more straightforward sense because he

---

see Robert H. Gundy, *The Use of the Old Testament in St. Matthew's Gospel: With Special Reference to the Messianic Hope* (Leiden: Brill, 1967), esp. pp. 147–52; Jobes and Silva, *Invitation to the Septuagint* (n. 26), summarize these complex issues neatly: for Matthew "the LXX form is often more suitable than a literal translation of the Hebrew" (193–94).

29. The exceptions are not without interest: Jesus' final words according to Mk 15:34 and Mt 27:46 are a quotation of Ps 22:1, directly transliterated first by the evangelists *before* they translate it, probably in order to explain why the bystanders mistook his appeal to God (in Aramaic, "Eli" or "Eloi") for an appeal to "Elijah." Thus Christ founds his church in death as in life—with a pun.

embodied it typologically. According to this patristic commonplace, writ large across the cycle plays, Christ on the Mount could simultaneously fulfill and nullify the Law received by Moses on Sinai because Christ was his *antitype*.[30]

One particular quotation of Moses via the Septuagint especially stands out in this respect: "You have heard it said, an eye for [*anti*] an eye and a tooth for [*anti*] a tooth," Christ tells his listeners. "But I say to you, do not resist [*antistēnai*] the evil one" (Mt 5:38–39a).[31] Rhetorically linking the two halves of the antithesis is the Greek preposition at the heart of the present study, used in both of its central meanings. We see here on the one hand *anti-* as a principle of representation or exchange whereby one thing must answer for another as its pseudo-equivalent ("eye *for* an eye"); on the other, a kind of opposition: *anti-* as "against" in the verb "to resist," which Wyclif renders literally as "ayenstonde," that is, "stand against." (In *The Antichrist*, Nietzsche not incidentally called this "the most profound phrase of the gospels, their key in a certain sense" [§29].)[32] Incredibly Christ calls here for an *end* to any resistance of evil, that is, for a certain acquiescence to adversity, as he sees in the refusal to retaliate what we might call the vindi-cation of the talion: such refusal would fulfill, with its own "injustice," the *vindictive* prescription whereby one thing "justly" replaces another under the legal fiction that both are equal and therefore fairly traded in the scales of righteous discipline. Jesus would answer the inherent injustice of the Law (an eye for an eye), that is, with yet a further injustice (the cooperation with wrongdoing that is "mercy"). By this means he would extract from the Law a *higher* justice and so fulfill its spirit by violating the letter.

Whatever Jesus himself understood by his sermon, or the evangelist, in light of subsequent theological developments one could be forgiven for seeing the fiction of Christian fulfillment, in the broadest possible sense, pri-marily as a supplemental function of this prior, entirely "legal" yet contra-

30. See the Gloss: "Christ, whose type Moses bore" (PL 113:188D); also Dale C. Allison, *The New Moses: A Matthean Typology* (Minneapolis: Fortress, 1993), with helpful appendices summarizing the previous literature.

31. Quoting verbatim from LXX Exod. 21:24; Lev. 24:20; Deut. 19:21 (the Hebrew Bible omits the word "and"). I have intentionally chosen the most perverse way of translating Christ's counter-commandment, which could also be rendered "do not resist evil" or "an evil person," though Greek-speaking Fathers sometimes also took it as a reference to Satan: see, e.g., Chrysostom, *Comm. in Matt.*, Hom. 18.1 (PG 57:265; NPNF 10:124). The New Tes-tament makes reference to talionic law three more times: Rom. 12:17, 1 Thess. 5:15, and 1 Pet. 3:9. For further analysis, see Ingo Broer, "Das Ius Talionis im Neuen Testament," *New Testament Studies* 40 (1994): 1–21.

32. *The Portable Nietzsche*, trans. Walter Kaufmann (New York: Viking Penguin, 1954), p. 600.

factual premise: Christ's personal sacrifice will remain consistent with the talion, despite the felicitous immunity he confers on a guilty humanity, insofar as the very identity which that Law imposes, the Law, too, also suspends.[33] With an eye for an eye, the second eye, the "payment," cannot really in any way be the same as the eye it supposedly equals, or else its loss would not be *punitive*. Talionic punishment rests on the basic differential of any economic or mimetic substitution, only unlike exchange or mimesis, the talion requires that the fiction of sameness be inscribed on the flesh—that it be imposed *by force*. This practical violation of the mimetic and economic differentials presupposed by the legal theory legally violates the lawbreaker. The transfer of all human sin onto one divinely innocent victim would then somehow make of him the restoration or even the radicalization of the Law's originally fictive premise. His absolute uniqueness now coincides with his purely representative status:[34] Christ is subject to the Law's adequation even while being the *least* worthy of punishment, the *least* adequate representative of all human sin (because he is God, and innocent), and this inadequacy, already inherent to the Law's operation, becomes through him the superabundance of mercy. By dying as though he were guilty, he allows for humanity's "legal" survival as though we were innocent.

Over time there have evolved a lot of other explanations for Christ's complex teaching. The most traditional, which goes back at least as far as Tertullian in his battle against the Marcionite rejection of the Old Testament, says that the Jewish laws *necessitating* retaliation had obviously been designed to *prevent* retaliation. The spirit of the talion lay not in its real-world application but, as with Jonah's prediction of destruction, in the threat's resounding emptiness: simply fearing for your own eyes would cause you to spare others'. Or as Tertullian puts it, "By the fear of vengeance all iniquity is bridled" (*Adv. Marc.* 4.16 [CCSL 11:583; ANF 3:371]). Equally ancient is the frank acknowldgement that such a harness does not work: the threat of commensurate retribution sooner or later invariably spirals into ever more excessive cycles of vengeance with no easy cessation—other than, on Girard's view, the sacrifice of some impotent

---

33. Cf. Milgrom, *Leviticus 23–27* (n. 19), p. 2138: "It is plainly impossible to execute talion with absolute equality.... It must have been the primary experience of jurists (not legists!) over the ages that talion in cases of personal injury was not only impracticable, but unjust. In other words, *in such cases the very retributive equality that forms the basis of talion is totally vitiated*" (my emphasis).

34. A phrase I borrow, along with this chapter's epigraph, from some penetrating remarks on sacrifice by Theodor Adorno and Max Horkheimer, *Dialectic of Enlightenment: Philosophical Fragments*, ed. Gunzelin Schmid Noerr, trans. Edmund Jephcott (Stanford: Stanford University Press, 2002), pp. 6–7.

party who has no power to retaliate and whose impotence is typically worshipped thereafter as a divine form of innocence.[35] "Woe to the earth for its failures!" exclaims the anonymous writer of the *Opus imperfectum* (an Arian of considerable influence on Origen, as well as Jerome, and mistaken through the rest of the Middle Ages for Arianism's opponent, John Chrysostom).[36] "While the Law wanted to make evil good, it also made the good evil" (PG 56:699). Hence the need for Christ's dialectical innovations, which would redeem the Law from itself *by means of* itself: no longer giving evil for evil, but in exchange for evil, an incommensurate good. Such uneven trade would have been unfair, were not eye-for-eye justice itself already compromised by inequality and thus able to prefigure its "end" in Christian mercy.

Long before the gospels it had been anyway possible, when sinning, to preempt the Law's retaliation by offering more immediate goods to the injured party. When reporting the Sermon on the Mount, Matthew would in all likelihood have known that the synagogue had also taken concrete steps to avoid the escalating violence that the Law itself could appear to license: in certain cases rabbis used the law of retaliation to legitimate the payment of money as the preferred form of moral restitution.[37] It was preferable because completely ersatz. So for example in the verse preceding the

35. See René Girard, *Violence and the Sacred*, trans. Patrick Gregory (Baltimore: Johns Hopkins University Press, 1977). It will be obvious by now that I take exception to the exceptionalism of Girard's subsequent books, whereby Christianity, far from being a myth among others and so conforming to the impeccable logic of *Violence and the Sacred* (outlined in the sentence to which this note has been appended), entirely escapes that logic, even if no one ever realized this fact before the "scientific" reading of scripture bestowed on humanity by…René Girard. See, for example, *Things Hidden Since the Foundation of the World*—a title that on my view ranks with the messianic pretensions of Nietzsche's late essays in *Ecce Homo.*

36. See Franz Mali, *Das "Opus imperfectum in Matthaeum": Und sein Verhältnis zu den Matthäuskommentaren von Origenes und Hieronymus* (Innsbruck: Tyrolia-Verlag, 1991). The passage I quote in the next sentence has been translated in *Matthew 1–13*, ed. Manlio Simonetti (Downers Grove, Ill.: InterVarsity Press, 2001), p. 117.

37. Luz 1:330. See also the next two notes, plus those cited by Adrian Schenker, *Versöhnung und Widerstand: Bibeltheologische Untersuchung zum Strafen Gottes und der Menschen, besonders im Lichte von Exodus 21–22* (Stuttgart: Katholisches Bibelwerk, 1990), p. 50 n. 83, along with the discussion on pp. 61–73. This issue touches on another of comparable difficulty, namely, the much contested etymology of the Hebrew word for "atonement"—*kippēr* and its derivatives (e.g., *kōper*), which have been said to involve everything from expiation and ransom to bribery, propitiation, and vicarious substitution. For bibliography and discussion, see Baruch J. Schwartz, "The Prohibitions Concerning the 'Eating' of Blood in Leviticus 17," in *Priesthood and Cult in Ancient Israel*, ed. Gary A. Anderson and Saul M. Olyan (Sheffield: Sheffield Academic Press, 1991), pp. 51–60; also Baruch A. Levine, *Numbers 21–36: A New Translation with Introduction and Commentary*, AB 4a (New York: Doubleday, 2000), p. 559.

famous "eye for an eye" formulation in Leviticus, we read that "anyone who kills an animal shall make restitution for it, life for life " (Lev. 24:18). Scholars have thought that the phrase "life for life," coming so closely on the heels of an openly monetary call for "restitution," cannot easily mean "life for life" in a literal sense, so was probably taken in practice as just another *euphemism* for economic exchange. In fact it has been argued that nearly *all* the Hebrew laws demanding tit-for-tat retribution were equally euphemistic.[38] What these laws really entailed—or in any case could be mercifully interpreted as requiring—was for a person to give something of "equal" *value* to what he had destroyed, however objectively different the replacement might turn out to be; he could sometimes offer a substitute for the loss that, so to speak, materialized its absence. This substitute could then act as a makeshift stopgap against the threat of metastatic blood feuds.

Of course this was precisely the kind of ersatz stand-in that according to other passages in the Old Testament its retributive God refused to condone or accept—above all in cases of homicide, where the Hebrew jurists, too, seem least likely to have allowed monetary recompense: "Whoever sheds the blood of a human," God says to Noah, "by a human shall that person's blood be shed" (Gen. 9:6).[39] There was no obvious escape from this mandate other than interpreting such stipulations, wherever one could, as an allegory for money, which we know people often enough did, very early on, because the Bible expressly forbids it: for example, the commandment in Numbers, "You shall accept no ransom for the life of a murderer...but he shall be put to death" (35:31). Throughout the Hebrew Bible its legal prescriptions in other words seem to present a nearly perfect hermeneutic circle: the insistence on *blood* payment in places probably counters a cultural habit of reading that insistence elsewhere allegorically as licensing less painful, *fiscal* payments.

For Christians the allegory's historical fulfillment was supposed to be the blood money of Christ, and as usual their supposition got some help from the Septuagint. When the legendary Seventy came to a critical passage from Leviticus asserting, "It is the blood that makes atonement by reason of the life" (17:11), they rendered the instrumental *beth* (by means of) with the same preposition they had used (on surer grounds)[40] to translate talionic law: *anti*. So that for Greek-speaking Jews such as the writers of Christian

38. J. K. Mikliszanski, "The Law of Retaliation and the Pentateuch," *Journal of Biblical Literature* 66 (1947): 295–304; for critique, see Milgrom, *Leviticus 23–27* (n. 19), pp. 2122–24.

39. Cf. Lev. 24:17; Deut. 19:11–13; also Ezek. 3:18ff., 18:4ff.; and Ps 49:7–9.

40. Cf. Jakob Weismann, "Talion und öffentliche Strafe in Mosaischen Rechte," in *Um das Prinzip der Vergeltung in Religion und Recht des Alten Testaments*, ed. Klaus Koch

scripture, there would subsequently be an even stronger implication that the blood of a sacrificial victim could make atonement *"in place of* [*anti*] the life."* In place, that is, of the *sinner's* life! The sacrificial victim implicitly dies here *instead of* the atoning party, whose spiritual debt the victim pays with his life's blood so the guilty will not have to pay anything at all.[41] By most accounts biblical law traditionally forbade all such vicarious atonement, but then again the Bible contains more than the biblical: it contains as well "the basic motif of classical Greek literature, the representative death of a victim (ἀποθνῄσκειν ὑπερ: διδόναι ἑαυτὸν ὑπέρ), [which] first occurs in Jewish literature under Hellenistic influence"[42]—most pointedly in the suffering servant of Isaiah. This would be of tremendous aid to Christian syncretism by providing a proleptic, "Jewish" model for Christ's atoning death (e.g., Mt 12:18–21).[43] Matthew and Mark, in describing that death as a payment of sorts, both transfer the Septuagint's use of *anti-* in the talionic and Levitican laws to Christ's bloodied body, such that he offers himself on the cross as "ransom for (or in place of) many [*lutron anti pollōn*]" (Mk 10:45; Mt 20:28; cf. 1 Tim. 2:6). "It makes little difference," writes a modern commentator on this New Testament usage, "whether the word [*anti*] denotes an actual replacement, an intended replacement, or a mere equivalent in estimation (Heb. 12:16) or similarity (1 Cor. 11:15)....In Mk 10:45 and parallels...the saying still contains in substance the thought of representation or substitution....What he [Christ] does on their behalf is simply to take their place."[44]

(Darmstadt: Wissenschaftliche Buchgesellschaft, 1972), p. 350, who explains that the Hebrew preposition in the phrase "eye for [*tāḥăt*] an eye" means "originally 'under, in the position under someone,' in a transposed sense, 'in place of, instead.' So then it largely means replacement [*Ersatz*], in particular reimbursement [*Ersatz*] for an injury, damages." Cf. Joachim Jeremias, "Das Lösegeld für Viele (Mk. 10,45)," in *Abba: Studien zur neutestamentlichen Theologie und Zeitgeschichte* (Göttingen: Vandenhoeck & Ruprecht, 1966), p. 226.

41. So argues A. Metzinger, "Die Substitutionstheorie und das alttestamentliche Opfer mit besonderer Berücksichtigung von Lev. 17.11," *Biblica* 21 (1940): 159–87, 247–72, 353–77; here 356–64. His views have not been without controversy. For a discussion siding reluctantly in his favor, see Robert J. Daly, *Christian Sacrifice: The Judaeo-Christian Background before Origen* (Washington, D.C.: Catholic University of America Press, 1978), pp. 129–31 and 140–41; more generally on the topic of vicarious substitution, pp. 120–27; also Martin Hengel, *The Atonement: The Origins of the Doctrine in the New Testament* (Philadelphia: Fortress, 1981), esp. p. 50; and see the next note.

42. Karl-Heinz Menk, *Stellvertretung: Schlüsselbegriff christlichen Lebens und theologische Grundkategorie* (Freiburg: Johannes, 1991), p. 39.

43. See William H. Bellinger Jr. and William R. Farmer, eds., *Jesus and the Suffering Servant: Isaiah 53 and Christian Origins* (Harrisburg, Pa.: Trinity Press, 1998).

44. F. Büchsel, *Theological Dictionary of the New Testament*, trans. and ed. Geoffry W. Bromiley, 10 vols. (Grand Rapids: Eerdmans, 1964–76), 1:372–73.

For medieval Christians things were maybe not quite so simple as this commentator would have it, however, since they took pretty seriously the ambiguities of representation (of whatever kind) and saw in these a version of mysteries divine. To earlier generations the ransom verse, in conjunction with several others, meant that Christ had hung on the cross in humanity's place *as if* he were a criminal, that he effects payment on behalf of the truly corrupt only if he is *not* those whom he *only* represents. Christ may be "fully" human, but his humanity necessarily omits the one defining quality that, reckoned with the lawless (Isa. 53:12; Mk 15:28; Lk 22:37), he only *appears* to possess: sin. The whole of human salvation then ultimately turns on a mimetic or, more specifically, a *dramatic* distinction between Christ's real innocence and the guilty party he merely playacts; between his pure divinity, that is, and the sin that he "assumes," as an actor wears a frightful costume. According to the traditional gloss, when Paul wrote that God had made Christ "to *be* sin" (2 Cor. 5:21), actually this meant he costumed his son "in the *likeness* of sinful flesh" (Rom. 8:3) that Christ might become, at a strictly *figurative* level, "a curse for us" (Gal. 3:13) and so fulfill the Hebrew dictum, "Everyone is cursed who hangs on a tree" (ibid.; citing Deut. 21:23, LXX).[45] Visions of Judas! "Some of our own people, less learned in the scriptures," Augustine acknowledges, "unduly fearful about this passage and with due piety approving the ancient scriptures, do not think that this refers to the Lord but to Judas his betrayer."[46] Not true. Because just as Judas had feigned holiness, so too had Jesus posed as a traitor: "For 'our old humanity' would not have been 'crucified together with him,'" Augustine explains (paraphrasing Rom. 6:6), "unless in the Lord's death there had hung a *figure* of our sin [*peccati nostri figura*]" (op. cit.; my emphasis). The historical crucifixion offered no less "satisfaction" than if God had hung a fine painting—or staged a tragedy. Later, God will come openly, according to the psalmist (Ps 50:3). "Not disguised [*occultus*]," Augustine stresses, "the way he came the first time" (*Serm.* 263.1 [PL 38:1209;*WSA* III/7:219]).

Just how deeply entrenched this theatrical understanding of atonement had become in medieval culture can be easily gathered from a later Augustinian's description of the cross, such that God effectively stars there

45. On Paul's relation to the LXX in this passage, see George Howard, *Paul: Crisis in Galatia: A Study in Early Christian Theology*, 2nd ed. (Cambridge: Cambridge University Press, 1990), pp. 54 and 59. For the commentary on this verse which is cited by the medieval Gloss, see Jerome, *Comm. in Galatas* 1.2.11–13 (PL 26:364D; quoted in the introduction, p. 38; cf. PL 26:360A); also next note.

46. Eric Plumer, *Augustine's Commentary on Galatians: Introduction, Text, Translation and Notes* (Oxford: Oxford University Press, 2003), pp. 158–61.

in the lead role as the guiltiest of all humans: "All the prophets saw this, that Christ was to become the greatest thief, murderer, adulterer, robber, desecrator, blasphemer, etc., there has ever been anywhere in the world" (*In Gal.* 3.13 [WA 40.1:433; *LW* 26:277]). To Luther, as to his orthodox predecessors, Christ "becomes" such an awful litany of villains, however, only in the sense that a medieval actor took on a *persona*.[47] The antichristian *imitatio Christi* in other words finds its answer in Christ's *imitatio diaboli*. God exchanged his divinity for the costume of the damned, thereby allowing the damned to play, for all eternity, a part in salvation:

> He clothed himself in our person [*induere personam nostram*], laid our sins upon his shoulders, and said: "I have committed the sins that all men have committed."...By this fortunate exchange with us he took upon himself our sinful person and granted us his innocent and victorious person. Clothed and dressed in this [*Hac induti et vestiti*], we are freed from the curse of the Law, because Christ himself voluntarily became a curse for us, saying: "For my own person [*persona*] of humanity and divinity I am blessed, and I am in need of nothing whatever. But I shall empty myself [Phil. 2:7]; I shall assume your clothing and mask [*assumam vestem et larvam vestram*]; and in this I shall walk about and suffer death, in order to set you free from death." Therefore, when, inside our mask [*larva*], he was carrying the sin of the whole world, he was captured, he suffered, he was crucified, he died. (*In Gal.* 3.13 [WA 40.1:442–43; *LW* 26:283–84])

Except of course that Jesus doesn't "really" die, any more than he is "really" a thief; or to put it more radically, he actually does die (and maybe he actually did steal something—more on this in a moment), but historical actuality as such then itself amounts, at worst, to *a play*. Neither death on the cross, nor death as such, nor the disaster of a fallen history is ultimately real (because none of it is eternal). On the contrary, everything temporal has been by definition merely "enacted."

That so much of the Christian attitude toward theater is elsewhere so relentlessly negative, even while Christ's atonement was itself understood in some sense "theatrically,"[48] receives here in Luther's sermon perhaps its

---

47. On which see Meg Twycross and Sarah Carpenter, *Masks and Masking in Medieval and Early Tudor England* (Burlington, Vt.: Ashgate, 2002).

48. E.g., Calvin, *Institutio Christianae Religionis* (1559) 2.16.5, ed. Guilielmus Baum et al. (Brunswick, 1869), vol. 2, col. 372; trans. Ford Lewis Battles, ed. John T. McNeill, 2 vols. (Philadelphia: Westminster Press, 1960), 1:509: "Thus we shall behold the role [*personam*] of a sinner and evildoer represented [*repraesentatam*] in Christ, yet from his shining innocence it will at the same time be obvious that he was burdened with another's sin rather than his own." Cf. the implicit costuming metaphor of the 1587 Genevan gloss on Rom. 8:3: "Therfore God clothed his Sonne with flesh like vnto our sinful flesh" (side note 4).

most perverse explanation: Christ himself was just as empty (Phil. 2:7) and just as cursed (Gal. 3:13) as drama, condemned like every other player in the antitheatrical writings of the Fathers to his own personal *descensus ad infernos*. If Christ was for a time damned to hell, on the medieval view, because of his evil persona, it was hardly surprising that dramatic players should be reckoned as equally hell-bound for also daring to play villains. The reception that Christ first got from the religious authorities, that the primitive church then got from subsequent pagan powers, was in other words the same welcome that players could expect in places to receive from the church and later from puritans. And yet the contempt historically directed at players—as those same puritans liked to point out—had been equally earned by the church. In the following two sections I want to argue for an unexpected unity in how the church saw demonic, lucre-loving players and how the vernacular plays saw Christ—which is further to say, how plenty of churchmen on the eve of the Reformation were beginning to see themselves. "Two kinds of men use masks," writes a fourteenth-century preacher in England, "those who play and those who rob. For players in the play which is commonly called a *Miracle* [also] use masks, beneath which the persons of the actors are concealed. Thus do the demons, whose game is to destroy souls and lure them by sin."[49] What this leaves unsaid is that Christ himself was commonly thought to have answered the demons with a game of his own, wherein he concealed his divinity beneath a mask of sinful flesh and so deprived the devil of his rightful due and humans of their just comeuppance; it also omits how the church used that promise of impunity and the same dissimulation to plunder other religions, along with its own adherents.

Christian Appropriation

"The fact must be emphasized," writes Martin Hengel, "that only the Christianized LXX permitted the church to adhere to the Old Testament. The alternative would have been its total rejection, as Marcion and some Gnostics had done."[50] The church had "Christianized" its LXX by adding favorable verses to it like one supposedly from Jeremiah cited by Justin Martyr against his Jewish opponents and then later by Irenaeus against the church's intramural heretics, predicting Christ's descent into hell: "The Lord God remembered his dead . . . and descended to preach to

49. John Bromyard, *Summa predicantium*, in G. R. Owst, *Literature and Pulpit in Medieval England* (Cambridge: Cambridge University Press, 1933), p. 395.

50. Hengel, *Septuagint as Christian Scripture* (n. 2), p. 41.

them his own salvation."[51] On just this point, however, Marcion's rejection of the Old Testament appears to have been less than total. He accepted the wrathful divinity of creation, all right, but saw him as a malevolent demiurge whom Christ, the better God, had come to combat. Marcion thought of Christ's trip to hell as part of the fight. Only, when Jesus arrived, Marcion imagined, all the Old Testament's supposed heroes—Abel, Moses, Noah—long duped by their Hebrew deity, mistook the new gospel for the latest trial afflicting them and refused to give in: "For since these men, [Marcion] says, knew their God was constantly tempting them, so now they suspected that he was tempting them, and did not run to Jesus, or believe his announcement: and for this reason he declared that their souls remained in hell" (*Adv. haer.* 1.27.3 [SC 264:352; ANF 1:352]). Meanwhile the *villains* from the Old Testament, those who had been smart enough all along to *oppose* the orthodox God of creation—"the Sodomites, and the Egyptians, and others like them, and, in fine, all the nations who walked in all sorts of abomination"—these were the ones according to Marcion whom Jesus managed to save.[52] He even raised Cain (ibid.).

Irenaeus was among the first to develop a counter-doctrine that could explain to the orthodox why Christ had been condemned to hell and whom specifically he had come to save. Rather than rejecting the Old Testament's deity of rage, Irenaeus helped engineer the classic figure of Satan to stand in his place; like Marcion's demiurge, Satan too was an impostor posing as God. Underneath his posturing, or rather, by its means, the apostate angel proved a robber and thief (as would Irenaeus' Antichrist), for he "insatiably snatched away what was not [his] own" (*Adv. haer.* 5.1.1 [SC 153:19–21; ANF 1:527])—namely, the humans beings whom he falsely promised could also be like gods. According to Irenaeus, the whole point of the Harrowing, then, and of salvation more generally, was for Jesus to give his soul talionically "in place of [*anti*] our souls, his flesh in place of

51. Justin Martyr, *Dial.* 72 (PG 6:645B; ANF 1:235); Irenaeus, *Adv. haer.* 3.20.4; 4.22.1, 33.1 and 12; 5.31.1 (SC 211:394; 100:684f., 802f., 834f.; 153:388f.; ANF 1:451, 493–94, 506, 510, 560).

52. A Marcionite doctrine also reported by Theodoret, *Haereticarum fabularum compendium* 1.14 (PG 83:376), and Epiphanius, *Panarion haer.* 42.4 (GCS 31, Epiphanius Werke 2:99–100). For further discussion, see Robert M. Grant, *Irenaeus of Lyons* (London: Routledge, 1997), p. 17. Markwart Herzog, *"Descensus ad Infernos": Eine religionsphilosophische Untersuchung der Motive und Interpretation mit besonderer Berücksichtigung der monographischen Literatur seit dem 16. Jahrhundert* (Frankfurt am Main: Joseph Knecht, 1997), pp. 274–75, raises but does not answer "the question as to how far the Descent-theory of the Catholic Church represented a reaction to Marcion's doctrine, or vice versa" (275). This is given fuller analysis by Raymond Schwager, *Der Wunderbare Tausch: Zur Geschichte und Deutung der Erlösungslehre* (Munich: Kösel, 1986), pp. 7–31.

[*anti*] our flesh" (ibid.), and so to steal—or, if you prefer, to buy—God's rightful property *back*: "since 'none can enter a strong man's house and spoil his goods, unless he first bind the strong man himself' [Mt 12:29; Mk 3:27]....The Word bound him [the devil] securely as a fugitive from himself, and plundered his goods" (*Adv. haer.* 5.21.3 [SC 153:276; ANF 1:550]).[53] No wonder Christ dies between thieves. He is the original Robin Hood.

Other readers of scripture, in particular its copyists, were less graceful than Irenaeus at assimilating the robbery it continually linked to Christ's mission. Where the Greek text implies that Jesus was as criminal as the thieves who died alongside him, for instance, a number of scribes invented a spurious emendation inverting the word order: the "two other criminals" (Lk 23:32)—that is, *besides* Jesus—become instead "two others, criminals." A couple of Old Latin manuscripts, along with the Sinaitic Syriac and the Sahidic versions, solved the problem by leaving the Greek word for "other" untranslated.[54] As late as the late medieval stanzaic *Gospel of Nicodemus*, scribes were still coping in a similar fashion: some of its manuscripts, in a verbatim repetition of authentic scripture, say that Christ died "with other theues him by" (Galba and Hartley), while two more replace that suspect line with stock piety: now he dies "on a rode rewefully."[55] In any event his association with thieves could hardly be suppressed. It was constantly abetted elsewhere in scripture and was a standard accusation among non-Christians;[56] Jesus himself claims to be a representative of the kingdom that will come "like a thief in the night" (Mt 24:43; Lk 12:39;

---

53. Cf. *Adv. haer.* 3.23.1 (SC 211:445–47; ANF 1:455–56); also Hippolytus, περὶ τοῦ ἁγίου πάσχα: "The Body [of Christ] lay in the grave, not robbed of the Divinity, but indeed He...robbed Sheol with the Soul" (GCS 1:268–69); trans. J. A. MacCulloch, *The Harrowing of Hell: A Comparative Study of an Early Christian Doctrine* (Edinburgh: T & T Clark, 1930), p. 96; also Origen, *Comm. in Rom.* 5.10.10–12 (PG 14:1051A–52B; trans. Thomas P. Scheck, FC 103:372–74).

54. See Bruce M. Metzger, *The Text of the New Testament: Its Transmission, Corruption, and Restoration*, 3d ed. (New York: Oxford University Press, 1992), p. 202. The RSV resolves the ambiguity by translating "Two others also, who were criminals, were led away." For an anxious defense of this resolution and of Christ's innocence on philological grounds, see *The Expositor's Greek Testament*, ed. W. Robertson Nicoll, 5 vols. (Grand Rapids: Eerdmans, 1979), 1:639, note on Lk 23:32.

55. William Henry Hulme, ed., *The Middle English Harrowing of Hell and the Gospel of Nicodemus*, EETS e.s. 100 (London: Kegan Paul, Trench, Trübner, 1907), p. 106; §112, line 1340. More on the complex provenance of *Nicodemus* to follow.

56. E.g., in Lactantius, *Div. inst.* 5.3 (SC 204:140; ANF 7:138), where it is reported that Hierocles "affirmed that Christ Himself was put to flight by the Jews, and having collected a band of nine hundred men, committed robberies." My next chapter will touch on the passing mention of robbery in Phil. 2:6 (such as it is).

cf. 1 Thess. 5:2; Rev. 3:3). Betrayed by Judas, a thief (Jn 12:6), Christ asks the Romans when they come to take him, "Have you come out to arrest me...as if I were a thief?" (Mt 26:55; Mk 14:48; Lk 22:52). He then allows them to capture and punish him as though he *were* a thief and, while on the cross, slots one of the other "real" thieves for paradise (Lk 23:43). (Some manuscripts of Luke attempt to specify more clearly which thief Christ forgave so as to exclude the outrageous possibility—outrageous because so unjust, so positively *criminal*—that he rescued the *impenitent* one [*TC* 155]. *Nicodemus* will name the saved one Dysmas to prevent confusion.) Last but not least: Jesus hangs in place of the robber Barabbas (Jn 18:40), for the Middle Ages as for Marlowe an obvious type of the Antichrist, whom the Jews, to their spiritual peril, had conspired to release.

Unbeknownst to the Jews, Jesus himself was also conspiring and acted as their accomplice in the switch, yet did so, according to one strain of the Christian tradition, in order to transfer their blessings to the gentile nations. Historically the dispossession began in earnest with the adoption of Jewish scripture by a non-Jewish church—a process epitomized by Christians' attachment to the Septuagint: "The appropriation of these Scriptures by the Christian Church," writes Sidney Jellicoe, "—'one of the most remarkable take-over bids in history,' as C. F. D. Moule has so aptly described it—was fraught with far-reaching consequences for a people who felt themselves to have a proprietary right in them."[57] The translation helped legitimate, in other words, a broader *translatio spiritus* that added a worldly dimension to the underworld robbery accomplished by Christ.

By the Middle Ages the Christian usurpation of the Jews' spiritual inheritance, along with more tangible assets, could be read back into the Old Testament without much effort regardless of the translation. The *Glossa ordinaria*, for example, allegorizes Genesis in such a way that Jacob plays the second-born "Christian" to Esau's first-born "Jew," while Rebecca, a.k.a. Mother Grace, "causes the Gentiles, who greedily [*avide*] accept faith, to steal [*auferre*] the blessing owed to the Jews" (PL 113:150B).[58] Readings like these increasingly functioned as the exegetical counterpart to political structures across Europe that included Jews as "an indispensable source of fiscal revenue,"[59] then soaked them with special taxes or subjected

---

57. Sidney Jellicoe, *The Septuagint and Modern Study* (Winona Lake, Ind.: Eisenbrauns, 1993), p. 75.

58. For the rabbinic reading, plus a lot more, see the marvelous essay by Gerson D. Cohen, "Esau as Symbol in Early Medieval Thought," in *Jewish Medieval and Renaissance Studies*, ed. Alexander Altmann (Cambridge: Harvard University Press, 1967), pp. 19–48.

59. Salo W. Baron, Arcadius Kahan et al., *Economic History of the Jews*, ed. Nachum Gross (New York: Schocken Books, 1975), p. 25; see esp. pp. 44–47. For a compressed account of

them to arbitrary seizures as a penalty for sins that could be proved with reference to scripture whenever their actual behavior seemed innocent. The circle became vicious: a lot of Jews had to charge usurious rates, one twelfth-century rabbi explains, "because there is no end to the yoke and the burden king and nobles impose on us. Everything we take is...needed for subsistence. Moreover, we are condemned to live in the midst of other nations and cannot earn our living in any other manner (except by money lending)."[60] The predictable result was that this lending of money, as the roughly contemporaneous Jew in a dialogue by Abelard ruefully says (ca. 1125), "just makes us more hateful to them who think they are being oppressed by it."[61] The Christian exegesis that defended this situation, even as the rise of centralized nation-states with far less tolerance had started to change it for the worse through mass expulsions,[62] extended to the stagings of liturgical and, eventually, vernacular drama.[63] The drama would then come to reflect the economic structure of a thoroughly Christian social order that was predicated as much on universal exploitation as on depriving Jews specifically: thus Marlowe's *Jew of Malta*.[64]

But I anticipate. One could object that the didactic purpose of medieval drama, by contrast, was primarily to demonstrate, through the demonization of existing social abuses, some higher, wholly symbolic social order predicated on the virtue of "charity." Yet an ideal society based on charity is little more than an inverted image of the real social order, which survives through exploitation. Without exploitation, there would be no surplus

the changing details in different countries over the long term, see Immanuel Wallerstein, *The Modern World-System*, 3 vols. (New York: Academic Press, 1974–89), 1:147–51; also the next note.

60. Quoted in Shael Herman, *Medieval Usury and the Commercialization of Feudal Bonds* (Berlin: Duncker & Humblot, 1993), p. 70.

61. *Dialogus inter Philosophum, Judaeum et Christianum* (PL 178:1618C); trans. Pierre J. Payer (Toronto: Pontifical Institute of Mediaeval Studies, 1979), p. 33; quoted and discussed by R. I. Moore, *The Formation of a Persecuting Society: Power and Deviance in Western Europe, 950–1250* (Oxford: Blackwell, 1987), p. 85.

62. A classic account is given by Moore, *Formation of a Persecuting Society*; see esp. the section "From Exploitation to Expulsion," pp. 42–45.

63. For Jacob and Esau in particular, see *DMC* 2:259–66, where a chorus "sings sweetly the allegory of the story" (259), and the allegory is basically the same as what one would have found in the Gloss. Shakespeare will replay the scene along similar lines in *The Merchant of Venice*: see John Scott Colley, "Launcelot, Jacob and Esau: Old and New Law in *The Merchant of Venice*," *Yearbook of English Studies: Literature and Its Audience* 1, Special Number, ed. G. K. Hunter and C. J. Rawson (Leeds: W. S. Maney and Son, 1980): 181–89. For Marlowe's reprise, see next chapter.

64. See David H. Thurn, "Economic and Ideological Exchange in Marlowe's *Jew of Malta*," *Theatre Journal* 46.2 (1994): 157–70, esp. 163.

available for charitable redistribution. *That* is the sad moral behind a so-called morality play like *Mankind*: the medieval "community" cohered only if your average person could be persuaded, by drama if not by force, to labor on behalf of others. Or as John Cox writes of the cycle plays, "Commemorating the broken body of Christ was, paradoxically, the foundation of liturgical community, the establishment of the social body by whom and for whom the mystery plays were performed, sometimes and in some places actually on the Feast of Corpus Christi."[65] There was less of a paradox here than a lot of people would care to admit. The members of this "social body," stratified and scarred by class, accepted the broken body of Christ as the highest symbol of their collectivity because their collective was founded on antagonism so deep, a systematic appropriation so vast, that they themselves were powerless to effect any meaningful redemption from it.

Christ's apparent condemnation as a thief consequently took on in medieval English drama a profound overdetermination. "No wonder, as it standys, / if we be poore," says the first Pastor of the Second Shepherds' Play,

> We ar so hamyd [hamstrung],
> Fortaxed and ramyd [overtaxed and beaten down],
> We ar mayde handtamyd
> With thyse gentlery-men. (*Towneley* 13.18–19, 23–26)

Though "no wonder," their misery nonetheless becomes the stuff of miracles insofar as it prefigures Christ's solidarity with the abject and put-upon everywhere. Social inequality on the widest possible scale, like any antichristian calamity,[66] here awaits its corrective in an event at once similar to the inadequacies it supplements and yet, by virtue of the similarity's messianic opposition to what it resembles, weakly transcendent of them. The systematic problem of expropriation, for example—the way the thefts

---

65. John Cox, *The Devil and the Sacred in English Drama, 1350–1642* (Cambridge: Cambridge University Press, 2000), p. 34.

66. Linda Marshall, "'Sacral Parody' in the *Secunda Pastorum*," *Speculum* 47.4 (1972): 720–36, has pointed out how catastrophes such as the storms and floods suffered by the shepherds conventionally prefigure in accounts of Antichrist's coming (e.g., Adso, *Cursor Mundi*) the impending revelation of apocalypse. Following the lead of William Manly she has consequently drawn various parallels between Mak and Antichrist himself (see p. 728). As Manly puts it, "The expansive quality of the complaints, and the echoes of Antichrist in Mak, *all explicitly operate in the midst of the secular scenes* to control the play as religious drama and to focus the immediate action on the final scene of Christ's birth" ("Shepherds and Prophets: Religious Unity in the Towneley *Secunda Pastorum*," *PMLA* 78.3 [1963]:151–55;

of the aristocracy engender a starving class of thieves represented by
Mak—will be answered by one final, absolute theft:

> For now is he borne
> That shall take fro the feynd
> That Adam had lorne [what Adam lost]. (*Towneley* 13.921–23)

All that need happen is for Mak and Gill to transform themselves, through
a miracle of theatrical doubling, into the angel and Mary,[67] while the stolen
lamb they disguised as a baby and joked (in full earnest) of eventually
eating (772–76) becomes the edible Christ child, born in a manger. At last
with his advent, sums up an angel, "The fals gyler of teyn/Now goys he
begyled" (1030–31).

Who is the real beguiler here? The vernacular plays that were given to
staging Christ's righteous deceit could hardly present the action of redemption as something other than a distant version of their own mimetic
duplicity. They had after all inherited a plethora of theological rationaliza-
tions for the way Christ and his blood money might combine the imitation
of sinful humanity ("incarnation") with an ostensibly unequal exchange
("redemption") toward the end of a *just* salvation, on the grounds that
such iniquity was a "fair" response to the iniquity of God's worst imitators:
in recompense he imitates *them*. Christian justice, such as it is, is in this
case above all "poetic." It fell to poetry to demonstrate this fully. In fact
the fullness of the demonstration showed a world in which poetic fictions,
and aesthetic activity more generally, had become a primary instrument
in the maintenance of the hierarchical if not also hieratic dispossessions
from which these fabrications pretended to offer utopian deliverance.
The solace of drama was for that reason always a little demonic, even if
the rhetorical and visual powers it exercised did not actually belong to demons. They were bad enough. The drama arose, after all, from the worldly
roots of evil, from money and trade and the deceptive pleasures of imitation. Hence, also, its potential godliness—invariably pseudo because *only*
potential.

---

here 155); I underscore the phrase that I want to extend, via Marlowe, to secular drama
as such. Míceál F. Vaughan, "The Three Advents in the *Secunda Pastorum*," *Speculum* 55.3
(1980): 484–504, also equates Mak with Antichrist.

67. A conventional staging. See, e.g., Wallace H. Johnson, "The Origin of the *Second
Shepherds' Play*: A New Theory," *Quarterly Journal of Speech* 52 (1966): 47–57; here 52–53.

The Deceiver Deceived and the
Cycles' Descent

Dramatic poetry took its cue with respect to Christ's beguiling of Satan above all from the *Gospel of Nicodemus*, whose latter and substantially older half gives the definitive "biblical" account of Christ's descent into hell. It was definitive in the sense of inspiring a vast amount of medieval artwork, and so by ramification medieval devotion as such, with as much if not greater force than the canonical scriptures. It was no less authentic than the Septuagint, no less inspiring, nor less inspired, and it goes to some lengths to advertise their parity. Toward this end an early Latin version of the *Gospel* borrows the story of its authoring more or less directly from Septuagint legend,[68] now grown well beyond Aristeas. Among those raised by Jesus, we learn, were Leucius and Charinus, dead sons of the proto-Christian Simeon (about whom more in a moment). Mute to the living like all the dead, notwithstanding their resurrection, they set pen to paper during the brief interval between their harrowing and ascension and in this way memorialized for posterity what happened in hell after the arrival of Jesus, which would have been otherwise known, after all, only to the dead. The brothers "were separated one from another in different cells,"[69] each with his own roll of papyrus, exactly as the legendary translators were separated—according to Irenaeus, lest they collude against Ptolemy and use their translation to *conceal* from him the scriptural truth (*Adv. haer.* 3.21.2 [SC 211:402–7; ANF 1:451–52]). (That Philadelphus specifically sequestered them in "cells" comes to the tradition through Pseudo-Justin [*Cohortatio ad graecos* 13.2], who says he personally went to Pharos, laid eyes on the traces of their foundations, and can therefore confirm that the miraculous stories one hears are neither "myths" nor "feigned histories" [13.4], a fiction from then on widely taken at face value. Jerome was chagrined: "Who the first author was to erect with his lies the seventy cells [*cellulas*] of Alexandria, I do not know," [*Apol. c. Rufinum* 2.25 (CCSL 79:62)]; or knowing, he hardly cared.)[70] In *Nicodemus* a miraculous unanimity of

---

68. A correspondence also noted by Josef Kroll, *Gott und Hölle: Der Mythos vom Descensuskampfe* (Leipzig: B. G. Teubner, 1932), p. 87.

69. Latin B-text, 1.8. Original in Constantinus de Tischendorf, ed., *Evangelia Apocrypha*, 2nd ed. (Leipzig, 1876), p. 421; trans. J. K. Elliott, *The Apocryphal New Testament: A Collection of Apocryphal Christian Literature in an English Translation* (Oxford: Clarendon, 1993), p. 200. The same phrase, "in singulis cellulis," appears in the account of the LXX translation given by Isidore, *Etym.* 6.4.3 (PL 82:236B), and Rabanus Maurus, *De univ.* 5.4 (PL 111:121D), among others.

70. Jerome repeats his disdain in the *Praefatio in Pentateuchum* (PL 28:181A); cf. *Praefatio in lib. paralipomenon* (PL 28:1393A). For the "first author," so far as we know (quoted above), see the "οἰκίσκους μικρούς" in Ps.-Justin (Markell von Ankyra?), *Ad Graecos de vera*

the separate transcriptions likewise ensues: before vanishing away (the least of the brothers' feats), Leucius gives his account to Joseph and Caiaphas; Charinus his to Annas and Nicodemus, all of whom then compare notes. As the Middle English stanzaic version describes it:

> togeder þan þai gan þam luke
> þat serely [separately] wretin was,
> and þat one wrate noght a letter noke [not one iota]
> bot euyn als þat oþer has.[71]

Divine inspiration! The brothers' texts, though of separate birth, were anyway identical twins.

A lot of people, still unconvinced, have seen in the names of these inspired brothers a coded reference to the man they suspect of authoring the original gospel in a less divine fashion: this was one Leucius Charinus, a second-century Manichean exposed by Augustine and Evodius as the author of "alleged apostolic acts,"[72] whose writings thereafter only gained in popularity, notwithstanding their repeated condemnation as forgeries—both by legitimate witnesses (Innocent I, Turribius of Astorga)[73] and in texts that are of equally false provenance. For example, whoever compiled Pseudo-Matthew (another hugely influential gospel) prefaced it with a forged exchange between Jerome and two bishops expressing their deep concern over the proliferation of apocryphal books, in which "are written many things contrary to our faith."[74] The bishops worry especially that in mistaking apocrypha for authentic scripture, they might accidentally "transfer the joy of Christ to Antichrist" (op. cit.), and so they propose the wholesale rejection of every potentially spurious document—with one telling exception. What if one of those rejected documents turned out to be the real thing? Would it not be possible, in rejecting Antichrist, unwittingly again to condemn the true Christ? The two bishops have heard that Jerome possesses a Hebrew volume, for instance, "written by

religione (bisher "Cohortatio ad Graecos"): Einleitung und Kommentar, ed. Christoph Riedweg (Basel: Friedrich Reinhardt, 1994), pp. 315–16 (commentary), 548–49 (Greek), 595–96 (German).

71. Hulme, *Middle English Harrowing* (n. 55), p. 126, §137, Galba ms.

72. Augustine, *C. Felicem* 2.6 (CSEL 25:833.12); Evodius, *De fide* 5 and 38 (CSEL 25:952, 968–969).

73. Innocent I, *Ep.* 6.7 (PL 20:502A); Turribius Asturicensis, *Ep. de non recipiendis in auctoritatem fidei apocryphis scripturis* 5 (PL 54:694D).

74. Original in Tischendorf, *Evangelia Apocrypha*, pp. 51–53; trans. Elliott, *Apocryphal New Testament* (both n. 69), pp. 91–92.

the hand of the most blessed Evangelist Matthew" (ibid.). Could he perhaps render it for them in Latin, so "as to counteract the craft of heretics who, in order to teach bad doctrine, have mingled their own lies with the excellent nativity of Christ" (ibid.)? Pseudo-Jerome naturally accedes: Pseudo-Matthew, though entirely authentic, had come under suspicion of being pseudonymous, he explains, only on account of the reputation of the huckster who made it public against Matthew's stated desire that the book be kept secret. This publisher was none other than "Leucius, who also wrote the falsely styled Acts of the Apostles" (ibid.).[75]

We can get a pretty good idea of what those lost Acts contained from the people who again and again had to denounce them. Photius—a ninth-century Patriarch of Constantinople and possibly the contemporary of Pseudo-Jerome (whoever he was)—found the collection "stuffed with foolishness, inconsistency, and incongruity." His indignation soon grows into a more descriptive fury: "for it says that there is One who is God of the Jews, who is evil, whose servant Simon Magus became; and another is Christ, whom it calls good." Who ever heard of such a thing? Furthermore, "it concocts senseless and childish [stories about] resurrections of dead men,"—which presumably he could tolerate—"and of cattle and other animals," which he could not. "In short this book contains innumerable childish, improbable, ill-conceived, false, foolish, self-contradictory, profane, and godless things; and if anyone called it the source and mother of all heresies he would not be far from the truth."[76] The events contained in the *descensus* episode of *Nicodemus* allegedly penned by Leucius and Charinus are of course no less foolish, nor less false, but that did not stop them from constituting the latter half of one of "the period's most prestigious, culturally most significant texts,"[77] or from influencing literatures as disparate in time and purpose as the cycle plays are from *Paradise Lost.* That the name of Leucius Charinus has been encoded within the gospel as the name of its author(s) naturally does not prove Leucius Charinus originally wrote it,

---

75. For other pseudonymous or falsely attributed denunciations of Leucius, see Melito of Laodicea (PG 5:1239) and the sixth-century Pseudo-Gelasian decree, in E. von Dobschütz, *Das Decretum Gelasianum de libris recipiendis et non recipiendis* (Leipzig: J. C. Hinrichs, 1912), p. 298.

76. Photius, *Bibliotheca*, cod. 114 (PG 103:389B–C). This has been translated, with an exceedingly helpful account of Leucius' alleged books, by Knut Schäferdiek in *NTA* 2:87ff.

77. Zbigniew Izydorczyk, "The *Evangelium Nicodemi* in the Latin Middle Ages," in *The Medieval "Gospel of Nicodemus": Texts, Intertexts, and Contexts in Western Europe*, ed. Zbigniew Izydorczyk (Tempe, Ariz.: Medieval & Renaissance Texts & Studies, 1997), pp. 43–102; here 75.

though plenty of scholars have argued he did.[78] The point is that the names of Simeon's sons actively transpose a heretical signature into a form of authorship that the orthodox were, for the most part, happy to embrace.

What happened to the *Gospel of Nicodemus* over the course of the Middle Ages ironically fulfilled its internal fiction of divine authenticity, and the cycle drama played no small part in the apocryphon's popular apotheosis. In particular the drama helped widely disseminate its theology of Christ's (possibly) salvific deception.[79] Apparently "done to ded now late / and dampned for his misdede,"[80] according to *Nicodemus*, Jesus in the Harrowing plays at last meets on stage the godlike demon with whom he had been for more than a millennium locked in dramatic dialogue, two dueling impersonators, each jockeying for advantage, each loving the spoils. And ultimately, as Jesus explains, the spoils are humans:

> Þe feende þame wanne with trayne [won with deceit]
>   Thurgh frewte of erthely foode;
> I haue þame getyn agayne
>   Thurgh bying with my bloode. (*York* 37.9–12)[81]

This formulation clearly balances the economics of Christ's atoning work—"buying with blood"—against the satanic guile or "trayne" that created a need for atonement in the first place. Christ touts in effect his superior

78. Beginning, perhaps, with a ninth-century scribe: see Izydorczyk, "The *Evangelium Nicodemi*," p. 76; see also those cited by Hulme, *Middle English Harrowing* (n. 55), p. lxi n. 5, and Josef Kroll, *Gott und Hölle* (n. 68), p. 86.

79. The direct influence of the Middle English stanzaic *Nicodemus* on the cycle drama was demonstrated long ago by W. A. Craigie, "The Gospel of Nicodemus and the York Mystery Plays," in *An English Miscellany: Presented to Dr. Furnivall* (Oxford: Clarendon Press, 1901), pp. 52–61. On the deception of the devil and his "abuse of power" in the cycle plays, see the scholars criticized by C. W. Marx, *The Devil's Rights and the Redemption in the Literature of Medieval England* (Cambridge: D. S. Brewer, 1995), p. 114. His criticisms are not entirely earned, as Henry Ansgar Kelly explains on the last page of his review in *Speculum* 72.3 (1997): 861. For other problems with Marx's argument, see the review by Ronald Waldron in *Modern Language Review* 92.3 (1997): 685–86.

80. Hulme, *Middle English Harrowing* (n. 55), p. 90, §91, lines 1085–86, Galba ms.

81. A play taken over by Towneley with some changes of disputed significance. In this instance Towneley has "thrugh fraude of erthly fode," and the editors point out that York's redundant "fruit" is likely a corruption of "fraud" (*Towneley* vol. 2:593 n.14). For a more detailed discussion of the two plays' relationship, see M. G. Frampton, "The Towneley 'Harrowing of Hell,'" *PMLA* 56 (1941):105–19; Chester Curtis, "The York and Towneley Plays on 'The Harrowing of Hell,'" *Studies in Philology* 30 (1930): 24–31 (who argues that Towneley's changes bring the text closer to *Nicodemus*). For the argument that the plays, despite all their substantial identity, are in reality "quite distinct," see Michelle M. Butler, "The York/Towneley *Harrowing of Hell*?" *Fifteenth-Century Studies* 25 (2000): 115–26.

cunning: where Satan "wanne" Adam and Eve by persuading them to eat from the tree of knowledge, Christ has outmaneuvered the devil by offering, in place of that "frewte," his own flesh and blood. The comparison between satanic guile and this redeeming purchase then implicitly extends to the drama of the Eucharist, where the "*un*earthly food" of Christ's redeeming body was always on offer and where the offer could seem no less sinister than Satan's original deception: first and foremost because the flesh and blood were there disguised to your senses as something else entirely.

In fact, as the Harrowing plays (among others) all go on to illustrate, the flesh of Christ had to be grasped, quite independently of communion, as in itself a "righteous" form of deceit. According to a commonplace stretching from the Eastern Fathers through a long list of Latins, patristic and medieval, God had wrapped his divinity in the flesh of Jesus the way fishers bait hooks, in order to capture through just treachery the satanic Leviathan.[82] Augustine's idiosyncratic, alternate formulation was enshrined in Lombard's sentences and, most brilliantly of all, on the Mérode altarpiece, where Jesus' fleshly "father" is shown in his carpenter's workshop, opposite the crucifixion, fashioning a mousetrap: "What did our redeemer do to our captor?" asks Augustine about the passion. "As our price, he held out his cross as a mousetrap and set his own blood as bait upon it."[83] This black sacrament, once swallowed by Satan, freed

---

82. Origin, *Comm. in Rom.* 5.10.10–12 (PG 14:1051B–1052A; trans. Scheck, FC 103:372–74), where Christ is swallowed by death/the devil just as Jonah was swallowed by the whale; Cyril of Jerusalem, *Catecheses* 12.15 (PG 33:741C; trans. Leo P. McCauley, FC 61:236), for the first time introduces explicitly the image of Christ's body as bait. Repeated by Gregory of Nyssa, *Oratio catechetica magna* 24 (PG 45:11–105; NPNF II, 5:494) when speaking of Christ's triumph over Satan—*and* (less often noticed) when speaking of Satan's initial deception of humanity: "for this deception would never have succeeded, had not the glamour of beauty been spread over the hook of vice like a bait" (*Oratio* 21 [ibid.]). The bait image enters the Latin tradition with Gregory the Great, *XL hom. in ev.* 25.8–9 (PL 76:1194C–1196A); trans. David Hurst, *Forty Gospel Homilies* (Kalamazoo, Mich.: Cistercian Publications, 1990), pp. 195–98, and again in Gregory's seminal *Moralia* 33.7.14ff. on Job 40:19ff. (CCSL 143b:1884ff.); trans. J. Bliss (Oxford, 1844–1850), 3²:569ff. From there it spreads far and wide throughout the Middle Ages, including Luther. For a catalogue of instances, see Schwager, *Wunderbare Tausch* (n. 52), p. 36.

83. *Serm.* 130.2 (PL 38:726; *WSA* III/4:311); cf. *Serm.* 134.6 (PL 38:745; *WSA* III/4:344), *Serm.* 263.2 (PL 38:1210; *WSA* III/7:220); repeated by Lombard, *Sent.* 3, dist. 19.1 (PL 192:796). For the iconography of this image, see Meyer Schapiro, "*Muscipula Diaboli*: The Symbolism of the Mérode Altarpiece," in *Late Antique, Early Christian, and Medieval Art: Selected Papers* (New York: George Braziller, 1979), pp. 1–19; on Christ's deception of the devil more generally, Ruth Mellinkoff, *The Devil at Isenheim: Reflections of Popular Belief in Grünewald's Altarpiece* (Berkeley: University of California Press, 1988), pp. 28–31. Presentations like these kept Augustine's view alive quite independently of other theological

humanity from the dominion of his deceptions by deceiving Satan the *same way* he himself first scammed humanity into consuming their fall. Such talionic reciprocity spoke to the ultimate justice of Christ's triumph, in that a triumph without trickery, over a trickster, would have been *less* fair.

The York and Towneley plays of the Harrowing give a Mametesque twist to God's holy fraud: their Satan is fully aware of the satanic trickery practiced by his opposite yet is therefore all the more readily duped. Warned that Jesus, "þe Jewe þat Judas solde/For to be dede þis othere daye" (*York* 37.147–48), has arrived outside hell's gates and is demanding the doors be opened, Satan rebuffs his sub-demons' fear with a cool estimation of this wily Jew's transparent con artistry:

> I knowe his trantis [tricks] fro toppe to taile,
> He leuys with gaudis and with gilery.
> Þerby he brought oute of oure bale [captivity]
> Nowe late Lazar of Betannye. (*York* 37.159–62)

According to Satan, *Jesus* is the Antichrist, or at the very least a sorcerer claiming a close relation to God but actually living with "gaudis"—a word that could mean deceitful tricks as well as courtly amusement (cf. *York* 31.236). In the cycle plays the miracles of Jesus were both. As far back as the gospels the charge had been leveled against him that such marvelous deeds as the resurrection of Lazarus were at best a form of "guilery" without which Jesus could never have bewitched so many; the same charge was a major theme of the stanzaic *Nicodemus* (§4, §§38ff., §142). Here in the York Harrowing (based largely on *Nicodemus*) Jesus manages again to charm the multitudes, only in this case his followers, who include the audience, are transported explicitly by drama. Those whom his *miracula* momentarily deceive, by contrast, are not Christians but overseers of the underworld. It was by means of this chicanery, Satan admits, that Jesus recently "brought oute of oure bale...Lazar of Betannye."

Satan's complaint regarding Lazarus' premature resurrection begins to touch on the peculiarly economic component of Christ's deception of the devil in rescue of the damned. "Fro paradise he [God] putte þame doune / In helle here to haue þer hyre [reward]," Satan observes, ironically

---

developments. Its survival may well begin to explain so late an icon as the entertainment that Hamlet designs to catch the conscience of his villainous king. See John Doebler, "The Play within the Play: The *Muscipula Diaboli* in *Hamlet*," *Shakespeare Quarterly* 23.2 (1972): 161–69.

speaking as an advocate for absolute, tit-for-tat justice. Every deed ought to have its fair return, he says to Christ:

> And thyselfe, day and nyght,
>   Has taught al men emang
> To do resoune and right,
>   And [yet] here werkis þou all wrang. (*York* 37.259–64)

Acting as hell's chief warden—that is, as the officer employed by a just God in the eternal confinement of the righteously condemned—Satan takes the "miracle" of resurrection for an illicit jailbreak. When Jesus removed Lazarus from the "bale" of hell without officially "bailing" him out or paying Satan his due ransom, he effectively *stole* Lazarus from prison, and that is how Satan "knows" Jesus is nothing more than a thieving magician or some other sort of mountebank. Even after the crucifixion, when Christ makes his way into hell and claims the property he has (by now) "legitimately" bought with his priceless blood, Satan just takes this for another, perhaps more elaborate fraud—which it is, according to the plays, in that Satan has been fooled into thinking that Jesus, when he died, was *merely* human. If Jesus has all along had the power to free the damned, Satan asks, why has he waited so long to redeem them (223–24)? "Nowe is þe tyme certayne," responds Jesus, "Mi fadir ordand before" (225–26). Here Satan seems to have him. By what authority does Jesus' *father* ordain the time of anyone's redemption? "Thy fadir knewe I wele be sight," says Satan,

> He was a write his mette to wynne,
> And Marie me menys þi modir hight—
> Þe vttiremeste ende of all þi kynne. (*York* 37.229–32)

Joseph, Satan says, was a normal workingman who won his meat the same as anybody else and who, along with Mary, made up the full extent and highest degree ("uttermost end") of Jesus' familial relations. How then can Jesus appeal to his "father" for the authority to take hell's chattels? Jesus replies, of course, that his father is actually God, but Satan isn't buying it. The great deceiver is deceived by God's flesh and blood:

> *Sattan:* God sonne? Þanne schulde þou be ful gladde,
>   Aftir no catel neyd thowe crave!
>   [i.e., you don't need to worry about property]
> But þou has leued ay like a ladde,
>   And in sorowe as a simple knave.

> *Jesus*: Þat was for hartely loue I hadde
> Vnto mannis soule, it for to saue;
> And for to make þe mased and madde,
> And by þat resoune þus dewly to haue
> Mi Godhede here, I hidde
> In Marie modir myne,
> For it schulde noȝt be kidde [known]
> To þe nor to none of thyne. (*York* 37.241–52)

According to this, the hidden God of Isaiah "appears" to Satan as the un-canny double of Satan's own imposture. The incarnation "reveals" the god-head the same way the host reveals Christ's flesh, namely, by not revealing it: God in this way *intends* to deceive the deceiver, "to maze" and madden him by performing seeming miracles in the guise of a "simple" knave. Satan saw through these ruses but mistook the agent for a mere trickster like himself, and therefore did not hesitate to orchestrate his death (at least not before he sent the dream to Pilate's wife).

C. W. Marx is no doubt right to point out that the deception of Satan by Christ in medieval literature had the ability to function independently of any specific theory of the atonement, though Marx never says *what* function it might serve on its own other than that of "traditional interpretations."[84] In fact the need was the same as what tasked every typological exegete: namely, to explain why Jesus makes for such a poor god. According to the deception theory he is literally *faking* it—faking, that is, his non-divinity. God's calculated deception of the devil now justifies why, for example, he asked that the cup of death pass from him even while knowing he could never die permanently, why he remained silent at his trial, why he cried out on the cross in desperation and abandonment.[85] "A man he ys fullye, in faye," logically deduces the Chester Satan from such behavior,

> for greatly death hee dread todaye,
> and these wordes I hard him saye:
> "My soule is threst [tormented] to death."[86]

---

84. Marx, *Devil's Rights* (n. 79), e.g., p. 45.

85. See the various authorities cited and discussed by Martin Werner, *The Formation of Christian Dogma: An Historical Study of Its Problem*, trans. S. G. F. Brandon (New York: Harpers & Brothers, 1957), p. 97. Also Ambrose, *Exp. Lucam* 2.1–3 (SC 45:70–73), Leo the Great, *Serm.* 22.4 (PL 54:196–97; trans. Jane Patricia Freeland and Agnes Josephine Conway, FC 93:84–85). The basic idea persists well into the late Middle Ages; see Marx, *Devil's Rights* (n. 79), pp. 33–34, 45 and passim.

86. *Chester* 17.105–8, quoting Mt 26:38; cf. *Chester* 12:213–16.

Christ's intention to deceive Satan could likewise account for details as simple and troubling as his comically fraudulent birth to a married "virgin." Was she not, as critics had been saying from time immemorial, obviously an adulterer? According to the cycle plays, not to mention the Fathers and schoolmen, Mary's chastity was *supposed* to seem suspicious, it was *supposed* to look as if (in the alleged words of Marlowe) "Christ was a bastard and his mother dishonest,"[87] *so that* his incarnate godhead would be hidden from Satan.

At bottom we are probably witnessing here a way of handling the various Docetic and Gnostic heresies that would see in Christ's humanity some kind of deception or illusory appearance. His all-too-human aspect on earth was by this late date generally accepted as historical reality, but the *reality itself* had been effectively raised to the level of a divine "illusion" (or "miracle") meant to deceive demons; paradoxically Satan is tricked into thinking Christ really is as he appears in historical reality: a deceptive man, like Marlowe's heroes, whose gargantuan pretense is inversely proportional to the humility of his origins. Theatergoers were then supposed to see Satan's "dowte" about Christ's divine claims as itself produced by divinity on their behalf. That is the essence of the paradox: Christ is *more* deceptive than even Satan suspects; those who perceive this are saved from his doubts. "Fayn wolde I knowe who were fadyr his," says the N-Town Satan,

> For of þis grett dowte I am sore dysmayd,
> Indede.
>   If þat he be Goddys childe
>   And born of a mayd mylde,
>   Than be we rygh sore begylde.[88]

Satan was of course not the only one so "dysmayd" by God's birth to a "mayd" to doubt the authenticity of Christ. Satan stands here for the majority of humans on earth. Only those in the know, know that an inauthentic savior is part of God's historical *act.* Faith for them is the pleasure of suspended disbelief.

---

87. *CM* 221. Cf. the view attributed to Richard Cholmeley "that Jhesus Christe was a bastarde St Mary a whore & the Anngell Gabriell a Bawde to the holy ghoste" (*CM* 216).

88. *The N-Town Play: Cotton MS Vespasian D.8*, ed. Stephen Spector, EETS s.s. 11–12 (Oxford: Oxford University Press, 1991), 1:214 (play 23, lines 20–25).

Virgin Birth, or the Septuagint Redux

These cognoscenti find perhaps their best representative in Chester's Simeon—a person only briefly mentioned by Luke (2:25–35) though central to the *Gospel of Nicodemus*, where he fathers its author(s) Leucius (and) Charinus. In the Chester Purification he makes for that most emblematic of stage creatures: a figure plagued by doubt who eventually becomes the very image of Christian belief. (So too in the play's second half, where Christ disputes as an adolescent with the temple priests, is "the most skeptical" of them "the first to recognize Christ's divinity.")[89] When Simeon consults the book of Isaiah regarding the virgin birth, for example, he reacts with indignant incredulity:

> A wonder I fynd written here.
> It sayth a mayden clean and cleare
> shall conceive and beare
> a sonne called Emanuell.
> But of this leeve I never a deale [believe not at all];
> it is wronge written, as have I heale [so may I prosper],
> or elles wonder yt were. (*Chester* 11.26–32)

Unable to credit anything that wonderful, but nonetheless longing for a savior—this longing, for the moment, is the whole of his "faith"—Simeon sets about rewriting the Bible so as to bring it in line with a more credible reality:

> I will scrape this awaye anon;
> thereas "a virgin" is written on
> I will write "a good woman"—
> for so yt should be. (37–40)

Some of the comedy here turns out to be self-referential: the Lukan Simeon does *not* worry about Isaiah's impossibilities, nor does he single out the virgin birth for skepticism. It takes a dramatic "translation" of Luke to raise these concerns, which are intimately connected to the play's own mission: first, because the drama also excises material from the Bible that it finds unworkable while interpolating materials that work better; second, because the Bible by itself, which these dramatic adjustments mean to *legitimate*, presents a radical discrepancy between what it says happened

89. Peter W. Travis, *Dramatic Design in the Chester Cycle* (Chicago: University of Chicago Press, 1982), p. 139.

and what falls within the realm of the possible, and religious drama formally encodes this latter discrepancy in its inherently contrafactual arrangements: here an actor stands before his audience and pretends to be a biblical personage it was no longer possible to see. Chester will make of that formal "miracle"—or fraud, depending on your view—a central element in the episode's narrative content as well.

Simeon's coming conversion to faith in Christ will require in other words the realization that the way it "should be," according to the dictates of the possible, and the way it *is*, according to divine mystery, are completely at odds. He must learn to accept, even to celebrate, everything in the Bible he knows is not possible—including what in the text is plainly a mistake or fabrication—as the highest expression of God's contrarian power. He has to learn, in short, what the audience watching him already allows as a matter of course: they accept what is happening on stage as an expression of divine truths only because it is not happening; they "believe" *on account of* its rank artificiality. If someone were publicly to announce outside the cycle's charmed circle, behold, he was Simeon, and he found the Bible manifestly in error and planned to obliterate its absurdities, medieval bystanders would have looked on him quite differently. The stage directions by contrast stress vehemently that the radical discrepancy between what appears on stage and what is actually happening needs itself to appear on stage, as though this discrepancy were itself the essential aspect of biblical revelation that the drama meant to convey: "Then he [Simeon] will make with the book as if [*fabricabit librum quasi*] he were deleting this word (virgo); and afterwards he will put the book on the altar. And an angel will come and take the book, making a sign as if [*faciens signum quasi*] he were writing; and he will close the book and vanish" (*Chester* 11.40 SD). Subsequent iterations then instruct Simeon to make like before, a second and third time: *tunc iterum fabricat ut antea.* Precisely where the stage directions go out of their way to underscore how the action on stage should be (literally) "fabricated," that is, Simeon is confronting the full contrafactuality of his nascent faith, particularly its dependence on an oxymoronic "virgin birth." Mary's chastity is no more nor less believable, the episode suggests, than the contrafactual appearance of any drama: the persons playing Simeon and the angel are neither Simeon nor an angel; both are acting, both making "signs" *as if* (*quasi*) they were deleting and rewriting—as if, that is, they were defacing the Bible. In this way the actors confirm its miraculous authenticity. "Simeon" does not *actually* erase Isaiah's "virgin"; and in any case Simeon is not Simeon and the word is not "virgin," according to the stage directions, but "virgo," for which "Simeon" gives a vernacular translation.

Not that the word "virgin"—in any language—had been written by Isaiah. Audience members who laughed at Simeon's (ultimately faithful) incredulity, whether they knew it or not, were laughing at the comedy of early Christian debates about the Septuagint: for it is the Septuagint that first renders the word for "young girl" (*almā*) in Isaiah's prophecy with a word meaning "virgin" (*parthenos*).[90] (The change is what inspired critics of Christianity to allege that the name of Mary's adulterous lover, with whom she produced the love child Jesus, was Pantheras.)[91] Greek translations made after the Septuagint (Aquila, Symmachus, Theodotion) meanwhile gave a word closer to Simeon's substitution (*neanis*, or "young woman"), with the result that Christian apologists like Justin Martyr accused the Jews of having changed the Bible in order to make it *more credible* and therefore *less serviceable* to Christian doctrine.[92] Now at last eyewitness evidence for Justin's accusation! Simeon, a Jew, literally rewrites the Bible out of his misplaced faith in a different, less incredible savior. His dismay at scripture's *impossibilium* only increases when, during a chat with the prophetess Anna about the coming messiah, an angel invisible to them both walks on stage, changes the word back, then disappears (or leaves the stage, anyway). Simeon returns to his book and finds the word "virgin" there again, though this time in red ink. Still, he refuses to believe. "Nay, faye, after I will assaye / whether this miracle be verey" (*Chester* 11.60–63). He scratches out the virgin again, turns again to Anna, who reminds him that the Bible contains "no leasinge [lies]," since for God almighty nothing is "impossible" (76–79). Simeon checks Isaiah one last time and, behold, the word "virgin" is back, this time in "goulden letters" (84). Unbelievable! Now he believes.

90. See Raymond E. Brown, *The Birth of the Messiah: A Commentary on the Infancy Narratives in Matthew and Luke* (New York: Doubleday, 1977), pp. 145–53; he remarks that "the variation between 'young girl' (MT) and 'virgin' (LXX, Matt) has given rise to some of the most famous debates in the history of exegesis, ranging from...Justin Martyr...to debates provoked by ultraconservative readers of the RSV translation in 1952," which "was burned by fundamentalists in some parts of the United States because it used 'young woman' rather than 'virgin' in Isa 7:14" (p. 146 n. 37). They burned it, in other words, because it followed the *Hebrew* rather than the LXX and was therefore antichristian.

91. See in particular *C. Celsum* 1.32–40; for further references, Joseph Klausner, *Jesus of Nazareth: His Life, Times, and Teaching*, trans. Herbert Danby (New York: Macmillan, 1953), pp. 23–24.

92. See, e.g., *Dial.* 84 (PG 6:673B–676A; ANF 1:241); also *Dial.* 67 and 71 (ibid.). Also Tertullian, *Adv. Marc.* 3.13.4–5 (CCSL 11:524–25; ANF 3:331–32); Jerome, *Comm. in Esaiam* 3.7.14 (CCSL 73:102–5), a portion of which is taken over by the Gloss (PL 113:1245D–1246A). For more general background, Adam Kamesar, "The Virgin of Isaiah 7:14: The Philological Argument from the Second to the Fifth Century," *Journal of Theological Studies* n.s. 41 (1990): 51–75.

After this much shtick you have to ask yourself what it is about the last iteration that finally convinces old Simeon, and the answer lies, I think, in the iteration's difference: the color of the letters changing first to red, then to *gold*. (It's probably worth emphasizing that the change takes places only when Simeon says. His audience has to take it on faith.) I know those colors are usually associated with the rubrics and gilt illuminations of a bookish culture, but I do not think we are that far, either, from the sort of symbolism we've already seen in *Mankind*'s golden red royals—which is to say, we are not far from the symbolism of blood money. The golden letters finally convince Simeon of Christ's virgin birth because, like Everyman, he takes the monetary value that gold represents as the most convincing approximation of God's future advent. He believes without knowing, like Aristorius and the Jews of Croxton, in the common standard through which everything is potentially an object of exchange—hence a standard without any identity itself other than a showy and shadowy glimmer. Gold's real power rests in its promise of becoming something even more sensuous. In itself it gives sensuous form only to an objective difference. (This "difference" is the object for which gold can always be traded.) To Simeon, gold means everything, because it could potentially be anything; thus it promises to be and always risks becoming God.

On some level people knew better. A version of the labor that Jesus' conception would actually precipitate was the real common substrate of the manifold translations and exchanges that brought a Bible and biblical drama to the Middle Ages. Adulating Mary as the mother of God not so secretly celebrated the human contribution in producing divinity (and was for that reason in time generally excised from the cycles), even as her virginity posited an inhuman force that could remake humanity—some cooperation of the Spirit that might prevent human reproduction from devolving into the simple reproduction of the means and relations of production. The Septuagint here above all had done more than reproduce the Hebrew, just as the craftsmen of Philadelphus had done more, by means of their art, than reproduce nature's ivy and acanthus. In Chester it was the blacksmiths who staged Mary's Purification; in Coventry, the weavers; in York, the hatmakers, masons, and laborers. Once again there were workers participating in the production of a Bible whose variance with the original, as with reality, confirmed the possibility of a single woman's generating more than seemed possible.

"If it is the necessity of labor that makes humanity the creature who in transforming itself also transforms its environment," writes Sarah Beckwith, "then it is this always excessive and non-self-identical creature who will permanently inhabit the gap between the actual and the possible. It is this gap between the actual and the possible that renders both inevitable and compelling the political struggle to redeem 'what is possible from what is real, our reality being but the systematic obstruction of the possible.'"[93] Belief in the potential of any sort of labor to overcome the limits of what passes for reality takes faith in something almost as hard to conceive as virgin birth. Reasonable doubts like Simeon's or that of his better-known counterpart Thomas (for whom, of all the guilds, York's *scriveners* were responsible) function in these plays as the higher form of belief insofar as these characters learn at the point of their conversion to doubt, even further, what should ultimately count as impossible. This does not mean that medieval audiences were especially gullible or confused about reality, but that reality same as now weighed so heavily, and biblical drama sided with them against it.

Or anyway seemed to. At Simeon's appearance in the Towneley Purification (17.59–72), somebody has scrawled in the manuscript's margin "no Maters ben as sade [said]." The editors suspect that this has to be some sort of "Protestant objection" to the extravagance of assigning so many extra-scriptural lines to Simeon (*Towneley*, vol. 2:532), and maybe it is. Yet in that case the Protestant objection just reiterates with respect to medieval drama what Chester's Simeon already doubts in the Bible. His skepticism there *makes possible* Christ's special revelation: real matters could never have been as scripture reported; thus scripture professed that things in the end would likewise be different, if for the moment that possibility appeared mainly just in performance. The coming Protestant dismissal of more than a thousand years of Christian culture for being at bottom mere theater, we're going to see in the next chapter, created a new drama that was equally dubious.

93. Sarah Beckwith, *Signifying God: Social Relation and Symbolic Action in the York Corpus Christi Plays* (Chicago: University of Chicago Press, 2001), p. 55, quoting John Brenkman, "Theses on Cultural Marxism," *Social Text* 7 (1983): 19–33; here 27.

CHAPTER 4

The Curious Sovereignty of Art

Marlowe's Sacred Counterfeits

He affirmeth...That if there be any god or any good Religion, then it
is in the papistes because the service of god is performed with more
ceremonies, as Elevation of the mass, organs, singing men, Shaven
Crownes, &cta. That all protestantes are Hypocriticall asses.
                            —RICHARD BAINES on the opinions
                                of Christopher Marlowe, 1593

Marlowe the Antichrist

Two future adversaries and scholars of Antichrist overlapped at
Cambridge, probably unknown to each other, in the 1580s. One attended
Jesus College, the other Corpus Christi. As one was getting his bachelor's,
the other received a master's. Afterwards they might both have taken the
orders toward which their training inclined them, but only one did. The
other was accused of nefarious activities and blasphemous opinions, of es-
pionage, sodomy, and atheism. The accusations were eventually strengthened by his former schoolmate, now a minister and pedagogue, whose
maiden publication included an account of his fellow graduate's sacrilege,
then murder, a few years previously. Two men, one training. One of the
them a clear-cut Christian, the other his demonic opposite. The other, in
all senses, is Christopher Marlowe.[1]

1. For Marlowe's life (and death) I have depended primarily on *CM*; David Riggs, *The
World of Christopher Marlowe* (London: Faber and Faber, 2004); Charles Nicholl, *The Reckoning: The Murder of Christopher Marlowe* (London: Jonathan Cape, 1992); and John Bakeless,
The Tragicall History of Christopher Marlowe, 2 vols. (Cambridge: Harvard University Press,
1942).

His doppelgänger is Thomas Beard, a puritanical preacher, Oliver Crom-
well's schoolmaster, and the best-selling author of *Antichrist the Pope of
Rome*.[2] He wrote in addition the compendious catalogue of God-sent af-
flictions meant to illustrate virtue by way of its opposite, fittingly called
The Theatre of Gods Iudgements, where Marlowe, as already mentioned,
briefly figures. Beard's titles alone help formulate our central inquiry:
How different, finally, is the antichristian theater of Marlowe from the
writings of his pious contemporaries? The question is so difficult to answer because it touches on issues with no graspable edges: the history of
real opposition to Christianity and the extent of its symbolic internalization, for one thing; for another, the relation of such opposition to the
doctrinal conflicts of the Reformation; for yet another, how the reformers' iconoclasm impinged on the much vexed issue of English drama's
secularization.

Beard makes for a pretty good microcosm of the initial complexities.
The cycle plays and moralities may have been happily on the wane from
his perspective,[3] but he nonetheless carried the old traditions forward
into a new world, as would Marlowe, by writing a passion play. Beard intended his religious drama, so far as we know, for a strictly "humanist"
student performance, and he modeled it, as medieval English dramatists
never had, on the five-act canon of the classics.[4] The gospel of Mark thus
returns at long last to its formal roots in pagan antiquity. Elsewhere Beard
follows the convention, not unrelated to scripture's pagan heritage, of
attacking "Plaies & Comedies, and such like toies...which haue no other
vse in the world but to depraue and corrupt good manners."[5] To prove it
he needed only quote such familiar authorities as Tertullian, Augustine,
Chrysostom, and, lastly, the pagan Plutarch, who was made to speak once

2. For an account of Beard's life, see the entry on him by Alexandra Walsham, *Oxford
Dictionary of National Biography*, ed. H. C. G. Matthew and Brian Harrison, 60 vols. (Oxford:
Oxford University Press, 2004), 4:537–38.

3. Harold C. Gardiner, *Mysteries' End: An Investigation of the Last Days of the Medieval Religious Stage* (New Haven: Yale University Press, 1946), gives the once standard interpretation
of the cycles' demise. For a powerful restatement of his view in a much broader context,
see James Simpson, *Reform and Cultural Revolution, 1350–1547*, vol. 2 of *The Oxford English
Literary History*, ed. Jonathan Bate (Oxford: Oxford University Press, 2002), pp. 536–39.
I have been greatly influenced on this question by Michael O'Connell, *The Idolatrous Eye:
Iconoclasm and Theater in Early-Modern England* (New York: Oxford University Press, 2000).

4. See Walsham, "Beard, Thomas" (n. 2), p. 537.

5. Thomas Beard, *The Theatre of Gods Iudgements* (London, 1597 [STC 1659]), p. 374.
The book is, by the way, an augmented translation of Jean de Chassanion, *Histoires memora-
bles des grans et merveilleux jugemens et punitions de Dieu* ([Morges?], 1581).

more, through and against impersonated dialogue, for the reform of the-atergoers.[6]

It is probably no surprise, given these sources, to find that Beard's an-titheatricalism coexists with, or even arises from, his embrace of the well-established view that history as such had been structured dramatically for the benefit of Christians. In explanation for the writing of his *Theatre*, for example, he paraphrases scripture to the effect "that the workes of God are wonderfull, and his iudgements past finding out" (cf. Job 9:10, Rom. 11:33), then adds this theatrical and somewhat tautological gloss: "For if we turne ouer euery leafe of Gods creatures...we shall find, that euery leafe and letter of this great volume, is admirable and wonderfull: and such as doth not onely demonstrate a diuine power to sit at the stern of the world, but also our owne weaknes, which is not able to comprehend the least part thereof" (Epistle Dedicatory). According to this, God is the real playwright, events his script, and the "theater of his judgments" simply the place where the leaves and letters in creation's "great volume" now live in the flesh. The course of the actual world duly confirms God's artistic sublimity, as usual, by failing to convey his true intention: his judgments are "wonderfull" *because* "past finding out." Beard concentrates on the hu-man weakness that cannot "comprehend the least part" of God's heavenly directives paradoxically so as better to study the transcendence of his un-known power.

When Beard considers drama itself (as he frequently does), the same an-cient paradox convinces him that players, rather than performing fictions, are unwittingly caught up and rent by the "reality" of history, which is to say, by the punishing calculus of God's more severe artifice. Beard borrows from Melancthon a typical story—akin to one we've already heard from an earlier German reformer, Gerhoch of Reichersberg[7]—about a passion play gone horribly wrong, which is to say, from God's perspective, a play gone perfectly right: the man who acted as Christ was *actually* wounded to death on the cross "by him that shou'd haue thrust his sword into a bladder full of blood tied to his side" (192). This wound then caused the play-Christ, playing no longer, to fall off the cross, whereupon the velocity of his descent slew an actor beneath who had been pretending to mourn Christ's death. The mourner, too, pretended no more. Then the brother of "Christ," incensed at seeing him killed, "slew the murderer, and was

---

6. For exact citations of his sources, see this excerpt as edited by Tanya Pollard, *Shake-speare's Theater: A Sourcebook* (Oxford: Blackwell, 2004), pp. 168–69.

7. For Gerhoch's story, see chapter 1, pp. 77–78.

himselfe by order of iustice hanged therfore: so that this tragedie was concluded with four true, not counterfeit deaths, and that by the diuine prouidence of God" (192). Another recent performance of a passion play at Oxford, we further learn, had similar results: Christ went stark raving mad, while "three other actors in the same play were hanged for robbing" (192).

It would appear we are not at all far in Beard's *Theatre* from the blood-baths at which Marlowe and his roommate Kyd would excel. Does Beard not also aim to titillate with gore? By this means he, too, sold books. The difference is that Marlowe—or better, Kyd—would have staged these scenes as plays-within-the-play, had they been legally able, whereas Beard could circumvent accusations of blasphemy by presenting the overall play in which these episodes occurred as *historical fact*. Historical reality is then made to signify the artistry of God.

Such Christianized history leads Beard inexorably to tales of the Jews, who, "being vpon a time celebrating their accustomed plaies and feasts, in the midst of their iollity, as their vse is…got a Christian child and hung him vpon a crosse" (43). Where the Catholic players of Melancthon's story *accidentally* killed their Christ ("accident" being a direct result of Providence), the Jews do so intentionally, yet their malevolent intention, as in the Bible, again coincides with God's deep design: "Wherein could these deuils incarnate shew forth their malice more apparantly, then thus," Beard asks, "not content once to haue crucified Christ the Sauior of the world, but by imitation to performe it againe, and as it were to make known, that if it were vndone, they would do it?" (43). This discontented desire to make the crucifixion endlessly iterable—forever done, forever still to do—reflects more than Jewish malice. It arises primarily, I think, from the Christian view of salvation as something already accomplished and yet somehow still to come. As Beard well knew, medieval Christians had spent hundreds of years also imitating the crucifixion as it were to make known that they too would have done it. Beard himself would eventually write a dramatic imitation of it. He is writing one now. Only Beard's version introduces a supererogatory sacrifice, absent from the cycles' passions: the execution of Christ's would-be tormentors. In this latter-day crucifixion, "devils incarnate" suffer alongside whatever representative of God's own flesh was then dying at their hands. In recompense all the Jews are to a man "either hanged, burned, murdred, or put to some other cruell death, at the discretion of the magistrates" (44). Their own injustice, administered in return on them, in other words becomes a *just* means of punishment, however "cruell." When exercised with a semi-artistic "discretion," their cruelty becomes righteous.

Not every ruler was so discreet, but in that case the spectacle of pain could be just as satisfying if it happened to the magistrate himself as payback for the murderous violence of state punishment—especially if the Jews whom the ruler had wrongly subjected to it were Peter and James (the apostle John's brother). In Beard's version, stemming from Josephus, Herod imprisoned the one and killed the other, then "came betime in the morning to the Theatre, clad in a garment all wouen with siluer of a marueilous workmanship; vpon which, as the sunne rising cast his beames, there glittered out such an excellent brightnesse, that thereby his pernicious flatterers tooke occasion to call him with a loud voice by the name of God" (128–29). Toadies of this sort were precisely the people he himself has just killed for the crime of flattering Jesus; in allowing himself to be worshipped by a similar flock, Herod usurps the role of Christ and does so in a manner evoking more than a little his namesake on the medieval stage.[8] A bona fide "Antichrist" (135), Herod predictably relies for his authority, when not leaning on violence, on pure aesthetics, on the glimmer of silver and "marueilous workmanship"; then he maximizes the faux glamour of his costume by parading through the theater. Of course it is there above all, in the place of pretend, that his pretense links him most awfully to the real brilliance of Christian revelation; it is there that medieval drama lives on in Beard. Pranked up so godlike, Herod the hypocrite soon finds his bowels in the grip of "horrible dolours" (129). The relentless grip of the one true God! *This* is the genuinely *spiritual* spectacle, if only witnessed as such when the appearance of Herod in the theater is replayed in *The Theatre* of Beard. Both in their way are heavenly spokesmen.

The term "Antichrist," which Beard applies in this chapter to Simon Magus and many others as well as to Herod, had long since turned against the highest officials in Christendom; the second of Beard's large books, *Antichrist the Pope of Rome*, strives at great length to prove the case once and for all. People had been denouncing the pope as Antichrist for centuries already because the papacy seemed to fulfill the most ancient and respected criteria by means of which the Adversary had been expected all along to consolidate his power.[9] From time immemorial Christ's worst nemesis had always been his sine qua non, which was imitation; so too for Beard: "What is it that Antichrist shall not attempt, doing the works

8. For Herodes Magnus as Antichrist, see chapter 2, n. 24.

9. The specifically *papal* Antichrist seems to date, at the earliest, from the Amalricians in Paris around 1210 but was given new and lasting life in England by Wyclif. From there it exploded outward. See Bernard McGinn, *Antichrist: Two Thousand Years of the Human Fascination with Evil* (New York: Columbia University Press, 2000), pp. 153 and 181–87.

of Christ, and performing the offices of Christians before Christians?" he asks, quoting Chrysostom.[10] Somebody doing the works of Christ is frankly about the worst thing Beard can imagine. For in performing the office of Christians before Christians, Antichrist will eventually render all such rituals *nothing but* "performance." According to Beard, "Antichrist shall serue himselfe of the name of Christ, to fight against Christ, and vnder that faire pretext, introduce his owne pernicious Traditions amongst Christians" (4). One such "tradition"—the word is coded in English Protestantism the way it was coded in the Vulgate and effectively means "betrayal"[11]—was without question the Mass; another, that of calling the pope God's earthly "Vicar" (12), which for Beard was as much as confessing his vice. Yet another tradition was teaching "that the Scripture is imperfect, ambiguous, a leaden rule, a nose of waxe, obscure, the booke of Hereticks, the cause of errours" (13)—hence the alleged need for "traditional" interpretation to compensate for these textual inadequacies: "Read the Treatise of Cardinall *Peron* touching Traditions, or of the vnsufficiency of the Scripture" (13), is Beard's ironic recommendation. If in this case the Catholic teaching was prima facie true—what heretic had not appealed to the Bible's hard words?—no doubt this only confirmed from Beard's ironical viewpoint how Antichrist used the truth to facilitate lies.

Fortunately for him as for most other commentators God uses the false, *mutatis mutandis*, to further *his* truth. Being God how could he not? So the real joke was on the antichristian papists; albeit liars, they inadvertently promoted the gospel. Beard relates an occasion, for example, during a siege of "Mount Dragon in Naples" when the people were ready to yield to their heathen attackers for want of clean water. (The location at Mount *Dragon* would have suggested the Antichrist of Revelation, if Naples by itself did not already suggest sufficient evil.) In a last-ditch effort the priests of the town decided to perform a blasphemous ritual involving the sacrifice of an ass, and lo, "the besieged were deliuered" (330). That the sacrifice worked only confirmed for Beard how sinister the wiles of Satan really were, which strengthened in turn his faith in God: "Is not this an horrible miracle of Romish Priests and can any but the deuill be author thereof?...These be their miracles then that they vaunt so much of, either ridiculous Fables, or mens delusions, or Sathan['s] impostures. *And it is Gods mercy* that they bragge of them, seeing else wee should want

10. Thomas Beard, *Antichrist the Pope of Rome: or, The Pope of Rome is Antichrist* (London, 1625 [STC 1657]), p. 4.
11. See chapter 2, pp. 110–12.

one maine Argument to proue the Pope to be Antichrist, whose comming must bee with lying signes and wonders, and with the efficacy of Sathan to deceiue, if it were possible, the very Elect" (330; my emphasis). According to this, the satanic impostures and fables that so delude Catholics into vaunting of their blunders are but instruments in the exercise of "Gods mercy," without which men like Beard, though the very elect, would still be worshipping unwittingly an asinine Antichrist of their own making, as people before the Reformation had been slavishly doing from time past memory.

Catholics were probably right to object against Protestants and earlier heretics, however, that once you started entertaining the "blasphemous fiction that the Pope should be Antichrist" (2 Thess. 2:3; Douai-Rheims annotation) and traced his apostolic lineage back through the ages, sooner or later you had to arrive at Peter, and thus at the "folish and vvicked paradoxe, that Christes cheefe Minister is Antichrist" (2 Thess. 2:6; ibid.). It did not help that Christ had called Peter "Satan"—a title that, from the Pharisees of the Bible to later opponents, others awarded to Jesus. To call the pope Antichrist led in other words even further than Catholic commentators were willing to admit: it actually implies the paradox that Jesus *himself* had been some kind of Antichrist. Only who in the sixteenth century could ever say such a thing and live?

This is the accusation Beard attributes to Marlowe. Now several years dead, Marlowe wrote books, Beard says, "affirming our Sauiour to be but a deceiuer, and *Moses* to be but a coniurer and seducer of the people, and the holy Bible to be but vaine and idle stories, and all religion but a deuice of pollicie" (*Theatre* 148). The last charge can be clearly traced to Marlowe's extant writings, *The Jew of Malta* especially, where devices of "policy" figure large, beginning with the prologue. "Admired I am of those that hate me most," announces Machevil in comic *approval* of Christ's commandment to love your enemies, just so long as your enemy is Machevil:

> Though some speak openly against my books,
> Yet will they read me, and thereby attain
> To Peter's chair; and when they cast me off
> Are poisoned by my climbing followers.
> I count religion but a childish toy.[12]

12. Christopher Marlowe, *The Jew of Malta*, ed. N. W. Bawcutt, The Revels Plays (Manchester: Manchester University Press, 1978), prologue 9–14.

Nietzsche's dream in *The Antichrist* of a modern *Schauspiel* to rival the extinct drama of Greece, which would feature "*Cesare Borgia as pope*" and give occasion for "immortal laughter,"[13] is already enacted here in Marlowe. Machevil's speech probably alludes to the alleged poisoning of Pope Alexander VI, father of Borgia, when he accidentally drank from a cup his son had seasoned for someone else (cf. 3.4.98–99). If these lines mock the Christian "religion" in a proto-Nietzschean fashion, however, they do so mainly by mocking Catholicism. As we're about to see, the radical condemnation of historical Christianity was in Marlowe's day and in his plays a normative convention. It was the common view of Protestants.

In fact all of the other accusations that Beard attributes to Marlowe stem as much from a literal reading of scripture, so beloved by Protestants, as from atheistic skepticism. To say Moses was a conjurer—or as the Baines note has it a "Jugler" (*CM* 221; cf. 227)—is in some sense just a careful reading of the passages where he squares off against the magicians of Egypt; only after several draws can he manage to execute a "miracle" more stunning than their magic, and one obvious point to take was that Moses' tricks were of the same *kind* as the Egyptians' "secret arts" (Exod. 7:11, 8:7), merely of greater *power* (Exod. 8:18–19, 9:11). Moses had, after all, been "brought up in all the artes of the Egiptians," as Marlowe also allegedly liked to point out.[14] And it was to Egypt that his antitype Jesus fled as an infant, where he too according to legend exhibited the earliest instances of the miraculous works that would eventually make him equally subject to comparison with sorcerers. The comparison is drawn, for example, by the gospels, in the early attacks on and apologies for Christianity, and in a huge array of medieval literature—most pointedly in the "miracle" plays where Christ was yearly tried in England *as* a sorcerer.[15] For all we know Jesus may have really *been* a magus: the early church used his name in spells and exorcisms, and he "long continued to be represented in Christian art as a magician, complete with magic wand, as he appears on a fourth-century gold glass plate *in the Vatican library*."[16]

---

13. *The Portable Nietzsche*, trans. Walter Kaufmann (New York: Viking Penguin, 1954), p. 654.

14. *CM* 221. A similar accusation has been attributed to Richard Cholmeley, who supposedly said "that Moyses was a Jugler & Aaron a Cosoner the one for his miracles to Pharao to prove there was a god, & the other for taking the Eareringes of the children of Israell to make a golden calfe" (*CM* 216).

15. See n. 4 in the introduction and then chapter 1, pp. 65–66; on the typology between Jesus and Moses, see chapter 3, pp. 154–55.

16. Morton Smith, *Jesus the Magician* (San Francisco: Harper & Row, 1978), p. 64; my emphasis.

At its theological core the Reformation was largely an extended campaign to eradicate such representations—along with the medieval Bible on which they were based, and the vast number of parabiblical legends that had accrued to it. As a result people like Beard were campaigning, in effect, to eradicate the foundation of all preceding Christian culture for having offered little more than "vaine and idle stories."[17] Beard's own critique and that which he attributes to Marlowe are therefore genetically akin—not only to each other but also to precisely those "vaine and idle stories" they claimed to dismiss. These frequently emphasize, as we've already seen, that the legendary events recorded in "scripture"—however defined—were divine only insofar as they would have been all but impossible save for God... or the devil, or mortal liars or their close familiars, the artists. The distance between all these duplicitous figures had if anything grown more slight over the course of the Reformation. Yet through some broad cultural shift, far deeper than doctrine, certain powerful people had started to wish it were not so common or easy to revel in the proximity.

Revel people did nonetheless. "But see what a hooke the Lord put in the nosthrils of this barking dogge" (*Theatre* 148), Beard writes, with no small delight, of Marlowe's gruesome demise. What he is affirming, to anyone who had read or heard preached the books of Jonah and Job as interpreted from Origen and Gregory to Luther and after, is the prerogative of God to outwit—more strongly, to deceive—anyone who calls him a deceiver. Such is the justice of his unsearchable mercy. For the hook here in Marlowe's nose is the same by which God had promised to raise the satanic Leviathan: it is the fishhook of his deity which he baits with the likeness of sinful flesh; it is the incredible paradox of incarnation and the sweet affliction of the Lord's crucifixion.[18] For Beard, the death of Marlowe signifies God no less than does the murder of Christ, and in a way it signifies better, since the most iconic testimonies to the suffering of Jesus had all been suppressed. Marlowe's dying figure here acts as their replacement: "The manner of his death being so terrible," Beard writes, "that it was not only a manifest signe of Gods iudgment, but also an horrible and fearefull terrour to all that beheld him" (148). A sign of this sort might well inspire terror: on the surface it showed only business as usual in a godforsaken world. And yet Beard discerns in that horror, as in the cultivated "terror" of theater, the hand of God at work in the hand of his opponents, just as for

17. A point whose relevance to Shakespeare has been brilliantly demonstrated by Stephen Greenblatt, *Hamlet in Purgatory* (Princeton: Princeton University Press, 2001).
18. On the incarnation as a fishhook for Leviathan, see chapter 3, p. 173–74.

Augustine the hand of Judas had acted as God's personal instrument: "But herein did the iustice of God most notably appear, in that he compelled his owne hand which had written those blasphemies to be the instrument to punish him, and that in his braine, which had deuised the same" (148). The momentary confusion over the pronoun's antecedent at the beginning of the sentence bespeaks Beard's theodicy: God's merciful justice "appears," so to speak, "in that *he* compelled *his owne* hand" to issue hard discipline, while neither the compulsion nor the hand is actually God's but rather that of a satanic blasphemer. God appears *in* Satan. Thus his actions conform again to the poetic justice of talionic law, as the same hand that sins is the instrument of sin's punishment. Had Beard known exactly where in "the head" Marlowe received the fatal blow—as we do from the coroner's report (*CM* 222–26)—he could have demonstrated even more precisely how this random bar fight illustrated God's will. The terror of those who "beheld" the scene was that of seeing a man, committed in his lifetime to feigning such spectacles, stabbing himself *in the eye*. Fracture for fracture, measure for measure...

One of the earliest contributions to the Marlowe industry, Beard's *Theatre* has the merit of sharing, ultimately, the same objective as its object of study; where Marlowe's "atheistic" drama tantalized viewers, in place of the old supreme deity, with the tribulations inflicted on humanity by human megalomania, Beard offers the same in hopes of producing a like consolation. The point of rehearsing such gruesome scenes, Beard explains in his preface, is "to lay open the nature of morall virtues"—though not, of course, by describing them outright. Virtue is approachable in the present world only if the approach has been bent; so instead he will anatomize "on each side the contrarie and repugnant vice; to the end that at the sight of them, being so out of square, so hurtfull and pernicious, vertue it selfe might be more amiable and in greater esteeme" (*Theatre*, preface). It is this procedure that lends to the book its Marlovian cast: in it Beard dwells, for the greater glory of God—or at any rate, for the entertainment of his readers—exclusively on the most devious of sinners, with the result that he seems in the end as much to foment as lament the world's current, apocalyptic state: "All things being as it were ouerthrowne and turned vpside downe, men speake euill of good, and good of euill, accounting darknesse light, and light darkenesse: sower sweet, and sweet sower. And by such disorder it commeth to passe, that the most vertuous are despised, whilest naughty packs and vicious fellowes are esteemed and made much of" (3). In fact the book's half-knowing adulation of wrongdoing as an ideal, ersatz icon in place of more pious imagery reads a lot like a synopsis of the plots then storming the stage of London in the absence of any more "direct" revelation. Beard presents, as do Marlowe and his fellow playwrights, the tragic fall of personages who reveled in their pleasures a while too long, as though they were gods. Their pleasures are practically infinite, these satanic but all-too-human aspirants; defiance of the Absolute they pretend to, their absolute favorite. Naturally when these characters come to their preordained end, they only testify there all the more eloquently to that impossible transcendence which had always eluded them. It has to elude, else lose all claim to transcend its earthly representatives, such as them. What else, in the age of iconoclasm, was the lesson to be drawn from the cross or from the historical successes of Antichrist? The lesson Marlowe drew is the key to his dramatic aesthetic.

Jesus Barabbas, Son of God

No episode in the life of Jesus captures more concretely the vicarious exchange by means of which he was supposed to redeem humanity than his last-minute substitution for that "remarkable criminal" (Mt 27:16), Barabbas. Christ consequently hangs on the cross *in place of* another and does so "in keeping" with the tradition of Passover—or perhaps better said, he hangs there in keeping with the symbolic demands of Christian soteriology: "Do you not marvel [*mireris*]," Origen questions, "if the Jews had newly taken up the yoke of the Romans, that it would be given to them to demand at Passover 'anyone whom they wanted' [Mt 27:15], even if he seemed guilty of a thousand murders?"[19] God might be willing to free an insidious sinner from due torment, but Romans? A similar doubt concerning the historicity of this incredible custom, though without Origen's concomitant wonder, has been detected by more recent scholars in Luke's refusal to mention it. A group of early scribes, likewise struck, corrected the omission by interpolating a verse (Lk 23:17) based on precisely the passage (Mk 15:6) that Luke had tried to omit. Their correction, deemed a corruption, has since been dropped (*TC* 153).

Independent of scripture there is no suggestion that the Roman government ever freed a political prisoner out of deference to Judaism. On the contrary, what testimonials exist about the character of Pilate have often served to discredit the biblical episode even more radically: for instance, Philo records a letter supposedly written by Agrippa I to Caligula in which the king complains of Pilate's "briberies, the insults, the robberies,

19. *Comm. in Matt.*, no. 120 (GCS 38, Origenes Werke 11:253; *KEM* 3:319).

the outrages and wanton injuries, the executions without trial constantly repeated, the ceaseless and supremely grievous cruelty" (*Ad Gaium* 38, §302; LCL vol. 10). We know further from Josephus, as E. P. Sanders summarizes, that Pilate was in fact "eventually dismissed from office because of large-scale and ill-judged executions."[20] In this light, the reluctant, philosophical Pilate of the gospels—cowed into cruelty by a fickle mob of Jews—has seemed to many less convincing as history than as a great stock figure in "world literature."[21] Even the scholars who see beneath Pilate's exquisite offer to free either Barabbas or Christ some historical kernel nonetheless acknowledge that the episode as written bears all the marks of a "dramatization."[22]

It certainly lays the groundwork for the drama that would be *The Jew of Malta*. As one of "the few Elizabethan poets who took a serious interest in Greek,"[23] Marlowe was in a good position to grasp, and to imagine his own writing could surpass, the details of New Testament fiction. His supposed speculation "that if he were put to write a new religion, he would undertake both a more Exellent and Admirable methode" (*CM* 221) is not exactly an imaginary proposition: playwrights of the late sixteenth century *had* to write a new religion; the old one, which up to then had sustained the best dramatizations, was no longer in fashion, due in part to the same worldview, then overtaking the schools, that could lead an educated man to make another remark attributed to Marlowe: "All the new testament is filthily written" (ibid.). By classical standards, the New Testament, like medieval drama, overflows with crudity—the style of Paul notwithstanding and despite his attempts at learned allusion or Mark's theatrical trappings. Early Christians did what they could to turn the tables on the first versions of Marlowe's criticism. "Do not be offended by the simplicity of holy scripture," Jerome admonishes, "or its almost vile phrases [*quasi vilitate verborum*]." That is the fault of the translators, he says, or rather part of God's

20. E. P. Sanders, *The Historical Figure of Jesus* (New York: Penguin, 1993), p. 274. For a full-scale study of the earliest accounts, see Helen K. Bond, *Pontius Pilate in History and Interpretation* (Cambridge: Cambridge University Press, 1998).

21. Robert Carroll and Stephen Prickett, eds., *The Bible: Authorized King James Version* (Oxford: Oxford University Press, 1997), p. 413.

22. Raymond E. Brown, *The Death of the Messiah: From Gethsemane to the Grave: A Commentary on the Passion Narratives in the Four Gospels* (New York: Doubleday, 1993), p. 820; W. D. Davies and Dale C. Allison, *A Critical and Exegetical Commentary on the Gospel According to Saint Matthew*, 3 vols. (Edinburgh: T & T Clark, 1988–97), likewise call the release of Barabbas "a circumstance which Christian imagination subsequently dramatized" (3:583) and further note that the ambiguity surrounding Barabbas' name (which we'll look at in a minute) "heightens the drama" (3:584).

23. Riggs, *World of Christopher Marlowe* (n. 1), p. 186.

own design: "for in this way it is better fitted for the instruction of an unlettered congregation" (*Ep.* 53 [PL 22:549; NPNF II, 6:102]). Against the charge that Christian scripture presents only a degraded parody of paganism's better achievements, Jerome and others argued that every classical genre actually derived from the Bible: any comparison between them was therefore always to the credit of Christian letters.[24] Marlowe's remark strikes me as only a slightly more twisted sally in this ancient agon between Christian and pagan writers. In this case the twist is that a "pagan" Marlowe, or someone speaking on his behalf, is made to repudiate his single greatest influence—the Bible.

Marlowe openly derives from the drama of scripture his antihero Barabas, and he furthermore attributes to him a veneration of lucre drawn straight from scripture's most "filthy" expressions for the rewards and means of entering heaven. As even Luther admitted, in the Bible God practically speaks of "nothing but *minae,* talents, riches, and *denarii*" (*Res. de indulgentiarum virtute* 62 [WA 1:616; *LW* 31:230]). Being God's "will" in every sense of the word, the Bible was above all a testamentary disposition of his immeasurable riches. According to Luther, the purpose of the bequest was of course not to license the grotesque commerce that so dominated every dealing with the church but rather the opposite—"to show by these terms which speak of temporal treasures that the gospel is the *true* treasure" (ibid.; my emphasis). This "true" treasure then empowered Luther to denounce the "false" treasury of the church, which scripture had long been said to underwrite: after all even salvation had had to be bought. Judas sold the flesh and blood of Christ. The freedom of Barabbas just added, as it were, to the revolting cost: as both Luther and Marlowe might

---

24. Judaism had admittedly preceded Christianity in deriving pagan literature and its philosophical-literary techniques from the Bible (that is, from the Septuagint): see, e.g., Philo, *De aeternitate mundi* 19 (LCL vol. 9), and Josephus, *Against Apion* 2.281 (LCL). For some examples of the Christian version, see Clement of Alexandria, *Stromata* 1.21–25; 5.4, esp. 5.14 and 6.2–3, more passim (GCS 15, Clemens Werke 2:64–104, 338–42, 384–421, 422–48; ANF 2:324–38, 449–50, 465–76, 481–88); Origen, *C. Celsum* 4.21, 8.30; Eusebius, *Praeparatio evangelica* 11.5 (GCS 43.2, Eusebius Werke, 8.2:11–12); trans. Edwin Hamilton Gifford, *Preparation for the Gospel,* 2 vols. (Oxford: Clarendon Press, 1903), 2:551; Jerome, *Praefatio in chronicorum Eusebii* (PL 27:223–26), *Praefatio in Job* (PL 28:1140–41). All of this more or less culminates in Bede, *De schematis et tropis* (PL 90:175–86); ed. and trans. Calvin B. Kendall, *Libri II: De arte metrica et De schematibus et tropis = The Art of Poetry and Rhetoric* (Saarbrücken: AQ-Verlag, 1991). For discussion and further citations, see Ernst Robert Curtius, *European Literature and the Latin Middle Ages,* trans. Willard R. Trask (New York: Pantheon, 1953), pp. 46–47 and 219–20. The issue was still alive and well at the time of Milton. See Barbara Lewalski, *Milton's Brief Epic: The Genre, Meaning, and Art of "Paradise Regained"* (Providence: Brown University Press, 1966), pp. 10ff.

well have known, his epithet—"remarkable" (Gr: *episēmon*; Lat: *insignem*)—
could also denote the representational mark on a coin, by virtue of which
empty and inverted image bullion receives its official worth.[25] Behold the
man in exchange for whom Christ ransoms humanity so that others just as
guilty might also escape. Barabbas *personifies* blood money.

Whatever Marlowe or Baines may have meant by the remark "that Crist
deserved better to dy then Barrabas and that the Jewes made a good choise,
though Barrabas were both a thief and a murtherer,"[26] there is without
question far more to the words than casual blasphemy: it registers precisely
what was structurally undecidable about the economics and aesthetics of
Christian salvation. The "Jewish" choice to forgive Barabbas' crimes while
holding Jesus to account for them is, in the end, a shadow of God's enigmatic preferences. "We do not censure [you], O Jews, because you set free
a guilty man by reason of the Pasch," writes Augustine of their deciding
for Barabbas, "but because you kill an innocent man. Albeit, unless this
happened, the true Pasch would not happen. But the shadow of truth was
held on to by the erring Jews; and by the wondrous dispensation of divine wisdom, through deceitful men the truth of this same shadow was
fulfilled."[27] We have seen again and again this Augustinian dialectic at work,
whereby evil, deceptive, and erring "shadows" command a certain veneration and afford clear enjoyment as the indispensable prefiguration of goodness at the moment of its greatest absence. We have seen it for example
in the teachings of heretics whose deceptions and errors essentially shape
the true church, and in the actions of biblical opponents like Judas, to
whom Marlowe's Barabas specifically owes a part of his costume: "The hat
he wears," says Ithamore, "Judas left under the elder when he hanged himself" (4.4.67).[28] Barabas is thus accoutered as his once great predecessor on

25. On the term, see Luz 3:496–97. See also Rom. 16:7. Frederick W. Danker, ed.,
A Greek-English Lexicon of the New Testament and Other Early Christian Literature, 3d ed. (Chicago: University of Chicago Press, 2000), s.v. ἐπίσημος, takes it here strictly in the sense
of "notorious" and has amassed various examples to prove it. L&S give the numismatic
significance, which the others omit, s.v. ἐπίσημος II.1.

26. *CM* 221. Cited by Harry Levin, *The Overreacher: A Study of Christopher Marlowe* (Cambridge: Harvard University Press, 1952), p. 64, with the incisive remark that "if Christ died
for all men, he died most immediately for Barabbas.... Marlowe, in instinctively taking his
side, identifies his Jew with the Antichrist." On the (exceedingly long) history of reading
Barabbas as Antichrist, see below.

27. *Tract. in Joh.* 115.5 (CCSL 36:646; trans. John W. Rettig, FC 92:26); cf. *Tract. in Joh.*
112.2–3 (ibid.).

28. That Judas hanged himself on an elder tree was a "widespread tradition" according to
Wayland D. Hand, *A Dictionary of Words and Idioms Associated with Judas Iscariot: A Compilation
Based Mainly on Material Found in Germanic Languages* (Berkeley: University of California

the English stage, now retired by force of religious change and the innovations of a strictly commercial drama. Yet in the absence of icons the London theater had clearly become only the latest shadow of deceitful men. The larger part of its power, as with the shadowy liturgy, was the illusion it created of fulfillment.[29] It too seemed to offer a sublime satisfaction.

John Cox has demonstrated in some detail that while overt mention of God was slowly ebbing from English drama, the devil remained in all his preposterous glory; so that ultimately its "secularization" amounts in the end to something more like a demonic re-sacralization.[30] Never before the Reformation could clerically trained men with a taste for playacting find work where Satan's shadow was at its longest, in those novel "Seminaries of pseudo christianit[y]," that "den of spiritual thieves," the commercial theater.[31] And none of these for-profit playwrights or "Counterfeit Christians"[32] was more dependent on and attracted to Satan than Christopher Marlowe.[33] Effectively it was through the *devil* that his writing managed, in the words of Don Beecher, "to revitalize...the powerful symbolic drama of the Middle Ages."[34]

Press, 1942), s. v. "Judas Tree" (p. 350). Cf. G. K. Hunter, "The Theology of Marlowe's *The Jew of Malta*," *Journal of the Warburg and Courtauld Institutes* 27 (1964): 211–40, here 221: "Judas' choice, preferring thirty pieces of silver to the life of his Lord, is easy to conflate with the general Jewish choice of Barabbas rather than Christ." According to Robert Greene, it was *Marlowe* who "inherited the portion of *Iudas*" (*Greene's "Groatsworth of Wit Bought with a Million of Repentance" (1592)*, ed. D. Allen Carroll [Binghamton, N.Y.: Medieval and Renaissance Texts and Studies, 1994], p. 82).

29. For this reading of the Mass, see chapter 2, pp. 121–25.

30. John D. Cox, *The Devil and the Sacred in English Drama, 1350–1642* (Cambridge: Cambridge University Press, 2000).

31. From Stubbes's *Anatomie of Abuses* (London, 1583) and Thomas Randolph's *The Muses' Looking Glass* (1630), respectively, both quoted and discussed by Jeffery Knapp, *Shakespeare's Tribe: Church, Nation, and Theater in Renaissance England* (Chicago: Chicago University Press, 2002), pp. 142 and 144; his argument in places overlaps with my own, though I am dubious about the theater's homiletic function and would want to stress instead the entertainment value of homilies; also I think the theater's commercialism ought to take center stage, so to speak, in any account of its religious heritage.

32. From a sermon of John Walsall (1578), quoted by Knapp, *Shakespeare's Tribe*, p. 142.

33. For Marlowe's reliance on the myth of Satan (e.g., *Faustus* 1.3.63ff.) as well as his attraction to its classical analogues—Icarus (*Faustus* Prol. 20–22; *Dido* 5.1.243–46; *Massacre* 2.46–47) and Phaeton (*Edward II* 1.4.16–17; *2 Tamburlaine* 5.3.230–34)—see Harry Levin, *Overreacher* (n. 26), pp. 52–53 and 112; Douglas Cole, *Suffering and Evil in the Plays of Christopher Marlowe* (Princeton: Princeton University Press, 1962), p. 196 n. 12; A. Bartlett Giamatti, "Marlowe: The Arts of Illusion," *Yale Review* 61.2 (1972): 530–43, here 535; also Marjorie Garber, "'Infinite Riches in a Little Room': Closure and Enclosure in Marlowe," in *Two Renaissance Mythmakers: Christopher Marlowe and Ben Jonson*, ed. Alvin Kernan (Baltimore: Johns Hopkins University Press, 1977), pp. 3–21, here 4–6.

34. Don Beecher, "*The Jew of Malta* and the Ritual of the Inverted Moral Order," *Cahiers Élisabéthains: Études sur la Pré-Renaissance et la Renaissance Anglaises* 12 (1977): 45–58; here 55.

The name of his hero Barab(b)as, for example, means either "son of the teacher," as Jerome in one place suggests,[35] or—more likely—"son of the father," as he suggests in another (probably following Hilary).[36] Given Jesus' extraordinary custom of addressing God as "Abba," or "Father," the title "son of the father" strongly implies "son of God," which in turn implies a claim to *be* God; at least, that is the claim inferred from Hilary onward in the commonplace that Barabbas is Antichrist.[37] As usual Christ's alter ego absorbs and atones for Christ's hubris: according to the religious accusers at his trial it was *Jesus* who "called God his own father, making himself equal with God" (Jn 5:18). That accusation became, in effect, an article of faith among later Christians who *affirmed* the Son's coequality, however blasphemous: "All Israelites can be said to be 'sons of God' (see e.g. Rom. 9.4)," writes E. P. Sanders, "and it is only the subsequent Christian claim that Jesus himself was divine that clearly constitutes blasphemy";[38] in medieval terms, anyone who would take for himself the attributes belonging exclusively to God actually commits a form of "robbery," insofar as this "deprives" (*rapit*) God of his due honor,[39] and in that case,

---

35. Jerome, *Comm. in Matt.* 4 (SC 259:278–81 on Mt 27:16); literally "son of their teacher." For a discussion of the puzzling personal pronoun in the context of Jerome's probable source, see *NTA* 1:156–57.

36. Jerome, *Liber de nominibus hebraicis*, de Joanne (PL 23:889–90); Hilary of Poitiers, *In Matt.* 33.2 (SC 258:248–50).

37. After Hilary (above note) the next to call Barabbas Antichrist is I think Ambrose, *Exp. in Luc.* 7.239 (SC 52:98). At any rate this identification, together with both etymologies for the name (see previous two notes), becomes standard throughout the Middle Ages: see, e.g., Isidore, *Allegoriae quaedam s. script.* 244 (PL 83:129A); Bede, *In Matt.* 4.27 (PL 92:121B, 122A), verbatim *In Luc.* 6.23 (PL 92:613C); verbatim in Rabanus Maurus, *Comm. in Matt.* 8.27 (PL 107:1133A); more by Maurus himself in *De universo* 4.1 (PL 111:83C–D). See also the Gloss on Mt 27:16, 21, 26 (PL 114:173C–D, 174B) and on Lk 23:18 (PL 114:345C); Haymo Halberstatensis, *Comm. in Isaiam* 3.39 (PL 116:1025B), and *Hom. de tempore* 64 (PL 118:373D–74A); Rupert of Deutz, *De trin. et operibus*, in Leviticum 2:31 (PL 167:819D–20A); in Num. 2:27 (908B); in Deut. 1:19 (939C); in Osee 4 (PL 168:158C); Gerhoch of Reichersberg, *Comm. in Ps.* 9.20 (PL 193:767A). The patristic and scholastic interpretation has been brought to bear on Marlowe's play already by Hunter, "Theology" (n. 28), p. 214; Eric Rothstein, "Structure as Meaning in *The Jew of Malta*," *Journal of English and Germanic Philology* 65 (1966): 260–73, here 261; Beecher, "*Jew of Malta*" (n. 34), p. 55; and Sara Munson Deats, "Biblical Parody in Marlowe's *The Jew of Malta*: A Re-examination," *Christianity and Literature* 37.2 (1988): 27–48.

38. E. P. Sanders, *Jesus and Judaism* (Philadelphia: Fortress, 1985), p. 298.

39. Anselm, *Cur Deus Homo* 1.7, 11 (SC 91:230ff., 264ff.); likewise for Calvin, *Institutio Christianae Religionis* (1559) 1.2.2, 1.4.2; ed. Guilielmus Baum et al. (Brunswick, 1869), vol. 2, cols. 35, 29; trans. Ford Lewis Battles, ed. John T. McNeill, 2 vols. (Philadelphia: Westminster Press, 1960), 1:41, 48: "We should learn to seek every good from him [God], and, having received it, to credit it to his account [*illi acceptum ferre discamus*]"; those who don't, "despoil [*spoliantes*] him of his judgment and providence." Cf. Marlowe's "paganization" of the motif when Hero is said "to rob" Venus of "her name and honor" by vowing *chastity* (1.303–5).

again, Jesus better deserves to die than Barabbas, because Jesus, according to the Bible, "did not consider equality with God to *be* robbery [*rapinam*]" (Phil. 2:6).[40] New Testament Jews, by contrast, apparently did, and considered such "equality" a far worse crime than any more mundane theft, so that given their options they chose the *lesser* of two criminals.

This decisive choice in the New Testament—effectively between Christ and Antichrist, between Christianity and its internalized opposite—was made all the more challenging in some early manuscripts of Matthew, understandably not much favored since the third century but currently thought authoritative as the *lectio difficilior.*[41] According to these witnesses, Jesus and Barabbas share even more than the honorific "son of the Father": Barabbas also goes by the name of "Jesus."[42] Jesus is, so to speak, his *Christian* name. So when Pilate appears before the crowd, people have to choose between Jesus, son of God, and *another* Jesus, the so-called Christ. "Whom do you want me to release for you?" Pilate now asks. "Jesus Barabbas, or Jesus who is called the Messiah?" (Mt 27:17; NRSV). Jesus? or Jesus? For Christ's sake . . .

The episode obviously marks a serious departure from the view that God has an unsayable name that applies only to him, was spoken to Moses then never again (Exod. 3:13–14).[43] Woe to the thief on the cross who

40. I give "robbery" here following the Vulgate and every English Bible before the twentieth century, so far as I know. That's probably not what the Greek ἁρπαγμός means. Thus the RSV: "He did not consider equality with God *a thing to be grasped*"—a more accurate rendering that, however, presents doctrinal difficulties of its own (to say the least). On Christ's other "thefts," see chapter 3, pp. 164–68.

41. An editorial principle, by the way, fully articulated in Augustine, *De consensu evang.* 3.7.29 (PL 35:1174–75). Mentioned by Elias Bickerman, "Some Notes on the Transmission of the Septuagint," in *Studies in Jewish and Christian History*, vol. 1 (Leiden: Brill, 1976), pp. 137–66; here 140 n. 12.

42. See *TC* 56; Davies and Allison, *Matthew* (n. 22), 3:584 n. 20 on the current consensus that "Jesus Barabbas" is the original reading (more on its preservation and transmission in a moment). There are those like Luz who see nothing in the coincidental names, both being so common; others like Hyam Maccoby, *Revolution in Judaea: Jesus and the Jewish Resistance* (New York: Taplinger, 1980), pp. 163ff., and S. L. Davies, "Who Is Called Bar Abbas?" *New Testament Studies* 27 (1980–81): 260–62, argue that Jesus and Barabbas were originally the same man and that the episode handed down by the gospels is the fabrication of a later gentile church intent on writing its animosity against Jews back into its founding documents. For criticism of this compelling but precarious view, see Brown, *Death of the Messiah* (n. 22), pp. 811–14.

43. Cf. Kenneth Burke, *The Rhetoric of Religion: Studies in Logology* (Berkeley: University of California Press, 1970), p. 2: "As for a unitary concept of God, its linguistic analogue is to be found in the nature of any name or title, which sum up a manifold of particulars under a single head"—except that in the case of Jesus the "single head" has been multiplied hydra-like.

calls out for "Jesus" without specifying the one from Nazareth! (Lk 23:42). Throughout the New Testament Jesus warns precisely of this: that others *just like him* will deceive many by coming *in his name.*[44] Not even his "real" disciples will be immune from the deception. Hence Christ's admonishment that on the final day, "many will say to me, 'Lord, Lord, did we not prophesy in your name, and cast out demons in your name, and do many mighty works in your name?' And then I will declare to them, I never knew you: depart from me, you evildoers" (Mt 7:22–23). These words as much as any extramural opposition to Christianity cast a suspicious light on the "signs and wonders" of the apostles which brought such "fear on every soul" (Acts 2:43; cf. 3:6). When Caiaphas and Annas specifically ask Peter "by what power, or by what *name,* have you done this?" (Acts 4:7b), Peter responds that he and his fellow apostles act "in the name of Jesus" and that "there is no other name under heaven given among men, whereby we must be saved" (4:10, 12). Yet a major trouble with the gospels was that in some versions *two* men went by the name of Jesus, and both had proven literally interchangeable; meanwhile the one accepted as God by the church specifically warned that to do things "in his name" was an insufficient guarantee of true devotion (cf. Mk 16:17).

The enormous emphasis throughout the New Testament on the singularity and power of "the name that is above every name" (Phil. 2:9; cf., e.g., Acts 4:10, 16:18; James 5:14) takes on in this light the look of a symptomatic compensation for the founding confusion between Jesus and the demonic others whose names might not necessarily differ. "Jesus does not trust himself to one who believes in his name," writes Origen of an enigmatic passage in John (2:24); "we must cling therefore to him rather than to his name" (*Comm. in Joh.* 10, §310 [SC 157:574; trans. Ronald Heine, FC 80:324–25])—provided only you could tell who he himself was. The Genevan explanation of "Barabbas" as "son of confusion,"[45] elsewhere unattested so far as I know, certainly helps gloss this whole situation and is probably alluded to by Marlowe in his hero's final confession before boiling to death in a vat of his own devising (as was traditional for Antichrist)[46]: "had I but escaped this stratagem, / I would have brought confusion on you all, / Damned Christian dogs, and Turkish infidels!" (5.5.83–85). If ever there was a play to dramatize the lack of distinction among Christian dogs,

44. For further discussion, see the introduction, pp. 6–10.

45. *The Geneva Bible: A Facsimile of the 1560 Edition* (Madison: University of Wisconsin Press, 1969), appendix, first table, s.v. "Barabbas."

46. For discussion of the vat, with pictures, see Hunter, "Theology" (n. 28), pp. 234–35, who notes (p. 218) that Barabas quotes verbatim from the Geneva Bible at 1.2.197–99.

Turkish infidels, and their Jewish antagonist—all of them equally venal, all of them equally vicious—this play is it.

Just as Marlowe's supposed blasphemies arise in at least one case from a tract written *against* doctrinal heresy (i.e., John Proctour's *Fall of the Late Arrian*), the "heretical" embarrassment of Barabbas' first name was likewise preserved and transmitted by the person partly responsible for its removal from the Bible—Origen, that problematic Father of the church, whose censorious remarks on the manuscripts reading "Jesus Barabbas" were for many scholars thereafter the only available testimony to the existence of that reading. In his commentary on Matthew, parts of which Marlowe could have read courtesy of Archbishop Parker,[47] Origen puzzles over the omission of Barabbas' first name from so many copies: "maybe rightly," he concludes, "so that the name Jesus does not join with one of the iniquitous."[48] You can easily understand Origen's worry, considering what he writes in his great apology: "Perhaps it is no less dangerous," he speculates there, "for a man to degrade the name of God or that of goodness to a thing to which these names ought not to be applied, than it is for a man to change names the nature of which is in accordance with a certain mysterious principle, and to apply the names of what is bad to what is good and of what is good to what is bad" (*C. Celsum* 1.25). The Barabbas episode, as Origen knew, threatened to accomplish exactly this transposition, and the danger now was that you could no longer tell the true religion from its demonic counterpart. The Jews were supposed to be the ones who "think and do the things of robbers," who "made the house of God 'a den of thieves'" by choosing as their God the robber Barabbas: "So, up to this day," Origen extrapolates, "the Jews do not have Jesus, for they have not believed in the Son of God. Instead, they have among themselves Barabbas, the thief. . . . Barabbas, the thief, rules

---

47. The comedy and coincidence of names! The Parker scholarship that supported Marlowe was at the time overseen by his son John. For a catalogue of the books that Parker maintained, see *The University and College Libraries of Cambridge*, ed. Peter D. Clarke (London: British Library, 2002), pp. 240ff. This list bears comparison with the library of Marlowe's earlier schoolmaster John Gressop (transcribed in *CM* 182–90), which includes among the expected Protestant authorities Philo, Gregory of Nyssa, Cyprian, Eusebius, Boethius, Bede, Lombard, Albert the Great, Scotus, Gabriel Biel, and John Proctour's *Fall of the Late Arrian*. I give this list because I want to demonstrate, within Marlowe's immediate orbit, the continual persistence of patristic and medieval theological debate.

48. *Comm. in Matt.* no. 121 (GCS 38, Origenes Werke 11:255; *KEM* 3:320–21). GCS prints a parallel fragment, variously ascribed to Peter of Laodicea or Athanasius, concerned with the reverse problem—not the omission of the name, but rather that in *all* of "the oldest manuscripts [*antigraphois*] Barabbas was called Jesus."

the unbelieving Jews."[49] The synagogue is in other words an anti-church with the wrong "Jesus, Son of God" at its head. Elsewhere in the same commentary, however, Origen himself can hardly distinguish among the infidels and true believers: "It is possible to find many places," he grudgingly confesses, "where the affairs of the so-called church have in a short time led to so evil a condition that a group having gathered *in the name* of Christ does not differ from a den of thieves."[50] The name of Christ Jesus, son of God, had always applied to too many; the robbers who went by the name of Christians and called themselves the true church now were also legion.

The Reformation brought this ancient critique of the faith to a new point of crisis. "Will you then steal my goods?" Marlowe's Barabas asks his Christian tormentors. "Is theft the ground of your religion?" (1.2.95–96). The question encapsulates how the confusion at the heart of the Bible between his scriptural namesake and Jesus had grown increasingly acute after a millennium and more of continual plunder in the name of Jesus; what in the end belonged to the church that had not been borrowed from others? There were of course many different sorts of transfer, yet nevertheless, as Clement of Alexandria writes, for example, of the similarities between Christian doctrine and Greek philosophy, "the thief possesses truly what he possesses [illegitimately] by stealing, whether gold, or silver, or ideas, or dogma" (*Strom.* 1.20 [GCS 15, Clemens Werke 2:64; ANF 2:323–24]). Clearly the language describing one form of appropriation could metaphorically describe the other, and the identity this posits between them is worth taking seriously: first, because Christianity's strictly "cultural" borrowings from classical antiquity, as from Judaism, directly *aided in* the maintenance of more concretely appropriative social hierarchies during the "Christian" Middle Ages. Augustine counsels that "when the Christian severs himself in spirit from the unhappy community of pagans, he must take their treasures from them and use them righteously for the proclamation of the Gospel,"[51] even though such proclamations,

49. *Comm. in Matt.* 16.23 (GCS 40, Origenes Werke 10:556; *KEM* 2:204). Repeated verbatim, *In Luc.*, fragment 246 (GCS 49 [35], Origenes Werke 9:331–32; trans. Joseph Lienhard, FC 94:223–24).

50. *Comm. in Matt.* 16.22 (GCS 40, Origenes Werke 10:551; *KEM* 2:202–3); my emphasis. Cf. Origen's preceding commentary on Mt 16:21 (ibid.) and *C. Celsum* 1.6: "In fact the name of Jesus is so powerful against the demons that sometimes it is effective even when pronounced by bad men." *Ex opere operato*!

51. Quoted by Hans Blumenberg, *The Legitimacy of the Modern Age*, trans. Robert M. Wallace (Cambridge: MIT Press, 1983), p. 70, who offers the following comment: "This formula of *debet ab eis auferre christianus* is one of those unbelievable licenses that are supposed to

as Augustine's entire polemical corpus helps witness, could not readily assure any more happy community among Christians. The metaphoric "treasures" stolen by Christians from others deserve literal consideration, second, because as the church became more rich, and more directly concerned with the management of an unprecedented wealth, it grew into its founders' language for grace. With the indulgence redemption had literally become a kind of theft. That is the real substance of Luther's critique.

In the aftermath of Luther's first explosive comments some powerful English factions felt licensed to steal their faith back. When Barabas asks if "theft is the ground of your religion," his question draws into the scope of its reference, along with these ancient issues of Christian thievery, a more recent dissolution. The "ground" on which several commercial theaters now stood had been subject to the largest transfer of land in English history. (Small wonder that Cranmer codified in the Book of Common Prayer the Lord's Prayer as rendered by Tyndale, though he had long been condemned: "forgive us our *trespasses*," it says, in place of the traditional *debita*.)[52] As David Riggs has noticed, the transformation of Barabas' impounded house into a nunnery, through some sort of symbolic comeuppance, "recalls and reverses the conversion of St. Sepulchre's nunnery at Canterbury [where Marlowe grew up] into a private dwelling."[53] This may give in turn one of several indications for the play's belated revival and first printing: in the 1630s fears were fast growing that under the crypto-Catholic plotting of Charles and Laud certain private estates might revert *back* to the church.[54] History fulfilled, as an ironic antitype, Marlowe's feigned plot.

The dissolution is hardly the sole historic theft given a reprise by *The Jew of Malta*. Instead of Christians stepping into the promise owed to the Jews according to the Pauline theory of "adoption" (Rom. 8:18; Gal. 4:5; Eph. 1:5), here the Jewish Barabas "adopts" his Muslim slave Ithamore, gives him the keys to the kingdom that Jesus gave to Peter (or promises them,

---

justify the possessors of the truth in putting to their own use everything held by those who cannot or will not know anything of this truth" (71). Cf. the passages regarding paganism's "debt" to Judeo-Christianity cited above n. 24.

52. On this and other issues of translation, see my "God among Thieves: Marx's Christological Theory of Value and Literature of the English Reformation" (Ph.D. diss., University of Pennsylvania, 1999), pp. 145–66.

53. Riggs, *World of Christopher Marlowe* (n. 1), p. 15.

54. See my "Barabas and Charles I," in *Placing the Plays of Christopher Marlowe: Cultural Contexts of His Drama*, ed. Sara Munson Deats and Robert A. Logan (Burlington, Vt.: Ashgate, 2008).

rather), then visits destruction on his own flesh and blood. "I here adopt thee for mine only heir," Barabas tells his one apostle:

> All that I have is thine when I am dead,
> And whilst I live use half; spend as myself;
> Here, take my keys—I'll give 'em thee anon.
> Go buy thee garments—but thou shalt not want.
> Only know this, that thus thou art to do.
> But first go fetch me in the pot of rice
> That for our supper stands upon the fire.... [exit Ithamore]
> Thus every villain ambles after wealth,
> Although he ne'er be richer than in hope. (3.4.41–47, 52–53)

It has been often enough pointed out that this diabolical speech, like many others in Marlowe, is a pastiche from the Bible. In this case Barabas tempts the way God tempts, with pledges of providence: after all if the Lord is your shepherd, you shall not want, either (Ps 23:1). More scandalous still, the "movement from servant to friend, the promise of adoption, and the guarantee of reward," Sara Deats writes, "recall Christ's assurance to his disciples in John 15:15–16, a passage particularly familiar to Elizabethans as part of the ritual of *The Book of Common Prayer*."[55] Barabas leads his servant on in this quasi-sacred fashion so that Ithamore will do the dirty work for him and deliver a "mess" (3.4.61) of poisonous porridge as alms to Barabas' former house, now Abigail's convent. The word "mess" was pointedly used in the Geneva Bible to describe the dish of porridge in exchange for which Esau rerouted his rightful inheritance.[56] The standard typological reading, and a liturgical drama, had once presented this episode as the moment when Christianity "justly" carried off from the Jews their Father's spiritual blessing through a "greedy" acceptance of faith in Christ.[57] Now the same mess causes Abigail, maybe the play's one genuine Christian, to lose her patrimony to a murderous infidel, while the inverted allegory is glossed with sarcasm: "What a blessing has he given't!" (3.4.106).

Barabas' dependence on Ithamore is typical of all his crimes in that he regularly resists committing them *in propria persona*. Rather, like God, he

55. Deats, "Biblical Parody" (n. 37), p. 29.

56. See editorial note on 3.4.64 and Garber, "'Infinite Riches'" (n. 33), p. 10, and recall that Barabas earlier (1.2.182ff.) quotes verbatim from the Geneva, as pointed out by Hunter, "Theology" (n. 28), p. 218.

57. See the previous chapter, pp. 165–66.

prefers the use of proxies. Barabas first employs Abigail, for example, to retrieve some money from the convent, then to seduce Lodowick so that he kills off her real love interest, his own friend Mathias, and is himself simultaneously killed. Although Barabas would seem to lend a more direct hand to the murder of Bernadine, he is actually throttled with his fraternal girdle, and there's the distinct implication, strengthened by the play's unremitting anticlerical satire, that Bernadine has been strangled not so much by Barabas or Ithamore as by his own monastic disingenuousness. Barabas disposes of Friar Jacomo in an even more vicarious fashion: by tricking the credulous cleric into thinking *he* killed Bernadine, confessing it, and getting himself condemned. "I never knew a man take his death so patiently as this friar," reports Ithamore; "he was ready to leap off ere the halter was about his neck" (4.2.24–26). Even when Barabas personally poisons the blackmailing triad of Ithamore, Bellamira, and Pilia-Borza, he does it disguised in the person of a French musician. So comes full circle his promise to pay Ithamore the wages he earned by acting on Barabas' behalf: "I'll pay thee," says Barabas, "with a vengeance" (3.4.116). Even more literal repayments likewise involve a form of impersonation: "I hope our credit in the custom-house," Barabas tells a factor he sends on a business errand, "Will serve as well as I were present there" (1.1.57–58). The wealth of this particular "son of God" in other words sometimes derives from the Catholic officials and other merchants who "credit" his "presence" in a vicarious substitute.

His fortune would be even more incredible, were it not through the credit of an audience that the character Barabas is at all made "present" in the first place. Really there *is* no "Barabas," only an actor standing in his place. That mysterious substitution enriched the players, however, just as it had long enriched the church.[58] On the secular stage, thanks to Barabas, greed could be again "transfigured," as F. S. Boas once wrote, such that it "ceases to be a sordid vice and swells to the proportions of

---

58. Against Riggs, *World of Christopher Marlowe* (n. 1), p. 247: "The poetic 'suspension of disbelief' in what the spectator knows to be false is radically different from religious faith"—the least Marlovian sentence in the book (see, for one obvious counterargument, the epigraph to this chapter, drawn from the Baines note). A lot of people living in Marlowe's age did not see any radical difference at all: that is why the theater in antitheatrical writings so easily *competes with* the (Protestant) Church and why, in those same writings, the (Catholic) Church appears *as nothing but* theater. For the relation between religious faith and the "suspension of disbelief," see the disbelief of Chester's Simeon discussed in the previous chapter, pp. 178–82, or the way the Jews of Croxton are explicitly converted by the sheer artifice of a speaking "ymage" (chapter 2, pp. 132–35), or the miracle of Paul's conversion in Digby (later in this chapter).

a passion for the infinite."[59] The countinghouse soliloquy at first curtain gives perhaps the best and most famous example of that transformation: "The needy groom that never fingered groat," Barabas complains, "would make a *miracle* of thus much coin" (1.1.12–13; my emphasis). Needy grooms composed the better part of Marlowe's audience. At the moment what they saw on stage was almost literally the money they had given, despite their neediness, to witness some relief. That the spectacle of their money pooled on stage could relieve them, when the pence in their pockets could not, *was* a miracle—or a novel analogue, anyway, to the glories historically offered through the Offertory procession and other lucrative rituals, not all of them abandoned by the Elizabethan church. Their money on stage brought them something more than they might otherwise buy: a momentary surfeit. They saw there a fleeting image of what they elsewhere prayed for, namely, that "scarcity and dearth," as in the Prayer Book, be "turned into cheapness and plenty."[60] The necessary expiration, at the play's end, of its temporary plenitude, when an audience went home poorer than they came in, only reinforced the need for hope.

The ship bearing Barabas' goods, christened the *Speranza* (1.1.71), arguably reflects for that reason the perversely *virtuous* longing that Barabas awakens in Ithamore as in all his spectators and that he himself feels most keenly of all with his desire for some contrafactual, vaguely Christological bounty that could take up less space the greater its increase—"infinite riches," he famously says, "in a little room" (1.1.37).[61] Barabas deals literally in the metaphors for Jesus—or for that matter the metaphors used of Marlowe's own vagabond-thief, who with miraculous words and incredible feats also aspired well beyond the station of his base birth, "the man that in the forehead of his fortune / Bears figures of...miracle," between whose shoulders

59. F. S. Boas, *Shakspere and His Predecessors* (1896; repr., New York: Greenwood Press, 1969), p. 50; cited and dismissed by Hunter as "ludicrously inappropriate" ("Theology" [n. 28], p. 221), though it seems to me, as it were, right on the money.

60. *The Book of Common Prayer, 1559: The Elizabethan Prayer Book*, ed. John E. Booty (Charlottesville: Published for the Folger Shakespeare Library by the University Press of Virginia, 1976), p. 75.

61. A traditional way of describing Christ in Mary's womb, as Hunter points out in "Theology" (n. 28), pp. 222–25; see esp. the quotation from Donne on p. 224: "And then, that there might bee *omnis plenitudo*, all fulnessse, as God, for the paiment of this debt, sent downe the Bullion, and the stamp, that is, God to be conceived in man, and as he provided the Mint, the womb of the Blessed Virgin, so hath he provided an Exchequer, where this mony is issued; that is his Church."

a pearl more worth than all the world is placed
Wherein by curious sovereignty of art
Are fixed his piercing instruments of sight,
Whose fiery circles bear encompassed
A heaven of heavenly bodies in their spheres.[62]

A kindred artistic sovereignty, by bringing such heavenly visions demonically down to earth, seems to have made every Marlovian spectacle entirely worth whatever the spectators paid in return. This, according to many an antitheatricalist, was the real deception of early modern drama and had long been the chief deception, according to those same reformers, employed by the church as well.

"Few viewers can escape the ambiguities which result from a partial submission to this play world," writes Don Beecher of *The Jew of Malta*, "whereby certain evil impulses may be privately and vicariously expressed."[63] To this I would add only two modifications: that the expression was, for one thing, public and, for another, a form of *expiation*. When your sins appeared in Barabas, they achieved through Barabas a kind of innocence.[64] The keys to Christ's promise, if no longer to be found in the church, could now be petitioned where Barabas first played, at the Cross-Keys Inn.[65] And the relocation gives new meaning, I think, to the observation Stephen Greenblatt makes in a seminal book that "while never relinquishing the anti-Semitic stereotype and the conventional motif of the villain-undone-by-his-villainy, Marlowe quickly suggests that the Jew is not the exception to but rather the true representative of his society."[66] The one "true representative" of society's members in premodern England, according to its

62. Christopher Marlowe, *Tamburlaine the Great*, ed. J. S. Cunningham, The Revels Plays (Manchester: Manchester University Press, 1981), part I, 2.1.3–4, 12–16. For more in this vein, see the next section.

63. Beecher, "*Jew of Malta*" (n. 34), p. 57. Following more or less directly in the footsteps of Freud, "Psychopathic Characters on the Stage," in *The Standard Edition of the Complete Psychological Works of Sigmund Freud*, trans. James Strachey, vol. 7 (London: Hogarth, 1953), pp. 303–10, an essay applied directly to Marlowe by Thomas Cartelli, *Marlowe, Shakespeare, and the Economy of Theatrical Experience* (Philadelphia: University of Pennsylvania Press, 1991), see esp. p. 21.

64. For another reading of Barabas using the same terms, still refreshing in its nonconformity, however conservative, see Alfred Harbage, "Innocent Barabas," *Tulane Drama Review* 8.4 (1964): 47–58.

65. In late 1589, according to Bakeless, *Tragicall History* (n. 1), 1:105.

66. Stephen Greenblatt, *Renaissance Self-Fashioning: From More to Shakespeare* (Chicago: University of Chicago Press, 1980) p. 203. Cf. his other fine essay on the play, "Marlowe, Marx, and Anti-Semitism," in *Learning to Curse: Essays in Early Modern Culture* (New York: Routledge, 1990), esp. p. 44.

own authorities, was supposed to be Christ. In his forced absence from the stage it was left to antichristian characters like Barabas to indulge the same old audience. Now the spectacle at the Cross-Keys Inn, rather than the usual crucifixion, provided the farcical uplift.[67]

The allegiance of this Marlovian drama to earlier passions is made explicit at the point of Barabas' dispossession. To his question "Is theft the ground of your religion," Ferneze answers,

> No, Jew, we take particularly thine
> To save the ruin of a multitude:
> And better one want for a common good
> Than many perish for a private man. (1.2.97–100)

A lot of editors and critics have been quick to point out that the same reasoning justifies the deprivations suffered by Jesus according to "the Jews" of the Bible: "It is expedient for vs, that one man die for the people," says Caiaphas, "and that the whole nation perish not" (Jn 11:50; 1587 Geneva). It normally goes unsaid, however, that the Geneva glosses this heartless remark of a heartless High Priest as a shadow of Christian *mercy*: "Christ doeth sometimes so turne the tongues, euen of the wicked, that euen in cursing, they blesse" (ibid., side note 9). According to this the Jews' curse against Jesus *is* the blessing. And what a blessing have they given!

The bounty traditionally reaped by Christians from Jewish "evil" begins to explain, I think, how Barabas continues to work as the sole force of "good" in the play long after his dispossession redeems Malta and he has dedicated himself entirely to bloodlust. Without his excessive vengeance Abigail would never have "truly" converted (in a reenactment of her first, faked conversion). "Admit thou lovedst not Lodowick for [i.e., on account of] his sire," she tells her absent father before returning to the nunnery:

> Yet Don Mathias ne'er offended thee.
> But thou wert set upon extreme revenge,
> Because the prior dispossessed thee once,
> And couldst not venge it, but upon his son,
> Nor on his son, but by Mathias' means,
> Nor on Mathias but by murdering me.

---

67. The considerable comedy of Barabas' antics and "tragic" boiling has caused past critics to worry about the play's precise genre, as well as its textual integrity; for a rehearsal of the usual positions, see the opening of Beecher, "*Jew of Malta*" (n. 34). Also Patrick Cheney, *Marlowe's Counterfeit Profession: Ovid, Spenser, Counter-nationhood* (Toronto: University of Toronto Press, 1997), pp. 138–41.

> But I perceive there is no love on earth,
> Pity in Jews, nor piety in Turks. (3.3.43–51)

Abigail's speech laments the vicarious substitutions by "means" of which Barabas' vengeance (and commerce) operates. The lament then leads her to embrace a supposedly alternate deity—worshipped by neither Jews nor Turks—who is actually, however, the apotheosis of Barabas' own procedures: having been dispossessed of due honor (through the theft of a fruit), the Christian God is also so set upon extreme revenge that he venges it "upon his son"—his *own* son. For Abigail, such divine "love" is compensation for the loss of her monstrous father—which loss her embrace of Christ causes. When Barabas carries out for real the murder of his child that she prophetically glances at here, it effectively merges with her wish to convert. Barabas kills off, as it were, her unbelieving self.

"Now experience, purchased with grief," she says at the point of entering the nunnery where she soon finds salvation and death,

> Has made me see the difference of things.
> My sinful soul, alas, hath paced too long
> The fatal labyrinth of misbelief,
> Far from the Son that gives eternal life. (3.4.63–68)

Except for this kind of reference, Christ had not been seen on stage for a long time. What Marlowe's Malta and Württemburg, his Rome and Damascus all displayed instead was the earth as Abigail sees it, wholly devoid of pity or piety. In this very abyss was the hidden God's last vestige. And he hid there as he always had, by virtue of the theater's difference from the world it staged, particularly where it showed its own impenitent will to profit encircling the globe. The difference of things inhered *in* its profits, which gave you this vanishing product: *The Jew of Malta* performed at full tilt. At bottom the performance offered to audiences Barabas' opening vision as an allegory of their playhouse experience: infinite riches in a little room, if only by the gratuitous transport of an "imaginative superflux,"[68] which a pittance could purchase. *Hermoso placer de los dineros*! (2.1.64).

Apostolic Conquest (Tamburlaine and Paul)

No opponent of Christianity proved as troublesome to the primitive church, or as definitive later, as the apostle Paul. He was the one figure

---

68. A phrase I borrow from Cartelli, *Marlowe, Shakespeare* (n. 63), p. 14.

of the canonical Bible (barring Judas) who explicitly acted both as Christ's antagonist and as his champion, whose conversion would epitomize to subsequent ages the dialectical relation of unbelief to faith, whose polemical writings against other believers, plus a rash of letters forged in his name, would eventually constitute nearly a third of the New Testament and far outstrip in length, if not also in consequence, the reported teachings of Jesus.

It was a strange fate for the one apostle who never actually met Jesus and long despised those who had. "You have heard of my former life," Paul tells the Galatians, "how I persecuted the church of God violently and tried to destroy it" (Gal. 1:13). He means by this admission to remove any doubts about his current authenticity: for someone once so dead set against the church now to act as Christ's advocate, he must really be feeling the spirit: "I do not lie!" (Gal. 1:20). Such was the integrity and intensity of his enthusiasm after Damascus, in fact, that he dared to attack Peter in public for showing deference to Jewish tradition (Gal. 2:11–12). Others may have been duped by Peter's "hypocrisy" (Gal. 2:13), but not Paul. He had a personal revelation from on high to guide him. He saw through the first pope.

Paul wrote his letter to the Galatians, however, because a powerful faction of Christians had arisen with "a different gospel" (Gal. 1:6) that must have accused *him* of hypocritical dissimulation.[69] As Peter's later apologists tried to point out, Jesus insisted on the Mount (Mt 5:18) and in his apocalyptic speech (Mt 24:35) that heaven and earth might pass away but not one jot or tittle of the law would ever perish (*Letter of Peter to James* 2.5 [GCS 42, Pseudoklementinen 1:2; *NTA* 2:494]). From their perspective, Paul's zealous devotion to an indiscriminate concept of grace made for a "lawless and absurd doctrine" (*Letter to James* 2.3; ibid.) every bit as dangerous as his earlier dedication to Pharisaic "legalism." His embrace of Christianity only increased the threat: now he was the false apostle par excellence. To prove their case, they composed (portions of) the Pseudo-Clementines, from which I've been quoting, as a

---

69. Paul's attack on Peter in particular was still an issue of contention much later. Jerome thought it was "mere playacting"; Augustine disagreed. For their combative letters on this topic, with background and discussion, see *Augustinus-Hieronymus Epistulae mutuae = Briefwechsel*, trans. Alfons Fürst (Turnhout: Brepols, 2002). For the late medieval continuation of the argument, see Erasmus (siding with Jerome), *Paraphrasis in Galatas* 2.11–12, in *Desiderii Erasmi Roterodami Opera Omnia*, 10 vols. (Hildesheim: Georg Olms, 1961–62), 7:949–50; trans. John Payne et al., *Paraphrases on Romans and Galatians*, ed. Robert D. Sider (Toronto: University of Toronto Press, 1984), pp. 104ff.; and Luther (siding with Augustine), *In epist. ad Gal.* (WA 40¹:191–203; *LW* 26:106–12).

kind of counter-scripture in which Paul appears "thinly disguised" under the name of Simon Magus.[70] Where Paul had claimed to be some sort of second-order incarnation—"it is no longer I who live, but Christ who lives in me" (Gal. 2:20)—his opponents accused him of saying something far worse: "Instead of [*anti*] our true Christ," reports Pseudo-Clement, "he proclaims himself" (*Hom. of Clement* 2.22.6 [GCS 42, Pseudoklementinen 1:44; *NTA* 2:512]).

The *Homilies* (and the closely related *Recognitions*) then describe their hero, Simon Peter, chasing this Pauline magus from country to country, rectifying his errors. It did not matter that Peter had thrice denied Jesus—or if it mattered, it seems to have made Peter all the more fitting a person to deny everyone else's divine transmissions. Spectacular phantasms like the one that supposedly reversed Paul's antichristian mission were to Peter just another demonic trick meant to pervert the true doctrine. Had someone actually seen the risen Christ on the road to Damascus, his flesh would have melted like Semele's. If he somehow managed to survive the vision and attacked other Christians using this revelation as leverage, then almost by definition he had seen "the work of a wicked demon"[71] and was furthering the work of Satan. Fortunately for Peter and his followers, Satan, too, fulfilled God's good plan, so they were not left entirely comfortless when faced by their adversary. There was always the lesson of Antichrist. "As the true prophet has said, a false gospel must first come from an impostor and only then…can a true gospel be sent forth for the correction of the sects [*haireseōn*] that are to come. And thereafter in the end Antichrist must first come again and only afterwards must Jesus be revealed as our actual Christ" (*Hom. of Clement* 2.17.4–5 [ibid. 42; 512 = ANF 8:232]). This was in ways a rather Pauline thing to say (cf. 1 Cor. 11:19), yet ironically Paul himself had become for these early

---

70. Bart D. Ehrman, *Lost Christianities: The Battle for Scripture and the Faiths We Never Knew* (Oxford: Oxford University Press, 2003), p. 183. For a more detailed reading of the anti-Pauline aspects of the Pseudo-Clementines, see Gerd Lüdemann, *Opposition to Paul in Jewish Christianity*, trans. M. Eugene Boring (Minneapolis: Fortress, 1989), pp. 169–96. For more on Simon, see next section.

71. *Hom. of Clement* 17.16.6 (GCS 42, Pseudoklementinen 1:238; *NTA* 2:536 = ANF 8:323). Paul's visions (2 Cor. 12:2 in particular) would eventually inspire a vast apocryphal literature. On its dissemination, see Théodore Silverstein, "The Vision of Saint Paul: New Links and Patterns in the Western Tradition," *Archives d'histoire doctrinale et littéraire du moyen âge* 34 (1959): 199–248; for text and the authorities who repudiate the *Visio S. Pauli* as a fiction (among them Augustine), see *NTA* 2:712–48. Cf. the 1560 Geneva side note to another of Paul's personal revelations in Acts 16:10: "We oght not to credit visions, except we be assured thereof by the Spirit of God."

heretics the first forerunner of the final days. The widespread success of his Antichristianity darkened the stage so the true gospel of Christ might one day shine all the brighter.

The orthodox church condemned Paul's opponents, but it agreed with them on this point: it too saw a few of his staunchest allies, like Marcion, as members of Antichrist. Tertullian's description of Paul as "an apostle to the heretics" (*Adv. Marc.* 3.5.4 [CCSL 1¹:513; ANF 3:324]), for example, reproves the sects that followed him *too* devoutly. (In time Tertullian was equally suspect on other grounds.) Nietzsche's friend Franz Overbeck put the problem something like this: with one exception nobody in the early church really understood Paul, and the exception, who did understand him, misunderstood him.[72] So much for Marcion—to say nothing of the Gnostic groups that also drew inspiration from Paul's difficult vision.[73] It would seem that interpreters of Paul as often as not were compelled by his letters to screw up his message; more strongly, that Paul's personal journey and theological musings continually posed a threat to the coherence of "true" Christianity, even as the threat itself became essential to the religion's self-definition. The orthodox embrace served also to hold him at a distance.

Not so the embrace of Paul by Protestants.[74] "Protestantism," writes C. S. Lewis, "was either a recovery, or a development, or an exaggeration of Pauline theology. Propositions originally framed with the sole purpose of praising the Divine compassion as boundless, hardly credible, and utterly gratuitous, build up, when extrapolated and systematized, into something that sounds not unlike devil-worship."[75] Lewis here repeats in regard to the sixteenth century a complaint first voiced during the earliest formation of the church—often by people who thought they were speaking on Paul's own behalf against his bad interpreters. By putting things so plainly Lewis helps underscore the dark continuity between the theological ferment of the late Middle Ages, which brought on the Reformation, and the "Pauline" heresies of a much earlier period that have sometimes

---

72. Quoted in Martin Werner, *The Formation of Christian Dogma: An Historical Study of Its Problem*, trans. S. G. F. Brandon (New York: Harper & Brothers, 1957), p. 7.

73. Elaine Pagels, *The Gnostic Paul: Gnostic Exegesis of the Pauline Letters* (Philadelphia: Fortress, 1975).

74. Cf. A. G. Dickens, *The English Reformation*, 2nd ed. (University Park: Pennsylvania State University Press, 1989), p. 376: "Colet, Luther, Calvin and the English Puritans display...that growing tendency among the critics of Catholicism—the tendency to turn from the veneration of many saints to the veneration of the great Saint" [i.e., Paul].

75. C. S. Lewis, *English Literature in the Sixteenth Century, Excluding Drama* (Oxford: Clarendon Press, 1954), p. 33.

been linked to Marlowe.[76] What all these strains share in common, I want to argue, is the longing for a God so transcendent that any worldly appearance breaches his sanctity and therefore looks grotesque or demonic, while the demonic then takes on, in its opposition to the divine, something like a refracted halo.

Scholarship on Marlowe is only beginning to stress that with respect to supposed "deviations" like Gnosticism, however, what explains their persistence and resurgence (for example, in Protestantism) "is much more the early Christian texts *of the New Testament* than texts or traditions deriving from ancient heresies."[77] Paul is again the textbook case—not just because he had been specially embraced by (Marcionite and Gnostic) heretics or specially denounced by Ebionites but because he had himself once stringently opposed Christianity as itself a (Jewish) heresy, and his personal opposition above all others was a founding element in the new faith. Had not Paul's violent sins against the church when persecuting it operated in the last instance to the church's betterment? "So Christ vseth the rage of his enemies," comments the Geneva Bible on Paul's pre-conversion havoc, "to the spreading foorth and enlarging of his kingdome" (Acts 8:1; 1587 ed., side note 1). As Paul scattered the church by "breathing out threatnings and slaughter against the disciples of the Lord" (Acts 9:1), so he caused it to spread. Converted to orthodox partisanship, his rage would then enlarge the kingdom even further with yet greater and more extraordinary conquests—as for example when he overcame the magician Bar-Jesus. "The deuill maketh the conquest of Christ more glorious," say the Geneva commentators on this conflict, "in that hee setteth himselfe against him (Acts 13:8; 1587 ed., side note 4). In other words they discern in the opposition of Bar-Jesus the same augmentation of Christ's reputation that they saw in Saul's own prior hostility. Saul does not so much convert to Christianity as become, through conversion, what he already was. Both he and Bar-Jesus, even when servants of sin, are equally servants of God.

The whole episode should have a familiar and rather Marlovian ring to it by virtue of this all too curiously named "Jewish false prophet" (Acts 13:6b).

---

76. See Roger Moore, "The Spirit and the Letter: Marlowe's *Tamburlaine* and Elizabethan Religious Radicalism," *Studies in Philology* 99.2 (2002): 123–51; for more on Marlowe and "Gnosticism"—or rather, the Gnostic elements of Protestantism—see A. D. Nuttall, *The Alternative Trinity: Gnostic Heresy in Marlowe, Milton, and Blake* (New York: Oxford University Press, 1998), esp. pp. 41–70.

77. Simone Petrement, *A Separate God: The Christian Origins of Gnosticism*, trans. Carol Harrison (San Francisco: HarperSanFrancisco, 1990), p. 15, my emphasis; quoted by Moore, "The Spirit and the Letter," p. 128 n. 28.

Acts feels an understandable need for some translation of "Bar-Jesus," but then renders it "Elymas" (Acts 13:8), which is strange, since everybody could see it ought to mean something closer to home. (Originally, Bede ventures, the text must have read "Bar-Jeu," not "Bar-Jesus"; "for it is not appropriate that a disgraceful man and magician be called the son of Jesus—that is, of the savior.")[78] Saul sarcastically translates it "son of the devil" (Acts 13:10), as though "Jesus" in this case meant its opposite, immediately after the narrator bizarrely refers to Saul himself, for the very first time, as "Paul" instead (13:9); from then on he will not be called anything else. Saul takes on the new man, so to speak, as he casts off the old in a superior act of legerdemain. It is as if in besting the magus he at last overcomes his former antichristian personality: "And now behold," the newly christened Paul tells Bar-Jesus, "the hand of the Lord is upon you, and you will be blind, unable to see the sun for awhile" (Acts 13:11). Eventually there appeared among exegetes a certain, divine symmetry to this punishment: "It was the sign," says Chrysostom, "by which [Paul] was himself converted, and by this he wanted to convert this man" (*Hom. in Act.* 28 [PG 60:210; NPNF 11:179]). Just as Jesus had blinded Saul outside Damascus for his opposition to the church, so now Paul darkens the eyes of Bar-Jesus in recompense for his blindness to the "doctrine of the Lord." Blindness for both is their first Christian insight.

According to other readers, the spectacle of Paul's thaumaturgy actually caused the scales to drop from the eyes of the Roman proconsul, Sergius Paulus, whom Bar-Jesus up to then had held in thrall (Acts 13:8), thus causing *Paulus* to convert. This then explained why Saul's name suddenly changes to his: "Just as when Scipio conquered Africa he took for himself the name Africanus," writes Jerome, "so too Saul after he was sent to preach to the gentiles, carried away a trophy of his victory from the first spoils of the church, Sergius Paulus, and raised his flag, so that, from Saul, he was called Paul" (*Comm. in Philem.* 1.1 [CCSL 77C:83]).[79] When taking a name from his defeated convert, Paul merely follows the custom of imperial conquest.

I suspect Marlowe owed more than a little to the clashing similarity everywhere attested in Acts between the "myscheuous craftes" of non-Christians

---

78. *Exp. Act.* 13.6 (CCSL 121:61); trans. Lawrence T. Martin, *Commentary on the Acts of the Apostles* (Kalamazoo: Cistercian Publications, 1989), p. 117.

79. Repeated in *De vir. ill.* 5 (PL 23:615A; trans. Thomas P. Halton, FC 100:12) and thereafter by Bede, *Exp. Act.* 13.9 (CCSL 121:61; trans. Martin [n. 78], p. 118); Rabanus Maurus, *Enn. in epist. Pauli* 26.1 (PL 112:696Cff.), the Gloss (PL 114:455A and 469C), among others. Some modern commentators have subscribed to the conquest view; for citations and a catalogue of the other opinions among the Fathers about Paul's name, see *The Beginnings of Christianity*, pt. 1, Acts of the Apostles, ed. F. J. Foakes-Jackson and Kirsopp Lake, 5 vols. (London: Macmillan, 1920–33), 4:145 n. 9.

like Bar-Jesus and the new imperium of Paul, "the heauenly oratour."[80] He owed to it not just his figuration of the (anti-)Christian magus in *Dr. Faustus*, as we'll see in a moment, but also his complex renewal of Pauline theology in the person of Tamburlaine—most especially when that great rhetorician and conqueror, the highest of the high, is faced with the choice, outside Damascus, to "repent" of his bloodlust. Among the stranger reports we have of Marlowe's "monstrous opinions," one remark of Thomas Kyd's stands out in this connection. Recall that Kyd was a playwright as fully invested as Marlowe in depicting scenes of gargantuan bloodshed. Yet in his second note to Puckering we find him recalling a time when he and Marlowe debated, of all things, the best way to write a (dramatic?) "poem of St. Paules conversion" (*CM* 231). According to Kyd, for him to proceed with his plan, Marlowe "said wold be as if I shold go wryte a book of fast & loose, esteming Paul a Jugler" (ibid.). The last word has a history and lexical range that touches on the calling of both men: it extends one root into the ludic traditions of ancient Rome and had an equivalent in Middle Latin synonymous with *mimus*; in English, "juggler" served among Wyclif and later reformers as a word for priests.[81] At the same time it covered witches, sorcerers, wizards, conjurors, and magicians—or their close kin, the trickster, who like the mime also plays in a sense, but in this case is one, as the O.E.D. has it, "who plays fast and loose" (s.v. "juggler" 3). Marlowe's alleged use of the word to describe Paul could have involved all of these meanings and suggests that for him to retell Paul's tale would be in effect to rewrite the book of Acts with Paul once again playing his own opposite.

Marlowe and Kyd were in any event not the first English dramatists to turn their attention to Paul's cataclysmic conversion, or to want to play it fast and loose. That is probably why there is only one example of Paul's drama left in English: the others were likely allowed to perish for looking so blasphemous. "Most dowtyd man I am lyuyng vpon the ground,"[82] announces the Digby Saul at his entrance. "Dowtyed" means here "dreaded," and yet the same word signals what makes this one man so feared—namely,

80. *The First Tome or Volume of the Paraphrase of Erasmus upon the New Testamente* (London, 1548 [STC 2854]), fols. xlvii[r] and xlviii[v], respectively.

81. See E. K. Chambers, *The Mediaeval Stage*, 2 vols. (Oxford: Clarendon Press, 1903), 2:230–33; also the quotation from Wyclif in the O.E.D., s.v. "juggler" 3, and the prefaces of Tyndale to Genesis and Jonah, passim.

82. *The Late Medieval Religious Plays of Bodleian MSS Digby 133 and E Museo 160*, ed. Donald C. Baker et al., EETS o.s. 283 (Oxford: Oxford University Press, 1982), pp. 1–23; here line 14. Cited hereafter by line number.

his doubts about the divinity of Christ, which stem from his own divine self-regard. "My pere on lyue," he goes on to say, "I trow ys nott found" (16; cf. 152–54). Audiences would have already met this figure: his boast is the same as Lucifer's, as Pharaoh's, the same as the boasts of Herod, whom earthly peoples also "Drede...and dowtys" (*Towneley* 16.65); elsewhere in Digby a Roman emperor is likewise "wythowtyn pere" (*Mary Magdalene*, line 1294). It is expressly the absence of any possible parallel, in all these parallel figures, which draws the higher parallel to God; that is, the repeated emphasis on their lack of any earthly peer highlights their warped kinship with the overriding authority inhabiting heaven.

This sort of "peerlessness" occurs so often on the medieval stage, I think, because medieval drama so often sets for itself the impossible task of making the God of monotheism, who has no peer by definition, "apere" before an audience. The satanic vaunts of its villains (or, for that matter, of the God they imitate, who is no less bombastic when on stage) articulate the drama's own highest, most hubristic aspiration. Theater would represent that which transcends representative equivalence; it would make the invisible visible—above all in a play of Paul's conversion, since here the whole plot literally turns on the sudden appearance of a transcendent apparition; or at any rate, on the meretricious effects meant to convey that God "himself" is speaking: "*Here comyth a feruent, wyth gret tempest, and Saule faulyth down of hys horse: þat done, Godhed spekyth in heuyn*" (182–83 SD). I take it from the stipulation "in heuyn" that the godhead as such does not show its face. In biblical tempests like this, there may be strong winds, but no Lord in the wind; then after, an earthquake, but the Lord is not in the earthquake; then after, a fire, but the Lord is not in the fire, either; till finally a still small voice (1 Kings 19:11–12)—"Saule, Saule! Why dost þou me pursue?" (183). That disembodied question, more than the storm, is what leaves Saul lame and blind. Later to confirm the message there descends a complementary figure when the stagehands lower down a literal deus ex machina—"*Hic aparebit Spiritus Sanctus super eum*" (291–92 SD)—but the spirit in this case keeps quiet. It would seem that God in the play presents either a disembodied voice *or* a mute form, never both speaking and appearing at once. Evidently at least one aspect of the divinity has to be withheld from the stage for its true transcendence to escape falsification.

Or rather, a transcendent divinity escapes the falsifications of drama, in whose "tokyns" the godhead was nonetheless supposed to find some true substance, only if God's proxies, the drama included, could be shown as *fully* inadequate. The magisterial Word might then arise immanently as their lacking "supplexion" (359), or supplement—the drama's absent center and sublime referent, against whose genuine grandeur both the drama and demons could at best measure their gaudiness. So for example when a hypocritical figure like Belial (the divinity avowed by Saul before his conversion to Christ) wrongly puts himself forward as God—also entering, not incidentally, "wyth thunder and fyre" (411–12 SD)—he represents God more fully than the Lord's still voice or the mute *Spiritus Sanctus*, and this garish "fullness" is precisely what marks him as specious in the extreme, and so especially threatening, because so stupefying, and therefore potentially so *winning*. He is as God would be, were God in this play ever to appear and speak at once—that is, Belial sounds exactly like God in other plays where his appearance does speak:

> Ho! Thus as a god most hye in magestye
> I rayne and I rule ouer creaturys humayne.
> With souerayne sewte sow3te to ys my deyte [my divinity
> is petitioned with urgent entreaty]. (426–28)

An audience could see here firsthand in the dramatic machinations needed to produce false thunder and lightning what Ananias earlier calls the "fendys pourys [i.e., powers] so fraudelent" (322). One inference to draw was that a miracle revealing the true God would be even more overwhelming than what demons or players could ever produce. Which is to say, it would have to look even more incredible. Hence the need for real faith: when Paul's attending bodyguards report to Caiaphas and Annas the "wonderfull myrable" (254) that they along with the apostle witnessed on the road to Damascus, for example, the high priests "maruayle gretly" (398) at the "tale" which, they believe, "ys not trw" (381)—or later thinking if it is true, then it has to be the work of some magician, or Satan. "I trow he ys bewytchyd by sum coniuracyon," says Caiaphas, "Or els the devyll on hym ys auengyd" (603–4). Even the devil himself cannot believe in the change when he first receives word that Saul has brought his (and the Jews') legal dominion at last to an end: "Yt ys not credyble!" Belial tells a subordinate. "Of fals tydyngys þou makyst here vtterance!" (442–43).

The apparent fictiveness of God's miracles, or alternately their appearance as "magic," has in this play directly to do with religious drama's inherent need to elaborate on the report of scripture, which unless performed in sermon and song, or otherwise pictured, was completely unavailable to an audience made up largely of illiterate people of "low degre" (362). Immediately preceding the scene where Caiaphas and Annas receive a spoken report of the same miracle that the audience has just directly witnessed in all its theatricality, a *poet* steps forward with an epilogue on the impossible wonder of it all and openly invites "þe correccyon of them þat letteryd be":

> Howbeyt vnable, as I dare speke or say,
> The compyler hereof shuld translat veray
> So holy a story, but wyth fauorable correccyon
> Of my honorable masters, of þer benygne supplexion. (355–59)

According to the poet, though he barely dares to speak or say it, the compiler of the drama was totally unable to translate in truth a story of such holiness except by leaving the drama open to the correction of (those who could read) scripture. Where the compiler has introduced naked fabrications, the lettered need only supplement and correct this with the corresponding moments from the "true story."

Not, be it said, history. The verities recounted in the Bible have to register if anything as far *more* fabulous than their inadequate dramatization, in order for the Bible to tell of a God beyond the limits of any pedestrian facticity. What is Saul in the beginning of the play if not a reader of scripture, devoted to the correction of the letter, who has to learn of its truly contrafactual spirit *from spectacle*? His conversion could be said for this reason to mediate the peculiar relation of scripture to theater, in which each term realizes its other: biblical spectacle calls out to the Bible for correction, yet in this case the Bible tells of a spectacle outside Damascus which fulfills its own letter. Just as the truth of the drama is its biblical message, the message of the Bible here proves to be that much more dramatic, if for that reason equally fantastic when measured against everyday reality. "Thus Saule ys conuertyd, as ye se expres," the poet instructs the audience:

> The very trw seruant of our Lord Jhesu.
> Non may be lyke to hys perfyʒt holynes,
> So nobyll a doctor, constant and trwe;
>   Aftyr hys conuersyon neuer mutable, but styll insue [striving]
> The lawys of God to teche euer more and more,
> As Holy Scrypture tellyth whoso lyst to loke þerfore. (346–52)

The idea here is that Saul's sudden conversion did not so much change as *realize* his previous convictions; or as today's lettered scholar of Holy Scripture will tend to put it: "The term 'conversion' in its common usage is inappropriate here. Neither Luke [the presumed writer of Acts] nor Paul saw the new movement as a new religion.... On the contrary, both would say that it was an awakening to the responsibility which had always been Israel's."[83] In the Digby staging, Paul's conversion allows him, through an almost Nietzschean paradox, to become what he already is: still unequaled in "perfyʒt holynes," so still more than a little satanic, still Jewish, still zealously struggling to teach "the lawys of God... ever more and more," just as he formerly did when opposing Christians for the illegality of their religion (e.g., 135–36), and just as he would continue to rebuke them for "heresy" in his canonical letters.

The poet can describe Saul, then, despite his "change," as a man of absolute constancy—a "trw servant... Aftyr hys conuersion *neuer mutable*"—only because what a lot of people thought all along was a tall tale about bolts of lightning and a voice from heaven effecting some inner transformation turns out, in another sense of the word, *not* to be "trw." Not even when "Holy Scrypture tellyth." (Paul's letters, by the way, conspicuously fail to mention anything at all outside Damascus.) What both the drama and scripture would convey is a higher form of truth usually called troth: Paul's unalterable loyalty to God. He proves trustworthy and faithful to an unearthly degree because of his fundamental intransigence. Otherwise the onset of faith at the moment of "conversion" would amount at best to credulity. His turn is by contrast more like an intensification, born in the trumped-up artificiality of stage lightning; the spectacle outside Damascus if anything *increases* his legalistic devotion to an overreaching, incredible letter. God does not abrogate that law, according to the poet, but rather, through a staged magnification of scripture's original artifice, calls once again for an all the more rigorous application, an even more radical scourge, and Paul is there, as always, to do the scourging.

Tamburlaine's over-the-top grandeur, from this perspective, does not strike me as any more fast and loose than Saul's pre-conversion cruelty or the later zeal for grace that his cruelty prefigured. So what if Marlowe dared "God out of heaven with that Atheist Tamburlan."[84] In Tamburlaine's case, as in Saul's, such demonic hubris actually works to the benefit of (the right

---

83. James D. G. Dunn, *The Acts of the Apostles* (Peterborough: Epworth Press, 1996), p. 119; he goes on to explain the ways "conversion" is an appropriate term after all. For a more uncompromising version of the first view, however, see Daniel Boyarin, *A Radical Jew: Paul and the Politics of Identity* (Berkeley: University of California Press, 1994).

84. Robert Greene, *Perimedes the Blacksmith* (1588), in *Life and Complete Works of Robert Greene*, ed. Alexander Grosart, 15 vols. (1881–86; repr., New York: Russell and Russell, 1964), 7:7–8.

sort of) Christians, "Whose state he ever pitied and relieved."[85] The divide among critics over the presence or absence of a Christian agenda in the play has probably always arisen from just this traditionally Pauline conundrum: the villain here is both heaven's representative and its opponent; "the scourge of God" is both subjective and objective genitive.[86]

In no other play of the period does the rhetoric of satanic mimesis resound quite as loudly. Some critics have consequently looked on Tamburlaine the same way others have looked on Barabas, as "a glaring symbol of the anti-Christ. A new Lucifer."[87] And to be sure, like Lucifer, Tamburlaine appears as "the chiefest lamp of all the earth, / First rising in the east with mild aspect," a man who aspires, as had that other Star of the Morn, to set himself on heaven's throne by assuming heaven's exclusive role and affecting "thoughts coequal with the clouds" (1.2.65). Such coequality, an audience would have supposed, belonged by rights to another no longer allowed on stage—definitely not to "this devilish shepherd" trying

> With such a giantly presumption
> To cast up hills against the face of heaven,
> And dare the force of angry Jupiter. (2.6.1–5)

It would come as no surprise that according to Tamburlaine's enemies, he deserves for his presumption to land in "hell / Where flames shall ever feed upon his soul," even though, as another lord explains, Tamburlaine is only playing out the fate imposed on him by an apparently supernatural parentage: "Some powers divine, or else infernal, mixed / Their angry seeds at his conception" (2.6.9–10). He is, it would seem, either a son of some god or hell incarnate.

Of course the pagan deity Jupiter had also dared the face of heaven by revolting against his own father, and although this is the precedent that Tamburlaine later cites in explanation for the "aspiring minds" (2.7.17, 20) of all humanity, it would be a mistake, I think, to insist on the importance of classical mythology for Marlowe over and against the Christian

85. *Tamburlaine*, ed. Cunningham (n. 62), part II, 5.1.32; cf. part I, 3.3.44–58, 250. All subsequent quotations are from part I of this (the Revels) edition, unless otherwise noted.

86. A great deal has already been written on the background to this phrase, "the scourge of God"; for references and discussion, see R. M. Cornelius, *Christopher Marlowe's Use of the Bible* (New York: Peter Lang Publishers, 1984), pp. 65–66.

87. Henry W. Wells, *Elizabethan and Jacobean Playwrights*, 2nd ed. (New York: Kennikat Press, 1964), p. 80. For more on Tamburlaine as Antichrist, see Cornelius, *Marlowe's Use of the Bible*, pp. 71, 146; as Christ, pp. 66–71, 75.

tradition—in part because Christian tradition even at its purest has never been free from classical influence. Marlowe's schoolmate Thomas Beard was more than happy to dwell at length on everything in "Catholicism," a.k.a. historical Christianity, that mirrored or derived from the heathen; we'll soon see in *Faustus* how Marlowe does Beard one better by including among the derivatives Protestantism too. For now, suffice it to say that in Marlowe's plays the effect of this hybridity was not to discredit Christianity but to preserve on a newly "secularized" stage what Marlowe most enjoyed in his religious heritage. The genus of the "Graeco-Roman sage promulgating poetic theology,"[88] to which Tamburlaine belongs according to Riggs, hardly excludes Paul, to say nothing of Christ: on the contrary, Christ was supposed to be its finest exemplar and celestial progenitor. From the Fathers onward, according to Ernst Curtius, the *poeta theologus*, however originally pagan, proved "eminently adaptable to Christian reinterpretation"—no doubt because such borrowings made it easier to convert cultivated pagans. They too could become through Christ what they already were, which was lovers of rhetoric; "not only the *poeta theologus*," Curtius goes on to add, "but the word 'theology' itself is borrowed from Paganism."[89] Marlowe's gesture is to revel in the contaminant. Without it there would be no recognizable Christianity, least of all on the "Renaissance" stage. Marlowe's paganism preserves the residue of Christian thought where less refracted thinking on stage had become increasingly difficult—or worse, was getting passé.

The conclusion of Tamburlaine's supposedly classical speech about humanity's "aspiring mind," for example, reverberates with parallels—if not deliberate allusions—to a passage from Calvin's *Institutes* (1.15.6) defining the powers of the soul.[90]

> Our souls, whose faculties can comprehend
> The wondrous architecture of the world
> And measure every wand'ring planet's course,
> Still climbing after knowledge infinite
> And always moving as the restless spheres,
> Wills us to wear ourselves and never rest
> Until we reach the ripest fruit of all,
> That perfect bliss and sole felicity,
> The sweet fruition of an earthly crown. (2.7.21–29)

88. Riggs, *World of Christopher Marlowe* (n. 1), p. 206.
89. Curtius, *European Literature and the Latin Middle Ages* (n. 24), p. 219.
90. See Anthony Brian Taylor, "Tamburlaine's Doctrine of Strife and John Calvin," *English Language Notes* 27.1 (1989): 30–31. Riggs points out that the speech also follows Ovid, among others (*World of Christopher Marlowe* [n. 1], pp. 205ff.).

Those who did not pick up on the allusion to Calvin could still have heard an obvious Christian valence in "the ripest fruit" at the apex of "knowledge infinite." That these aspirations come to full fruition in an *earthly* crown, rather than the heavenly coronet some critics have thought more appropriate, would be more of a shock if the Christian Fall had not promised—and also delivered—a human likeness of God crowned by thorns here on earth. If Tamburlaine's satanic aspiration toward God, in view of the theology he rephrases, is a version of what caused humanity's damnation, then he also becomes an image of the remedy. This ancient dialectic of the *felix culpa* comes particularly to the fore in the passage from Calvin that Marlowe appears to have absorbed wholesale: "Surely a man shuld want the principall use of his understandyng, if he shuld be ignorant of his own felicitie," writes Calvin (in translation), "whereof the perfection is that he be ioyned with God, and therefore it is the chiefe action of the soule to aspire therunto."[91]

I am not content with the predictable description of Tamburlaine's version of this passage as "an heretical Pauline parody,"[92] when a similar verdict could be leveled against the theology of Calvin itself, if not also against the "orthodox" Pauline thinking his protest refined. Tamburlaine can speak Calvinese because Calvin spoke for that strain of Christianity, historically linked to the figure of Paul, that was in itself already Marlovian. Marlowe does not so much parody as repeat its more dramatic bits verbatim. In a passage resembling the one from which Tamburlaine arguably borrows, Calvin goes so far as to declare, for example, that the miraculous artistry of human fiction best demonstrates the supernatural in us: "also the ingeniousnes by which it [the soul] inuenteth things incredible, & which is the mother of so many marvelous arts, are sure tokens of diuine nature in man."[93] If there were ever any doubt about the iconoclast's appreciation for artistic sublimity, let these words lay it at last to rest. Marvelous arts, the invention of unbelievable things in stark contradiction to the hard facts—surely these tokens produce, as their highest effect, the divinity they are here said to indicate. What would Calvin know of a divine nature that was "entirely other,"[94] and thus wholly unavailable

91. *Institutes*, 1.15.6; trans. Thomas Norton (London, 1561), fol. 55ʳ.

92. Taylor, "Tamburlaine's Doctrine of Strife" (n. 90), p. 31.

93. *Institutes* 1.5.5; trans. Thomas Norton (London, 1561), fol. 9ʳ; quoted in relation to *Tamburlaine*, though to a different purpose, by Paul Kocher, *Christopher Marlowe: A Study of His Thought, Learning, and Character* (Chapel Hill: University of North Carolina Press, 1946), p. 76.

94. Carlos Eire, "The Reformation Critique of Images," in *Bilder und Bildersturm im Spätmittelalter und in der frühen Neuzeit*, ed. Bob Scribner (Wiesbaden: Otto Harrassowitz, 1990), pp. 51–68; here 56.

to apprehension by the senses, without the scriptural rhetoric that, marvel of marvels, nonetheless conveys it? *Sola scriptura!*

This is what Tamburlaine shares most of all with Pauline tradition: he too conquers by virtue of the almighty Word. The writer of Acts apparently wants to present Paul, particularly in Athens and on trial, the way later Fathers would sometimes also hope to see him—as a classical orator of no mean talent. In Acts, writes Hans-Josef Klauck, "a new world-view is just beginning to conquer a world empire, not with a mighty army and the force of weapons, but only by means of itinerant messengers of the gospel and by the might inherent in the word they proclaim."[95] Marlowe, a real Protestant in this if nothing else, returns *ad fontes.* Throughout part I, Tamburlaine conquers his enemies (at the same stroke often converting them to friends) less through force than by "vaunts substantial" (1.2.212)—that is, an eloquence so mighty it proves Tamburlaine's exceeding strength in the absence of anything other than a rhetorical exercise. Paradoxically the substance of his speech (absolute might) develops after the fact from what at the start is a purely metaphorical power:

> Forsake thy kind and do but join with me,
> And we will triumph over all the world....
> See how [Jove] rains down heaps of gold in showers
> As if he meant to give my soldiers pay. (1.2.171–72, 181–82)

In this case the contrafactual "as if" turns out to be so persuasive that his fantastic words are soon realized, and Tamburlaine's army grows to the proportions of his vast rhetoric. His talk of divine payments—what the Pauline corpus would call the unfathomable riches of grace (e.g., Rom. 11:33; Eph. 1:7)—here *creates* an army of infinite capability; so too had Paul's airy promises expanded the church militant. If Tamburlaine's success provided the audience with a displaced image of how the church had come to possess its real-world blessings, it pictured even more directly what was actually then happening on stage, where the mere talk of wealth, when sufficiently grand, also enriched Marlowe's players.

It is surprisingly difficult to find in the literature on Marlowe any mention of a connection between Tamburlaine and Paul by way of Damascus, but in setting the final siege of the play outside this one city, Marlowe makes a deliberate choice about what to cull from the historical

---

95. Hans-Josef Klauck, *Magic and Paganism in Early Christianity,* trans. Brian McNeil (Edinburgh: T & T Clark, 2000), p. 11.

record.[96] Damascus to most Renaissance theatergoers, as to a lot of modern Americans, was nothing if not a religious symbol, and it pretty much meant one thing: conversion. That is what happens when a man hell-bent on bloodshed, utterly devoid of mercy, makes his way there. Tamburlaine's heartless speeches, the supplicating virgins before his black tent of death—in short, the culmination of the whole drama depends more than the scholarship has so far allowed on the cultural expectation that if ever so dastardly a man were to turn away from his inbred demonism, it ought to be here. And sure enough, despite Tamburlaine's grandiloquent and manly refusal of every plea for "events of mercy" (5.1.54), he nonetheless begins to buckle outside Damascus before a heavenly vision—his future bride, Zenocrate. Her intervention both converts him and doesn't: she fails to soften his resolve insofar as he still lays waste to the town, but she succeeds insofar as he spares her own father, whose blessing is needed to validate their marriage. The bloody spectacle thus turns at its end into the comedy it had often enough threatened to become.[97]

Zenocrate's name, which is not to be found in any historical source whatsoever, means in translation "the power of Zeus"; fittingly she alone strikes all-surpassing Tamburlaine with the limiting force of a higher god. Using slightly different words, Paul had called Christ "the power of God" (1 Cor. 1:24), which was likewise what appreciators called Simon Magus (Acts 8:10). In Tamburlaine's case the pagan variant literally occupies the same place as Christ, outside Damascus, and the power of this god, "appearing" via Zenocrate, has on him the same effect that a divine miracle formerly had on Paul; only now the revelation, such as it is, is explicitly called what it had in any case always already been: an aesthetic and political effect. "Ah fair Zenocrate, divine Zenocrate" (5.1.135), Tamburlaine repeatedly sings. The point to take from these epithets is that she can appear as divine Zenocrate *because* she is so fair—and she is fair, in large measure, because of her father, whose wealth and social station (Soldan of Egypt) will at last legitimate the upward mobility that Tamburlaine would otherwise still, for all his prowess, have failed to deserve. Besides this she is fair for the rather more metatheatrical and Marlovian reason that she is not as she seems, being actually a boy.

96. For the city in Marlowe's (probable) source, see Vivien Thomas and William Tydeman, eds., *Christopher Marlowe: The Plays and Their Sources* (London: Routledge, 1994), pp. 113–14.

97. Cf. the prefatory letter "To the Gentlemen Readers," lines 8–17, where the printer claims to have done what he can to eliminate comic elements; also the editor's commentary (n. 62), pp. 21–22. Many previous studies have noticed the bathos of Tamburlaine's violence; none that I have read mentions the generically comic ending in marriage.

The overdetermination of Zenocrate's beauty, a version of which we will see again in Faustus' Helen, perhaps explains why Tamburlaine's own soliloquy on the topic has proven so hard to understand: in it, he would hold together for an impossible moment the political issue of legitimacy with the moral question of showing mercy to a town he has already sworn to raze; plus he has to rationalize how his indomitable manhood could ever be subjected to the whims of a subject (his future wife, after all, is just another war trophy)—and all this in relation to the religious and theatrical prehistory submerged not far beneath his crisis of conscience outside Damascus. The loveliness of Zenocrate can hardly resolve these heterogeneous tensions, though he nonetheless looks to her for resolution. He has nowhere else to look. The pain he consequently feels "in the face of beauty," to put this in the starkly theoretical terms of Adorno, "is as much the longing for what beauty promises but never unveils as it is suffering at the inadequacy of the appearance, which fails beauty while wanting to make itself like it."[98] If that formulation seems overly difficult, wait till you hear Tamburlaine's:

> What is beauty, saith my sufferings, then?
> If all the pens that ever poets held
> Had fed the feeling of their masters' thought
> And every sweetness that inspired their hearts,
> Their minds and muses on admired themes;
> If all the heavenly quintessence they still
> From their immortal flowers of poesy,
> Wherein as in a mirror we perceive
> The highest reaches of a human wit—
> If these had made one poem's period
> And all combined in beauty's worthiness,
> Yet should there hover in their restless heads
> One thought, one grace, one wonder, at the least
> Which into words no virtue can digest. (5.1.160–73)

The syntactical deferrals after "What is beauty?" are essential to the final answer, which in a way never comes. Tamburlaine seems to be saying that beauty, even if distilled and condensed to utmost power, has to leave the impression, for all its fullness, of a telling deficiency, and that this sublime omission is actually beauty's whole source. For by delineating what human wit cannot grasp, beauty makes unwitting contact with that "one thought, one grace, one wonder" *beyond* the capacity of any talent or virtue. This

98. *AT* 114; trans. 73, though speaking here of natural (rather than supernatural) beauty.

beyond is then at bottom nothing other than the exquisite, flamboyant staging of Tamburlaine's failure to get there. Eye hath not seen, nor ear heard, neither has there entered into the heart of a man so sublime (or so Pauline) a revelation.

As if on cue, the lines that immediately follow devolve into something of a morass. He now asks whether it is in itself "unseemly" for a man of his stature to find his heart battered by so slight a thing as the pleading looks of a beautiful woman, then gives yet another hard, hypotactic answer that would appear to reaffirm the capacities of his own surpassing "virtue"—etymologically the same word, by the way, as this "manliness" that is currently under assault by thoughts, "effeminate and faint," about his gorgeous fiancée:

> Save only that in beauty's just applause,
> With whose instinct the soul of man is touched—
> And every warrior that is rapt with love
> Of fame, of valour, and of victory
> Must needs have beauty beat on his conceits—
> I thus conceiving and subduing, both,
> That which hath stopped the tempest of the gods,
> Even from the fiery spangled veil of heaven,
> To feel the lovely warmth of shepherds' flames
> And march in cottages of strewèd weeds,
> Shall give the world to note, for all my birth,
> That virtue solely is the sum of glory
> And fashions men with true nobility. (5.1.178–90)

Most editors suspect some corruption in the passage, though arguably the lack of easy meaning can only contribute to beauty's negative power. The more impenetrable his speech, the more clearly Tamburlaine continues to be mastered by a beauty even he can't articulate—the same beauty, he barely manages to say, that once held the pagan gods also subject. Meanwhile the more impenetrably he speaks, the closer Marlowe gets to penning lines that exemplify beauty's unexampled ineffability.

Presumably by the speech's end Tamburlaine has resolved *not* to cave in to Zenocrate's plea that he save the town and, particularly, her father. And yet spare him he does after all as though overcome in the end by the divine force of beauty he had wanted to best. This striking exception to Tamburlaine's supposedly universal death sentence highlights a related omission from the drama as a whole that allows for *its* overall beauty: the reality of death. Throughout the play, as Sidney Homan writes, "literal deeds are continually set against the poetry itself as words alone convert what is physical and horrid to something metaphorically grand. The play in this sense is…a testament to the theater's own alchemic power."[99] In light of Tamburlaine's religio-aesthetic, we should probably take this one step further and point out that his "literal" deeds of violence, even at their most extreme, are no less abstracted from action than the words that sublate them. The actor playing Tamburlaine literally inflicts no harm, literally executes not one prisoner; hence the theater's real "alchemy," which might be better described in Christian terms as the magic of resurrection. Death is the mother of beauty on stage only insofar as nobody dies—not even when Tamburlaine tries to *show* people death: "Behold my sword," he commands the virgins, briefly holding up the sword's hilt, I would hope, in a proverbial and fleeting sign of the cross before brandishing the blade against them. "What see you at the point?" (5.1.108). Of course they see nothing. There is nothing to see:

> Your fearful minds are thick and misty, then,
> For there sits Death, there sits imperious Death,
> Keeping his circuit by the slicing edge.
> But I am pleased you shall not see him there:
> He now is seated on my horsemen's spears
> And on their points his fleshless body feeds.
> Techelles, straight go charge a few of them
> To charge these dames, and show my servant Death,
> Sitting in scarlet on their armèd spears…
> Away with them I say and show them Death. (5.1.110–18, 120)

Needless to say death nowhere appears. These lines can be beautiful, by Tamburlaine's own definition, only because during their delivery an audience effectively occupies the position of the virgins, unable to witness what awaits all its members; they face their terminal limit without having to face it by seeing instead the theater's limit, which was the restriction of mimesis. The lines are a coup de théâtre by virtue of teasing. For by playing at death, they toy with an absolute boundary which if crossed would for sure end the show. To the extent that this toying begins anyway to intimate the actual carnage historically forbidden, mainly by Christian prejudice, ever to *be* on stage but pursued almost everywhere else—often in the name of Christ—the lines completely cross over: they emerge in a realm where death does not ever constitute the final tally but initiates, at worst, a curtain

99. Sidney R. Homan, "Chapman and Marlowe: The Paradoxical Hero and the Divided Response," *Journal of English and Germanic Philology* 68 (1969): 391–406; here 395.

call and then the resurrection of each character again the next day. The fatal charades of the Roman Empire had literally killed condemned actors as a matter of course.[100] In the Marlovian theater, as with the liturgy that conquered Rome, death was less proud.

Faustus Magus

Between Paul's persecution of the church (Acts 7:58–8:3) and the transformation outside Damascus (9:1–31) that allows him, next we hear, to overcome the magician Bar-Jesus, then afterwards to convert many others (13ff.), there falls the story of Simon Magus (8:9–24). That is, the career of Paul, from antichristian to apostolic conqueror, frames the one story in Acts perhaps most concerned with the uncanny resemblance between Christ's legitimate apostles and their magical opponents.[101] The very possibility of conversion throughout the book could even be said to turn on this resemblance: first, because Christians here win their converts by showing off "great deeds of power" (8:10,13) that look to the naked eye the same as any magician's, only more powerful; and second, because the particular conversions of Paul and Simon Magus depend on their unwavering respect for spectacle. Like Paul, Simon begins as a dangerous antagonist of Christianity but ends as its problematic advocate after witnessing, with his own eyes, the "true" power of God. And again like Paul, Simon appeared to certain Christians as a far worse threat *after* his conversion than ever before. To orthodox apologists he was unquestionably "the first author of all heresy" (Eusebius, *Hist. eccl.* 2.13.6; LCL), who together with a Faustian concubine named Helen begat a whole family of pseudo-Christianities.[102] By the late Middle Ages it had become thoroughly ensconced in tradition that Simon, whose name earlier heretics had used as a moniker for Paul, was Antichrist, actually, or at least his chief member.[103]

---

100. See K. M. Coleman, "Fatal Charades: Roman Executions Staged as Mythological Enactments," *Journal of Roman Studies* 80 (1990): 44–73.

101. See Klauck, *Magic and Paganism* (n. 95), pp. 14–23 (on Simon) and pp. 45–55 (on Paul and Bar-Jesus), and Susan R. Garrett, *The Demise of the Devil: Magic and the Demonic in Luke's Writings* (Minneapolis: Fortress, 1989), pp. 65–87.

102. For a list of the patristic and apocryphal portraits of Simon, as well as a thorough commentary on the NT figure, see *Beginnings of Christianity* (n. 79), 5:151 n. 1. For the figure in medieval literature and art, William R. Cook and Ronald B. Herzman, "Simon Magus and the Medieval Tradition," *Journal of Magic History* 2 (1980): 28–43; further references and a very helpful overview are to be found in James Nohrnberg, *The Analogy of "The Faerie Queene"* (Princeton: Princeton University Press, 1976), pp. 247–60.

103. Origen, *Comm. in Matt.* nos. 33 and 41 (GCS 38, Origenes Werke 11:59–60, 82; *KEM* 3:94–95, 117); Hilary of Poitiers, *Comm. in Matt.* 25.2–4 (SC 258:180–84); Jerome, *Comm. in*

The word "magus" comes originally from Persian and "importes as muche" (writes King James) "as to be ane contemplator or Interpretour of Divine and heavenlie sciences."[104] The etymology is needed in part to explain how three magi could appear at Christ's birth without opprobrium, even though they do the same thing that will later damn Simon: they make an offering. The Magi's "treasures" (Mt 2:11) were supposed to materialize their apostasy from an alien, idolatrous mode of devotion, and their turn toward right worship to foreshadow how subsequent powers, no matter how pagan, upon learning of Christ would likewise "humble them selues to his crosse, to foster, enriche, adorne and defend his Church" (ibid.; Douai-Rheims annotation). Protestant princes who refused to enrich or adorn it any longer presented a recent exception to the church trium-phant and so signified to the writers of that annotation a major step back-wards: for all his demonism, the "Sorcerer" Simon according to them actu-ally "had more knovvledge of the true religion then the Protestants haue" (Acts 8:24; annotation). At least he *gave* something. His offering had to be condemned, but it was not formally different from the sort of transaction the church elsewhere accepted; one could say in fact that from the church's beginning, as described in the New Testament, the repudiation of Simon helped sanctify those other exchanges through a kind of ritual purifica-tion. Had not Paul himself also believed, after a fashion, that the grace of God was obtainable "at a price" (1 Cor. 6:20, 7:23)? Even if he meant in this case the price of Christ's blood, his letters nonetheless record various efforts to get money from converts in return for spiritual riches, such that even where Paul claims to sell the "the Gospel of God gratis" (2 Cor. 11:7; Douai-Rheims), he has to admit that he does so in part by robbing Peter: "Other churches I spoiled, taking a stipend, for your ministerie" (2 Cor. 11:8; Douai-Rheims). My sense is that some people might have more easily called this a form of simony, had Paul, the transfigured opponent, not explicitly

---

Matt. 24.5 (SC 259:186–88); Gregory the Great, *Moralia* 29.7.15 on Job 38:15 (CCSL 143b:1443; trans. J. Bliss [Oxford, 1844–50], 3¹:311); Bede, *In Matt.* 4.24 (PL 92:102C); *In Marc.* 4.13 (PL 92:260A); *In Luc.* 5.17, 6.21 (PL 92:545C, 585D); Rabanus Maurus, *Hom. in ev. et ep.* 144 (PL 110:424C); the Gloss on Mt 24:11 (PL 114:161B) and Mk 13:6, 21 (PL 114:226D, 227C); Hincmarus of Rheims, *De praed. dei et lib. arb. diss. post.*, epilogi caput 6 (PL 125:462A–463A); Adso, *Vita S. Mansueti* 1.12 (PL 137:630B). For a few other refer-ences, including a vernacular citation, see Richard K. Emmerson, *Antichrist in the Middle Ages: A Study of Medieval Apocalypticism, Art, and Literature* (Seattle: University of Washington Press, 1981), p. 248 n. 42–44; discussion on pp. 27–28, 30–31, 47, 75–76, 93, 122–24, 169, 211; also Morton Smith, "The Account of Simon Magus in Acts 8," in *Harry Austryn Wolfson Jubilee Volume*, English Section, vol. 2 (Jerusalem: American Academy for Jewish Research, 1965), pp. 735–49; esp. pp. 743–49.

104. *Daemonologie* (Edinburgh, 1597), p. 8.

warned against opponents like Simon: beware the false brethren, he says in the same passage, "craftie workers" who transfigure themselves into apostles of Christ: "And no maruel: for Satan him self transfigureth him self into an Angel of light" (2 Cor. 11:14; Douai-Rheims).

The multiform and vastly detailed story of Simon Magus came in the course of the Middle Ages to epitomize this constant rivalry between apostolic miracle and the commercial spectacles of Antichrist—commercial not just because of Simon's willingness to pay for the techniques of the apostles but because he (too) charged a fee for the exercise of his talents; that is presumably where he first got the money he offers in turn to Simon Peter. "If he [Simon Magus] is now willing to invest a large sum," writes Klauck, "he does so in hope of even higher earnings in the future: this new power of the Spirit will help him to offer a wider spectrum of services and so win new clients."[105] The animosity this earns him from Peter is, in effect, the animosity of a seasoned competitor unwilling to accept a bribe in exchange for trade secrets.

The trade they both practice is as theatrical as it is profitable according to the *Acts of Peter*—after the canonical Acts, the earliest account of their conflict. Christians and pagans alike assembled to watch them in the Julian Forum, we are told, each one paying in gold for a place.[106] In return for that fee, the audience eventually gets to witness both Simon and Peter trying their hand at Christ's most ravishing miracle, raising the dead. Simon appears to succeed, but it turns out this resurrection is appearance merely. Peter alone can truly cause a dead boy to walk, whereupon "from that same hour they adored him [Peter] as a god" (*Acts of Peter* 29). (So too had people venerated Paul as a god in human form after his canonical dazzlements [Acts 14:11, 28:6].) The boy's mother gives Peter two thousand pieces of gold to demonstrate her newfound reverence—money she would have otherwise spent on a funeral—and the revived boy himself comes up with four thousand. Later while Peter is preaching to another crowd, a wealthy woman of very loose morals, named Chryse (for "golden"), has a personal vision and coughs up ten thousand (*Acts of Peter* 30). There were the expected objections to Chryse's donation—word is she services even her servants—but Peter just "smiles," then reasons his way

---

105. Klauck, *Magic and Paganism* (n. 95), pp. 20–21.

106. *Acts of Peter* 23. The *Acts* comes down to us in myriad forms; for the "original," I have relied on *Les Actes de Pierre*, ed. Léon Vouaux (Paris: Letouzey et Ané, 1922). Translation in *NTA* 2:271–321; here 306. Further citations by chapter number only. For textual issues, provenance, and a full bibliography, see Christine M. Thomas, *The "Acts of Peter," Gospel Literature, and the Ancient Novel* (Oxford: Oxford University Press, 2003).

to acceptance: "for she was bringing it [the money] as a debtor to Christ, and is giving it to Christ's servants; for he himself has provided for them" (ibid.). The money comes in other words not so much from this prosperous harlot as from an even more indiscriminate, rich lover of man—the prodigal patron, Lord Christ.[107]

Where Peter used Chryse for the cause of the church, according to multiple other sources Simon used Helen, "formerly a prostitute" (Justin, *1 Apol.* 1.26 [PG 6:368B; ANF 1:171]), but now speciously promoted by him as some kind of goddess "brought down to the world from the highest heaven...as the all-bearing being and Wisdom" (*Hom. of Clement* 2.25.2 [GCS 42, Pseudoklementinen 1:45; ANF 8:233]). That characterization of Helen (common in the Fathers, too, and reappearing in Marlowe) is clearly meant to mimic the Wisdom of God as personified in the Book of Wisdom, which we'll consider in a moment, and in Proverbs, for another example, where instead of getting money from her lovers, Wisdom pays *them*: "I walk in the way of righteousness, along the paths of justice, endowing with wealth those who love me, and filling their treasuries. The Lord created me at the beginning" (Prov. 8:20–21a). So too did Simon claim Helen as "the first conception of his mind" (Irenaeus, *Adv. haer.* 1.23.2 [SC 264:314; ANF 1:348]) and was likewise enriched by her presence.

The charm for Simon's audience—and the deception—was getting to see not only a hot approximation of honest-to-God Wisdom but the zenith of pagan mythology also made flesh. A humanist *avant la lettre*, Simon pretended through Helen to reconcile the Bible with Homer; his celestial paramour turns out to have been both Wisdom incarnate and, according to patristic and apocryphal sources, none other than Helen of Troy; meanwhile the person whom Homer sang about, and every Greek fell for, was nothing more than a lovely mirage[108]:

> Because of her, he [Simon] says, the Greeks and barbarians fought, although having before their eyes but an image of the reality, for the true

---

107. For Christ as a Roman patron dispensing material rewards to his clients, see Robert F. Stoops, "Patronage in the *Acts of Peter*," *Semeia* 38.1 (1986): 91–100; in calling Peter "a broker of the benefits that flow from Christ" (95), he somewhat euphemizes a relation that in places mirrors that of pimp to prostitute. The regulation of female sexuality, often toward economic ends, is a major issue in the *Acts*; for analysis and bibliography, see Jan N. Bremmer, "Aspects of the *Acts of Peter*: Women, Magic, Play, and Date," in *The Apocryphal Acts of Peter: Magic, Miracles, and Gnosticism*, ed. Jan N. Bremmer (Leuven: Peeters, 1998), pp. 1–20; esp. 1–9.

108. By then an ancient permutation of (or against) Homeric myth. See Norman Austin, *Helen of Troy and Her Shameless Phantom* (Ithaca: Cornell University Press, 1994).

Helena dwelt at that time with the supreme God. Thus by credibly interpreting [*allēgorōn*] things of this sort, made up from Greek myths, he
deceives many, especially as he performs a lot of prodigious marvels, by
which we would ourselves have been deceived, had we not known that he
performs them by magic; but whereas in the beginning we were his colleagues, when his doing these things did not wrong the share of religion,
now when—completely raving—he has started trying to deceive the religious, we have withdrawn from him.[109]

Simon's presentation of Helen in this passage tellingly repeats the standard Christian polemic against Greek culture with which we are already
familiar: Clement too rejects the "false and bad myths" of the Greeks
because they express incorrect opinions about the gods (*Hom. of Clement* 4.8.6 [GCS 42, Pseudoklementinen 1:86; NTA 2:521]). Their opinions
could never be correct since according to Clement, "the whole of Greek
culture is a most irksome fabrication of an evil spirit" (*Hom. of Clement*
4.12.1; ibid., 87; 521). Christians should therefore "shun such myths of
theirs, as also their theaters and books, and if it were possible even their
cities" (*Hom. of Clement* 4.19.3; ibid., 90; 522). Seen in this light, Simon's
insidious genius is to preach to the gullible Greeks the *same* Christian message that Clement delivers, so as to deceive them all the better. He too
shows how groundless Homeric myth really is, then claims with his magic
to fulfill it. Greek devotion to the baseless image of Helen had according
to Simon inspired their most mythic conflict; here before them, by means
of his "prodigious marvels," stands now the real thing. In this way he wins
the devotion that his former "colleagues" (but present adversaries), by
means of their competing revelation, also were after.

This early cooperation and current competition obviously throws into
doubt how different the apostolic and Simonian religions ultimately were,
and yet the similarity actually works in the end to the benefit of Peter: if
his "acts" and their persuasiveness depend on the same radical disjunction
between reality and appearance as do Simon's, then precisely this disjunction transforms his apparent defeat at the hands of the Romans into a
spiritual triumph. In the episode of his martyrdom, which had a life and

---

109. *Hom. of Clement* 2.25.2–4 (GCS 42, Pseudoklementinen 1:45–46; ANF 8:233). As
with much else in the *Homilies* there is a parallel passage in the Pseudo-Clementine *Recognitions*, widely available in the Middle Ages through the translation of Rufinus, though this
calls Simon's mate "Luna," not Helena (GCS 51, Pseudoklementinen 2:58; ANF 8:100).
Justin, Irenaeus, and Eusebius, however, all go with Helen (for the relevant passages, see
citations in the main text).

popularity all its own,[110] we hear again that Simon's spirits are "only appearances [*phainomena*] without real existence" (*Acts of Peter* 31 [2]); that what he does, he does "in fantasia" (ibid., Latin); that when, attempting to fly, he falls and is broken at a word from Peter, his God has been "baffled" (*Acts of Peter* 32 [3]; lit. "blinded"). Trouble is, Peter also soon must fall. His defeat of Simon portends his own ruin. Why not then the ruin of his God, too? According to Peter's own words, his mission will survive because his decline, like Simon's ascent, is wholly other than it appeared—so different, in fact, that compared to its heavenly truth the historical reality of death is ultimately as insubstantial as Simon's apotheosis: "You who hope in Christ," Peter tells those who assemble to see his death, "the cross must not be for you this that appears [*phainomenon*]; for this passion, according to the passion of Christ, is something other than what it appears [*phainomenon*]" (*Acts of Peter* 37 [8]).

The visible crucifixion should give Christians hope, in other words, to the extent that its historical appearance finally diverges from some higher reality. The point is not that what happens on the cross (whether Peter's or Christ's) is pure illusion—though at the time there certainly existed opinions that Jesus was either not really a man or not really dead; that, for example, he changed positions with the Simon who carried the cross, then stood beside his own crucifixion disguised and laughing.[111] Peter's point in the passage above, familiar to us from later typology, is that reality itself, if in any way sacred, has to be more like a play than an actual happening, even when it happens. The mystery "concealed" in the cross, he declares while dangling head down, is the mystery of *felix culpa*: "the form in which you see me hanging is a type [*diatypōsis*] of that man who first came to birth" (*Acts of Peter* 38 [9]). It was Adam who rearranged with his fall the original divine schema, reversed good and evil, thus invited the coming of Christ to right things again. The way to intuit the divine in a fallen reality

110. As a result we now have, in addition to the Latin text of the *Acts* from which I've been quoting, a Greek *Vorlage*. In citations from the martyrdom episode, the first number is to the Latin chapter, the second (in brackets) to the Greek—now the basis of translation, unless otherwise noted. For the Latin (not printed by Vouaux [n. 106]) I have used the text in *Acta Apostolorum Apocrypha*, ed. R. A. Lipsius and M. Bonnet, vol. 1 (Leipzig: Hermannum Mendelssohn, 1891), pp. 78–103.

111. Irenaeus, *Adv. haer.* 1.24.4 (SC 264:328; ANF 1:349). For similar passages from the apocrypha, see Ehrman, *Lost Christianities* (n. 70), pp. 186–88; on the difference between the Valentinian Gnosis, or any other form of Docetism, and the "doctrine" here articulated by Peter, see "'Head Downwards': The Cross of Peter in the Lights of the Apocryphal Acts, of the New Testament and of the Society-Transforming Claim of Early Christianity," in *Apocryphal Acts of Peter* (n. 107), pp. 111–22; esp. 113. Throughout, the notes of Vouaux dwell on this point.

is therefore through the re-inversion accomplished by Jesus: "Concerning this the Lord says in a mystery, 'Unless you make what is on the right hand as what is on the left hand and what is on the left hand as what is on the right and what is above as what is below and what is behind as what is before, you will not recognize the Kingdom" (ibid.).

Upside down and on the verge of death—which is to say, of eternal rebirth—Peter sees the Kingdom better than most. He tries to communicate his vision at some length in his dying speech, and its length underscores the generic kinship, already noted by scholars,[112] between this apocryphon and drama—though here the real final speech, unlike any drama before Beckett, transpires in total silence:

> Since you have made known and revealed these things to me, O Word...
> I give you thanks, not with these lips nailed shut, not with the tongue, out
> of which come truth and deceit, not with this word that proceeds by the art
> of a physical nature; but I give you thanks, O King, with that voice which
> is understood in silence, which is not heard clearly, which does not pass
> through bodily organs, which does not enter ears of the flesh, which is not
> heard by corruptible beings, which is not in the world or uttered on earth,
> nor written in books, nor belonging to one but not to another, but with
> this, I thank you, Jesus Christ, in a silence of voice with which intercedes
> the spirit in me that loves you and speaks to you and sees you. You are
> known only to the spirit. (*Acts of Peter* 39 [10])

This remarkable formulation of Christian gratitude as that which resists identity with any material expression by voice or letter, but which is nonetheless expressed in the negative by means of Peter's own "drama," ultimately makes of the speech itself a version of Simon's groundless show: all this is mere talk, says Peter. The real expression of thanks none can hear but the spirit, whose movements are equally silent. As we'll see, the special power of professedly empty speech anyhow to convey Christian transcendence anticipates the magic of Faustus. The enactments of Marlowe's early modern magus also promote a kind of grace that cannot match its appearance, because such grace appears to exist but does not. Neither does Peter's negative spirit. Or rather this spirit exists, but only in negating the appearance that it ought to surpass. Its substance is what appearances lack.

All this might have remained at the level of a dematerialized theology save for the enormous emphasis given by the *Acts* to the mutual profitability of

---

112. E.g., Vouaux, *Actes de Pierre* (n. 106), p. 316 n. 4, p. 361 n. 8, and G. Poupon, "L'accusation de magie dans les Actes apocryphes," in *Les Actes apocryphes des apôtres: Christianisme et monde païen*, ed. François Bovon (Geneva: Labor et Fides, 1981), pp. 71–85; here 77.

both Christian and antichristian *miracula*. Finally the difference between Simon and Peter is that Peter redistributes his surplus. His money, like the spirit of his dying speech, cannot belong to one without belonging to others. (It follows in this the apostolic communism of the canonical Acts 2:44–45; 4:32–33.) Simon's "capitalist" drive toward personal increase signifies through contrast, lest the contrast collapse. He dogs the disciples as their disavowed greed and the fallen reality that foreshadows the church: in the end "simoniac" applies not to followers of Simon but to medieval priests. "Christians are the only ones," Origen admits early on, "who [still] speak of him" (*C. Celsum* 1.57). They continued to embellish and retell Simon's story so often because his name increasingly said to the church something about its commercialized structure which was otherwise unspeakable, except for "heretics." Already we can see here in the Roman market with Simon and Peter what Marlowe's play will make more visible in London with Faustus, though England had been supposedly purged of Romish religion for its shameless dependence on fraudulent commerce: we will see there again the empty plenitude of a commodified art form—empty because detached as by magic from the broken whole whose hierarchies of wealth made it happen in the first place; yet replete by virtue of that same detachment. From this dialectic stems both its socio-spiritual promise and its power to deceive.

Marlowe's portrait of Dr. Faustus borrows a great deal from the tradition of Simon Magus.[113] The most famous lines in the play, an encomium to Helen, resurrect Simon's consort, for instance, who first appears when Faustus' fellow scholars, presumably trained in the beauties of heaven, beg him to stage instead "that peerless dame of Greece" (5.1.14) and are dumbfounded by antiquity's ersatz goddess. According to one of them, her "heavenly beauty passeth all compare" (5.1.30)—which is to say, she compares quite favorably to the Christian notion of heaven, as had Simon's conjurations. This was because she, too, had as little real substance to spoil her beauty. By Faustus' own admission he has no power to present "true substantial bodies" (4.1.48), but merely "shadows," rather (B-text:

113. See Philip Mason Palmer and Robert Pattison More, eds., *The Sources of the Faust Tradition: From Simon Magus to Lessing* (New York: Oxford University Press, 1936), and Beatrice Daw Brown, "Marlowe, Faustus, and Simon Magus," *PMLA* 54 (1939): 82–121; more recently, Nuttall, *Alternative Trinity* (n. 76). For summary and bibliography of the intervening critics' interest in Simon (or lack thereof), see Christopher Marlowe, *Doctor Faustus, A- and B-texts (1604, 1616)*, ed. David Bevington and Eric Rasmussen, The Revels Plays (Manchester: Manchester University Press, 1993), pp. 7–8. All quotations are from the A-text of this edition unless otherwise noted.

4.1.104), which not incidentally was Elizabethan for actors. The confession is important because it puts Faustus in agreement with his skeptical on-lookers, one of whom appears on stage as an eavesdropping knight and immediately quips in response to the magician's professed impotence: "Ay, marry, Master Doctor, now there's a sign of grace in you, when you will confess the truth" (4.1.51–52). However offhand, the remark provides an entire theology for *Faustus*. The one sign of grace in a play famous for its lack is this truth: its actors are not the bodies they represent. One can grasp the boy who impersonates (the demon impersonating) Helen, but there is no grasping Helen "herself."

What makes Faustus' description of her so striking and famous is that in it he tries, à la Tamburlaine, to articulate a beauty beyond the powers of human speech. More pointedly, Faustus would overtop the mythological force of ancient poetry, the Bible's included, and so prove the superior grandeur of Marlowe's new verses:

> Was this the face that launched a thousand ships
> And burned the topless towers of Ilium?
> Sweet Helen, make me immortal with a kiss.
> Her lips suck forth my soul. See where it flies! (5.1.91–94)

That final, impossible deictic probably characterizes the work of Marlowe on its deepest level: he commands you to see the invisible. The soul of Faustus is of course no more on display than the "topless" spires of Troy—an architectural correlative to the aspirations of all Marlowe's heroes, but ashes now and dissipated, so doubly removed from earthbound reality. "Here will I dwell," Faustus next says, though what is "here" is that much harder to see: "for heaven be in these lips" (5.1.96). The archaic poeticism sounds to my ears nearly plaintive. It says let this, which is not, for once be. It cannot: playing Semele to Helen's Jupiter, Faustus will live to see heaven only at the brink of eternal deprivation. Until then, this substitute form, what Richard Halpern has called God's "more pleasant, pagan simulacrum,"[114] will be as close as Faustus gets. His poetic encomium to Helen really does confound hell in Elysium: it replaces the lost Christian heaven with an infidel fable.

More radically, his speech plays on the extent to which the Christian God derives his power, too, from fabulous poetry. Despite the classical allusions, there is a major scriptural intertext here, one that further connects the magic of Faustus to the way Simon Magus liked blending pagan myth

---

114. Richard Halpern, "Marlowe's Theater of Night: *Doctor Faustus* and Capital," *ELH* 71 (2004): 455–95; here 485.

with the Greek fabrications officially embraced by Christians: "O, thou art fairer than the evening air," Faustus tells Helen, "Clad in the beauty of a thousand stars / Brighter art thou than flaming Jupiter...And none but thou shalt be my paramour! (5.1.104–6, 110). So had the uxorious King Solomon, reputed a magician by medieval legend and canonically guilty of devil worship,[115] extolled the figure of Wisdom in the Septuagint: "For she is more beautiful then the sunne, and is aboue all the order of the starres, and the light is not to be compared vnto her....I haue loued her, and soght her from my youth: I desired to marye her, suche loue had I vnto her beautie" (Wisd. of Sol. 7:29, 8:2; 1560 Geneva). As usual, the perversity of Faustus' borrowing from this passage is considerably deeper than a "parodic"[116] appropriation of scripture toward atheistic or pagan ends. The biblical passage is itself a version of the Jewish, then Christian, polemic against Greek culture occurring throughout the book. Solomon constructs a sensuous allegory for the love of heavenly "Wisdom" that clearly resembles, and so acts as a suitable replacement for, the Platonic love of knowledge or, alternately, the heathen love of Isis.[117] Marlowe's gesture is both more and less scandalous than bastardizing scripture with the classics: in this instance, the words of Faustus work on the principle that scripture has already had to bastardize itself. Its best response to pagan letters, same as that of Simon and Clement, is to denounce, then assimilate.

Well before Marlowe believers already knew, by the way, that the impersonation of Solomon affected by the author of Wisdom (7:1–4, 8:17–19:18), however sacred by Christian standards, was a dramatic fiction: the Muratorian Fragment, an early list of canonical books, includes Wisdom even while pointing out that its authorial pose was a pretense: instead of the Wisdom of Solomon, we find *Wisdom Written by Friends of Solomon in his Honor.* In fact it's possible that this new title mistranslates an even earlier Greek text ascribing authorship not to Solomon's friends (*philōn*) but to Philo (*philōnis*),[118] the book's most likely author according to Jerome on account of its flair for Greek style, though he consequently excludes

---

115. 1 Kings 11:5–7; for the ensuing legends, see E. M. Butler, *The Myth of the Magus* (Cambridge: Cambridge University Press, 1948), pp. 35–43.

116. Michael Keefer, ed., *Christopher Marlowe's "Doctor Faustus": The 1604 Version Edition* (Peterborough, Ontario: Broadview, 1991), p. xlvi.

117. See James M. Reese, *Hellenistic Influence on the Book of Wisdom and Its Consequences* (Rome: Biblical Institute Press, 1970), esp. pp. 14–15, 34–35, 45–49; for some criticism of Reese's position and a more recent bibliography, see Lester L. Grabbe, *Wisdom of Solomon* (Sheffield: Sheffield Academic Press, 1997), pp. 68–80, 91–95.

118. Geoffrey Mark Hahneman, *The Muratorian Fragment and the Development of the Canon* (Oxford: Clarendon Press, 1992), p. 201.

it, as *pseudepigraphos,* from the true canon (*Praef. in libros Salomonis* [PL 28:1307B; cf. PL 29:427A]). Jerome's judgment made its way into the Gloss and was shared by a number of schoolmen, plus Luther, among later reformers.[119] Number six of Elizabeth's Thirty-nine Articles of Religion (1563) quotes Jerome to justify the secondary status of the apocrypha, which "the church doth read for example of life and instruction of manners, but yet doth it not apply them to establish any doctrine,"[120] even though, as Bruce Metzger has noticed, the Elizabethan Homilies at the very same time drew plenty of doctrine from the apocrypha. One of the Homilies specifically goes so far as to call the Book of Wisdom, whose impersonation of Solomon no one disputed, the "infallible and undeceivable word of God."[121] Knowing it was fiction evidently in no way lessened its impact. It was as if the emptiness of the fiction inadvertently supplied so fitting a vehicle for the numinous to communicate that it could not be eradicated without sacrificing the message.

Such emptiness had only been *enhanced* under the iconoclastic program of English Calvinists, to which Faustus seems also in his way dedicated. Vowing never to look "to" heaven, he explains in the same breath why his audience could no longer look at it, either, as he promises further

> Never to name God, or to pray to him,
> To burn his Scriptures, slay his ministers,
> And make my spirits pull his churches down. (2.3.96–98)

Only the resolution to give up prayer removes Faustus from standard Protestant practice. Radical iconoclasts had happily renewed the ancient tenet that no one could properly name God; hence the popularity among Protestants, when "figuring" him, to place the unpronounceable Tetragrammaton in a cloud.[122] Their animosity against more positive icons was in places what furthermore led them to slay Catholic ministers, strip their churches, and even at times to burn their scriptures. Barabas, whom Faustus here echoes, could not have been more enthusiastic than many Protestants

119. For a list of scholastics against the authenticity of Wisdom, see C. Larcher, *Études sur la Livre de la Sagesse* (Paris: Librairie Lecoffre; J. Gabalda, 1969), p. 65; overall pp. 36–84 give a thorough history of the debates over Wisdom from the beginning of the Christian era through to the Reformation.

120. Reproduced in *Doctor Faustus,* ed. David Scott Kastan (New York: Norton, 2005), p. 241.

121. Bruce Metzger, *An Introduction to the Apocrypha* (New York: Oxford University Press, 1957), p. 192.

122. See John N. King, *English Reformation Literature: The Tudor Origins of the Protestant Tradition* (Princeton: Princeton University Press, 1982), pp. 153–54.

(*Jew of Malta* 5.1.64–65). In fact, Marlowe has a real fondness for ethically compromised heroes proclaiming their agreement with hard-line reform: Edward, too, vows vengeance on Rome for its "superstitious taperlights / Wherewith thy antichristian churches blaze," and he longs to make the Tiber swell "with slaughtered priests" (1.4.98–99, 102).[123] These lines in turn repeat, or are repeated by, King Henry's promise to Queen Elizabeth in *The Massacre at Paris* to visit destruction on their mutual adversaries— coded, of course, not as Christians, but as members of the "antichristian kingdom"[124] ruled by the Vatican.

Exactly this animus accounts for the emergence of secular drama in the last quarter of the sixteenth century; exactly this animus eliminated Christ from the stage. The devil, however, had stayed. The stage itself remained. And on the Protestant view a devilish theater was all that the promises of Christ for a millennium had amounted to. After the Reformation the allure of the old Latin incantations might have left England altogether for a long while, had the theater not helped find a way to display the bad charms in a new sanctuary. Their exclusion from the rest of England intensified what the new drama now could offer. Theater fed the hunger that denuding the churches had radically strengthened. When Henslowe pays for additions that, so far as we know, would augment above all the business in Rome, he recapitulates the devotion that Marlowe originally attributes to Faustus—a mocker of Catholicism for sure, but a critic completely engrossed, more even than the pope he mocks, by the devil's showmanship, *especially* as the devil's pomp proved still a great means to accumulate wealth.

And yet for the first time in the history of English drama, London audiences had to content themselves with nothing more than what the damned see in *Faustus*: "Why, this is hell, nor am I out of it," Mephistopheles says with a gesture—one likes to think—at the surrounding theater:

> Think'st thou that I, who saw the face of God,
> And tasted the eternal joys of heaven,
> Am not tormented with ten thousand hells
> In being deprived of everlasting bliss? (1.3.78–82)

---

123. Christopher Marlowe, *Edward II*, ed. Charles R. Forker, The Revels Plays (Manchester: Manchester University Press, 1994), p. 165; for commentary, see corresponding notes in this edition.

124. Christopher Marlowe, *Dido Queen of Carthage and The Massacre at Paris*, ed. H. J. Oliver, The Revels Plays (Cambridge: Harvard University Press, 1968), p. 161 (sc. 24, line 59); see also the introduction of this edition, pp. lvi–lvii and lxxvi.

The description defines quite literally the new limits of a secular theater, where the face of God no longer appeared (to appear), either. At play's end Faustus will wish to share with his audience the briefest backward glimpse of a time long gone—"See, see, where Christ's blood streams in the firmament!" (5.2.78)—but as per Elizabethan policy no one could see a thing. By the 1616 printing even this mention of godhead had fled from the censor.[125]

In its place one saw Helen, however, and the other for-profit fables mounted by devils on behalf of the players. Mercifully these would have looked rather familiar to Christians raised on medieval drama:

> Chief spectacle of the world's pre-eminence,
> The bright shining of whose glorious acts
> Lightens the world with his reflecting beams—
> As when I hear but motion made of him,
> It grieves my soul I never saw the man. (4.1.30–34)

I think it is possible to hear in this (the Holy Roman emperor's description of Alexander the Great) an entire culture's longing less for antiquity than for its lost native drama. The playbill effectively calls here for a figure of divine caliber—someone like Digby's Saul or the God of the cycles—and Faustus will fill the order by summoning the demons who were that divinity's traditional imitators. In fact the players could easily have doubled the part of Alexander with Lucifer—another chief spectacle, even more divine in show, but not yet under erasure as the divine now was. That Lucifer and Alexander were in reality actors paid to be there would have all the more effectively raised the undead specter of medieval divinity.

"Faustus, we are come from hell," Lucifer at one point announces, "to show thee some pastime" (2.3.100). There follows a spectacle derived literally from a time now past: an allegorical parade of the Seven Deadly Sins. Faustus had hoped that the sight of these sins would please him as much as Paradise pleased Adam, but, like the cycle plays that once had staged God in creation, such talk now is silenced. The Fall, as it were, had happened a second time in England, only this time God himself was expelled: "Talk not of Paradise nor creation," says Lucifer, "but mark this show. Talk of the devil, and nothing else" (2.3.105–6). From a Wittenberg perspective, this was maybe just as well. Since the devil was defined by his hubristic likeness to God, plus a sinister ability, after his fall, to be

125. Roma Gill, ed., *The Complete Works of Christopher Marlowe*, vol. 2 (Oxford: Clarendon Press, 1990), p. xvii.

transformed back into an angel of light, for Luther the main difference between them was that God, when judged by fallen reason, appeared so much worse—far "*more* frightening and horrible than the devil" (*Predigten über das zweite Buch Mose* 9 [WA 16:141; my emphasis]). Luther goes on to say elsewhere that naturally a God of this nature is never believed by those mockers and mamelukes who hold the Old Testament "for a mere fable," but they will eventually learn the hard truth of Moses' unimpaired vision—namely, that God is a fire and "assails one and has such a passion for it that by jealousy and wrath he is driven to consume the wicked" (*Predigten über das fünfte Buch Mose* 4 [WA 28:559]).[126] Of course humans also have a passion for this sort of thing, especially when observing from a safe, aesthetic distance while it happens to somebody else. That, I suspect, is why audiences so adored yearly seeing the death and descent of the fraudulent magus, Jesus, and why they now liked *Dr. Faustus*. "In hell is all manner of delight" (2.3.167).

In Rome, too. After the parade of vices, Faustus asks to see their source in hell, but perhaps since hell has no geographical limits he winds up instead at the Vatican. These two seats of evil were in any case easily conflated: when Faustus first conjures, he abbreviates the names of the saints, among other things, and then makes the sign of the cross—all in a language that to many would have sounded like a version of the Roman liturgy: "signumque crucis quod nunc facio" (1.3.22). Latin, once the sacred tongue of the English church, was fast becoming hocus pocus (from *hoc est corpus meum*). "Protestant polemicists had a point when they claimed that Roman Catholic rites were no different from conjurations," writes Gareth Roberts, "as the latter had long since appropriated some of the formulae and rhetoric of the former."[127] One could extend his point far more deeply into the history of Christianity by noting the distinct possibility that the Christian liturgy historically originated in Christ's own magical practice and that of his disciples. This possibility is everywhere acknowledged in the magus legends and in medieval drama (where Jesus is always accused of sorcery), as it had been in the Bible—particularly when Christ, like Faustus, commands demons to obedience. Such exorcisms, say the Pharisees, are really the devil's work; and to this, as we've seen, Christ

---

126. These and other like passages from Luther are given more detailed analysis in Rudolf Otto, *The Idea of the Holy*, trans. John W. Harvey (London: Oxford University Press, 1958), pp. 94–108, esp. 99.

127. Gareth Roberts, "Marlowe and the Metaphysics of Magicians," in *Constructing Christopher Marlowe*, ed. J. A. Downie and J. T. Parnell (Cambridge: Cambridge University Press), pp. 55–73; here 61.

responds with a curse. Marlowe's Roman friars, whose "holy shape," according to Faustus, "becomes a devil best" (1.3.27), simply ask the Lord to curse once again: *Maledicat Dominus! Maledicat Dominus! Et omnes sancti! Amen.* (3.1.91ff.).

The patent anti-Catholicism of these scenes—or, if you like, their anti-Christianity—may place *Dr. Faustus* again on the side of iconoclastic Protestantism, yet it does so paradoxically by *reanimating* the excesses of religious theater and Catholic ritual: the old rites were not to be seen anywhere else in England. In part that was because the old religion, on the Protestant view that *Faustus* conforms to, was as demonic and lacking in substance as the commercial theater. Its being was no being at all, or to the extent it had any residual substance, its substance was the stuff of money. Embodying an objectively fictive equivalence between any two things, this universal, which Marx would call the *Stoffwechsel* or "metabolism" of abstract labor,[128] seems constantly to open the potential for an infinite return on finite investments. Hope for such returns long formed an explicit and indispensable centerpiece of Catholic culture: in the liturgy, the traffic in indulgences, and in the spectacle of the sacred sale resulting in "atonement." Now that the Reformation stemming from Wittenberg had choked off a lot of that traffic in its traditional forms, new forms were emerging where the old profits were still to be had.

So while "purgatory" and the "pardon" (3.1.74) that the friars think Faustus wants to beg of the pope may have been exposed in Reformation England as pure fictions of Antichrist and thus become a laughingstock, no one could afford to laugh at redemption as such. The problem faced by an Elizabethan audience at this historical moment was how to buy in without the old mechanisms. And this very problem, commercial drama was in the perfect position to solve. At least one critic has discerned an ironic parallel between Faustus' words about Christ's blood streaming in the firmament—"One drop would save my soul, half a drop"—and the words of the bull that authorized the indulgence: "not a meagre drop of blood, which would have sufficed for the redemption of all mankind; but rather it poured forth copiously like a stream."[129] The point to take from this parallel, I think, should less involve questions of source or influence than the relation between two modes of commerce, that of the medieval church and that of the London theater. Their relation is at the heart of

128. Karl Marx, *Capital*, trans. Ben Fowkes, vol. 1 (New York: Penguin, 1976), e.g., p. 207.
129. Charles Clay Doyle, "One Drop of Christ's Streaming Blood: A Gloss on *Dr. Faustus*," *Cahiers Élisabéthains: Études sur la Pre-Renaissance et la Renaissance Anglaises* 17 (1980): 85–87; here 86.

Faustus, as of Marlowe's work more generally. In the theater audiences could again pay for the momentary transport of a sensuous indulgence and come away, as they had in the past, morally strengthened by the wonder of it all.

The commodification of Faustus' soul in this way provides a visible correlative for the commodity of Christ's blood, admittedly absent now from the sacraments in all but symbol and invisible on stage because suppressed by fiat: "View here the blood that trickles from mine arm," Faustus tells Mephistopheles at the signing of the pact, "And let it be propitious for my wish" (2.1.57–58). After some stage business designed to heighten the suspense, using his blood as ink Faustus finally signs away his soul "in manner of a deed of gift" (2.1.59–60), which is to say, in the same manner that the blood of Christ also functions. The Bible, too, is signed in blood. That is how Jesus ratified his will and Testament (Heb. 9:15): "Christ must dye," the Geneva commentators elucidate further, "because the couenant or testament is of none effect without the death of the testator," and Christ's blood alone "wolde pacifie his Fathers wrath" (Heb. 9:17–18; Geneva 1560, side notes o–p). Faustus bequeaths his soul to Satan, that is, just as Christ surrenders to his bloodthirsty Father, whom Satan anyway had always imitated.

It's worth pointing out the way that this angry God, demanding the innocent blood of his son, had frequently driven "orthodox" theorists of atonement toward a rather Marlovian blurring of the boundary, such as it was, between the demonic and sacred: "Whereas the patristic view, in its extreme forms, tends to make the devil into a god," writes Robert Culpepper—meaning the patristic view concedes rights to the devil that God must respect—"the Latin view [of Anselm et al.], in its extreme forms, tends to turn God into a devil."[130] Culpepper means by this that in the latter case, the "just" God of the Old Testament acts like a demonic sadist, with Christ in the New Testament as his willing masochist.[131] Hence the

---

130. Robert Culpepper, *Interpreting the Atonement* (Grand Rapids: Eerdmans, 1966), p. 87.

131. For the masochist's "distinct talent for impersonation, mimicry, and masquerade," see Jonathan Dollimore, *Sexual Dissidence: Augustine to Wilde, Freud to Foucault* (Oxford: Clarendon Press, 1991), p. 200 and those he cites. Another way of putting Culpepper's point would be to say that the Latin view effectively puts God into the place formerly occupied by the devil as recipient of Christ's ransom. Cf. Aquinas, *Summa th.* 3a.48.4: "Christ therefore is not said to have offered his blood, the price of our redemption, to the devil, but to God"; against Origen, Gregory of Nyssa, Basil, Ambrose, and Jerome. For text and citations, see *Summa Theologiae: Latin Text and English Translation, Introductions, Notes, Appendices, and Glossaries*, 61 vols. ([Cambridge? Eng.]: Blackfriars; New York, McGraw-Hill, 1964–81), 54:86–87.

critique of the "Latin view" by Abelard, who was in turn fiercely attacked.[132] Given how difficult it had been for committed Christians to talk about Christ's death without falling into blasphemy of one sort or another, I do not see that Marlowe's reformulation of the problem ought to impress us as somehow preternaturally skeptical and modern. Rather, what the blasphemy inhering in historical discussions of atonement does is imbue the scandalous blood pact of Faustus with a belated and depraved divinity despite the theater's lost ability to picture atonement any more directly; any less indirection, any less displacement or distortion would have been, to contemporaries, *even more* scandalous. Only the so-called parody makes it possible for a man on stage to speak once again the words of Christ: "Consummatum est" (2.1.74; Jn 19:30). The difference is that where Christ's life ends, Faustus career as famed magician properly begins.

Both cases—one dominating the medieval stage, the other dominating the Renaissance—provided their onlookers with that peculiar satisfaction born of depicting calamity. In both instances the halfway faux humiliation that audiences purchased—first by way of the church, then at the theater—offered them momentary freedom from what James Simpson has called the pain of social existence.[133] The purchase, itself a component in the relations of production that so pained them, of course was not freedom. But then neither is a world in which such fabrications have existed a world from which freedom is entirely absent. When glossing the final words of Christ, and with them the future words of Faustus, Augustine takes *consummatum est* as a comment on the successful completion of God's plan for salvation at its apparent endpoint and failure: "Who can so arrange what he does," Augustine asks, "as this man arranged what he suffered?" (*Tract. in Joh.* 119.4 [CCSL 36:659; trans. John Rettig, FC 92:47]). God stage-managed the crucifixion, in other words, that he might appear not as God but "hidden," rather, in the figure of a magus condemned by the forces of (his own) evil. Such was the artistry of Christ's defeat that his true godhead appeared mainly in the signature arrangement of an invisible author. The death of Jesus, sold by Judas and fully suffering for the disbelief he inspired in Jews and Romans, therefore made God manifest, if manifest only to the sufficiently *cultivated* onlooker: "For the men through whom these things happened did not recognize the man as God; he who appeared [*apparebat*] as a man was hidden as God: he who appeared suffered all these things, and the same one, who was hidden, himself arranged

132. For Abelard's critique, see chapter 1, p. 71.
133. Simpson, *Reform and Cultural Revolution* (n. 3), p. 511.

all" (ibid.). Afterwards to be saved you had only to embrace this scriptural or dramatized image of a would-be god called out for his hubris, then to find in his (merely apparent) guilt the potential renewal of everyone's innocence. This may not quite be *l'art pour l'art*, but still.

Traditionally Antichrist and his henchmen like Simon had served to acknowledge the proximity of such a revelation to the fallacious impersonations of any devilishly talented con artist: the proximity did not discredit revelation but helped, rather, exonerate and explain its power. If such was the raw force of unsacred beauty, God's was the same, only better. God was emptier. Simply picture the most amazing spectacle ever, then subtract the picture. Imaging that absence was a stage trick as old as the *quem quaeritis*—older, if you count the abrupt ending of Mark at Christ's empty tomb; now that God could be by law eliminated, it worked even more effectively. Marlowe's money-hungry villains, and the dramatic catastrophes they orchestrate, seem especially to have lent a dark shape to this otherwise banished, inscrutable deity. Between Jesus and Barabbas was no longer a choice. Jesus was gone. Barabas, Tamburlaine, and Faustus now stood in his place. If you still thought you could bear to see God, the players were glad to provide, for a price, a distant, tantalizing glimpse.

Index

Abelard, Peter, 71, 166, 244

actor: Antichrist as, x, 38; Christ as, 160–62; distinct from character, 54, 69, 179, 205, 227–28, 235–36; and hypocrite, 17n37; indistinct, 69, 77, 185–86

Acts, 89, 213–15, 223

Acts of Peter, 64, 230–35

Adorno, Theodor, x, 86, 156, 225

Aeschylus, 15

aesthetics, x–xi, 10–11, 21, 83, 123; Aristotelean, 67–70; in Beard, 187; in *Letter of Aristeas*, 148–51. *See also* beauty; fetishism; likeness

alms, 102, 116, 166–67

Ambrose, 41, 47, 53, 91–92, 97, 105

Anselm, 71, 118, 198, 243

anti, 163, 211; meaning of, 49, 155, 158–59

Antichrist, x, 1–4, 38–39, 41, 43–46; Barabbas as, 198; Herod as, 96; Judas as, 112; and money, 92–93, 95–98, 101–102; other members of, ix, 5, 212; pope as, 187–89; Simon Magus as, 228. *See also* Christ

antipope, 4, 77

anti-Semitism, 5n11, 127n80, 207

antitheatricalism, xi, 11–12, 70, 72–79, 162, 185. *See also* iconoclasm

apocalypse, x–xi, 8–10, 21, 167n66. *See also* eschatology; second coming

apocrypha, 3n5, 140, 191, 211n71. *See also Acts of Peter*; Charinus, Leucius; *Gospel of Nicodemus*; Judas, *Gospel of*; Pseudo-Clementines; Pseudo-Matthew; Wisdom of Solomon

Aquinas, Thomas, 72, 129–30

Arianism, 157, 201

Aristotle, 15, 18, 67–69, 145

atonement, theory of, 38, 71, 87–89, 157–61, 176, 243–44

audience: Elizabethan, 207–8, 209, 223, 239, 242; an ideal, 67–70, 134; medieval, 136–37, 177–78, 182

Augustine, 6, 41, 49n, 135, 202; on Christ's *commercium*, 91, 93; Christ's last words, 244; cross as mousetrap, 173–74; heretics, 108; Jews, 196; Jonah, 31–33; Judas, 109–10, 160, 192; land of unlikeness, 57–58; lies and likeness, 52–55; miracles, 64, 72; theater, 72–74, 84–85, 123

Aune, David, 7

Bacon, Francis, 62

Barabbas, xi, 46, 165, 193–202

Bar-Jesus, 213–15, 228

Basil the Great, 51

Bauer, Walter, 36

Beard, Thomas, 183–93, 221

beauty, xi, 23–24; of apocalypse, 8; Augustine on, 41; of blood money, 106–7; of Helen, 236–37; of host, 133–34; of props in sacrifice, 148–51; Tamburlaine on, 225–28